Varieties of Criminology

Varieties of Criminology

READINGS FROM A DYNAMIC DISCIPLINE

EDITED BY
Gregg Barak

PRAEGER SERIES IN CRIMINOLOGY AND CRIME CONTROL POLICY
Steven A. Egger, *Series Editor*

Westport, Connecticut
London

Library of Congress Cataloging-in-Publication Data

Varieties of criminology : readings from a dynamic discipline / edited
  by Gregg Barak.
    p.   cm. — (Praeger series in criminology and crime control
policy, ISSN 1060–3212)
  Includes bibliographical references and index.
  ISBN 0–275–94485–9 (alk. paper)
  ISBN 0–275–94774–2 (pbk. : alk. paper)
  1. Criminology. I. Barak, Gregg. II. Series.
HV6025.V29   1994
364—dc20   93–14138

British Library Cataloguing in Publication Data is available.

Library of Congress Catalog Card Number: 93–14138
ISBN: 0–275–94485–9
      0–275–94774–2 (pbk.)
ISSN: 1060–3212

First published in 1994

Praeger Publishers, 88 Post Road West, Westport, CT 06881
An imprint of Greenwood Publishing Group, Inc.

Printed in the United States of America

∞™

The paper used in this book complies with the
Permanent Paper Standard issued by the National
Information Standards Organization (Z39.48–1984).

10 9 8 7 6 5 4 3 2 1

Contents

Illustrations

MAPS

Acknowledgments

I would like to acknowledge first the contributors to this volume for their willingness to participate in the project. A venture like this inevitably pits their diverse theoretical works against others of different persuasions. I would also like to acknowledge the support and interaction from my criminological colleagues at Eastern Michigan University (EMU): Mark Lanier, Stuart Henry, Christina Johns, Joe Rankin, and William Shay. I especially want to thank Stuart for our dangling theoretical conversation, his intellectual and scholarly agenda, and his never-ending energy. Whatever intellectual endeavor I pick up, Stuart is always right there with the necessary feedback.

I am grateful to the *Journal of Human Justice* for permitting me to reprint Chapter 13, which originally appeared in the Autumn 1990 issue.

There are others who have made this book possible. I acknowledge three in particular: Praeger sociology and criminology editor Anne Kiefer, for her attitude and perspective and for her belief from the start in the project and me; Praeger criminology and criminal justice series editor Steve Egger, for his appreciation of this work's importance and for input and discussion; and EMU graduate assistant, Karen Schaumann. Without Karen's input and work on this anthology, it would not have reached the publisher's desk. Karen not only brought all of the various computer disks and manuscripts from three continents into painstaking uniformity, but she also assisted in the editing of this manuscript. Last but not least, Karen was the indexer for this book. Finally, I would like to acknowledge the Project and Copy Editor, Katie Chase, for a superb copyediting job.

Gregg Barak

Varieties of Criminology

Introduction: Criminological Theory in the "Postmodernist" Era

GREGG BARAK

In the 1990s, the discipline of criminology, defined here as the study of "crime" and social control, is characterized by some criminologists as "very viable" and by others as "very liable." When it comes to the study of criminological theory in particular, "some criminologists will view the relatively large number of competing theoretical explanations as a sign of the vitality of the discipline. Others, however, will view the array of competing explanations as a sign that the discipline lacks coherence" (Stitt and Giacopassi, 1992: 4). It may very well be that both of these points of view are correct. It could be argued, as this volume will demonstrate, that the study of crime and its causation has primarily been a multidisciplinary rather than an interdisciplinary enterprise. Explanations and theories are derived from diverse fields such as biology, psychology, sociology, and the law. Approaches to criminology stem from very different core assumptions and values about human nature, society, and change. Hence, this anthology attempts to capture *the varieties of criminology* created by the various explanations and approaches to crime and deviance. It does not pretend to represent all theoretical perspectives or schools of criminology equally, but it does claim to indirectly if not directly cover a very wide range of theoretical approaches.

To assess "the degree of connectivity between theory and research over the last twenty-eight years," Stitt and Giacopassi (pp. 3–4) conducted a content analysis of the journal *Criminology* and found that the articles increasingly embodied "a traditional theory-testing paradigm." In the most recent five-year period studied, nearly half of the articles involved tests of criminological theory. Stitt and Giacopassi were pleased to discover that both the types and diversity of theories tested over time had increased and that the discipline's theoretical orientations had broadened. They found a criminological world where the motivation for research had been enriched by the contemporary incorporation of explanations of crime and criminal behavior grounded in such theoretically oriented models as deterrence, economic/structural, biosocial, and typological. In addition, there were the more traditionally dominant sociopsychological and sociocultural explanations, as well as the less dominant biological and psychological ones.

Those criminologists who are not impressed by these theoretical developments point to the confusion. Thomas Kelley says in his contribution to this anthology (Chapter 2), the "understanding of the causes of crime appears to be lost in an entanglement of criminological theories and concepts that, while often clever and intellectually sophisticated, are more often misleading or incorrect." He maintains that in attempts to explain or justify the exceptions and contradictions of the so-called integrated and interdisciplinary theories of our field, "we have either designed forced and intricate explanations, or we have ignored or twisted... irregularities to fit our established theoretical models." Nevertheless, Kelley has himself been going about the business of advancing a newly developed and integrated model of crime and crime prevention.

While the contributors to this volume disagree about the "best" analysis for integrating the study of crime and social control, they all share, at varying levels of theoretical development, the presentation of work that represents (in this editor's opinion) the vitality of criminology in the 1990s. *Varieties of Criminology* is essentially an expression of the intersecting criminological and social discourses of the early 1990s. Criminological discourse is rather narrow and specialized; it typically refers to offenders, victims, theories, state policies, the public, and scholarly research. Social discourse by comparison is broad and diverse. It may include the vast reaches of popular speech, the writings of the cultural elite, and all other facets of mass communications media. Taken in its hybrid formation, contemporary criminological-social discourse includes perspectives or schools of thought referred to as positivist criminology, neoclassical criminology, neofunctionalist criminology, critical criminology, realist criminology, cultural criminology, feminist criminology, peacemaking criminology, biosocial criminology, anarchistic criminology, deconstructionist criminology, postmodernist criminology, and various combinations of these. While this text is not a comprehensive study of all the different criminologies in depth, it does provide the widest theoretical discussion of primary (or first-person) criminological accounts ever assembled in one book. Moreover, as one anonymous reviewer of the prepublished manuscript wrote: "undoubtedly the most original collection of essays in theoretical criminology to appear in many years." We hope that teaching faculty and advanced undergraduate and graduate students agree.

History will reveal whether or not this is the "postmodernist" era as postmodern theorists claim. Is our social reality characterized by a rejection of the Enlightenment belief in scientific rationality as the main vehicle to knowledge and progress? Or is our social reality, instead, characterized by an intellectual development surrounded by the importance of the unconscious, a plurality of viewpoints, and the free-floating signs and images of a consumerist society? It may very well be that we are simply entering a phase of the modernist period characterized by a more realistic or modest regard for scientific rationality. Time will tell, but in the meanwhile, contemporary discourse reflects a period of rapid national and international change. Referred to by different groups as the New World Order, as the internationalization of capital, or as the globalization of order and ecological stability, this period of transition cannot be disconnected from the emerging and changing political and social discourses.

All discourses are part and parcel of historical, political, and economic contexts. As such, criminological discourses are sociohistorically specific and cannot be separated from the development of the human condition. As a part of the history and language of social change, these discourses have both liberating and constraining potentials. Theoretical models of any kind may be liberating in that they identify and define phenomena in question and help to make sense of or to construct order out of relative confusion. Accordingly, criminological schools serve as necessary conduits not only for purposes of conceptualization and identity, but also for guiding action and reaction. On the other hand, these theoretical models or schools of criminology—with their competing assumptions, world views, and agendas—have also served to limit or restrict criminological inquiry. Because of the mutually exclusive and often antagonistic orientations of competing schools, favored criminological discourses may often constrain students of crime and justice in their pursuit of theory advancement and policy refinement. Although most criminological textbooks at least attempt to provide discussions that allegedly represent the differing approaches to crime and justice, most, nevertheless, tend to be one-dimensional, reifying the value of one or possibly two perspectives while dismissing the value of virtually all the others.

Consequently, most undergraduate students in criminology and criminal justice are exposed to a review of criminological theory (and practice) that provides, at best, a superficial gloss of the varieties of criminology and, at worst, a distorted and myopic view of their potential for both social control and social justice. Even at the advanced undergraduate or graduate levels, students of criminology/criminal justice are often forced to delimit their areas of understanding to only one or perhaps two criminologies, depending for the most part on the chance historical circumstances of where and with whom they study. In an effort to provide an alternative to this traditional approach to criminological-pedagogical discourse and inquiry, this anthology presents original theoretical pieces representative of the full array of contemporary criminological discourse.[1]

The reader of this text will find examples of the latest expressions of both the older and newer types of criminological theories, including but not limited to the following: genetics and brain functioning, personality theory, psychological learning, psychoanalytic theory, ecological/socioeconomic theory, social learning, social integration/anomie, social disorganization, differential association, structural strain theory, relative deprivation, social control, labeling, subcultural theory, conflict theory, routine activity/opportunity theory, class theory, postmodernist and semiotic theory, and sex roles/gender effects theory. However, this is not a relativistic undertaking. Nor is it one that accords equal significance to each perspective. It is not assumed, for example, that there are strengths and weaknesses in all criminological approaches. Nor are we advocating some kind of eclectic criminology that takes a pinch from here and a pinch from there.

Rather, recognition is given to the critical pluralistic and dynamic world of criminology, and to the serious theoretical and conceptual endeavors of criminologists working in a variety of "old" and "new" criminological traditions. My desire from the outset has been to provide a selection of the latest thinking and research from each of several broad areas of contemporary criminological theory. It is not to rank order or weight the relative importance of these theories, nor to attempt to synthesize or integrate what we believe are lines of continuity between the differing theoretical orientations. For the most part, anyway, attempts to produce integrated theories of crime causation have not been very compelling. See Groves and Sampson (1987) for a relatively interesting attempt at the integration of mainstream and critical criminology.

Like many criminologists, I have my own rank order of theories and/or theoretical orientations. Nevertheless, in the context of the contributions to this volume I have chosen not to reveal these. I have, instead, left the task of evaluating and judging each of the theoretical contributions found within to students and teachers during their classroom discussions. Hence, I have consciously tried not to prejudice the reader with my own particular assessment of a given chapter's theoretical value. Even so, I would be surprised if my own critical orientation does not contaminate my efforts to some degree, especially in the following comparative overview on the differences between "mainstream" and "critical" criminology.

Contrary to the views of those criminologists who believe that the criminological discipline is currently experiencing a crisis in theory and practice, and that state-sponsored administrative and instrumental approaches have taken control of criminological inquiry, the implicit argument here is that the field of criminology is undergoing a dynamic, vibrant period of development and change. Before I briefly highlight this dynamism as reflected in each of the contributions and its relationship to the development of criminological thinking in the past and present, I would like to make a few comments concerning some of the underlying similarities and differences between mainstream and critical criminology.

To a degree all of the chapters whether identified here as "mainstream" (read: classical/neoclassical or positivist theories) or "critical" (read: inter-actionist/labeling, Marxist, feminist, or postmodernist), are engaged in efforts that seek to link, connect, or integrate various levels of criminological analysis. Most typically, these involve linking character or agency variables with some kind of structural or cultural or policy variables. Put simply, they address the individual-society relationship. Four of the seven mainstream contributions and three of the six critical contributions also share a focus on delinquency and/or youthful deviance. While not necessarily represent-ative of the field of criminology in general or of criminological theory in particular, this reflects, after some two decades of relative indifference, a reemergent interest in adolescent deviance.

The last point also raises the issue of discursive difference between main-stream and critical criminology. It is not by chance or accident that the chapters found in Part I discuss "delinquency" and "individual interven-tion," while those in Part II discuss "youthful misbehavior" and "cultural change." Such differences are indicative of what perhaps best distinguishes mainstream and critical orientations. I refer specifically to their respective epistemological positions as well as to the boundaries of their criminological inquiry. The mainstream contributors take crime, law, and justice as a given. They ground their theoretical endeavors in the official ideology of the pre-vailing socioeconomic order that neither investigates nor questions the "so-cial reality" of crime and crime control. By contrast, the critical theorists, to varying degrees, find the "social reality" of crime and crime control to be problematic, and subject to a myriad of questions and interpretations. They call for different and alternative forms of social control, and for a restructuring of aspects of the sociopolitical order.

To more fully elaborate the meaning of mainstream and critical crimi-nology, one needs to underscore the way in which the assumptions of these criminologies differ in three important respects: First, unlike classical/neo-classical theories, which assume that human beings are free-willed, and positivistic theories, which assume that human beings are determined, either in a hard or soft way, critical theories assume that human beings are both determined *and* determining. Second, in contrast to both classical/neoclass-ical and positivistic theories, which assume that a given society is distin-guished fundamentally by a consensus over moral values, whether by social contract in the former or collective conscience in the latter, critical theories assume that conflict is the norm; that society is characterized primarily by contention over moral values. Third, unlike positivistic theories, which as-sume that social scientists, including criminologists, can be value-neutral or objective in their work, critical theories assume that such a position is impossible. In sum, perhaps the most fundamental difference between main-stream and critical criminology is the belief by the latter that human beings are not only the creators of the institutions and structures that ultimately dominate and constrain them, but that they are capable of changing those institutions and structures (and not just individual offenders and their associated environments).

Varieties of Criminology is divided into two parts. Part I, Mainstream Criminology, contains seven chapters, and Part II, Critical Criminology, six chapters. In Part I, the chapters are originally reflective of or have their roots in the nineteenth-century works of such diverse disciplinary persons as biologist Charles Darwin (1809–82) and sociologist Emile Durkheim (1858–1917), or in the twentieth-century works of psychoanalyst Sigmund Freud (1856–1939) and sociologist Talcott Parsons (1902–). Accordingly, as a group these mainstream chapters are derived from a positivist philosophy, which holds that science's most important aim is the establishment of stability and order through an understanding of determined or cause and effect relationships. Politically conservative, these contributions serve to avert social and political change while they tend to reinforce the status quo by attempting to delineate biological, psychological, and sociological differences between criminals and noncriminals. At the same time, these mainstream chapters virtually ignore the criminalization process; separating the study of crime from a theory of the law and the state. Following Durkheim and Parsons, these contributions echo the belief that crime is both "normal" and "functional" to society. All societies, in other words, require crime as a necessary part of the whole social system. The fundamental task for mainstream criminology, therefore, is to discover the most efficient means for controlling criminals or the necessary evils of crime.

In Part II, the chapters are initially reflective of or have their roots in the nineteenth-century work of philosopher and political economist Karl Marx (1818–83), the early twentieth-century work of social-psychologist George Herbert Mead (1863–1931), and the more contemporary writings of criminologists Richard Quinney (1934–) and William J. Chambliss (1933–) that first appeared in the 1970s. As a group these critical chapters are part and parcel of a demystification of crime and society that questions the functionalist belief in the necessity of crime. Less concerned by the peculiarities in the criminal actor than with the criminalization process, these critical contributions each, to varying degrees, focus their attention on the meaning of crime and criminality as it is socially constructed. At the same time, these critical chapters employ a cultural and historical materialism that integrates the capitalist mode of production, the state, the law, and the crime control apparatus with the development of crime. Generally underlying these critical contributions is the belief in the need for progressive changes in society's prevailing institutional orders. As a prerequisite for treating the crime problem as primarily a social and not an individual activity, critical criminology pursues the roots rather than the symptoms of crime.

The opening chapter of Part I, "Biological and Neuropsychiatric Approaches to Criminal Behavior," by C. Ray Jeffery, is reflective of the two oldest traditions in the scientific study of criminal behavior, traditions that emphasize the importance of biology and psychology. Before moving into a contemporary discussion of modern biocriminology and psychiatry, Jeffery provides the reader with an historical introduction to the field typically not found in textbooks on crime, criminal behavior, or crime control. He contends that the insights and perspectives suggested by the forerunners to today's biocriminologists were closer to an understanding of individual criminality than any of the contemporary sociological theories that commit the twin sins of examining crime in the aggregate without ever enunciating a theory of human behavior. Jeffery calls for an integrated theoretical approach to behavior first and foremost, as well as for an interdisciplinary focus for the whole field. The linchpins in Jeffery's analysis of criminal behavior and its prevention are neuropsychiatry and the interaction of genetics and brain functioning within biology.

In Chapter 2, "Crime and Psychology of Mind: A Neo-Cognitive View of Delinquency," Thomas Kelley considers how the recent development of two interrelated models, Psychology of Mind and Neo-Cognitive Learning Theory, contribute to the explanation and prevention of delinquency. Kelley elaborates on the assumptions and/or principles of these models and on empirical research that apparently supports the neo-cognitive view of human interaction. He also contends that this perspective on learning provides a more precise understanding of the relationship between cognition, emotion, and criminal behavior, and offers a significant improvement over first-generation cognitive and reciprocal social learning models of deviance. Finally, Kelley discusses the implications of the neo-cognitive learning perspective for prevention and early intervention strategies with youth at risk.

In Chapter 3, "Human Ecology and Social Disorganization Revisit Delinquency in Little Rock," Jeffery T. Walker reexamines the theory and research of Shaw and McKay in light of a half century or more of change in Arkansas. His study is grounded in the criminological traditions of "human ecology" and "social disorganization," dating back respectively to the work of the early-nineteenth-century French criminologist, André Guerry, and to the late-nineteenth-century French sociologist, Emile Durkheim. Walker addresses the relationship between delinquency and urban environmental change since World War II. Specifically, he revisits Little Rock to measure delinquency rates and to test various conclusions reached by Shaw and McKay in their study of the city conducted some fifty years earlier. Walker provides a detailed discussion of the background and development of Shaw and McKay's theory of criminality, and then updates and utilizes their measures to empirically test the value of their theory in the 1990s. He concludes that "the tenets of ecological research and social disorganization continue to be valid explanations of delinquency in modern urban cities."

Chapter 4, "Strain, Relative Deprivation, and Middle-Class Delinquency," by Velmer Burton and Gregory Dunaway, exemplifies contemporary efforts to conceptualize strain theory from both individual and structural perspectives. Utilizing the recent reformulations of strain advanced by Agnew, they specifically examine the explanatory power of relative deprivation theory. Grounded not only in an appreciation of Agnew's neostrain contributions, but also in the traditional formulation of strain as introduced by Merton and modified by Cohen and by Cloward and Ohlin, they assess the effect of relative deprivation on delinquency of high school youth. Their findings support inclusion of relative deprivation measures in efforts to predict self-reported delinquent behavior. Their approach also suggests that researchers can find common ground for fusing the older structural and newer individual explanations of strain.

In Chapter 5, "Social Control, Family Structure, and Delinquency," Joe Rankin and Ed Wells provide another statistical analysis of social control theory in regard to explaining the broken homes and delinquency relationship. Building on their own research and analyses of family structure and social control that have appeared over the past decade in such journals as *Criminology, Social Problems,* and the *Journal of Research in Crime and Delinquency,* Rankin and Wells contend that the time has certainly come for delinquency (and criminal) analysis to go "beyond simple bivariate descriptions" to include "social control (family process) variables and social contingencies." They operationalize measures from the 1981 National Survey of Children for separate indices (i.e., delinquent behavior, status offense, runaway, and official trouble). With respect to family structure, "a variety of family process factors were included to reflect differing aspects of the social control model." Finally, utilizing regression and multivariate analysis, Rankin and Wells move beyond social control variables to factor in socioeconomic status, social environment, sex, race, and age. Their findings and conclusions are both interesting and complex, suggesting that a mixed assessment of social control theory is in order—with social control factors explaining the less serious types of adolescent deviance, but not the more serious forms of criminal behavior.

In Chapter 6, "The Collective Reality of Crime: An Integrative Approach to the Causes and Consequences of the Criminal Event," Frank Schmalleger and Ted Alleman present a conceptual model of the collective reality of crime and crime control. Their integrative approach to the causes and consequences of the criminal event is similar in framework to the "square of crime" advocated by realist criminology. Using the crime of rape as an illustration, they urge criminologists and victimologists to transcend traditionally one-dimensional explanations of rape as simply acts of violence and domination. Their chapter reflects cultural or postradical feminism, historical as well as contemporary schools of criminological theory, and traditional sociological perspectives such as "symbolic interactionism," "character and social structure," "social constructionism," and "labeling and social control." Having recognized the holistic or integrative nature of crime and crime control on both the personal and societal levels, Schmalleger and Alleman proceed to describe a typology of heterosexual rape that can not only distinguish various forms of rape, but that also connects various agents of causality and reform.

The final contribution to Part I, Thomas O'Connor's "A Neofunctionalist Model of Crime and Crime Control," introduces the relationships between criminology, neofunctionalism, and the revival of Parsonian-like analyses. Neofunctionalism departs significantly from the functionalism of post–World War II: gone is the older technology of explaining causes by effects; gone, too, is the tacit approval of social problems as functional for change and social control. Neofunctionalists contend that the ideas of Parsons are more compatible with those of Marx and Weber than of Durkheim and Merton, and that neofunctionalism can facilitate identification of structural points of intervention and social change. O'Connor develops his neofunctionalist model of crime and crime control and sets out not to test, but to illustrate, the value of neofunctionalism as an integrative rather than co-optive criminological strategy. His chapter is a theoretical specification of Philippine terrorism prior to the use of the model for empirical inquiry. He maintains that neofunctionalist models such as his provide a way to study society, law, justice, legitimacy, and order as connected phenomena and concludes that this type of macro-level neofunctionalism, "rounds out the criminological repertoire by adding a pluralistic consensus theory to existing typologies."

In the opening chapter to Part II, "Confronting the Agenda of Authority: Critical Criminology, Anarchism, and Urban Graffiti," Jeff Ferrell exemplifies the tradition of doing criminology from "inside out" rather than "outside in." His examination of urban graffiti lays the groundwork for an anarchist critical criminology, and his cultural approach is ethnographic in content and grounded in the postmodernist movement. Ferrell calls for and develops an agenda for confronting authority and domination. His analysis integrates the interactionist tradition with that of political economy, but he also presents a social reality that stresses the "foreground of criminality" rather than the background. Influenced by critical sociology, British cultural studies, and feminist debates, Ferrell argues that the antigraffiti campaign and the criminalization of graffiti represents yet another "moral panic" successfully created by defenders of moral order. They also represent an "epistemic clamp down, a paradigm of fear and condemnation," and result in increased arrests and "degradation ceremonies" that reinforce dominant authorities and hierarchies.

In Chapter 9, "Young People, Culture, and the Construction of Crime: Doing Wrong versus Doing Crime," Mike Presdee provides insights for making sense out of the recent riotous and rebellious actions of young people in England. Influenced by Baudrillard's *America* and Katz's *Seductions of Crime*, and by such classic works as Veblen's *The Theory of the Leisure Class* and Foucault's *Discipline and Punish*, Presdee believes that the task for criminologists is to "mend the fracture of subject from society." Working within the traditions of radical and critical criminology, he provides an ethnographic account of British youth transgressing the boundaries of proper society. Presdee contends that criminologists should make their object of study the realm of cultural practices rather than crime per se, be it official or unofficial. He maintains that such an approach does not negate or devalue either the effects of poverty or inequality. Indeed, Presdee calls upon criminologists to locate our understanding of "doing wrong" in both the deregulation of economies on a global scale and the resolution between structure (or social economic situation) and agency (or sensuality). Put differently, Presdee believes that the origins of deviance are to be found in developing cultural relations between individuals and society rather than between offenders and law enforcement.

In Chapter 10, "Crime, Excitement, and Modernity," Pat O'Malley and Stephen Mugford deliver a provocative discussion and conceptualization of criminal action and emotional states. Stimulated by such seminal postmodern works as Barthes' *The Pleasure of the Text*, Elias' *The Civilising Process*, and Baudrillard's *Simulations*, they set out to rescue agency or individual action in the explanation of criminal behavior. In so doing, they provide a phenomenological as well as an objective-materialist account of the moral, sensual, and emotional attractions of crime. Beginning with an extended discussion of Jack Katz's work on "moral transcendence," and other related theorizing, O'Malley and Mugford present a broader historical perspective and analysis that can accommodate questions of class, race, and gender. They conclude that Katz's relevance to criminological theory lies in a connection between his "historically contextualized phenomenology of the attraction of crime" and a "Mertonian analysis of structural opportunity."

In Chapter 11, "Gender and Justice: Feminist Contributions to Criminology," Susan Caulfield and Nancy Wonders acknowledge differences within feminism, yet they choose to focus on commonalities within feminist thought. Specifically, they call for a "feminist-oriented" criminology rather than a "feminist criminology." Caulfield and Wonders contend that the development of a feminist-oriented criminology is an on-going process, and they identify five major contributions of feminist scholarship and practice that have already begun to alter the way that some criminologists conduct their work: (1) the focus on gender as a central organizing principle for contemporary life, (2) the importance of power in shaping social relations, (3) the sensitivity to the way that the social context shapes human relations, (4) the recognition that all social reality must be understood as a process and that methodology must develop accordingly, and (5) the emphasis on social change as a critical part of feminist scholarship and practice. Finally, in discussing the five contributions made by feminist analysis, they describe both the impact and the potential impact of these contributions on criminology.

In Chapter 12, "Law, Ideology, and Subjectivity: A Semiotic Perspective on Crime and Justice," Dragan Milovanovic provides a critically informed, psychoanalytic semiotic analysis of law and justice. His postmodernist approach to discourse examines how the "what happened?" in the courtroom is constructed. Milovanovic reconstructs the way lawyers present events of an alleged crime for jurors in accordance with the ideologically established rules of law. Anchored in a Lacanian postmodernist framework, he enriches this analysis by creatively blending his own work with insights from Marx, Hegel, and Althusser, as well as literary and film theory. The product of such a synthesis is a materially and subjectively based semiotic conceptualization of law and the judicial process. This effort on the part of Milovanovic, and others such as Peter Manning, represents the emergence of one of the newest schools of critical criminology.

In the final chapter, "Crime, Criminology, and Human Rights: Toward an Understanding of State Criminality," I reproduce an article published in *The Journal of Human Justice*, where I explore the potential of critical criminology to deal with state criminality through investigation of such issues as state interventions, overlapping activities of criminal versus noncriminal organizations, and the distinction between individual and state actors. I specifically examine state criminality via analysis of the activities of the Central Intelligence Agency and the Federal Bureau of Investigation. These activities include the usual methods of surveillance, wiretapping, mail tampering, and the use of *agents provocateurs*. I also consider issues related to the definition of terrorism and the use of terrorism by the state. In short, I stress that unless criminologists begin to address these kinds of issues, we may find ourselves in the awkward position of aiding the criminalization of noncriminal peoples around the world. I conclude that the adoption of basic human rights obligations as part of a progressive criminological practice are absolutely essential for future study and reduction of state criminality.

In closing this introduction to *Varieties of Criminology*, I would like to commend the contributors to this volume. The richness of their contributions is testimony both to criminology's maturity and its coming of age. While disagreeing with each other on several issues, these criminologists have all agreed to participate in this novel and risky project. Without their diverse theoretical insights and preparedness to let their work stand against others of different, and often critical persuasions, the field of criminology would be that much worse off.

NOTE

1. What is not represented here are the underdeveloped theoretical and multicultural perspectives on crime, minorities, and crime control that are only now beginning to be articulated. For the most comprehensive treatment of the subject, see Coramae Richey Mann's *Unequal Justice: A Question of Color* (Bloomington: Indiana University Press, 1993).

Part I

Mainstream Criminology

1

Biological and Neuropsychiatric Approaches to Criminal Behavior

C. RAY JEFFERY

The purpose of this chapter is to review the history and present status of biological approaches to criminal behavior. It will begin with a review of the early history of criminology, to be followed by a discussion of modern biological criminology and psychiatry. It will conclude with a statement on the policy implications for a criminal justice that integrates theoretical approaches to behavior, including the development of crime prevention programs in place of the politically fashionable "build more prisons and execute more people" approach of the Reagan-Bush administrations.

THE EARLY YEARS

Biology and Criminology in the Nineteenth Century

The history of criminology does not reflect the early beginnings as found in medicine and biology because in the 1920s the term "criminology" was used to apply to sociology. Criminology started with the positive school of Lombroso and others in an attempt to apply science to the study of human behavior. The main figures in this movement were Charles Darwin, Cesare Lombroso, Gregor Mendel, and Sigmund Freud.

However, before Lombroso's time there were a number of prominent figures who were developing the study of the brain in relationship to human behavior. In 1806 P. Pinel published his *Treatise on Insanity*, Francis Gall had published his work on phrenology and behavior in 1826, J. Pritchard had published *A Treatise on Insanity* in 1835, Darwin published the *Origin of Species* in 1859, and Paul Broca's work on the brain was emerging at the same time. Mendel's original work on genetics appeared in 1866. Herbert Spencer's *First Principles* appeared in 1862 using a bioevolutionary model for the study of society, and his *Principles of Psychology*, published in 1896, was naturalistic, evolutionary, biological, and positivistic (H. Ellis, 1897; D. N. Robinson, 1977; Wolfgang, 1972). Thus, the influence of biology on the study of man was very great in the nineteenth century, and Lombroso's work was only a small part of the movement.

The works of Rush, Maudsley, and Ellis in particular are a background to the study of biological criminology. Benjamin Rush was a physician who was prominent in colonial history, having signed the Declaration of Independence. He is also known as the father of American psychiatry. His book, *Medical Inquires and Observations Upon the Diseases of the Mind*, was published in 1812 (Carlson, Wollock, and Noel, 1981). Rush was instrumental in focusing on the physical causes of mental disorders—in other words, the relationship between brain and behavior. He ended his treatise with a plea to physicians to understand the role of the human brain in behavioral problems.

The work of Henry Maudsley, M.D., was critical to the development of a neuropsychiatric approach. His book, *The Physiology and Pathology of the Mind*, was published in 1867 and it still stands as a classic in neuropsychiatry (D. N. Robinson, 1977). Maudsley worked to integrate physiology and the pathologies of the mind by focusing on the structure and function of the brain. He viewed mental illnesses as a result of brain pathologies.

Maudsley identified the several parts of the brain and nervous system according to the neurology of his time, and he discussed free will as a problem in nervous energy. He related mental illness to the "chemical changes in the nerves" (p. 222), which is identical with the current concept of the neurotransmitter system. He dealt with the problems of classification and treatment of mental disorders but without the benefit of Computerized Axial Tomography (CAT), Magnetic Resonance Imaging (MRI), and Positron Emission Tomography (PET) scans. He also mentioned diet and nutrition as aspects of mental health, another contemporary idea.

Other works cited by Robinson (1977) as contributions to the history of psychology include Alexander Bain's *The Senses and the Intellect*, published in 1855; Alfred Binet's *Alterations of Personality*, published in 1896; Binet's *The Mind and the Brain*, plublished in 1907; and David Ferrier's *The Functions of the Brain*, published in 1886. In the late nineteenth and early twentieth centuries, Ramon Y. Cajal and Charles Sherrington introduced the idea of the synapse as a gap between neurons, a major stepping stone in the development of modern neurology. In 1881 Moriz Benedikt published a landmark book entitled *Anatomical Studies Upon Brains of Criminals* (Benedikt, 1881) in which he found major differences between normal brains and the brains of criminals. This book contains a wealth of information that has never been made a part of criminology. It can be said that by 1920 many significant works had emerged in biological criminology.

A major landmark in biological criminology was the publication of *The*

Criminal (H. Ellis, 1897). Havelock Ellis is better known for his later work on human sexuality, but his book on criminality established the biological approach firmly within European thought. Ellis followed Lombroso in discussions of criminal types from biological to social, and he found the causes of crime to range from genetics to brain structure to diet, geography, and social environment. He observed that many criminals had childhood problems such as behavioral problems, fire setting, cruelty to animals and to other children, epilepsy, left-handedness, and poor sexual adjustment. He cited many current studies of criminals, including a Scottish study of 5,000 criminals that found major physiological defects in this population. Ellis also cited insensitivity to pain, moral insensibility, and a desire for strong sensory stimulation as characteristics of criminals, and all of these are today considered important indicators of criminality and psychopathic behavior. He noted that female criminals are more like males than their noncriminal female counterparts.

Ellis argued for a treatment and prevention approach to behavioral problems in place of the prison/punishment approach. He noted that executions were used sparingly and that prisons were improving. He also supported the positivistic notion of indefinite sentences in place of fixed sentences, since the purpose of the criminal justice system is to reform and prevent, not to punish. I can only imagine that Dr. Ellis would be horrified to wake up to the criminal justice system of the early 1990s, which is dependent upon executions and long, fixed prison sentences.

It is worth noting that Ellis placed great emphasis on nutrition, which is still a novel approach today and one I will explore in more detail later on in this chapter. In his concluding chapter he emphasized a scientific approach to criminal behavior and the resolution of the conflict between legal and scientific criminology, a major theme of this chapter.

At the turn of the century, three books appeared in the United States devoted to criminology and a Darwinian/Lombrosian perspective. Arthur MacDonald's (1893) *Criminology* had a introduction by Lombroso, as did *The Criminal* by August Drahms (1900). Drahms' book presented a Lombrosian interpretation of criminality for an American audience, including detailed discussions of heredity, instincts, and brain organization. Philip Parsons (1909) in his *Responsibility for Crime* cited Ellis, Lombroso, Drahms, and Maudsley as the great figures in criminology. Parsons classified criminals according to the Lombrosian system, and he noted that crime is the normal functioning of an abnormal mind. His formula for crime was *Criminal Personality* × *Stimulus* = *Crime*, or *Organism* × *Environment* = *Crime*. In his work, Parsons discussed the environment but only in interaction with the individual or *Heredity* × *Environment* = *Individual*. He noted the high rate of alcoholism and insanity among criminals, a factor still important in contemporary criminology.

The focus of most criticism of biology came from sociologists and was directed at Lombroso. Wolfgang (1972: 288) responded to these criticisms, saying "Lombroso illuminated the scientific study of criminal behavior with many provocative ideas and deserves a place of honor in his own field." Such ideas as brain damage, alcoholism, and epilepsy, which were present in this early work, have assumed new importance in recent years, owing to the emergence of a new neurology and scientific knowledge that was not present at the time Lombroso was writing.

The Early Sociological Years

In 1829 A. M. Guerry and Adolphe Quetelet published separate but nearly identical works on the social statistics of crime. They looked at such factors as age, sex, poverty, geography, education, race, and crime. Quetelet referred to his work as "Social Physics," whereas Guerry labeled his "Moral Statistics" (Rennie, 1978: 35–37; Radzinowicz, 1966: 31–38). With these two statisticians we observe a shift from the *individual* offender to statistical correlates of crime as found in official government data banks. Interest moved from the structure of the criminal's brain to the number of criminals who were male or in poverty. This research methodology has characterized much of sociological criminology to this day.

These works were followed by the appearance of Emile Durkheim in 1895 with the argument that all facts were social to the exclusion of biology and psychology. For Durkheim crime was a social fact that helped to maintain the social order by upholding the common values of society that the criminal had violated (Rennie, 1978: 107–108; Radzinowicz, 1966: 72–74).

The sociological work of Durkheim and Karl Marx ignored the work of Auguste Comte as the father of sociological positivism. Comte argued that sociology must be based on biology and must be scientific in nature following the model of physics. Sociology followed the model of statistical analysis and aggregate data rather than scientific observations of individual events, as well as the concept of the socialized individual (Jeffery, 1990: 251).

The social approach was strengthened by the appearance of Marx's *Das Capital* in 1859, the same year Darwin's *Origin of Species* appeared. Marx argued for a class-conflict interpretation of social evolution. He borrowed the ideas of conflict and evolution from Darwin but placed them in a social rather than biological form. Other writings followed Marx in the class conflict approach to crime, a movement that reemerged in the 1960s and 1970s as part of the conflict/critical/radical approach to crime analysis. This approach totally ignores the biological basis for conflict as found in studies of brain structure, neuroendocrine systems, and male/female differences (Jeffery, 1990: 288).

The conflict between biology and sociology came to a head at the 1889 second Congress of International Criminology held in Paris. This meeting was sponsored by the faculty of the Medical School of Paris, a point worth noting as to the interest of medicine in criminology at that time in history. Lombroso, Raffaele Garofalo, Enrico Ferri, and Gabriel Tarde were present along with a distinguished gathering of biologists, physicians, and sociologists (H. Ellis, 1897: 307). Rennie (1978: 99) has labeled this the great debate between biology and socialism. At this conference Tarde presented his ideas of social environmental determinism and set the stage for the theory of imitation and differential association.

The sociological image of humankind is one of a socialized individual who committed crime only because of defective socialization. This view is in stark contrast to the psychobiological image of man as a dangerous animal, or as Desmond Morris (1967) expressed it in *The Naked Ape*, an ape in a gray flannel suit with a veneer of culture.

The Early Psychological Years

Three types of psychology have emerged over the years. Psychology has always reflected the division between mind and body, or mentalism and physicalism. Psychology reflects the philosophical divisions between mind-body dualism as found in Plato, René Descartes, Immanuel Kant, and others, and the physicalism of science and positivism as found in Isaac Newton, John Locke, Thomas Hobbes, David Hume, J. S. Mill, and others. We have already reviewed some major works in nineteenth-century psychology that showed the attempt of some writers to overcome the dualism of mind and body and to regard the brain/body system as a monistic one. The concept of a mind or "psyche" is well ingrained in psychology as found in introspective psychology, which is based on data from the mind as reported to the psychologist through written tests and verbal comments. Mentalistic psychology has been challenged by both behavioral and biological psychology in the twentieth century. Early psychology was founded in physiological psychology, as illustrated by *Elements of Physiological Psychology* by Ladd (1887). Experimental psychology received a major boost from the work of Wilhelm Wundt who was an M.D. trained in physiology. His *Principles of Physiological Psychology* (1873) set a standard for the development of psychology as a laboratory science, and his laboratory in Leipzig became a model of laboratories in England and the United States. The International Congress of Physiological Psychology was founded during 1889 in Paris and it was devoted to biology and genetics. This occurred before the founding of the American Psychological Association in 1897 (Hilgard, 1987).

Another major interpretation of the human behavior perspective was that of Sigmund Freud. Freud was a physician and neurologist who engaged in psychotherapy with neurotic patients in his practice in Vienna. He introduced conflict, psychosexual development, unconscious processes, dream analysis, and free association as major concepts within clinical psychology.

Psychoanalytic psychology depended on interpretations of dreams, thought processes, verbal statements, the Rorschach inkblot test, the Thematic Apperception Test, and other indirect measures of internal mental/physical processes (Hilgard, 1987; Jeffery, 1990).

Freud did not have the neurological knowledge needed to put forth an integrated theory of behavior, so he used mentalistic concepts such as Id, Ego, and Superego to explain the human personality. The basic biological instincts of food, sex, thirst, and survival are to be found in the Id, whereas the Ego and Superego develop from experiences with the social environment. When the three are in conflict personality disorders appear, such as psychoses or neuroses or character disorders.

Freud in his *Project for Scientific Psychology* (1895) attempted to find a neurological basis for his system, and he argued that ultimately psychiatry and medicine would be joined. Freud is considered by some as the father of psychobiological psychology (Jeffery, 1990: 214). Freud would be very happy and comfortable with the new neuropsychiatry that has emerged in the past twenty years, which will be discussed in detail later.

The behavioral school of psychology emerged with I. P. Pavlov, J. B. Watson, and B. F. Skinner. Behaviorism is based on a denial of introspectionism and mentalism as approaches to the study of human behavior, and in their places the behaviorist used the direct observation of behavior within a controlled laboratory setting. Behavior was studied as a response to a stimulus or environmental condition—that is, the environment determined behavior. This psychological environmentalism totally denied the role of human genetics and brain functioning in the study of behavior. The behaviorist ignored or minimized these topics. According to this psychology, the environment impacted upon behavior without an organism, or the organism was an "empty organism." Environmental determinism as found in behaviorism ignored the role of the brain in learning theory, even though Pavlov had emphasized the unconditioned or biological relationship between stimulus and response. The role of learning theory in criminology is discussed further later in this chapter (Hilgard, 1987; Jeffery, 1990).

The third model of behavior to emerge was that of biological psychology and neuropsychiatry. This is the model now used in psychology and psychiatry and the one put forth in this chapter as a basic model of human behavior.

Three Models of Behavior

To summarize, we are dealing with three models of behavior:

1. Introspective psychology or mentalism, which assumes that the environment changes the mental processes, which in turn control behavior or *Environment→ Mind→ Behavior*. The mental processes are never directly observed but are

inferred from behavior. This theory of behavior is found in introspective psychology and in sociology, where it is assumed that attitudes and values determine behavior. These are often referred to as self-concepts or role models.

2. Behavioral psychology, where the environment or stimulus produces the behavior, or *Environment→ Behavior*, usually treated as Stimulus-Response relationships.

3. Biological psychology, where the environment interacts with the individual by means of the brain, and in turn the brain controls behavior. This is an *Environment→ Brain→ Behavior* model of behavior, sometimes referred to as an *Environment→ Organism→ Behavior* approach. Only in this model is there an integration of biology and psychology, and this type of psychology recaptures the movement of the nineteenth century as found in Rush, Maudsley, and Havelock Ellis to make the brain sciences a basic foundation for psychiatry and psychology.

THE NEW ERA

Interdisciplinary Criminology

The compartmentalization of knowledge as it occurs in universities means that the biologists never talk to the economists or criminologists, whereas the problems each is involved with call for knowledge from other fields. Criminology must integrate the knowledge from biology, psychology, sociology, and law, as well as other fields (Jeffery, 1990). The major components of such an approach to criminology include genetics and brain functioning within biology; learning theory and personality development within psychology; the social environment within sociology; and the legal aspects of crime and criminal behavior within the law. Each level of analysis is based on the other levels.

Criminology must begin with a basic theory of behavior, not of criminal behavior. Criminal behavior is a subcategory of behavior based on the legal/criminal justice system. We need a theory of behavior to explain the behavior of judges, jurors, police officers, prosecutors, and the like. This is a *theory of crime*, or why certain acts are reacted to by society as criminal acts. We also need a theory of behavior to explain the behavior of those individuals whom we classify as criminals. This is a *theory of criminal behavior*. In turn, we must develop an interdisciplinary theory of behavior and then apply it to the explanations of crime and criminal behavior.

Behavioral Genetics

Genetics and environment interact to produce the individual or the phenotype as known in genetics. From the time of conception until the time of death, genes interact with other genes and with the internal and external environments of the individual. In turn, the phenotype interacts with the environment to produce behavior, and the important combination of phenotypic traits for behavior is the brain, which is a product of *Genetic* × *Environment* interaction as well. The *Genetic* × *Environment* interaction produces the Phenotype ($G \times E = P$), and the phenotype interacts with the environment to produce behavior ($P \times E = Behavior$). The phenotype/environment interaction is by way of *Brain* × *Environment* = *Behavior*.

Several points must be made. Phenotypic traits are the product of both genes and environment. It is not heredity or environment, but heredity in interaction with the environment. Genes do not produce behavior, only phenotypic traits such as the brain in interaction with the environment produce behavior. Arguments that genes cause or do not cause crime are false because the brain produces behavior, not genes. Genetic factors have been related to schizophrenia, for example, and the linking variable is the neurotransmitter system in the brain, especially the dopamine system. Violent behavior has been related to serotonin levels in the brain. To understand behavior we must first understand the linkage between genes and brain structure.

Each individual, except for identical twins, inherits a different genetic system, so no two individuals are alike. Genetic variation in interaction with environmental interaction creates the variation in the phenotype ($Vg \times Ve = Vp$). Since no two individuals are alike, criminological approaches that deny or ignore individual differences are faulty, and 99 percent of criminological research uses aggregate data that ignore basic individual differences.

Crime and Genetics

Good reviews of crime and genetics are to be found in L. Ellis (1982), Mednick and Volovka (1980), L. Taylor (1984), Mednick, Moffit, and Stack (1987), and Fishbein (1990). The issue of genes and behavior is a most controversial one as seen in the opposition to and cancellation of a conference on Genetic Factors in Crime, which was to be sponsored by the National Institutes of Health in October 1992. The argument also can be found in several recent articles published in *Criminology* by Walters and White (1989a), Brennan and Mednick (1990), and Walters (1990). Genetics is still too hot to be discussed openly as a scientific topic, which in turn greatly limits our ability to treat criminals and prevent crime.

THE BRAIN AND BEHAVIOR

Brain Development and Evolution

Brain development is a combination of genetics and environment. That is why any model of behavior that uses mentalistic concepts or environmental explanations of behavior is in error. All environmental experiences go into the brain. Summaries of brain/behavior relationships can be found in Kalat (1992), Jeffery (1990), and Graham (1990).

The genetic endowment interacts with the environment to determine brain development. This interaction starts at the fetal stage when the environment of the uterus determines fetal development, including brain development. Drugs such as tobacco, alcohol, or cocaine in the mother's bloodstream will impact on the fetal brain. Diet and the level of protein in the mother will also impact, since low protein levels result in incomplete brain development. Early environmental experiences in the postnatal period determine how the immature neurons in the brain connect and how the brain is ultimately organized. A lack of environmental stimulation will also result in a poorly developed brain.

Brain Structure and Evolution

The brain is organized to receive sensory information, organize and store information, and control behavior via the motor system. Sensory input and motor output are controlled by the emotional and rational parts of the brain. The emotional part of the brain (the limbic system) is a system of primitive parts of the brain shared by lower animal forms, and has been referred to as the "crocodile brain." In the limbic system are the emotions of violence, rage, hunger, fear, sex, and thirst. These behaviors are basic to survival, but they are also basic to human conflict and passion and are expressed in murder, assault, rape, robbery, and burglary. The limbic system contains what are called the "pleasure and pain centers" of the brain. The one basic rule of behavior is that of the maximization of pleasure and the minimization of pain. This pleasure/pain principle is found in Plato, in Jeremy Bentham and the classical school of criminology, in Freud, in behavioral psychology, and in neuropsychiatry and psychobiology.

The hypothalamus regulates the autonomic nervous system, or the internal functions associated with the heart, kidneys, digestion, respiration, sexual behavior, and the blood vessels. The hippocampus consolidates information and is critical to memory. The thalamus relays sensory information to the cortex. The cortex or higher brain controls the integration of sensory and motor processes into an integrated behavioral system. The temporal lobes receive visual and audio information, the occipital lobes receive visual information, the parietal lobes receive somatosensory information from the body such as touch, and the frontal lobes contain the motor cortex as well as the prefrontal lobes, which are responsible for thought processes, rationality, decision making, memory, and planning, or what we refer to as the human qualities of life. Sensory information flows from the sensory systems to the several lobes in the cortex where it is channeled through the sensory/motor system. The final output is through the prefrontal lobe, which can inhibit emotions from the other parts of the brain. The impulse to kill can be stopped by the prefrontal lobes with what we call ethical behavior or a decision process based on socialization and learning. The impulse will not be stopped if the prefrontal lobes are damaged.

Neurochemistry of the Brain

The critical part of brain functioning is the communication between millions of neurons that takes place biochemically in the synapses between neurons. These messengers, called neurotransmitters, are a product of the food we eat. Acetylcholine is a product of choline; tyrosine is the precursor of dopamine and norepinephrine; and tryptophan is the precursor for serotonin. These biochemicals are responsible for our behavior, including such aberrant behaviors as alcoholism, schizophrenia, and violence.

Learning and Human Behavior

Learning is the modification of behavior through experience. Human beings are born with certain basic innate responses to the environment, such as sucking and fear of falling, but due to the large cortex and association area in the human brain the individual can learn a multiplicity of responses to any given environmental stimulus. Ants and cats live by innate stimulus-response patterns—that is, given a stimulus a response occurs. The innate response patterns are modified by learning for the higher primates through associational learning. Pavlovian learning theory started with basic biological drives, which are then modified by experience, whereas Watsonian and Skinnerian behaviorism started with responses that produce a given stimulus. The behavior is maintained and learning occurs if the stimulus is rewarding, or reinforcing in the language of the Skinnerian psychologist. In either case learning occurs because the stimulus is biologically necessary, such as food, water, sex, or shelter. The individual learns in this way to gain pleasure and avoid pain (Hilgard, 1987; Jeffery, 1990).

Learning is biologically based in another way. When learning occurs the brain structure is modified in terms of the synaptic connections and the neurotransmitter systems. The reason we learn and have memories is that the biochemistry of the brain is changed by experience. In recent years the major development in learning theory has been in the development of a physiological basis for learning. Skinnerian behaviorism has been replaced with biological learning theory.

The brain is made up of neural connections formed before birth or shortly thereafter as a result of genetic/environmental interaction, as well as the experiences with the environment from birth to death. Learning allows for much greater adaptation of the human animal to the environment than could occur through simple unlearned stimulus-response behaviors. Learning allows for elaborate environmental/organism interactions not possible otherwise, it permits the storage of this learning in the brain in the form of memory, and it allows for the transmission of such knowledge to others through associational learning, or what we call cultural transmission of learning.

Criminal Behavior and the Brain

Since all behavior is a product of brain action, any deficiency or defect in the brain can be related to criminal behavior. This includes problems with the neurotransmitter system, brain damage, underarousal of the autonomic nervous system, brain laterality, and nutrition and pollution (Jeffery, 1990; Fishbein, 1990).

Drugs are biochemicals that act on behavior by altering the neurotransmitter system of the brain. Drugs either block or increase the flow of neurotransmitters into the synapses. Drugs that block neurotransmitters are called antagonists, whereas those that increase the flow are called agonists. The drug AMPT blocks the synthesis of dopamine and norepinephrine by blocking the conversion of tyrosine into dopa and then dopamine, thus decreasing stimulation to the postsynaptic neurons. The amphetamines increase the release of dopamine and norepinephrine, thus increasing excitement and arousal. Caffeine and nicotine increase stimulation of neurons, which in turn increase the heart rate and blood pressure among other things (Kalat, 1992).

Drug therapies are now common in neuropsychiatry. Depression is treated by a series of drugs called tricyclic antidepressants that inhibit the absorption of dopamine, norepinephrine, and serotonin, thus increasing the flow of these biochemicals into the postsynaptic neurons and increasing neural stimulation. Schizophrenia has been treated by decreasing the amount of dopamine reaching the neural receptors (Kaplan and Sadock, 1991; Schatzberg and Cole, 1991; Yudofsky and Hales, 1992). Several medications have been developed for the treatment of drug addiction, such as stimulants for cocaine abusers that will increase the natural amount of dopamine in the brain. Aggressive individuals are low in serotonin and serotonin agonists, which increase the serotonin levels and thus reduce violent behavior. It is also possible to increase the dopamine and serotonin levels by increasing the tyrosine and tryptophan intake in the diet. Through medications and nutrition we can better control alcoholism, drug addiction, and violence, all of which are major problems for the criminal justice system.

Underarousal of the autonomic nervous system can result in thrill-seeking as a way of increasing the level of neural stimulation. Such individuals are often labeled psychopaths because of the high level of antisocial behavior associated with their thrill-seeking. Again, the alcoholic and the cocaine addict are self-medicating and increasing brain stimulation by the use of drugs.

Brain laterality is also related to criminality. Most individuals are right-handed and left-hemisphere dominant; however, 10 percent of the population is left-handed and either right- or left-hemisphere dominant. Many more males are left-handed, and many more left-handed males are criminals than right-handed males. Whatever is responsible for this pattern of hemispheric dominance, it does influence criminal and antisocial behavior.

Brain Damage and Criminal Behavior

Damage to the brain can occur as a result of brain trauma, nutrition, toxic pollution, drug and alcohol abuse, and hemispheric dysfunction. Frontal lobe damage is associated with antisocial behavior and violent behavior because the frontal lobes control the violent impulses from the limbic system as discussed above. Lewis (1986, 1988) found that 14 of 14 youthful offenders and 15 of 15 adult offenders on death row suffered from neurological damage and defects. Such damage can also occur as a result of alcohol or drug use by the mother during pregnancy, resulting in fetal alcoholism syndrome or the "crack baby" syndrome.

Diet and nutrition are also important because a lack of the proper diet during the pre- and postnatal period can lead to low birth weight, low intelligence scores, and brain damage. Heavy toxic mineral contamination has been related to aggression. Lead, cadmium, aluminum, and mercury have been found at high levels in aggressive individuals. The lead levels as determined by hair analysis of serial murderers has been extremely high. Research in California has revealed high manganese levels in prison populations (Gottschalk et al., 1991).

Biology, Sex, and Crime

One of the long-standing and unexplained aspects of criminal behavior has been the fact that many more males than females commit crimes. This is usually interpreted as due to social influences and socialization, but the biological differences between males and females are the critical beginnings of sex/gender differences (see Kalat, 1992; Jeffery, 1990; and Fishbein, 1992 for reviews). The female zygote has two X chromosomes, or is an XX. The male zygote has a Y chromosome in place of the second X chromosome, or is an XY. During the fetal stages of development, the presence of the Y changes the biochemistry of the development of the fetus, including the sex organs and general body build. What is critical for behavior, however, is the impact these biochemicals or sex hormones have on the development of the fetal brain. The male brain lacks the development of the left hemisphere that the female brain has owing to the impact of testosterone on the left hemisphere. Male brain development is typically (but not for every case) more right-hemisphere dominant, with more spatial abilities and less linguistic skills, which are in the left hemisphere. The left hemisphere is also more involved in the control of emotional behaviors. Males are more dominant, exploratory, and aggressive than females from birth on. They are also more susceptible to diseases, defects, learning disabilities, and other biological inadequacies.

Exposure of the female fetus to androgens during the gestation period, especially at certain critical periods in brain development, will result in an "androgenized female" who has many male characteristics and behaviors, including being more antisocial and more violent. The opposite case is that of the "androgen insensitive" male who was not exposed at the fetal stage to the proper amount of androgens and thus never developed androgen-sensitive neurons in the brain. At the time of puberty when the male hormones increase these males do not respond as males because the plasma testosterone does not attach to the neurons and thus does not influence their behavior.

Recent research findings on homosexuals has been released showing major differences in the hypothalamus of male homosexuals and nonhomosexuals. The development of the hypothalamus during the fetal stage is influenced by the androgens (L. Allen, 1992).

Fishbein (1992) in a review of the literature on the female criminal concludes that more attention must be paid to biological factors in female criminality. She cites such facts as the higher risk for aggression among those females who are exposed to androgens, and she notes that female criminals are more mesomorphic (male athletic body build) than are female noncriminals. She also notes that serotonin levels are higher in females in general, thus protecting them from violent outbursts. The female menstrual cycle is such that estrogen peaks at ovulation and progesterone peaks shortly thereafter, so that just prior to the new menstrual cycle both estrogen and progesterone are at a very low level. The premenstrual syndrome (PMS) has been related to these hormonal changes that produce anxiety, tension, and in some cases violent outbursts.

IMPLICATIONS FOR CRIME PREVENTION

New Prevention Strategies

Crime prevention means preventing the crime *before* it occurs rather than waiting for it to occur. This usually takes the shape of crime prevention through environmental design, but the discussion in this chapter suggests that some heavy attention be paid to the biological variables involved in criminal behavior. This would include early pre- and postnatal care for pregnant women and infants. Such care would be concerned with alcohol and drug use by pregnant women, the nutritional status of the mother, low birth weight of the infant, hyperactivity or brain damage of the infant, and other medical problems that could lead to later behavioral problems (Jeffery, 1990).

As the child develops, the early symptoms of behavioral disorders such as enuresis, child abuse, violence by the child against other children or animals, fire-setting, running away from home, inadequate family care, truancy from school, and school disciplinary problems must be dealt with at an early age. The cooperation of parents, teachers, pediatricians, and social counselors must be secured. Neurological examinations including CAT, MRI, and PET scans must be provided when the medical examination indicates that they are needed.

Attention must be paid to the 5 percent of the delinquent population that commits 50 percent of the serious offenses, and especially the core group of violent offenders who are drug addicts. This effort must identify the "high risk" group at an early age and move them into treatment programs before they have committed ten or twenty major felonies. We must look for individual differences rather than at statistical categories of offenders. In short, the question is not "what disease does the person have?" but "what person has the disease?" We should not ask "how many men are criminals?" but rather "what men are criminals?"

The Politics of Crime Prevention

The current U.S. policy is to control crime through the criminal justice system, waiting for the crime to occur before taking action retroactively. We spend millions of dollars on the police-courts-prison system, whereas we spend virtually nothing on research and prevention. In order to put a crime-prevention program into place we need to totally change our approach to crime, and the politicians are not willing to do this. The political system must move from a punitive to a preventive framework. There must be major changes in the legal system, which would relate criminal law much more to science and technology and much less to prisons and executions; otherwise, our high crime rate will continue in the future.

2

Crime and Psychology of Mind: A Neo-Cognitive View of Delinquency

THOMAS M. KELLEY

Our current thinking about the causes of crime and delinquency lacks precision and, thus, our solutions have been well off the mark. A more accurate understanding of the causes of crime appears to be lost in an entanglement of criminological theories and concepts that, while often clever and intellectually sophisticated, are more often misleading or incorrect (Cressey, 1979; Gibbons, 1972, 1989; Williams, 1984; Gibbs, 1987). Over the past century, the field of criminology has produced divergent theories of crime and delinquency with often inconsistent and contradictory implications for the prevention of crime and the treatment of criminal offenders. The field's frustration in trying to develop powerful solutions to the problem of crime is symbolized by the dysfunctional and fragmented alliances among our criminal justice agencies, the swinging pendulum from liberal to conservative crime control models, the impulsive shifts from one treatment fad to the next, and, perhaps most poignantly, by the trends toward the increasing complexity of our theoretical formulations and the diversification of our professional pursuits.

For every theory of crime or delinquency that exists in our field today, there are conspicuous exceptions to the established rules and predicted outcomes derived from those theories. For every theoretical explanation of crime, there are probably many more individuals touched by the conditions or circumstances proposed by these theories as causes who are not criminals or delinquents. In our attempts to explain or justify these exceptions and contradictions, we have either designed forced and intricate explanations, or we have ignored or twisted these irregularities to fit our established theoretical models. A prime example of the first response has been the recent proliferation of so-called integrated or interdisciplinary theories of crime (Knudten, 1970; Wilson and Herrnstein, 1985; Elliot et al., 1985; Pearson and Weiner, 1985). Yet in our best longitudinal studies based on these

interdisciplinary models of crime and delinquency, we find that the explained
variance ranges from 25 percent to 49 percent. Thus, the greatest percentage
of variance remains in the unexplained category (Elliot and Huizinga, 1984;
Clayton and Voss, 1981; Jessor, Chase, and Donovan, 1980; West and
Farrington, 1977; Elliot and Voss, 1974; Ginsburg and Greenly, 1978;
Jessor and Jessor, 1977; Kandel, 1978).

The variation that exists both within and among our theories appears to
have become as great as the variety of factors those theories are attempting
to explain. Instead of seeking some common factors that would break down
the variation into some comprehensible design, it has become commonplace
for the field to focus on the variation itself. Instead of connecting the diverse
variables of our field into a unifying framework of understanding, our
current formulations break up or fragment the concepts they are studying
to such an overwhelming degree that they are confusing rather than il-
luminating.

PSYCHOLOGY OF MIND

Therefore, what the field appears to need are principles that can provide
a basic or commonsense understanding of criminal and delinquent behavior
in most of its forms and reveal clearly how to prevent and reverse the process
that results in crime and delinquency. The purpose of this chapter is to offer
the field such a group of principles, which can become the basis of a new
model for criminological inquiry to which I have referred previously as
Breakthrough Criminology (T. M. Kelley, 1990).

The pioneering work on these principles was done in the field of psy-
chology by Suarez (1985a, 1985b), Suarez and Mills (1982), and Suarez,
Mills, and Stewart (1987). These researchers have formulated a set of four
psychological principles or constants which they called Psychology of Mind
(POM). The four major principles of POM are summarized by Suarez,
Phelps, and Blevens (1987: 5–6):

1. *The Principle of Thought.* Thought is a formulating agency of consciousness.
   Thought has two dimensions: (a) the content of details of specific cognitions (i.e.,
   ideas, interpretations, beliefs, etc.), and (b) the function that formulates the
   content. One basic premise of this principle is that people create their own
   thoughts and thought systems but are, to varying degrees, not aware of doing
   so. Thus, it is possible for people to experience reality to varying degrees only
   in terms of the end products of their thinking (images, beliefs, interpretations,
   expectations, etc.) and their associated perceptions, feelings, and behaviors.

2. *The Principle of Separate Reality.* Reality is a perceptual phenomenon that is a
   continuous product of thought. Personal reality is a *separate* and unique experience for each individual. Reality, as experienced by the individual, is a function
   of his or her thinking and the degree to which he or she is aware of thinking as

being the origin of all cognition. POM views "individual differences" as a principle rather than the source of error variance.

3. *The Principle of Feelings and Emotions.* Feelings and emotions, like physical pain, represent a continuous, moment-by-moment indication of the individual's adaptive/maladaptive level of psychological functioning. Whatever is felt at any given moment corresponds to the level of functioning at that moment. As such, feelings are not stored (i.e., repressed).

4. *The Principle of Levels of Consciousness.* The psychological state of functioning is not stable, it fluctuates. Each level is a qualitatively separate state of consciousness. So while an individual may possess a relatively fixed fund of stored information from past experiences (i.e., a thought system), this information will be recalled, utilized, and experienced differently according to the state. It is the "state" of consciousness that is the context within which the function of thought produces or reproduces (recalls) cognitions.

In a recent article (Kelley, 1990), I examined and then utilized the above principles of POM in an attempt to explain most forms of delinquent and criminal behavior. Recently, these same principles have served as the foundation for a group of new assumptions about learning that has now been formalized in the literature as Neo-Cognitive Learning Theory or NLT (R. C. Mills, 1987; 1988; Mills, Dunham, and Alpert, 1988; Shuford, 1986; Phelps, 1987; Suarez, Phelps, and Blevens, 1987; Kelley, 1990). This new perspective about learning provides an even deeper level of understanding about the etiology of delinquency, drug use, and other health-damaging youthful misbehavior. Therefore, the objectives of this chapter are to describe the major assumptions of NLT, to cite contemporary research evidence that supports each assumption of this new perspective, to distinguish how this model of learning offers a significant advance over first-generation cognitive and reciprocal social learning models of deviance, and to discuss the implications of the Neo-Cognitive Learning perspective for prevention and early intervention strategies with at-risk youth.

MAJOR ASSUMPTIONS OF NEO-COGNITIVE LEARNING THEORY

NLT Assumption 1: The Natural Mental Health of Children

NLT is based on a "wellness" model of human psychological functioning and contains three major principles or assumptions. The first is that every child begins life with a natural, inborn capacity for healthy psychological functioning. In other words, at birth, children do not have a mind-set that points them toward delinquency, drug use, or other forms of deviant behavior. To the contrary, the attributes of this innate ability for healthy functioning include the use of common sense, a natural desire to learn, and an intrinsic motivation to develop and utilize these abilities in pursuing prosocial life-styles. Furthermore, this innate mind-state incorporates unconditional, positive self-worth, a desire to learn for the basic satisfaction of learning, and a natural joy from the understanding and mastery of the environment (Suarez, 1985a; Suarez, Mills, and Stewart, 1987; Mills et al., 1988).

From this natural state of mind or psychological perspective, high self-esteem is automatic and effortless. It exists naturally and need not be taught, developed, or strengthened (R. C. Mills, 1990; Mills et al., 1988). Self-esteem, in this mind-state, is not derived from outside exploits, but serves instead as the motivation behind the ability to accomplish. In this mind-state, a child will experience his or her innate capacity to process new information with common sense and good judgment, will have genuine peace of mind, as well as a high capacity for insight. Furthermore, learning and performance in this state of mind are not experienced as particularly stressful or effortful. According to the Neo-Cognitive Model, all of the above capacities exist together in one cohesive package that is part and parcel of this intrinsic state of mind (Mills et al., 1988; R. C. Mills, 1987; Peck, Law, and Mills, 1987; Mills, 1990).

NLT Assumption 2: The Learning of an Alienated Frame of Reference

The second major assumption of NLT is that delinquency and other dysfunctional adolescent behaviors become possible to the degree that children begin to learn and incorporate into their belief systems alienated frames of reference. Such alienated mind-sets are molded by an on-going conditioning sequence starting early in the family environment with continuous exposure to conflict, negative beliefs, and other forms of unhealthy parental and family functioning. According to NLT, repeated exposure to such dysfunctional processes leads to conditioned feelings of insecurity often experienced by children at very early ages. To be more precise, NLT proposes two distinct types of learning (conditioned and unconditioned), both of which occur simultaneously and are experienced by all children. Unconditioned learning is a natural, basically effortless form of learning based on insight and intuition. Conditioned learning, on the other hand, is more stressful, forced, and motivated by feelings of fear and insecurity. Which type of learning predominates is dependent on the qualities of the particular child's early home and school experiences.

Within the neo-cognitive learning perspective, unconditioned belief systems are associated with higher states of mental health or higher levels of mood. In these more natural and unconditioned levels of functioning, a youth's ego or self-concept is less a source of motivation. According to the NLT, ego is defined as a conditioned system of beliefs through which a child comes to define his or her personal identity or self-concept as well as the measures of performance and personal expectations that must be met for this thought-created identity or image to be validated. In lower mood states or more conditioned levels of functioning, motivation is more highly ego determined. In lower mood states, anything (event, circumstance, etc.) perceived by a child to invalidate, differ with, or contradict his or her ego or self-image will result in some feeling of insecurity (e.g. anger, anxiety, depression, etc.). The more ego-based "learned insecurity," the greater the level of self-consciousness experienced by a child and the lower the child's natural experience of self-esteem. Thus, any time a youth's conditioned ego appears to be challenged or threatened, that youth will automatically experience insecure feelings. These feelings then serve as the breeding ground for dysfunctional behaviors such as delinquency, drug use, school failure, and such. Ultimately, it is through the relationship of ego or self-concept and insecure feelings that all forms of youthful health damaging behavior are fostered and maintained (Mills et al., 1988; J. Bailey, 1990; Pransky, 1990; Peck et al., 1987; Mills, 1990).

Thus, according to NLT, it is the internalization (i.e., conditioned programming) of a negative, alienated belief system that blocks the expression of the innate healthy psychological functioning described above. Therefore, learning and performance become effortful and deviant behavior desirable only when these products become connected in a child's thinking (through conditioned learning) with proving themselves to others in socially or culturally conforming ways. Put another way, children possess and will display natural feelings of emotional wellness and unconditional self-worth before learning beliefs that they must prove themselves in particular ways in order to reduce the intensity of insecure feelings and or achieve fleeting and artificial experiences of well-being and self-worth.

To summarize at this juncture, NLT proposes that children are not born with automatic thoughts and beliefs associating their worth and self-esteem with their mode of dress, personal acquaintances, neighborhood, possessions, or personal and school performance. It follows, therefore, that if youth do not incorporate an insecure, alienated belief system, through early cognitive programming, their innate capacity for healthy functioning will evolve naturally into mature behavior, unconditional self-esteem, and emotional well-being.

NLT Assumption 3: Drawing Out Children's Natural Healthy Functioning

The third major assumption or principal of Neo-Cognitive Learning Theory is that any child's innate capacity for healthy, mature psychological functioning can be rekindled and drawn out, regardless of that youth's prior history or record of delinquent or other self-damaging behavior. As discussed above, NLT proposes that insecure states of mind that foster alienated belief systems and the mind-state that allows for the ability to function in a more mature, commonsense perspective, are discontinuous or mutually independent states of functioning. According to NLT, these two qualitatively distinct states of mind are not interactive or related, although they are both produced through the agency of thought. Insecure feelings, negative attitudes, and dysfunctional behaviors like delinquency stem from distorted low-quality thinking in insecure, alienated mind states. Common sense or maturity, on the other hand, result from higher quality thinking in more unconditioned states of mind. According to this final NLT assumption, if certain essential conditions are present, alienated youth have the ability to understand how their thinking processes work and through this understanding can regain access to their natural healthy psychological functioning.

Thus, according to the neo-cognitive learning paradigm, a key to drawing out a youth's natural healthy functioning involves discerning what factors or conditions, at any given moment, determine whether a youth will function at unconditioned levels (learning and behaving by insight) rather than more conditioned levels of insecurity-driven learning and motivation. In other words, NLT proposes that while high-risk youths have comparatively higher levels of learned insecurity, they can be helped to function in frames of mind that are less likely to stimulate these insecure experiences. In these healthier mind-states, such youths can begin to understand and recognize the cognitive and perceptual distortions that occur during more insecure episodes. By so doing, they can be empowered to avoid being at the affect of their insecure feelings and related urges to engage in such dysfunctional behaviors as delinquency and drug use.

SUPPORTIVE EVIDENCE FROM CONTEMPORARY RESEARCH AND THEORY

There is considerable evidence from contemporary criminological research and theory that supports each major assumption of Neo-Cognitive Learning Theory. With respect to the first assumption of this model, that children are born with a natural capacity for healthy psychological functioning, Wilson and Herrnstein (1985: 222) conclude that "the infant cries to signal distress/hunger, not so far as we know, to control the behavior of others [and] devoted attention to the infant's needs at this stage does not produce a spoiled child." This statement underscores the fact that hundreds of examinations of infants and toddlers raised in nurturing settings reveal clearly that such youngsters possess a natural curiosity to explore and learn as much as possible about their surroundings. In fact, most early childhood research appears to support the assumption of the natural mental health of children. According to Mills (1987), the vast body of developmental research reveals conclusively that at birth, children do not have a mind-set that predisposes them toward delinquency, drug use, or other forms of deviant behavior. To the contrary, such studies point almost unanimously to the natural inborn state of healthy mental functioning for children, which includes a natural interest to learn; an intrinsic ability to act in mature, commonsense, nondelinquent ways; and a natural desire to use and expand their abilities in legitimate and prosocial directions (Mills, 1987; Mills et al., 1988; Wilson and Herrnstein, 1985; Stewart, 1985; Dodge and Frame, 1982; Patterson, 1982; Suarez, Mills, and Stewart, 1987; Arendt, Cove, and Sroufe, 1979; Sroufe, 1979; Ainsworth, 1982; Sroufe, Egeland, and Erickson, 1983). The bulk of contemporary early childhood development research further concludes that this natural state of healthy functioning includes a high capacity for learning new behaviors and skills along with little or no awareness or self-consciousness surrounding the learning process.

Further support for this first NLT assumption is provided by R. C. Mills (1990), who cites several current studies on motivation stemming from research demonstration grants on primary prevention at the University of Oregon in the late 1970s followed by research demonstration programs at a variety of sites in the 1980s. According to Mills, this research has produced a new look at what has been called the "higher self" or "true self," as a basically healthy, already actualized self as a source of intrinsic motivation (Mills, 1990; Mills, 1987; Mills, Dunham, and Alpert, 1988; Peck et al., 1987). Mills points out that several well known researchers in the field of motivation are beginning to point toward a recognition of this deeper or truer "meta-cognitive" self as an agent in producing and sustaining intrinsic motivation and in mediating external reinforcers (McCombs, 1991; Weiner, 1990; Bandura, 1989a, 1991; Carver and Schier, 1990; Deci and Ryan, 1991; Harter, 1988, 1990; Iran-Nejed, 1990; McCombs and Marzano, 1990). Mills (1990) states that while authors such as Maslow (1970) recognize the existence of this state, they felt that one had to first go through and satisfy lower need states to attain this actualized experience. The above research on motivation, however, tends to support the conclusion that everyone starts out in life in this actualized state and then learns or is conditioned to function in lower "need" states.

The second major assumption of NLT is that delinquency, drug use, and other forms of deviant youthful behavior result from the learning of an insecure, alienated belief system. Much of the evidence that supports this second major principle of NLT relates to delinquency and is summarized in recent articles by Mills (1987; Mills et al., 1988) and Kelley (1990), which review several relevant etiological studies, cross-sectional research programs, and youth panel surveys. According to Mills, this research indicates clearly that delinquency, drug use, and school failure appear to be related to a common set of social-psychological variables. The first group of common factors is well-documented and revolves around the family environment. At-risk youth tend to come from families experiencing high levels of turmoil or stress. Parent-child interaction involves excessive nagging and fault-finding. Discipline in such families is characterized by inconsistency and lacks fairness and empathy. Also, in these families, parents were found not to explain rules, to have little verbal or nonverbal caring, support, or sustained interest in the child's activities (Patterson, 1982; Loeber and Dishion, 1984; Tittle, 1980; Smith and Walters, 1978; P. Robinson, 1978; Hanson et al., 1984; Hershorn and Rosenbaum, 1985; Block, Keyes, and Block, 1986; Baumrind, 1985; McCord and McCord, 1959; West and Farrington, 1973; Conger, 1976; Hirschi, 1969; Schaefer, 1959).

Mills (1988) cites the results of the University of Minnesota's Mother-Child Study as being illustrative of this process. The Minnesota study examined a group of low-income, single-parent mothers and their children from infancy to age five. Researchers looked first at infants with a secure attachment to their mothers. At age five, most children in this group tended to be more creative in responding to environmental changes, and more persistent in staying with complex tasks. On the other hand, children with a less secure attachment to their mothers tended to decompensate when challenged with complicated tasks, were more likely to avoid their mothers, and were quicker to become angry, oppositional, overwhelmed, and depressed. Furthermore, at age four, children with secure attachments had generally higher self-esteem, were less dependent, and more mature. Those with less secure attachments at age four were more impulsive and aggressive (Arendt et al., 1979; Sroufe, 1979; Ainsworth, 1982; Sroufe et al., 1983).

According to R. C. Mills (1988) the bulk of contemporary longitudinal research concludes that, as a consequence of these dysfunctional patterns of familial interaction, these youths tend to develop behavioral, emotional, and learning problems at early ages. Subsequently, these problems tend to worsen as the child enters the school environment. Research on the early school experiences of these youths indicates that the process of acquiring an insecure belief system, which begins in the homes of such youths, tends to be reinforced or reconfirmed by the types of interactions these youths have with school personnel and other students. According to Mills et al. (1988: 648),

in the absence of understanding that these qualities of interactional patterns are a consequence of their parents' habitual states of mind, they will interpret them to mean that there is something wrong or inadequate about themselves, programming these biased attributions into their cognitive structure at a very fundamental level. This cognitive programming begins to obscure children's natural common sense, ability to learn by insight, and natural feelings of well being. As a result, they develop an insecure belief system. They then enter school with poor self-concept, insecurity about learning and performance, and mistrust of others, particularly adults in terms of perceiving genuine caring and interest.

Thus, these early negative childhood experiences appear to combine with later school and community experiences, with the result being even higher levels of alienation. Much research indicates that insecure belief systems foster high levels of self-consciousness, making it more difficult for children to concentrate, follow instructions, and to relax in the classroom setting. Another outcome of learned insecurity is strong urges in such children to prove themselves, which often leads to acting-out behavior and discipline problems in school. In other words, early childhood experiences, leading to conditioned insecurity, interfere with a child's ability to learn naturally via insight and inspiration.

Mills (1988) cites considerable research findings from several independent sources that reveal that at-risk youths develop a cognitive style or structure of interpretation that results in negative school attitudes and negative self-cognition related to school and learning. Dissatisfaction with the entire school experience appears to be one of the strongest factors leading to school misbehavior. High-risk youths are, in general, more alienated from school and from nondeviant life-styles (Dunham and Alpert, 1987; Cippolone, 1986; Stern and Catterall, 1985; Howell and Frege, 1982; Coombs and Cooley, 1986; Glasser, 1969; Polk and Schafer, 1972).

Mills (1988) points out that these findings are consistent with contemporary social process theories (Hirschi, 1969; Reckless, 1967), and the symbolic interactionist perspective (Blumer, 1969), all of which predict that youths develop more and more aversive points of view about school and prosocial peers owing to this repetitive pattern of perceived failure and learned insecurity in family, school, and community settings. Mills states further that recent studies of high-risk youths grounded in contemporary cognitive learning theory support the notion of a cumulative learning process that leads to stronger levels of alienation and predicts many forms of deviant, often criminal, behavior (Block, Keyes, and Block, 1986; Elliot and Huizinga, 1984; Ekstrom, Goertz, Pollack, and Rock, 1986; Jessor and Jessor, 1977; Elliot and Voss, 1974; West and Farrington, 1977; Wehlage and Rutter, 1986).

Furthermore, Mills (1988) cites many cognitive learning theorists who now support a model of the brain similar to a biological computer with comparable information processing, representational, and retrieval characteristics, capable of projecting thought as a sensory-motor experience (Penfield, 1975; Haugeland, 1985; Dodge, 1986; Lochman et al., 1985; Chandler, 1973; Selman, 1976; Cermack and Craik, 1979; Dodge, Murphy, and Buchsbaum, 1984). Several cognitive researchers suggest that a thought system works in much the same way as computers are programmed by a process known as nested programming (Miller, Galanter, and Pribram, 1960; Baylor and Gason, 1974; Anzai and Simon, 1979; Klahr, 1982).

The findings of these and other researchers would appear to support the conclusion that youth at risk are more likely to translate present circum-

stances through an already existing thought system mechanically programmed in memory as a result of their idiosyncratic interpretations of past
experience. These preprogrammed sets, expectations, or attributions have
been confirmed and validated by much empirical research (Blumer, 1969;
Burger and Luckman, 1966; Polk and Kobrin, 1972; Wilson and Herrnstein,
1985). For example, Dodge et al. (1984) and Lochman et al. (1985) have
found that aggressive delinquents are more likely to misperceive the intentions of others as hostile, are significantly poorer in recognizing neutral or
passive intentions, and are more apt to be biased in assuming continued
hostility. Mills (1988) points out that these flaws in attribution are not a
function of general intelligence but instead are related to youths' assessments
of the meaning of an event rather than the real properties of the event or
circumstance. To summarize, the evidence presented above would appear
to support the neo-cognitive interpretation of youthful deviance as a process
that begins at an early age and culminates with deviant episodes that tend
to become a self-perpetuating spiral.

Put another way, the above research lends support to the neo-cognitive
view that delinquent behavior is interpreted by insecure youths as one so-
lution to the problem of insecurity and low self-esteem. Legitimate persons,
values, and institutions tend to be rejected as they become connected more
strongly with insecure feelings. Seen through an insecure belief system, delinquency becomes a desirable behavior because it enhances self-concept
and/or serves as a way to reduce or avoid uncomfortable feelings of insecurity. Furthermore, within this framework the attraction to other delinquent peers is predictable and serves as another way of obtaining agreement
for distorted attributions and ego validation.

At present, considerable evidence can be found in the literature to support
the third NLT assumption that the self-perpetuating cycle described above
can be countered and that even high-risk youths possess a natural ability
to behave in more mature, commonsense, and noncriminal ways (Stewart,
1985; Dodge and Frame, 1982; Patterson, 1982; Suarez, Mills, and Stewart,
1987; Mills, 1987). For example, Patterson (1982) documented, by home
observations, an average of 3.1 (acting out) behaviors a day in the more
disturbed children he studied. Many researchers have concluded that even
highly insecure children are not, most of the time, in frames of mind that
result in deviant behavior. This final NLT assumption is further supported
by several evaluation research studies of national prevention programs focusing on substance abusers, drop-outs, and delinquents. Mills (1988) cites
several such studies involving programs in which at-risk youths—who became involved in certain types of positive, healthy, productive relationships
with adults, teachers, and peers—began to display higher levels of healthy
functioning as predicted by NLT (Peck et. al., 1987; Wehlage and Rutter,
1986; O'Conner, 1985; Stern, Catterall, Alhadeff, and Ash, 1985; Foley
and Warren, 1985; Gadwa and Griggs, 1985; Shure and Spivack, 1982).

According to Mills (1987), youth involved in such relationships showed significant improvement in positive attitudes, rational problem-solving ability, prosocial behavior, and motivation to attain educational goals and nondeviant life-styles. Mills (1987: 14) underscores that across the programs he reviewed, "the consistent predictors of program success were the observed qualities of interaction and therapeutic qualities of the relationship between program staff and project youth." These qualities or characteristics are summarized below (Mills, 1987: 15):

1. Consistent, unconditional positive regard (affection and respect), from trainers and program staff.
2. Emotional/psychological support from staff for the children addressing and solving problems in an objective, commonsense way.
3. The role of program staff as effective, attractive, and supportive role models for responsible and rational problem solving.
4. Support for the children solving problems for themselves, in a consistent nonjudgmental, noncritical, nonpunitive atmosphere.
5. The realization within this atmosphere on the children's part that there are alternative ways of looking at and resolving interpersonal problems that lead to more positive solutions.

Mills (1987: 17) concludes that the above conditions began to foster significant increases in healthy psychological functioning for at-risk youths because they created conditions that "(1) are least likely to 'trigger' a child's more insecure states of mind, (2) facilitate the child's ability to function in their more commonsense (mentally healthy) states of mind, while (3) developing cognitive skills that are characteristic of more mature, healthier cognitive processes."

In sum, the evidence presented above tends to support the conclusion that even high-risk children will tend to gravitate toward higher mood levels or more healthy psychological functioning when the conditions exist that tend to draw out this improved functioning. Over time, NLT would predict that this healthier, "commonsense" level of functioning will begin to take precedence over the child's alienated programming and learned insecurity. Further support for this prediction is presented later in a discussion of the implications and direct applications of NLT to the prevention of delinquency and other forms of deviant behavior.

NLT'S ADVANCE OVER RECIPROCAL SOCIAL LEARNING AND FIRST-GENERATION COGNITIVE MODELS OF DELINQUENCY

At the present time, social-psychological, integrated models appear to be the field's best predictors of delinquency and other deviant youthful activities such as drug use and academic failure. Elliot and Huizinga (1984), for example, formulated a predictive model of delinquency that combined elements of social control, strain theory, bonding theory, and social learning theory. These scholars tested this model in a longitudinal cohort study that followed 1,725 youths aged 11–17, between 1976 and 1983. Results showed that this model was capable of predicting about 50 percent of the variance in delinquent activity, and 34 percent of the variance in illegal drug use among project youth. Similar theoretical models have tested several combinations of social-psychological variables such as parental supervision and control, prosocial and antisocial bonds, peer group values, social modeling, and family dysfunction. There has been much empirical support in the literature for such models in explaining delinquency (Clayton and Voss, 1981; Akers et al., 1974; Jessor et al., 1980; Ginsburg and Greenly, 1978; Jessor and Jessor, 1977; Elliot and Voss, 1974; Kandal, 1978; West and Farrington, 1977; R. E. Johnson, 1979; Conger, 1976; Jensen and Erickson, 1977; Hindelang, 1973; Linden and Hackler, 1973; Meade and Marsden, 1981; Winfree, Theis, and Griffiths, 1981). While longitudinal and cross-sectional studies constructed on such interdisciplinary social-psychological models have shown the greatest power in predicting multiple-problem youthful deviance, they have several flaws. Mills (1987: 5) discusses their limitations:

Firstly, there is normally a fairly "loose" conceptual relationship between the variables involved. In the majority of these studies the relationship is derived from a path model or other form of statistical "clustering" technique for deriving the causal dimensions from the data that implies a uni-directional interpretation of cause and effect. Also, in the best of these studies, the "explained" variance is anywhere from 25 to 49%. That leaves the greatest percentage of the variance still in the "unexplained" category. Another limitation of these studies . . . is that they have not, as yet, led to preventive interventions that have successfully addressed the problems identified by this area of research.

First-generation cognitive models of delinquency are information processing models derived from contemporary research on the function of the brain in processing, interpreting, and storing information (Chomsky, 1989; Waugh and Norman, 1965; Bandura, 1977). In such models, the delinquent's developing thought system serves as the context for their attributions, expectancies, and predispositions about future experiences. Further, a child's self-concept, attitudes, beliefs, and values are considered to be derived from attributions, interpretations, and experiences stemming from that child's early cognitive programming. For delinquent youths and youths involved in other self-destructive behaviors, these models predict that the cognitive structures of such youths cause them to perceive their world in a manner that involves extreme systematic bias or distortion. As a result, these youths are more likely to have a low self-image and antisocial attitudes, values, and beliefs that generally increase the likelihood of dysfunctional behavior such as delinquency (Beck, 1970; A. Ellis, 1962; Meichenbaum, 1977). What these cognitive models appear to lack, however, is the ability to explain why the same youths will function at very different levels of perception, affect, and behavior at various moments in time.

The Neo-Cognitive Learning Model, based on the Psychology of Mind, is a reciprocal model of deviance that offers a significant advance over the cognitive models and other reciprocal social-learning models of delinquency cited above in that it describes "(1) how delinquent youth function at a conditioned level of awareness, (2) how delinquent youth function at unconditioned levels, and (3) what variables determine whether they will function at either one of these two levels of perception, affect, and behavior at any given moment in time" (Mills, 1987: 7). Mills underscores that the intervening variable, which accounts for the extent and direction of reciprocal affects of various experiences such as the attractiveness of delinquent peers, negative school experiences, and family conflict, is a youth's subjective organization of beliefs and perceptions (i.e., frame of reference) at the beginning of each experience.

Put another way, the advance of this model is that it represents the first "state" model of delinquency, as contrasted with traditional single and multiple "trait" models. Youths move through different states of mind in which their perceptions are affected to varying degrees by their prior conditioning. Lower, more negative, insecure states of mind are characterized by the introduction of negative, distorted, and maladaptive thoughts and the experience of the thinking process as being more involuntary. In more positive, mentally healthy states of mind, youths experience their thinking process as more voluntary. Furthermore, they understand that their personal experience of life is primarily a function of the quality of their thinking within the context of their existing mood level and only secondarily as a function of external circumstances.

PREVENTION IMPLICATIONS AND APPLICATIONS USING NLT PRINCIPLES

The major assumptions or principles of Neo-Cognitive Learning Theory, when applied to prevention programming, lead to a different set of intervention strategies and types of interactions with at-risk youth than those typically used in most contemporary prevention efforts. For example, interventions based on these assumptions differ significantly from those stemming from traditional behavioral, social learning, and first-generation cognitive learning theories of deviant behavior. According to Mills (1988: 7),

the premise that the natural state of mental health is something that is always potentially accessible and, which under certain conditions, naturally emerges from within the youth themselves, means that it must be drawn out of rather than "put into" youth. Put another way, it is not something that youth learn by being supplied from the outside with something that is considered missing. Thus, environmental reinforcements and external techniques for behavior change are not an integral part of this model. This more mature psychological perspective is not something that can be provided from the outside by external reinforcements, or other behavioral training, social skills or assertive training, cognitive restructuring, or other learning models based on the assumption that these youths are missing something that needs to be supplied from the outside.

It is interesting to note that contemporary approaches to delinquency prevention and control have, on the other hand, focused almost exclusively on supplying youthful offenders with some missing factor (e.g., values, discipline, punishment, jobs, self-esteem, limits, etc.), the presence of which would supposedly reduce the inclination to engage in deviant behavior. Hence, traditional behavior theory approaches (Patterson, 1982; Skinner, 1971; Rutherford, 1975; Klein, 1977; Bandura, 1977; Phillips, 1968) assume certain external reinforcement schedules are missing, and therefore the attempt is to supply offenders with behavior modification programs such as token economies, behavior contracting, and "scared straight" type programs. Also, social process theories (Agnew, 1985b; Hirschi, 1969; Reckless, 1967; Sutherland, 1939; Sykes and Matza, 1957) assume the absence of certain external constraints or limits on the behavior of offenders, who need more noncriminal beliefs and prosocial attitudes about school, community, and religion. Finally, first-generation cognitive theories (A. Ellis, 1962; Samenow, 1984; Burns, 1980; Walters and White, 1989b) utilize a variety of techniques, rituals, and numerous discussions in which offenders' criminal beliefs are monitored, analyzed, disputed, condemned, and judged so they can learn to identify and abandon thinking patterns that have supposedly misguided their behavior.

Prevention and early intervention programs based on this "something is missing" assumption have also been the focus of much evaluation research over many years. Programs utilizing reward- and punishment-based operant conditioning models, teaching coping skills, values clarification, cognitive restructuring, and the like, have all been evaluated (Patterson, 1982; Agnew, 1985b; Peck et al., 1987). While social learning, social process, and first-generation cognitive models of crime and delinquency may be on the right track, they all appear to lack the understanding that replacing bad thoughts with good thoughts, altering the frequency, intensity, or duration of pro-criminal relationships, or strengthening positive beliefs with regard to primary socializing institutions (i.e., bonding) all miss the point. Such conversion processes do not result in any transformation in level of understanding; offenders just move in and out of belief systems while staying at exactly the same level of consciousness concerning their thinking function.

In addition, within the neo-cognitive perspective, there is no value in focusing on the details, contents, or the sources of an alienated frame of reference. Results emerging from the applications of this approach to prevention suggest that to the degree it is practical, the less importance given to the child's alienated beliefs, past behavior, family dysfunction, early traumas, past and present failures, the better. First, these details are essentially irrelevant because they are only thoughts. Second, when we give credence to such details we only reinforce the level of understanding that creates the problem of delinquency in the first place. When we take these details seriously, we validate the child's idiosyncratic system of thinking. Avoiding this costly mistake will help children realize that they are at the affect of their pasts, their personalities, their negative conditioning, and learned insecurity only when they are not conscious that these things are all connected to and derived from their own thinking function. Thus, according to the NLT, the major priority of prevention efforts must be on creating a climate that minimizes the triggering of insecure attributions and that at the same time emphasizes the positive, nonthreatening, high mood environment in which the natural mental health of children has an opportunity to emerge.

Focusing on specific prevention efforts, there is considerable evidence in the school environment that children can learn to recognize the distinctions by which they move from healthier more unconditioned, to dysfunctional or more conditioned levels of psychological functioning. National research efforts to identify teachers capable of influencing high-risk youth who were likely school drop-outs found that such teachers were consistently positive, empathic, and showed such youths high amounts of respect and concern. These teachers consistently supported these youths and were optimistic about their ability to learn. Furthermore, they allowed these students to actively structure and determine their own learning, and were creative, flexible, and innovative in molding teacher methods to the particular attitudes, interests, and performance levels of each student. In such educational climates, even high-risk youths were enabled to see the distortions and illusions that emerge from an alienated thought system and were thus empowered to begin acting in more mature and objective frames of mind (Wehlage and Rutter, 1986; Mills, 1987; Stewart, 1985; Krot, 1983; Shuford, 1986).

There is also increasing evidence that parents of a high-risk youth can be instructed to alter the typical dysfunctional patterns of interaction in the home in ways that can assist such youths to improve their self-esteem, learning ability, and mental health. Shure and Spivack (1982), for example, found that they could train low-income, inner-city parents with low educational levels to teach their children improved interpersonal problem-solving skills. Mills (1988) found that parents of high-risk youths could be taught to monitor their own mood levels and significantly change their most frequent patterns of interaction with their children in a positive direction. In higher moods, parents generally exhibit the characteristics of more mentally healthy states of mind, experience higher self-esteem, see more positive characteristics in their children, are more understanding and patient, are less angry and defensive, and are more flexible and open minded.

At present, this Neo-Cognitive Learning Model has been applied directly in several prevention and early intervention programs with at-risk youth as well as in clinical treatment programs with different populations displaying deviant (frequently criminal) behaviors. Several clinical outcome studies have been published that demonstrate the effectiveness of the intervention model based on Neo-Cognitive Psychotherapy (NCP). These studies have demonstrated the effectiveness of this modality across cultures and across the entire spectrum of psychiatric diagnoses seen in outpatient settings. Significant reductions in clinical symptoms have been achieved (measured by standardized psychological inventories) for clinical samples ranging from 42 to 242. One noteworthy finding produced in each of these studies was that several patients, when measured posttreatment, improved in level of mental health to a degree that was significantly higher than that of the mean for the "normal" nonpatient control group (Bailey, Blevens, and Heath, 1988; Shuford and Crystal, 1988). In addition, Neo-Cognitive Psychotherapy has demonstrated success in the treatment of alcohol and drug abuse (Stewart, 1987), several forms of family violence (Crystal and Shuford, 1988), and for several other diagnostic groups of emotional disorders (Shuford, 1986).

One specific project, utilizing the Neo-Cognitive Learning Model, deserves special attention. This project, called the Modello/Homestead Gardens Program, was funded by the U.S. Department of Justice beginning in October 1987. Modello and Homestead Gardens are two housing projects located in Dade County, Florida, that were determined to be the worst areas in the county in terms of illicit drug trade, teen pregnancy, school drop-out rates, delinquency, truancy, gangs, and welfare dependents. A preproject survey revealed that approximately 85 percent of the heads of households were on public assistance, and approximately 67 percent of the families in these neighborhoods were either using or dealing with drugs. Furthermore, school truancy rates were around 80 percent, and youths in these neighborhoods were deemed to be the worst behavior problems in school, based on referrals for discipline expulsions and suspensions. The intervention methods used in this program were based on NLT and were adopted for use in parenting classes, leadership training courses for residents, teacher training programs, family and individual counseling, and in counseling groups for students in the schools. Adaptations were also applied in community development and in interagency coordination components of the Modello/Homestead Gardens Program.

Results from this program have been extremely positive. Following the second project year, truancy rates for youths decreased from around 80 percent to almost nothing. Improvements in grades revealed decreases in failure rates at the junior high level from 64 percent to less than 15 percent, and an overall improvement in grade point average for at-risk students in the senior high level of about 64 percent. Discipline referrals decreased by over 75 percent, while suspensions and expulsions for serious delinquent behaviors decreased by over 80 percent. Students showed significant improvement in self-esteem scores and overall mental health status. The number of teen pregnancies at the junior high level decreased by over 80 percent. The majority of parents of project youth also showed significant improvement in self-esteem, overall mental health, and either began working or going to school themselves. Finally, the overall rates of drug abuse and child abuse or neglect decreased by over 65 percent in both communities (Mills, 1990; Timm and Stewart, 1990).

CONCLUSION

At present, social-psychological, integrated models of deviance are the field's best predictors of delinquency, drug use, and other health-damaging youthful behaviors. These models are limited, however, in that among other things they leave "unexplained" the greatest percentage of the variance, have not led to particularly successful preventive interventions, and do not adequately explain why the same youths will display very different kinds of perception, affect, and behavior at different times. The Neo-Cognitive Learning Model presented here is a reciprocal, "state" model of deviance, which proposes that youths move through different states of mind in which their perceptions are affected to varying degrees by their prior conditioning. In other words, the reciprocal effects of a youth's experiences across settings are mediated by his or her subjective frame of reference. The major advance of this model is that it describes the principles of learning that determine the extent to which a youth is able to function at different levels of mental health at any given moment in time.

There is considerable evidence from contemporary delinquency research and theory that supports each major assumption of the Neo-Cognitive Learning Model. Furthermore, there is considerable evidence as well from evaluation research, naturalistic observations, and youth panel surveys that these NLT principles can be used successfully to reverse the cumulative process of learned insecurity and perceived alienation by drawing out the natural healthy psychological functioning of which even severely at-risk youths are capable. More innovative and effective programs are likely to emerge as researchers and youth advocates become aware of the accuracy and power of the comparatively simple principles of Neo-Cognitive Learning Theory and Psychology of Mind.

3

Human Ecology and Social Disorganization Revisit Delinquency in Little Rock

JEFFERY T. WALKER

In the early twentieth century, Robert Park and others at the University of Chicago began a new form of study related to the growing urban life-style in the United States. This area of study, called "human ecology," looked at the environmental and social impact of urban conditions on the life-styles of city dwellers. Clifford R. Shaw and Henry D. McKay (1942) used the techniques of human ecology research, created and popularized by the Chicago School, to study the relationship between the urban environment and delinquency. From this study, they developed what is now referred to as the theory of social disorganization. This theory posited increased criminal activity in neighborhoods characterized by breakdowns in social organization.

In their initial research, Shaw and McKay examined the ecological makeup of Chicago in terms of three categories of socioeconomic characteristics: physical status, economic status, and population status. They then analyzed the association between these variables and delinquency, which formed the basis of the theory of social disorganization.

After the initial study in Chicago, Shaw and McKay replicated their research in several cities throughout the United States; one of those cities being Little Rock, Arkansas. Although the full model employed in Chicago was not replicated, the findings in Little Rock were consistent with those in other cities and Chicago: ecological characteristics were associated with high rates of delinquency, and each tended to cluster in concentric rings surrounding the central business district. Shaw and McKay concluded from this distribution that the relationship between ecological characteristics and delinquency in Little Rock were consistent with those in Chicago.

This chapter will reanalyze the association proposed by Shaw and McKay between ecological characteristics and delinquency in Little Rock in light of changes that have occurred in the city since the original study which was conducted in the mid–1930s and published in 1942. This analysis will replicate, to the extent possible, Shaw and McKay's model in order to examine the current relevance of the earlier findings and to determine if the tenets of social disorganization and human ecology remain viable explanations of juvenile delinquency in the 1990s.

Due to the problems and criticisms associated with using social disorganization to explain delinquency, the focus of this chapter will be on the relationship between ecological characteristics and delinquency. Links between such characteristics, social disorganization, and delinquency will be put forth only in terms of the explanations used by Shaw and McKay in their original study.

HISTORICAL BACKGROUND OF
SOCIAL DISORGANIZATION

The historical roots of social disorganization are grounded in geographic studies of the 1800s and the study of plant ecology. These early studies would provide the impetus for the study of growing urban cities in the United States, called human ecology; and the focus on associated crime rates that would lead to the theory of social disorganization.

The ecological study of delinquency most likely began with research undertaken by André M. Guerry in 1833. Guerry compared the crime rates in eighty-six departments in France from 1825 to 1830. His study showed that crime rates had marked differences in different cities in the country. He concluded from this that there was a substantial relationship between geographical (later to be ecological) characteristics of certain cities and crime.

The relationship between a city's central district and juvenile delinquency was first explored by Cyril Burt in 1925. Burt proposed that areas in London that had the highest rates of delinquency were located adjacent to the central business district, and those areas with the lowest rates were located near the periphery of the city (Shaw and McKay, 1942).

The study of the geographical distribution of delinquency began in the United States with research undertaken in 1912 by Sophonisba Breckenridge and Edith Abbott. In that study, Breckenridge and Abbott looked at the geographic distribution of the homes of juvenile delinquents in Chicago. A map showing the location of these delinquents indicated that a disproportionate number of the juveniles' homes were located in particular areas of the city. Breckenridge and Abbott concluded from this distribution that there were characteristics of those areas that caused them to be associated with high levels of delinquency.

Although not directly related to social disorganization, at least part of the credit for the development of the theory of social disorganization must go to the Danish botanist Eugenius Warming. In his book, *Oecology of*

Plants (1909), Warming proposed that plants live in "communities" with varying states of symbiosis, or natural interdependence. Warming's (1909: 13) use of the term "community," he argued, "implie[d] a diversity but at the same time a certain organized uniformity of units," such that "some of the communities had a greater reliance on each other for survival." Of these "plant communities," those which contained plants predominantly of the same species seemed to be in competition with nature, but not with each other. Those with several different species, however, would often compete for limited resources more among themselves than with the environment.

Comparing plant communities with human communities, Warming proposed that there was a struggle for limited resources where the weaker were often suppressed by the stronger. Warming called this relationship a "natural economy" because of the use of resources by the plants. This "natural economy" was expounded on by a German biologist, Earnest Haeckel, who used the Greek word, *oikos*, from which economics was formed, to coin the term "ecology."

Robert E. Park, who is considered the father of human ecology, used the terminology of Haeckel and the concepts of Warming to describe what he called "human ecology." Specifically, Park used the concept of symbiosis, which described the interrelationships of plants in the struggle for survival, to describe the phenomenon found in human communities where people work together for common goals and at the same time compete for scarce resources. Park also applied the concepts of dominance and succession to denote the phenomenon where a stronger group would disrupt the community through change and eventually reestablish order by replacing (succeeding) a previously dominant group.

Park and Earnest Burgess (1969) expanded these hypotheses into the study of the characteristics of the urban environment. As a part of a class in social pathology, students were required to make maps of demographic and socioeconomic data of Chicago (Faris, 1967). As the maps were developed, Burgess noticed that patterns existed in the distribution of many of the characteristics being studied. One of the most enduring patterns observed by Burgess was that certain characteristics of the population tended to cluster in rings set at about one mile increments from the center of the city and that the patterns changed dramatically from one ring (or zone) to the next. For instance, Burgess found there was a zone of manufacturing enterprises that immediately surrounded the central business district of the city. Outside this "factory zone" was an area of very-low-income housing. In the third concentric ring, the predominate residential characteristic was working-class homes. Finally, in the fourth and fifth rings from the center of the city were middle- and upper-class homes. This pattern of housing, shown in Figure 3.1, which Burgess labeled the "Burgess' zonal hypothesis," represents one of the central elements of human ecology.

Figure 3.1
Burgess' Zonal Hypothesis

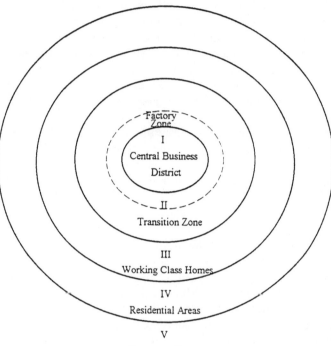

SHAW AND McKAY'S STUDY

Clifford R. Shaw and Henry D. McKay took the ideas of human ecology, which were then being used to describe the urban environment, to study the association between urban ecological characteristics and urban juvenile delinquency. In studying the relationship between ecology and delinquency, Shaw and McKay analyzed three general areas: physical, economic, and population characteristics.

Physical Characteristics

In analyzing the relationship between physical attributes and delinquency, Shaw and McKay used three variables to measure the physical characteristics of an area: population change, vacant and condemned housing, and proximity to industry. They proposed that areas with high delinquency rates tended to be physically deteriorated, geographically close to areas of heavy industry, and populated with highly transient residents.

The primary physical characteristic Shaw and McKay examined was the population shift associated with a given area. Shaw and McKay found that, as population rates changed (increased or decreased), there was a corresponding increase in delinquency. This was a curvilinear relationship in which a relatively slight change in the population was associated with a considerable change in delinquency rates, while large changes in population did not have the same dramatic effect. They proposed that population shifts affected delinquency because of the process of "invasion, dominance, and succession." This is the process in which the balance of power in a given area changes because one group "invades" (moves into) another group's neighborhood, grows in number, and eventually drives the first group out (Shaw and McKay, 1942). When an area is invaded by another group, an anomic condition results in a manner very similar to that proposed by Emile Durkheim, where the loss of social order results in a reduction in the informal social control that is responsible for enforcing social norms of behavior. In this interstitial area (so-called because the area is "in between" periods of social organization) the ability of the neighborhood to maintain informal control is reduced, resulting in a high delinquency rate.

While population change was proposed to be an integral part of social disorganization, it was not thought to be absolutely essential. Shaw and McKay proposed that physical deterioration and proximity to industrial areas also affected juvenile delinquency. They reasoned that, even if invasion, dominance, and succession do not apply and the city's growth is stagnant or only at the peripheries, ecological interpretations would still explain some deviance because the neighborhoods close to the industrial district would be physically less desirable than those farther away. The homes would be older (since a city grows from the center, and the central homes would have been built first); and the smoke, noise, and smell of industries would render the homes physically unattractive (Shaw and McKay, 1942).

To analyze the relationship between proximity to industry and delinquency, Shaw and McKay mapped industrial areas and the home addresses of juvenile delinquents. This mapping formed the core of their concentric ring hypothesis concerning ecology and delinquency. In their map analysis, they found that the central business district of a city usually lay at the place where the city was founded. Surrounding the central business district was a zone of manufacturing and industry. Surrounding the industrial zone was a ring characterized by high levels of the ecological characteristics Shaw and McKay were studying and a corresponding high delinquency rate. Moving toward the outskirts of the city, they found a reduction in the prevalence of these characteristics and the rate of delinquency. This pattern is the same as that described by Burgess and shown in Figure 3.1. From this analysis, Shaw and McKay concluded that there was a relationship between the proximity to industry and delinquency.

The final physical characteristic Shaw and McKay analyzed was the number of vacant and condemned homes in an area. Shaw and McKay also measured the number of vacant and condemned buildings through mapping and direct observation. They found that there was an association between maps showing the number of vacant and condemned homes in a given area and its rate of delinquency. This finding was thought to be a product of the desire of residents to move out of the area and a reluctance of others to move into physically unattractive areas with high delinquency rates.

In explaining the link between physical characteristics and delinquency, Shaw and McKay proposed that residential areas in close proximity to areas of heavy industry were physically unattractive, because of the noise, smoke, and smell of the area and because these homes were usually among the oldest in the city and therefore physically deteriorated. They further concluded that the physical unattractiveness of the area resulted in a residential population that would move out of the area as soon as it was economically feasible (demonstrated by a high population turnover), leaving many vacant housing units. Such migration of the residents would result in a disruption of the social organization of the area, producing high rates of delinquency.

Economic Characteristics

Next, Shaw and McKay analyzed the association between the economic characteristics of an area and its delinquency rate. Three variables were used for this analysis: the number of families receiving social assistance, the median rental price of the area, and the number of homes owned rather than rented.

First, Shaw and McKay found that, as the number of families receiving social assistance increased, there was a corresponding rise in delinquency rates. They did not contend that receiving social assistance was directly related to delinquency, however. They argued instead that social assistance was an indicator of the economic characteristics of residents in establishing where they might live: those with lower economic characteristics lived in areas dominated by the other ecological variables.

Next, Shaw and McKay analyzed the relationship between the median rental price and delinquency. They found that, for the most part, delinquency rates dropped as the median rental price of the area rose. This relationship was not completely linear, however. In some high delinquency areas, high rent rates were recorded, due to overpricing of living quarters by tenement owners. Median rental values were therefore thought to be an additional measure of the economic characteristics of a census tract as it related to a high presence of other ecological variables.

Finally Shaw and McKay looked at the relationship between the percentage of residents who owned their own homes and the delinquency rate for the area. Their findings revealed a significant negative relationship between home ownership and delinquency. This was not a linear relationship either, however. There were significant drops in delinquency rates as the percentage of homeowners rose only slightly. This relationship diminished, however, as the percentage of homeowners reached high levels. Shaw and McKay proposed from these findings that economic characteristics affected delinquency, in the case of owning one's home, in that those who could afford to own their homes had a greater stake in the neighborhood where they would be permanent residents, whereas those renting would expend less effort to maintain the social organization or decrease the delinquency rate of the neighborhood.

Explaining the impact of economic characteristics on delinquency, Shaw and McKay suggested that economic conditions do affect delinquency rates, but only indirectly. For instance, they asserted that affluent areas offered an atmosphere of social controls, whereas areas of low economic characteristics produce an environment conducive to delinquency for two reasons. First, delinquency "provides a means of securing economic gain, prestige, and other human satisfactions [which are often unavailable in areas of low affluence]" such that many juveniles are drawn to delinquency as a means of economic advancement (Shaw and McKay, 1942: 164). They also proposed that economic conditions affected delinquency because low economic areas typically had the most culturally diverse residents. This diversity of cultures affects rates of delinquency in the area owing to the great disparity in social norms, some of which may condone certain delinquent acts.

Population Characteristics

The final analysis included in Shaw and McKay's study was the relationship between the population composition of an area and its rate of delinquency. Shaw and McKay found that areas with the highest delinquency rates contained higher numbers of foreign-born and black heads of households. They cautioned, however, that this finding did not mean that nativity or ethnicity was the cause of crime. They argued instead that the area of study was the factor contributing to delinquency (Shaw and McKay, 1942). This argument was supported by their finding that delinquency rates in areas containing large percentages of foreign-born and minority heads of households remained constant despite the total population shift to another minority group. Delinquency rates also remained constant in areas where the displaced population moved. This argument was further supported by the findings that: (1) no group had a uniform delinquency rate in all parts of the city; (2) all groups had delinquency rates that encompassed the entire range of rates; (3) within the same general social area, all groups had very similar rates of delinquents; and (4) within similar areas, each natural group had a delinquency rate proportional to the rate for the entire area (Shaw and McKay, 1942). The overall delinquency rate for a particular group, therefore, was dependent on the number of individuals residing in the high delinquency zones and not on their origins.

Shaw and McKay concluded that, owing to their low economic characteristics, certain racial and ethnic groups were associated with high levels of delinquency because they were essentially forced to live in areas that were economically feasible and in close proximity to their sources of labor. Population characteristics were associated with delinquency because these areas were the ones exhibiting the highest levels of other ecological variables.

Conclusions of Shaw and McKay

Based on the findings of their study, Shaw and McKay concluded that the ecological conditions that existed in areas with high delinquency were contributing to a breakdown in the social order of the area, resulting in conditions conducive to delinquency. This proposal is similar to Durkheim's anomie theory that stated, in its simplest form, that deviance is caused by a breakdown in the social bonds, resulting in noncompliance with conventional norms.

It would be possible for one to argue from Shaw and McKay's conclusions that the people in areas of high delinquency do not adhere to the conventional norms of society. This is not the case, however. Shaw and McKay found that conventional norms are prevalent in high delinquency areas. Delinquency is a highly competitive way of life, though, because it "provides a means of securing economic gain, prestige, and other human satisfactions and is embodied in delinquent groups and criminal organizations, many of which have great influence, power and prestige" (Shaw and McKay, 1942: 164).

The findings do not indicate, therefore, that certain ecological characteristics result in the residents' abandonment of conventional values, increasing the level of delinquency. They suggest, rather, that people who live in high delinquency areas are subjected to an environment with a variety of contradictory standards, values, and behaviors rather than one (usually law abiding) environment. As a result, residents may choose a delinquent lifestyle rather than a conventional one (Shaw and McKay, 1942). Not only do juveniles who live in areas of high delinquency have the organizational environment conducive to delinquency, they have contact with criminals and may belong to groups (gangs) that actually sanction deviance and exert peer pressure to perform delinquent acts (Shaw and McKay, 1942). Areas with low delinquency are insulated from this atmosphere because consistent and universal attitudes and values are controlled and perpetuated in institutions such as the PTA and church organizations. Where these institutions are dominant, juveniles participate in only one way of life (conventional and law abiding). Although the children will have knowledge of delinquent life-styles, they will have little real exposure to it.

RESEARCH DESIGN AND METHODOLOGY

There is a need within criminology to determine if certain theories endure over time. Shaw and McKay's study was conducted in the mid–1930s and has not been replicated on a full scale since the studies that closely followed it (Lander, 1954; Bordua, 1958–59; Chilton, 1964). Many changes have occurred in the United States since the time of the original study and replications, including dramatic increases in delinquency, comprehensive changes in the demographics of urban residents, and a general decentralization and dispersion of modern cities. In addition to the changes that have occurred in cities since the original study, there have been many advancements in the quality and quantity of data available from the U.S. Census Bureau. Beyond the advantage of being able to examine data by census tract or block rather than by voting district (which was used in the original study in Little Rock), 1990 census data contain a number of variables that may enhance the ability of this research to more accurately measure the incidence of social disorganization: vacancies, physical deterioration, and others. It is therefore desirable to reexamine human ecology/social disorganization theory in light of these changes in the last half-century.

Delinquency data for the original study were drawn from all male juveniles who were brought before the Little Rock Juvenile Court; a total of 226 boys. Delinquency data for this study were drawn from all juveniles from Little Rock who were processed by the Pulaski County Juvenile Court in 1990: a total of 1,880 cases. Elimination of addresses that could not be matched to locations in Little Rock and those who fell outside the city limits reduced the total to 1,779.

Ecological data in the original study were drawn from the 1930 Census of Population and Housing. Because the population of Little Rock at that time was only 81,679, the only data gathered for units smaller than the city itself concerned sex, race, origin, and age of inhabitants, which were gathered according to voting wards. Because of this limitation, the full research design of the Chicago study could not be applied. Shaw and McKay therefore simply mapped the distribution of delinquency in the city, demonstrated that it followed the general pattern of other cities, and concluded that the theory was supported. Ecological data for 1990 were drawn from the Census of Population and Housing (File STF 1A). This contains 100 percent counts of population characteristics by census tract.

OPERATIONALIZATION OF CONCEPTS

Dependent Variable

Juvenile delinquency is measured in this study by the address of juveniles appearing in Pulaski County Juvenile Court in 1990, aggregated by census tract (the unit of analysis). One point where this study departs from others of its kind is in its treatment of recidivism, defined here as multiple delinquent incidents from the same address. Multiple incidents of delinquency by the same person are included in this analysis as separate incidents because an occurrence of delinquency, even though it may be by the same person, is a separate incident. Additionally, multiple delinquent incidents are included in this study because extra care was exercised not to include the names of juveniles in the 1990 delinquency data; and, since it is possible that more than one delinquent lives at the same address (which is how delinquency is measured), all incidents from the same address are included.

Physical Characteristics

The primary physical characteristic considered in the original study by Shaw and McKay was the percentage increase or decrease in the population of a census tract. In this study, *population change* is measured by calculating the absolute percentage difference in the population of census tracts in 1980 and 1990.

The second physical characteristic included in the original study was the number of vacant and condemned housing units in a particular tract. Instead of using a quantitative measure of the number of vacant homes, Shaw and McKay simply mapped the number of homes vacant and condemned by the city of Chicago and analyzed this map in relation to the geographical distribution of delinquency. In this study, *vacancy* will be measured by the census variable "vacant housing units."

The original study also included the proximity of housing to industry as a measure of the physical attractiveness and deterioration of an area. There was, and is, no census measure of this concept, however; and Shaw and McKay recognized the inaccuracy inherent in attempting to measure this variable through direct observation and mapping (which was the method used in the original research). This study, therefore, dropped proximity to industry in favor of a more accurate, empirical measure of the physical deterioration of an area. Physical *deterioration* of housing units in a census tract is measured in this study by the census variable "boarded-up status of vacant housing units."

Economic Characteristics

The original study used three concepts to measure the economic characteristics of an area: number of families receiving social assistance, median rental value, and number of homes owned. In this study, the number of families receiving *social assistance* is measured by the census variable "income type," where the primary source of income is "social security" or "public assistance." The *median rental* value is measured by the census variable "median contract rent." This is expected to be a complementary measure to social assistance in assessing the affordability of an area for residents. *Homes owned* is measured in this study by the census variable "owner occupied housing units."

Population Characteristics

In the original study, only the nativity and race of residents were considered as population concepts. The number of *black-headed households* of residents will be measured in this study by the census variable *race*.

This study included an additional concept to *race* in an effort to more accurately measure the effect of population characteristics on social disorganization and juvenile delinquency. The added concept is the number of *female-headed households*, which is measured by the census variable "female householder, no husband present, with related children."

The Concentric Ring Hypothesis

A fundamental component of Shaw and McKay's study, and the way in which they tied physical, economic, and population characteristics to delinquency, was through the concentric ring hypothesis. Drawing on Burgess' proposition discussed previously that socioeconomic characteristics of cities followed distinct circular patterns around the chronological center of the city, Shaw and McKay proposed that if delinquency was correlated with each of these categories of ecological variables, then delinquency should follow a similar concentric ring pattern.

Shaw and McKay first tested this hypothesis in Chicago. The findings of that study supported their contention: delinquency rates were the highest in the area immediately surrounding the central business district (Zone I) and rates decreased toward the outer limits of the city. Shaw and McKay and others then replicated the Chicago study in eight other cities across the nation, including Little Rock. In each replication the results were the same: delinquency was found to be associated with the physical, economic, and population characteristics of an area; and, except where natural features such as rivers interfered, the patterns of ecological characteristics and delinquency followed a concentric ring pattern surrounding the central business district.

Findings and Discussion

A present danger in drawing conclusions from ecological research is committing the associated ecological fallacy. It is very easy with findings such as these to be lured into the trap of inferring structural correlates of area characteristics and delinquency to the people who live in such areas. To avoid such error, it is emphasized that these findings are interpreted in terms of the association between the ecological conditions of "census tracts" and their differential levels of delinquency.

The method of analysis used by Shaw and McKay, and replicated in this study, was bivariate correlation of the ecological variables and delinquency. The zero-order correlations of this study are presented in Table 3.1. A side by side comparison of the findings of Shaw and McKay and the 1990 findings are presented in Table 3.2 and are discussed below.

Physical Characteristics

Physical characteristics are proposed to affect social disorganization owing to the lack of interest and attachment to the well-being of the neighborhood. The findings of this analysis were generally supportive of Shaw and McKay's conclusions concerning the relationship between physical characteristics and delinquency, although specific results differed somewhat.

The primary physical characteristic studied by Shaw and McKay was the population change associated with a given area of analysis. *Population change* is proposed to affect delinquency because those just moving into a neighborhood, and more important those moving out or wanting to move out, have less interest in the social organization or the well-being of the neighborhood. The length of residence is a very important factor in maintaining the social bond to the area—so much so that Janowitz (1978) proposed that length of residence was the most important variable leading to stronger social bonds. Additionally, neighborhoods with a high population turnover have a greater number of new faces, which makes it difficult to distinguish between new residents and strangers. When this occurs, juveniles in the area have more anonymity in committing delinquent acts because the people of the area do not know who is a resident and who needs supervision (Stark, 1987).

In Chicago, Shaw and McKay found a substantial (r = .68) correlation between the net change in population (increase or decrease) and the delinquency rate. This relationship was curvilinear, however, in which slight differences in the rate of change of the population were associated with a considerable change in the delinquency rate, while large changes did not have the same dramatic effect.

At first glance, the population change in 1990 does not appear to be associated with delinquency. The zero-order correlation between the two variables was very weak (− .01) and nonsignificant. These findings are somewhat misleading, however. An analysis of the relationship between the quartile distribution of population change and delinquency produced different results. The correlation between low and moderate levels of population change and delinquency was very low and nonsignificant. Large changes in population, however (above the 75th percentile), were significantly (p <

Table 3.1
Zero-Order Correlations of 1990 Data

	Population Change	Vacancy	Boarded-Up	Social Assistance	Median Rental	Homes Owned	Black House Head	Female House Head
Delinquency	-.01	.30-	.48***	.30*	-.39**	-.26*	.71***	.68***
Population Change		.20	-.22	-.20	.19	.02	.23	.26*
Vacancy			.27	.33*	.02	-.08	-.37**	.52***
Boarded-Up				.42**	-.63***	-.10	.44***	.46***
Social Assistance					-.25*	-.39**	.21	.24
Median Rental						.14	-.36**	-.30*
Homes Owned							-.20	-.18
Black House Head								.97***

N = 45   1 tailed significance: * < .05   ** < .01   *** < .001

Table 3.2
Comparison of Zero-Order Correlations

Variable	Shaw and McKay	1990
Physical Characteristics		
Population Change	.69	.54#
Vacancy/Condemned	Not Measured	.30
Physical Deterioration	Not Measured	.48
Economic Characteristics		
Social Assistance	.89	.30
Median Rental Value	-.61	-.39
Homes Owned	-.47	-.25
Population Characteristics		
Black Headed Households	.60	.71
Female Headed Households	Not Measured	.68

Population change above the 75th percentile

.05) and substantially (r = .54) correlated with delinquency. Small changes in population, in other words, do not appear to affect delinquency. Large migrations, either in or out of the area, however, are associated with higher levels of delinquency.

The second physical variable associated with delinquency by Shaw and McKay was the number of *vacant and condemned homes* in a given area. Vacancies are not expected to be directly associated with delinquency, but, instead, to be a measure of the attractiveness of the area to those wanting to move into the neighborhood and the probability of current residents wanting to move out. Areas where other ecological characteristics (and delinquency) have caused residents to want to move will exhibit high levels of vacancies when the people leave. In areas with the lowest levels of physical attractiveness, it will be harder to attract new residents; thus exacerbating the number of vacancies.

As discussed previously, Shaw and McKay measured vacancy through direct observation of maps of Chicago rather than quantitatively. As a result, they did not calculate correlations for this variable. This study added the number of vacant housing units in a census tract as an empirical measure of this characteristic. The results of this empirical analysis supported the proposals of Shaw and McKay. While the correlation between vacancy and delinquency was among the lowest in the analysis (r = .30) it was significant (p < .05). This lower correlation is possibly due to the depressed real estate market, which is leaving many homes vacant and for sale even in affluent areas.

The final physical variable considered by Shaw and McKay was the physical attractiveness and deterioration of a given area. *Physical deterioration* is expected to represent another measure of the attractiveness of the neighborhood to potential buyers and the probability of current residents wanting to move away, along with the commitment of the residents to the area. Deterioration leaves an area physically unattractive. In such areas, there is a reduction in the commitment of the residents to maintaining social control, resulting in higher delinquency levels. In fact, it is probably the physical attractiveness and deterioration that is driving the other two physical variables.

Physical deterioration was also analyzed by Shaw and McKay through map analysis of the geographic relationship between high delinquency areas and their proximity to heavy industry; hence no correlations between this variable and delinquency were calculated. This study measured the physical deterioration of census tracts in Little Rock with the census variable "boarded-up status of vacant housing units." The findings of this analysis were very supportive of Shaw and McKay's conclusions concerning the relationship between physical characteristics and delinquency. The zero-order correlation between physical deterioration and delinquency was the second highest correlation in the matrix (r = .48). Physical deterioration was also one of two variables that were significant at the .001 level.

The findings concerning physical characteristics and delinquency suggest that areas with high delinquency rates are unable to retain residents. Many of those who currently live in such areas want to leave and few want to move into areas of high delinquency and high deterioration. An area inhabited by a population that would like to move reduces the commitment of the residents in maintaining informal control. This proposal is supported by Stark's (1986: 901) proposition that "[h]igh rates of neighborhood deviance are a social stigma for residents" such that "living in stigmatized neighborhoods causes a reduction in an individual's stake in conformity." Stark goes on to argue that such apathy leaves juveniles of the area to determine their own behavior, which may more likely turn delinquent.

Economic Characteristics

The replication of Shaw and McKay's analysis of the relationship between economic characteristics and delinquency was fairly straightforward, since they used variables that are easily replicated with current census data. Except for specific correlational findings, the results of the replication were also very similar. Each of the variables used in this analysis were significantly correlated with delinquency and the signs of the associations were the same as those in the original study.

The first economic variable analyzed by Shaw and McKay was the number of families receiving *social assistance*. Social assistance is not interpreted as having a direct association with delinquency. It is expected to be associated with delinquency because of the neighborhoods in which people can afford to live. Those receiving social assistance will be forced to live in areas exhibiting the greatest cultural diversity and social disorganization, and will thus be exposed to the highest levels of delinquency.

The analysis of the association between social assistance and delinquency produced the highest correlation ($r = .89$) in the Chicago study. In this study, social assistance was significantly correlated with delinquency ($p < .05$) but the relationship was less substantial than other variables ($r = .30$). This may have been the result of the measurement used in this study. As previously discussed, social assistance was measured by the number of people in a census tract whose primary income was through social security or public assistance. Surprisingly, there was only one census tract that had a zero value for this variable. This may be due, however, to the fact that many residents, even in affluent areas, are retired and receiving social security.

Shaw and McKay also used the *median rental value* of an area as a measure of the economic characteristics. It is expected that the median rental value will represent an index of the economic status of housing in a particular area (low median rent should represent lower economic and physical characteristics of available housing, while high median rent should represent high economic and physical characteristics).

The findings of Shaw and McKay's analysis revealed an inverse relationship between median rental value and delinquency ($r = -.61$); as the median rental value rose, there was a drop in the rate of delinquency. The findings of this study support those of Shaw and McKay. In Little Rock, there was a substantial inverse ($r = -.39$) and statistically significant ($p < .01$) correlation between rental value and delinquency.

The findings of this analysis suggest that the median rental value is the best measure of the relationship between economic characteristics and delinquency in 1990. Contrary to previous ecological research (Lander, 1954; Bordua, 1958–59; Chilton, 1964), the median rental value appears to be the most statistically and theoretically supportable measure of economic characteristics in Little Rock. Statistically, the median rental value was the economic characteristic most highly correlated with delinquency, suggesting that it is the most accurate measure of the three variables used. Additionally, social disorganization does not propose that economic characteristics are directly associated with delinquency, but rather that they define the probability that a particular person will reside in an area affected by the other ecological variables. Since the explanatory value of home ownership seems to be diminished (see below) and social assistance is another measure of the likelihood of residing in a particular area, the median rental value probably represents the most accurate economic indicator of socially disorganized areas.

The final economic variable analyzed by Shaw and McKay was the *number of homes owned*. It is expected that home ownership will impact on delinquency due to the increased commitment of home owners to the areas in which they live. Those who can afford to own their home have a greater stake in the neighborhood where they will be permanent residents, whereas those renting will expend less effort to maintain the social organization or decrease the delinquency rate of the area.

Shaw and McKay found an inverse relationship ($r = -.47$) between home ownership and delinquency. This study also found a significant ($p < .05$) inverse relationship between the number of homes owned and delinquency, but the correlation was the lowest of any significant relationship in the analysis ($r = -.25$). The low correlation between home ownership and delinquency is actually quite supportive of Shaw and McKay, however. In their analysis, Shaw and McKay found that low levels of home ownership were associated with high levels of delinquency. Small increases in the number of homes owned reduced the delinquency rate substantially; however, as the number of homes owned reached moderate to high levels, the effect on delinquency diminished to near zero. Studies showing a general increase in the percentage of people owning their own homes since the Great Depression (the time of the original study) suggest that the current relationship between home ownership and delinquency should more closely resemble Shaw and McKay's upper quartile of the relationship where there is a significant but low correlation between the two.

In summary, economic characteristics are proposed to effect social disorganization because of the instability of the residents and the link between low economic conditions/characteristics and other ecological factors. Shaw and McKay did not, nor does this study, propose that economic conditions are directly related to delinquency. The hypothesis here is that low economic characteristics limit the areas where people can afford to live such that less affluent people are forced to live in areas where people from many different "cultures" come together. There is a great diversity of values and beliefs in these areas militating against the residents communicating with each other and maintaining the social order of the neighborhood. This diversity of cultures also affects the rate of delinquency in the area due to the great disparity in social norms that may condone certain delinquent acts. According to Shaw and McKay (1942: 187) "crime, in this situation may be regarded as one of the means employed by people to acquire, or to attempt to acquire, the economic and social values generally idealized in our culture, which persons in other circumstances acquire by conventional means."

Population Characteristics

Probably the most controversial finding of Shaw and McKay's study concerned the association between foreign-born and black heads of households and delinquency. The high correlation ($r = .60$) between race or

nativity and delinquency brought about questions concerning racial characteristics and criminal justice even in the 1930s. Shaw and McKay cautioned that this finding does not mean that nativity or ethnicity was the
cause of crime. Delinquency rates in areas containing these minority heads
of households remained constant despite the total population shift to another minority group. Delinquency rates also remained constant in areas
where the displaced population moved. Shaw and McKay concluded that
the ecological makeup of the area of study and not the nativity or ethnicity
of its residents was the factor contributing to delinquency (Shaw and McKay,
1942).

This analysis also produced a significant ($p < .001$) and substantial ($r = .71$) relationship between *black-headed households* and delinquency. This
finding resulted in an interpretive dilemma for this study. On the one hand,
it has become "an established finding of criminological research . . . that
blacks have offending rates several times those of whites" (Stark, 1986: 95).
Practically any statistical procedure will produce significantly high associations between minority characteristics and delinquency or crime. On the
other hand, it is also an established fact that few if any propositional or
theoretical links can be drawn between minority characteristics and offending, save for spurious relationships or explanations related to differential treatment by the criminal justice system.

Owing to these problems, this study included a second variable as an
additional measure of population characteristics in an attempt to gain a
more accurate picture of the relationship between population characteristics
and delinquency. The variable chosen for this study was *female-headed
households*. It is anticipated that a large number of female-headed households would indicate a situation where the mothers may be devoting a great
deal of time outside the home, thus reducing the social interaction and
organization of a neighborhood such that the ability of the neighborhood
to control its children is diminished, resulting in a higher delinquency rate.
This variable produced a significant ($p < .001$) and substantial ($r = .68$)
correlation with delinquency, along with a high degree of intercorrelation
with the other ecological variables. This supports Shaw and McKay's argument that delinquency is a product of ecological factors other than the
race or nativity characteristics of an area.

Concentric Ring Hypothesis

The final analysis of Shaw and McKay to be replicated by this study is
the geographical distribution of ecological characteristics and delinquency.
As previously stated, Shaw and McKay proposed that the ecological factors
discussed above and delinquency varied in concert with each other and
within different regions of urban cities. Specifically, Shaw and McKay proposed that these characteristics followed a concentric ring pattern around

the center of the city, with the highest levels near the center and decreasing levels toward the periphery of the city.

It is difficult to address the amount of change in ecological characteristics that has occurred in Little Rock since Shaw and McKay's study because, as previously stated, they did not map ecological variables but assumed instead that they followed the concentric ring pattern exhibited in other urban cities. There is little reason to argue with Shaw and McKay's findings, however, because the pattern of distribution of industry in Little Rock was similar to other cities in the research conducted by Shaw and McKay. Along with the similarities of distribution of industry was a corresponding concentration of workers in nearby residential areas. This was especially true of lower economic status workers who could not afford to live far from their place of employment. Finally, the distribution of delinquency in Little Rock in 1930 followed the concentric ring pattern exhibited in other cities. The heaviest concentrations of delinquency in Shaw and McKay's study were found in Zones I and II, which are the current census tracts 3, 4, 6, 7, 8, and 9 (see Map 3.1 at the end of the chapter). These findings support the expectation that the ecological characteristics of Little Rock at the time of Shaw and McKay's study followed the concentric ring pattern established in Chicago and the other cities studied.

There is support for the contention that changes in the characteristics of Little Rock and other cities would produce changes in the ecological characteristics. Since such characteristics are closely linked to the pattern of residential areas, one would expect to see a dispersion and decentralization of the pattern of ecological variables and delinquency studied by Shaw and McKay.

This proved to be the case in Little Rock. As shown in Maps 3.1–3.9 at the end of this chapter, the distribution of ecological factors and delinquency has moved from one distributed in concentric rings to an uneven distribution of characteristics spread across the city. The current geographical pattern of ecological characteristics and delinquency suggests "hot spots" of such characteristics spread throughout the community much like those described by Sherman (1987).

These maps continue to show some similarities with the distributions proposed by Shaw and McKay. Maps concerning the population change, median rental value, and homes owned still show significant levels in and around the central business district. The pattern of decreasing levels of ecological characteristics toward the limits of the city is not present though. In most of the maps, Tract 40.01, which is at the periphery of the city, exhibits the highest levels of ecological characteristics in almost every category. Furthermore, Tracts 24.01 and 24.02, which are also toward the periphery of the city, exhibit moderate to high levels in every category.

Some of the hot spots of delinquency are also near the central business district; however, the area most predisposed to delinquency according to

Shaw and McKay's hypothesis (tracts 3, 4, 6, 7, 8 and 9) exhibits among the lowest delinquency rates in the city. Some of the census tracts that were high in Shaw and McKay's study are still high in 1990 (specifically, Tract 4). This supports the proposals of Bursik and Webb (1982) that some areas of a city have "enduring" characteristics that do not change over time. Most of the tracts that were high in 1930, however, have decreased in terms of their delinquency rate, while others have greatly increased their delinquency rate where they were low in Shaw and McKay's study. Furthermore, instead of decreasing toward the periphery of the city, levels of delinquency remain strong, even to the city limits in some cases.

Such patterns would suggest that there is an, albeit broken, concentric ring at the very edge of the city rather than closer to the center. This might lead one to assume that the concentric ring proposition that cities expand from the center could explain the current distribution in Little Rock. This does not seem to be the case, however. While there are concentrations of ecological characteristics at the center and peripheries of the city, these patterns are not consistent across all ecological characteristics and they are often broken up by tracts with very low levels of the mapped characteristics. Furthermore, there is an area between the inner and outer concentrations that is very mixed in the levels of certain characteristics, not only between each of the ecological characteristics, but also between different areas of the same map. This provides the impetus for the argument that the concentric ring pattern of delinquency is no longer applicable in Little Rock.

Four changes that have occurred in urban cities since the time of the original study may account for this disruption of the concentric ring pattern of ecological characteristics and delinquency. First, urban cities have changed dramatically since the 1930s. As America has moved from a manufacturing to a service-oriented economy, cities once characterized by concentration and centralization are now better described as decentralized and dispersed, both in terms of sources of employment and residential areas (See also P. I. Jackson, 1991). In the original study, the heaviest concentration of homes was found in tracts 2, 3, 4, 5, 6, 7, 8, and 9, which surround the downtown business district and extend to the state capitol (Shaw and McKay, 1942). Current patterns of households show the heaviest concentrations in tracts 15, 24.02 and 22.05. This supports an argument for decentralization and diffusion of residential areas in Little Rock.

Along with a diffusion of the homes of workers, there has also been a decentralization of sources of employment. With the move from manufacturing-oriented economies to that of service-oriented economies, the location of businesses has moved from central "industrial parks" to malls and shopping centers closer to where people live. After World War II, retail trade and service establishments increasingly followed the population to suburban areas to maintain their level of sales. The proliferation of freeways, expressways, and loops in the 1950s and 1960s served to accelerate the movement of workers to the periphery of the city; which, in turn, caused a greater expansion of the businesses that catered to the people—shopping malls, grocery stores, restaurants, and other service establishments (Palen, 1981). This allowed residents to remain close to their work while increasing the dispersion of workers from centralized residential areas. Recent censuses of retail trade show that central business districts now account for less than half of all of the sales in personal and household items, while suburban shopping malls are rapidly increasing their hold on this corner of the service market (Palen, 1981).

Movement to the periphery also means that there is much more room for residential areas to spread out. As a result, urban areas have not replaced one concentration of residential areas with another. Instead, there are many pockets of residential areas spread throughout the city. In order to maintain contact with these residents, service industries have had to open multiple establishments in several areas of the city. This phenomenon is clearly shown in Map 3.9. Where Little Rock could have once been characterized as having a central business and commerce district accounting for the majority of sales in the city, it is now more accurately described as having a wide distribution of shopping centers and malls spread throughout the city.

The third change that has occurred in modern urban cities is that technological advances made in the mid-twentieth century have allowed cities to develop patterns that were previously not possible. For example, advancements in automobiles have allowed workers to live farther from their work and have made commuting easier. At the time of the original study, many individuals lived close to their work—with an average distance from home to work of only 1.5 miles (Janowitz, 1978)—due to a lack of available transportation. This was true especially of lower class workers who could not afford the luxury of living in the suburbs and commuting to work areas (Palen, 1981). In present times, however, commutes of tens of miles to work are commonplace, thus dispersing the possible residences of city workers.

Finally, there has been widespread construction of public housing since the 1960s. This may cause certain groups to move where the housing is offered, rather than within areas of the city identified by the type of businesses found there (Henig, 1980). This would result in areas with high proportions of the ecological characteristics discussed in this chapter, owing primarily to factors other than the natural movement of urban dwellers. Such migration would most certainly break up an established pattern of residential areas such as concentric rings.

CONCLUSIONS

The findings of Shaw and McKay concerning the ecological correlates of delinquency are supported by this study. All of the variables used by Shaw and McKay in their original study were found to be significantly correlated with delinquency. Furthermore, supplementary measures added by this study to enhance the ecological explanations of Shaw and McKay were also found to be statistically significant. These findings would suggest that the tenets of ecological research and social disorganization continue to be valid explanations of delinquency in modern urban cities.

This study validated the physical explanations of delinquency put forth by Shaw and McKay in that it supplemented their qualitative analyses with empirical measures of physical characteristics of urban cities. Shaw and McKay's conclusions concerning the association between vacancy and physical deterioration were supported by these latest findings; and were strengthened by the significance of the association between the quantitative measure of physical deterioration.

Shaw and McKay's findings concerning the relationship between economic characteristics and delinquency were also supported by this study. While the correlations between economic characteristics and delinquency were not as high as they were in Shaw and McKay's study, they were significant and do support an argument of the relationship between economic characteristics and delinquency.

Finally, Shaw and McKay's findings concerning the relationship between population characteristics and delinquency were also strengthened by this study. The additional measure of female-headed households clarified the argument that it is not any one race or nationality that is associated with delinquency, but that there are conditions under which certain groups exist that are highly associated with delinquency.

The findings of Shaw and McKay concerning the geographical distribution of these characteristics and delinquency, however, were not supported. The changes discussed above seem to have broken the pattern of residential living such that a concentric ring pattern may no longer be applicable. These findings suggest that, while some similarities remain in the pattern of ecological characteristics and delinquency that might represent the remnants of concentric rings, the dominant pattern supports an argument that concentric rings are no longer accurate in describing the geographical distribution of such characteristics in modern urban cities. Urban cities have changed dramatically since the time of the original study. Modern urban cities have a much more decentralized, service-oriented form of industry such that current industrial distributions, along with technological and other changes that have occurred in urban America in the last three decades, have changed the pattern of residential areas. The concentration and centralization that once characterized the residential distribution of industrial cities of the 1930s has been transformed into decentralization and dispersion. This diffusion is translated to ecological explanations of delinquency in that there have been mass changes in the distribution of residential areas of urban cities, especially those that are predominately higher in delinquency and the ecological characteristics analyzed in this study. Such changes have forced a reevaluation of the concentric ring hypothesis that has long been associated with Shaw and McKay.

This study does not propose that Shaw and McKay's findings were wrong. It argues instead that the nature of urban areas has changed since the time of the original study such that the geographical distribution characterized by their findings no longer applies to modern urban cities.

It should be noted in conclusion that there are problems associated with drawing such inferences between ecological characteristics, social disorganization, and delinquency. The strongest of these is the leap of faith that is required to move from the association between structural level indicators of socioeconomic and demographic characters and delinquency to the breakdown of informal controls produced by social disorganization. Shaw and McKay and others have drawn sharp criticism for making such assumptions; and this chapter is reluctant to brave the accusations of ecological fallacy to support such conclusions. It is possible, however, to propose that, although the concentric ring pattern of delinquency proposed by Shaw and McKay no longer appears to be applicable in modern urban cities, the ecological correlates used in the original research in Chicago appear to be valid in the 1990s as indicators of "delinquency in urban areas."

Map 3.1
Delinquency Rate per Thousand Juveniles by Census Tract[1]

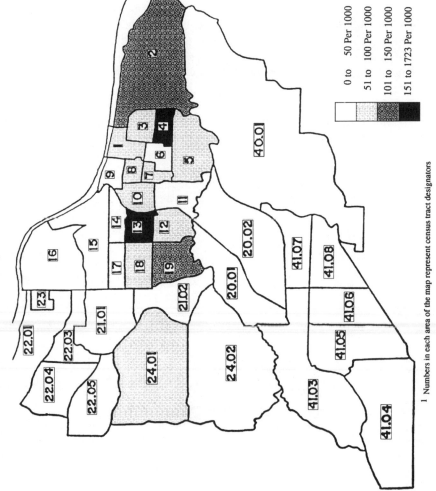

0 to   50 Per 1000
51 to 100 Per 1000
101 to 150 Per 1000
151 to 1723 Per 1000

1 Numbers in each area of the map represent census tract designators

Map 3.2
Percent Population Change by Census Tract[1]

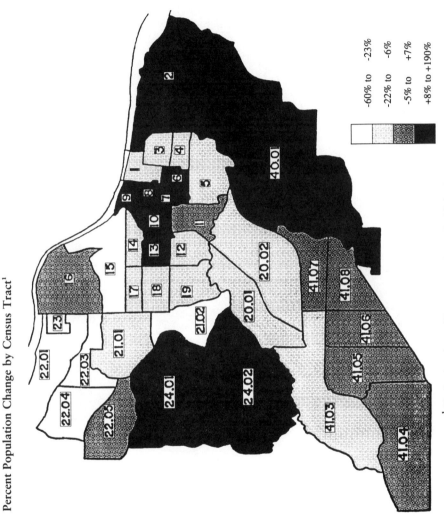

-60% to -23%

-22% to -6%

-5% to +7%

+8% to +190%

1 Numbers in each area of the map represent census tract designators

71

Map 3.3
Vacant Housing Units by Census Tract[1]

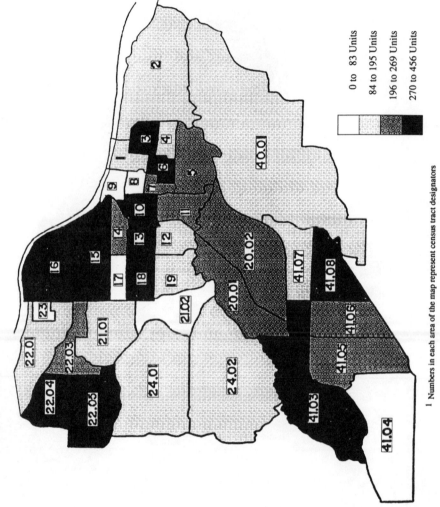

0 to 83 Units
84 to 195 Units
196 to 269 Units
270 to 456 Units

1 Numbers in each area of the map represent census tract designators

72

Map 3.4
Rate per Thousand of Boarded-Up Housing Units by Census Tract[1]

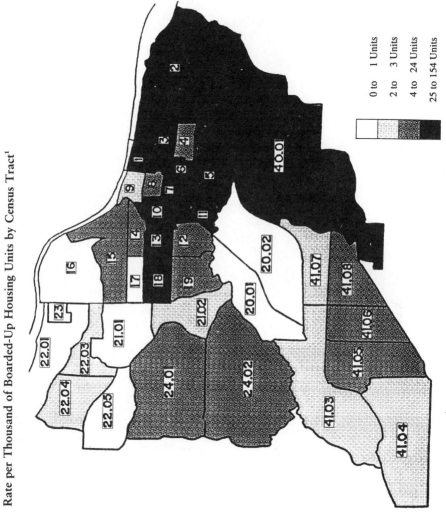

0 to 1 Units
2 to 3 Units
4 to 24 Units
25 to 154 Units

1 Numbers in each area of the map represent census tract designators

Map 3.5
Rate per Thousand of Families Receiving Social Assistance by Census Tract[1]

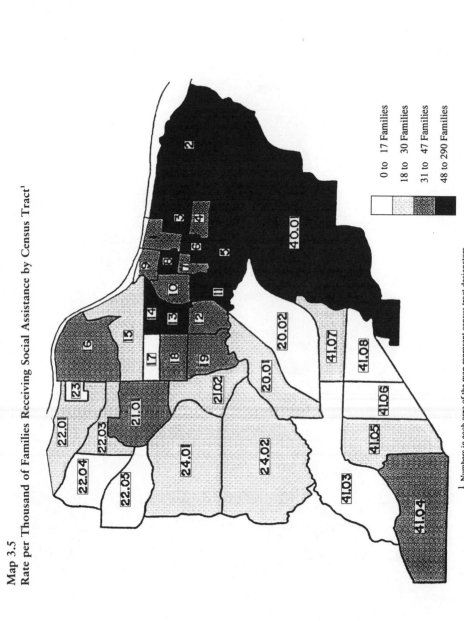

0 to 17 Families
18 to 30 Families
31 to 47 Families
48 to 290 Families

1 Numbers in each area of the map represent census tract designators

Map 3.6
Median Rental Value by Census Tract[1]

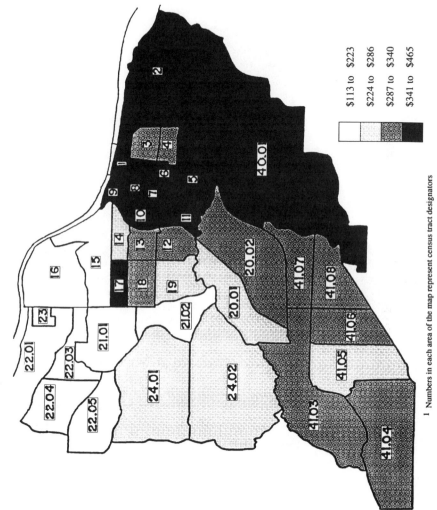

$113 to $223
$224 to $286
$287 to $340
$341 to $465

1 Numbers in each area of the map represent census tract designators

75

Map 3.7
Homes Owned Rather Than Rented by Census Tract[1]

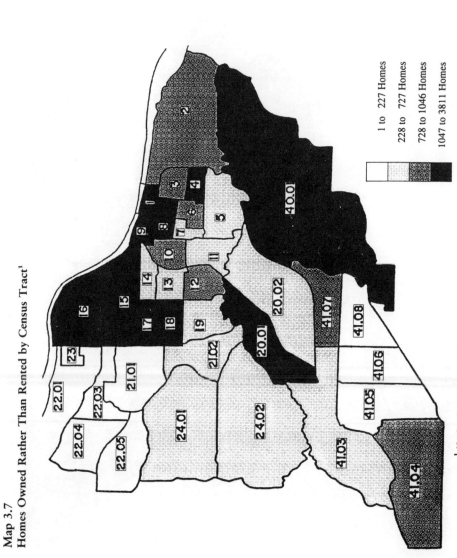

1 to 227 Homes
228 to 727 Homes
728 to 1046 Homes
1047 to 3811 Homes

1 Numbers in each area of the map represent census tract designators

Map 3.8
Ratio of Black to White Heads of Household by Census Tract[1]

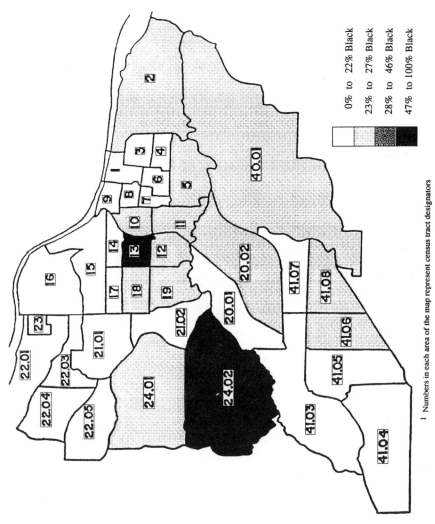

| 0% to 22% Black |
| 23% to 27% Black |
| 28% to 46% Black |
| 47% to 100% Black |

1 Numbers in each area of the map represent census tract designators

Map 3.9
Distribution of Manufacturing and Service Industries by Census Tract[1]

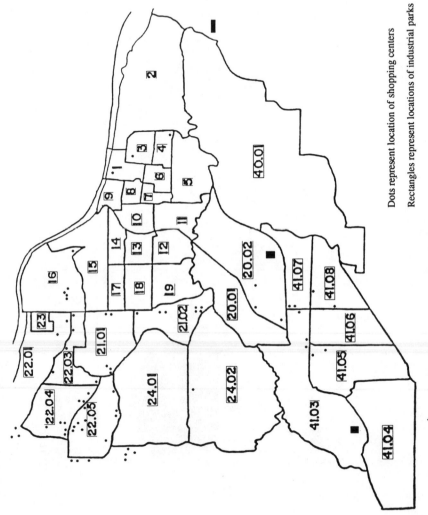

Dots represent location of shopping centers

Rectangles represent locations of industrial parks

1 Numbers in each area of the map represent census tract designators

4

Strain, Relative Deprivation, and Middle-Class Delinquency

VELMER S. BURTON, JR. AND
R. GREGORY DUNAWAY

Criminological theories, over the past several decades, have gradually shifted from structural explanations to more individualistic concepts of crime causation. For example, the prominence of traditional strain theories formulated by Merton (1938), A. Cohen (1955), and Cloward and Ohlin (1960) have been weakened by the recent emergence of individual-level models of criminality such as "revised strain" theory (see Agnew, 1984, 1985a, 1989, 1992) and stress theories (Kirkpatrick and Humphrey, 1991; Vaux and Ruggiero, 1983; see also Seltzer and Kalmuss, 1988). Further, both the development of competing crime models—such as Hirschi's (1969) social control and Akers' (1985) social learning theories—coupled with scholarly criticisms of strain theory (Kornhauser, 1978; R. E. Johnson, 1979) have resulted in strain theory's near demise as a useful predictor of criminal behavior (Burton, Cullen, and Link, 1989; Burton, 1991; Burton and Cullen, 1993).

Despite these developments, we believe that scholars (see Hirschi, 1969; Kornhauser, 1978; R. E. Johnson, 1979) may be a bit premature in dismissing the explanatory power of strain theories (Bernard, 1987). Accordingly, the work of Agnew has been timely in reviving interest in strain theories. In fact, the "individual-level" work of Agnew has provided an alternative, yet fruitful approach to measuring and testing strain theory (see Agnew, 1987).

Given this recent trend of conceptualizing strain from an individualistic perspective, we seek to examine a traditional conception of strain theory that allows for both structural and individual-level sources of strain, most notably relative deprivation theory.

This study examines the explanatory power of relative deprivation theory using a sample of high school youths. We follow the recent trend of measuring individual-level strain by operationalizing feelings of deprivation, which include anger, hostility, and frustration—the missing dimensions of most previous tests of relative deprivation theory (Vold and Bernard, 1986). Thus, the emphasis of this study involves assessing the effect of relative deprivation on delinquency.

Before embarking on this test of relative deprivation and self-reported delinquency, we trace the theoretical development of the strain school of thought. We attempt to underscore the movement away from structural operationalizations of strain toward the increasingly popular individual-level conception of strain.

THEORETICAL DEVELOPMENT OF STRAIN THEORIES

From Structural to Individualistic Models of Crime Causation

Sociology increasingly has become dominated by structural perspectives to explain social behaviors (see Collins, 1986; Mayhew, 1980). The influence of structural forces has been witnessed in the development of criminological theory and is greatly attributed to Merton's (1938) innovative essay: "Social Structure and Anomie" (Burton, 1991). Merton's social structure and anomie formulation, commonly referred to as "strain theory," was a prominent theoretical model of criminality throughout the 1960s (Cole, 1975). Since Merton's conception of social structure and anomie, however, "derivative theories" (Cole, 1975) of strain, most notably A. Cohen's (1955) *Delinquent Boys* and Cloward and Ohlin's (1960) *Delinquency and Opportunity* were introduced.

The core thesis of these traditional strain theories is that blocked opportunities to attain success goals generate pressures or frustrations that lead to criminality. These pressures or frustrations, however, are structurally produced and not at the individual level (Bernard, 1987). To be sure, Merton (1938; 1968a and b) proposed a theory of societal "anomie," not of individually felt strain. A closer examination of Merton's work suggests that there are "strains upon the individual" (1968b: 178), and he creates a "typology of individual adaptations" (1968a: 140), which implies that the personal experience of being blocked from economic success is strain-inducing and thus criminogenic (Agnew, 1987). However, even if Merton

wanders into the realm of the individual, ultimately he retreats from this level of analysis and reminds us that anomie is a societal condition and that his theoretical purpose is fundamentally sociological. Thus, Mertonian Strain theory is designed to explain rates of deviance/crime across the social structure, not to explain which individuals feel the pressure to engage in such wayward activities (Burton, 1991; Burton and Cullen, 1993).

The subsequent works of Cohen (1955) and Cloward and Ohlin (1960) come closer to addressing individual experiences with frustration and, thus, are precursors to current shifts toward individualistic strain theories. After all, the thesis that blocked opportunity and/or status frustration is a powerful force in producing the emergence, content, persistence, and effects of male delinquent subcultures/gangs concentrated in impoverished urban areas implied the existence of individualistic adaptations in the face of frustration. Further, in "studying subcultures, learning through social interaction, and the organization of neighborhoods, they rooted their thinking as much in the Chicago School and differential association theory as they did in the anomie tradition" (Burton and Cullen, 1993; Cullen, 1988; Kornhauser, 1978). Thus, early work on strain theory was primarily concerned with the structural barriers leading to criminality; not with individual feelings of strain (see Bernard, 1987).

The Rise of Individualistic Strain Theories

More recently, theoretical scholars have begun to focus on alternative or competing conceptions of strain theory (Burton, 1991; Farnworth and Lieber, 1989; Agnew, 1992). Several delinquency scholars have shifted away from broad-based structural explanations of criminality and toward individual theories of strain. Accordingly, we share insights into several alternative operationalizations of strain theory that view individual-level sources of strain and their predicted relationships to crime and delinquency.

Stressful Life Events

Though not yet a popular explanation of criminal behavior, "stressful life events" and stress models offer an avenue of investigation toward developing models of criminality. An assessment of causality from this perspective suggests that stressful or traumatic personal experiences generate a negative impact on the individual, which leaves the person more inclined to perpetrate deviant acts. Additionally, factors such as a period of stress over time and the existence of multiple or "clusters" of stressors may be responsible for criminal behavior, particularly violence (Kirkpatrick and Humphrey, 1991).

As noted, the development of this framework, though prominent in the sociology of mental health in studies of psychiatric symptomology (Pearlin et al., 1981; Shrout et al., 1989), has yet to be regularly applied to criminology (Burton and Cullen, 1993). However, Vaux and Ruggiero's (1983) research reporting a connection between "stressful life change" and delinquency suggests a plausible route of inquiry among delinquency researchers (Seltzer and Kalmus, 1988).

Revised Strain Theory

Recently, criminologists have begun to examine how competing sources of strain might influence criminality. For example, Robert Agnew (1984, 1985a, 1989, 1991, 1992) has embarked on a new path that has exceeded the bounds of traditional strain theory. Agnew (1984) laid the early groundwork by generating a multiple operationalization of "goals" and named it a "revisionist" strain theory. Shortly thereafter, his next contribution was the development of his "revised strain theory" (1985a; 1989; 1991).

Unlike traditional strain theories, which examined the ramifications of denied access to desired goals, Agnew's revised strain theory assessed the consequences of being blocked or restricted from escaping painful or uncomfortable stimuli, most notably a harsh or abusive family environment or a negative school environment such as mean teachers or having failing grades.

According to Agnew (1985a), when youths encounter the blockage of opportunities to escape these painful environments, two forms of delinquency may ensue. First, crime may be produced directly by encouraging unlawful means of escape such as running away from home or skipping school. Second, in these circumstances, criminal behavior may be the indirect product of induced anger, which culminates into violent acts (e.g., striking a teacher or a family member). In testing his theory with National Youth Survey data (a male-only sample and a juvenile sample), he found support for his hypothesis that strain generated from the blockages of escaping painful stimuli (environments) produced anger and aggressive forms of delinquency (see Agnew, 1985a; 1989).

In his most recent work, Agnew (1992) set forth an outline for a "general strain theory" of crime and delinquency. Succinctly, he identifies three potential sources of strain that may afflict individuals: (1) the failure to attain socially positive goals, (2) the restriction or denial of socially and positively valued goals, and (3) the presence of negative stimuli or forces. According to Agnew, it is under these conditions that individual-level strains emerge and both "nondelinquent and delinquent coping" may arise (Burton and Cullen, 1993).

The appeal of Agnew's revised strain theory (1985a; 1989) and general theory of strain (1992) is that their explanatory power is capable of transcending class lines (Burton, 1991). In his writings, Agnew (1985a; 1987) is cognizant of the limitations of traditional strain theory, most notably that it concentrates and "examines only lower-class populations" (Burton, 1991: 34). Accordingly, Agnew states that "middle-class adolescents (like lower-class youths), may encounter aversive situations from which they cannot escape" (Agnew, 1985a: 162).

Relative Deprivation Theory: A Return to the Individual-Level Dimensions of the Theory

The use of individual-level explanations, while not found in traditional strain theories (Bernard, 1987), is a component of relative deprivation theory. More specifically, relative deprivation theory assumes that structural sources of inequity lead to groups feeling deprivation and frustration, which may be crime-producing. Thus, while drawing its intellectual roots from early strain theory, relative deprivation theory recognizes that feelings of "hostility and anger" can be generated by structural level sources of inequality (Box, 1981; Blau and Blau, 1982; Stack, 1984). Though the idea of relative deprivation became popular during the 1960s, the work of Blau and Blau (1982) in "The Cost of Inequality: Metropolitan Structure and Violent Crime" rekindled interest in the theory (Burton, 1991). A number of researchers have examined the relationship between structural inequality and crime rates (Sampson, 1985), homicide rates (Rosenfeld, 1982; Parker and Liftin, 1983; Krahn et al., 1986), property crimes (Jacobs, 1981), and rape rates (Maume, 1989). Despite these studies demonstrating a significant relationship between economic inequality and criminal behaviors, all have failed to "tap into the feelings of anger, status frustration, and resentment that are at the core of relative deprivation theory" (Vold and Bernard, 1986; Burton et al., 1989; Burton, 1991). Instead, while relying only on aggregate data of crime rates, Blau and Blau (1982) suggest that feelings of relative deprivation play a role in the etiology of violent criminal behavior. Yet they do not directly test this hypothesis.

The failure of delinquency researchers to measure individual-level feelings of deprivation no doubt is partly attributed to Merton's (1938) "failure to integrate relative deprivation with his deviance theory," which was nonetheless a "curious moment in intellectual history" (see Merton and Rossi, 1968; Burton and Cullen, 1993). Had relative deprivation theory been incorporated into his theoretical conceptualizations, he could have avoided criticisms that his theory was for the lower class. Furthermore,

subsequent scholars might have explored more fully how feelings of deprivation (such as hostility, anger and frustration) and the pressures toward crime they engender are not confined to those absolutely deprived of economic opportunity but are found wherever in the class structure people see themselves as less well off than the "Joneses" (Chester, 1976; Cullen, 1984; Passas, 1987; Thio, 1975; Burton and Cullen, 1993).

In light of the empirical oversight to examine the individual-level dimension of relative deprivation theory, we attempt to fill this void through a test of relative deprivation theory with a sample of middle-class high school youths from an affluent midwestern community. The selection of a middle-class sample seems plausible on two counts. First, given that individual-level strain theories are not class-specific theories, the individualistic aspect of relative deprivation theory should be applicable to explaining middle-class delinquency. Second, the investigation of middle-class delinquency is timely in light of the recent scholarly interest in this segment of the population (Richards, 1981; Hagan, Gillis, and Simpson, 1985, 1987; Raskin-White, Pandina, and LaGrange, 1987; Raskin-White, Labouvie, and Bates, 1985; Morash and Chesney-Lind, 1991).

Finally, by investigating relative deprivation theory we seek to extend the work of Blau and Blau (1982) and others (see Maume, 1989; Sampson, 1985; and Jacobs, 1981) by examining the individual dimension (e.g., individual feelings) of structural strain theories.

METHODS

The Sample

The data for this study were gathered from a survey of high school students attending a suburban high school located near a large midwestern city, during the spring of 1991. The socioeconomic status of the community from which the high school draws its students can be best characterized as middle to upper-middle class.

All students that were attending on the day the survey was administered were asked to participate in completing a "1991 Youth Lifestyle Survey." The instrument consisted of nine pages of items that sought answers concerning youth attitudes about their families, friends, school, and community. Additionally, the survey measured youth participation in various conforming and nonconforming behavior (including delinquency).

Surveys were administered at the beginning of each first-period class by the teacher of that class. Teachers were informed only to distribute surveys to students and not to provide instructions. All instructions and directions were attached to each survey for each student to read. To insure anonymity of the respondent, students were instructed not to make any personal identification marks on the survey. A total of 263 valid questionnaires were obtained, representing 94 percent of the high school's students.

Dependent Variables

Consistent with delinquency literature, we make use of multi-item measures of delinquency (Elliott et al., 1983; Hindelang, Hirschi, and Weis, 1979, 1981). We have included fifty-seven individual items that assess some form of delinquency. Our items are borrowed largely from the National Youth Survey delinquency scales (see Elliott et al., 1983). The work of

Elliott and his associates (1980, 1983) stands out as having one of the most complete and varied sets of measures of delinquency. We have derived three delinquency scales from the individual items, including a general delinquency scale, a drug use scale, and a felony crime scale. The items comprising each scale along with their reliabilities can be found in Figure 4.1.

Additionally, each scale is measured two separate ways. Following the work of Hindelang and his associates (1979, 1981), we include both incidence and prevalence of delinquency in the past year for our three scales. Incidence scales are computed by summing the reported frequencies for each individual item within the scale. Prevalence scales are derived by recoding the reported frequencies of individual items into dummy variables, where 1 = participation and 0 = nonparticipation in a delinquent act. The recoded individual items within each scale are then summed to indicate the prevalence of delinquent involvement. Thus, while the incidence scales have no upper limit, the prevalence scales' upper limit will not exceed the number of items that comprise the scale.

General Delinquency Scales. The General Delinquency scales are comprised of 50 items (see Figure 4.1 for all scales). These scales include a wide variety of both minor and more serious delinquent infractions. Additionally, these scales contain a number of status offenses. The reliability of the two General Delinquency scales are rather high. The incidence of general delinquency and the prevalence of general delinquency have cronbach alphas of .81 and .91, respectively.

Drug Use Scale. The Drug Use scale is comprised of seven items assessing the respondents' consumption of illegal substances, including alcohol, marijuana, cocaine, heroin, barbiturates, amphetamines, and hallucinogens. The reliability coefficients were .69 for the incidence of Drug Use scale and .69 for the prevalence of Drug Use scale.

Felony Crime Scale. To assess more serious self-reported delinquency we have developed a Felony Crime scale. This scale includes individual involvement in theft over $50, burglary, robbery, auto theft, arson, aggravated assault, and rape. Our reliability coefficients were .89 for the incidence of Felony Crime scale and .76 for the prevalence of Felony Crime scale.

Independent Variable: Relative Deprivation

Relative deprivation is conceptualized as *actual* feelings of deprivation. We have included items that attempt to capture the negative feelings generated when youths "compare" their material conditions against others within their own "reference group" (Merton and Rossi, 1968). Thus, individual relative deprivation, as conceived of within this study, is a condition that can affect persons regardless of their socioeconomic status (Burton and Cullen, 1993).

Four Likert-type questions were used to create a Relative Deprivation

Figure 4.1
Individual Delinquency Items for Each Delinquency Scale

<u>General Delinquency Scale</u>

1. Smoked a pack of cigarettes in one day.

2. Cheated on a test or plagiarized a paper.

3. Skipped school without an excuse.

4. Avoided paying for such things as movies, bus rides, or food.

5. Committed acts of vandalism.

6. Been suspended from school.

7. Bought liquor.

8. Failed to return extra change that a cashier gave you by mistake.

9. Been loud, rowdy, or unruly in a public place.

10. Been late to school without an excuse.

11. Illegally copied cassette tapes, records or VCR tapes.

12. Hitchhiked where it was illegal.

13. Been drunk in a public place.

14. Begged for money or things from strangers.

15. Illegally copied computer software or video games.

16. Ran away from home.

17. Damaged another car but did not try to notify the owner.

18. Stolen things from school.

19. Gambled illegally such as betting on sporting events or card playing.

20. Been paid for having sexual relations with someone.

21. Stolen money from family members.

22. Drove a car while drunk.

23. Drove a car without a license.

24. Made obscene telephone calls, such as calling someone and saying dirty things.

25. Urinated in a public place (like behind a bush).

26. Been involved in gang fights.

Figure 4.1 (Continued)

27. Sold marijuana or hashish (i.e. pot, grass, or hash).

28. Sold hard drugs such as heroin, cocaine, or LSD.

29. Knowingly bought, sold, or held something that was stolen (or tried to do any of these things).

30. Taken a vehicle other than your own for a ride (drive) without the owner's permission.

31. Thrown objects (such as rocks, snowballs, or bottles) at cars or people.

32. Stole or tried to steal things worth $5 or less.

33. Stole or tried to steal things worth between $5 and $50

34. Stole or tried to steal things worth more than $50

35. Lied about your age to buy alcohol or to be admitted to a bar.

36. Carried a hidden weapon other than a pocket knife.

37. Purposely damaged or destroyed property belonging to your family members.

38. Purposely damaged or destroyed property belonging to your school.

39. Broken into a building or vehicle (or tried to break in) to steal something or just look around.

40. Stole or tried to steal a motor vehicle such as a car or motorcycle.

41. Used force (strong-arm methods) to get money or things from family members.

42. Used force (strong-arm methods) to get money or things from students at your school.

43. Used force (strong-arm methods) to get money or things from people other than family members and students.

44. Hit or threatened to hit a fellow student or teacher at school.

45. Hit or threatened to hit a family member.

46. Hit or threatened to hit someone other than a student, teacher, or family member.

Figure 4.1 (Continued)

47. Had or tried to have sexual relations with someone against their will.

48. Attacked someone with the idea of seriously hurting or killing that person.

49. Set fire to someone else's property.

50. Taped an album or compact disk onto a blank tape.

<u>Drug Use Scale</u>

1. Had alcoholic beverages (beer, wine, hard liquor).

2. Had marijuana or hashish (grass, pot, or hash).

3. Had Hallucinogens (LSD, Acid, Mescaline, or Peyote).

4. Had amphetamines (uppers or speed).

5. Had barbiturates (downers or reds).

6. Had heroin (horse or smack).

7. Had cocaine (coke).

<u>Felony Crime Scale</u>

1. Stole or tried to steal things worth more than $50

2. Broken into a building or vehicle (or tried to break in) to steal something or just look around.

3. Stole or tried to steal a motor vehicle such as a car or motorcycle.

4. Used force (strong-arm methods) to get money or things from <u>family</u>, <u>students</u>, or <u>others</u>.

5. Had or tried to have sexual relations with someone against their will.

6. Attacked someone with the idea of seriously hurting or killing that person.

7. Set fire to someone else's property.

scale. Youths were asked to what extent they agreed (where 1 = strongly disagree and 6 = strongly agree) with the following statements: (1) "In general, I don't have as much money as other students in this school"; (2) "It bothers me that most other students live in better homes than I do"; (3) "In general, my family is not as rich as other families in [community]"; and (4) "It bothers me that I don't have as much money to buy nice clothes as other students do." The scores of each item were summed and divided by four. Thus, the range of the relative deprivation scale (RELDEP) is from 1 to 6, where 1 = low relative deprivation and 6 = high relative deprivation. The reliability coefficient of the Relative Deprivation scale was .79.

Control Variables

In our attempt to assess the effects of relative deprivation on delinquency we have controlled for a number of variables. Respondents' race, gender, and age are controlled for. Race is coded as a dummy variable where 0 = white and 1 = black. Respondent's gender is also coded as a dummy variable where 0 = female and 1 = male. Our analyses also control for a number of variables that attempt to assess the socioeconomic status of the respondents. These variables include perceived social class of parents (PARCLASS) coded 6 = upper class, 5 = upper-middle class; 4 = middle class, 3 = working class, 2 = lower-middle class, 1 = lower class; whether parents own their home (OWNHOME) coded 0 = rent, 1 = own; respondent's employment status (EMPLOY) coded 0 = not employed, 1 = employed; hours a week respondent works (HOURS); amount of money in dollars respondent earns each week (MONEY); whether respondent owns a car (OWNCAR) coded 0 = does not own a car, 1 = owns a car; and whether respondent has access to a car (ACESCAR) coded 0 = no access to a car, 1 = access to a car. Finally, three educational variables were also controlled for: what grade the respondent was in (GRADE); the number of Ds the respondent received on their last report card (NUMBERD); and the number of Fs the respondent received on their last report card (NUMBERF). Table 4.1 contains the descriptive statistics for all variables included within our analyses.

FINDINGS

Ordinary Least Squares multiple regression analysis was used to assess the independent effects of relative deprivation on delinquency. Table 4.2 reports the standardized regression coefficients (Betas) for the relative deprivation measure and all control variables for all six delinquency scales. The Betas allow us to assess the strength of the effect of our independent variable relative to the effects of the control variables. Additionally, the amount of

Table 4.1
Descriptive Statistics for Variables Used in the Analyses

	Mean	Standard Deviation
Control Variables		
GENDER	.42	.50
RACE	.14	.34
AGE	16.42	.92
NUMBERD	.48	.83
NUMBERF	.14	.55
PARCLASS	4.55	.85
OWNHOME	.91	.28
ACESCAR	.72	.45
OWNCAR	.32	.47
EMPLOY	.50	.50
HOURS	5.99	8.67
MONEY	33.67	45.89
Independent Variables		
RELDEP	3.10	1.03
Dependent Variables		
General Delinquency (Inc.)	189.22	351.54
General Delinquency (Prev.)	9.73	7.14
Drug Use (Inc.)	29.37	60.82
Drug Use (Prev.)	1.00	1.13
Felony Crime (Inc.)	4.63	15.79
Felony Crime (Prev.)	.71	1.52

explained variance (R-Square) in the dependent measures by the model is reported.

As can be observed from Table 4.2, relative deprivation exerts a positive and significant effect on all six measures of delinquency. Relative deprivation is the strongest predictor in our models for both measures of general delinquency and the incidence of drug use. The number of Fs received on the student's last report card was the strongest predictor of delinquency among the control variables. Number of Fs was positively and significantly related to all measures of delinquency and exerted the greatest effects of all other variables on prevalence of drug use and both measures of felony crime. The effects of race and gender sporadically affected delinquency. Race was negatively associated with all delinquency scales and significantly affected prevalence of general delinquency and both measures of drug use. In other words, whites were more likely to engage in delinquent behaviors. The effect of being male statistically impacted both incidence and prevalence of general delinquency, as well as prevalence of felony crime. Finally, of all the measures of respondent's socioeconomic status, only student's employment status had any statistical effect on delinquency. Students who reported having

Table 4.2

The Effects of Relative Deprivation and Control Variables on Delinquency (Beta values reported)

	General Crime Scale (Inc.)	General Crime Scale (Prev.)	Drug Use Scale (Inc.)	Drug Use Scale (Prev.)	Felony Crime Scale (Inc.)	Felony Crime Scale (Prev.)
RELDEP	.269**	.395**	.247**	.295**	.139*	.231**
AGE	.034	.007	.057	-.121	-.074	-.032
RACE	-.023	-.135*	-.150*	-.157*	-.018	-.027
GENDER	.105	.160*	.031	-.057	.027	.177**
EMPLOY	.162*	.085	.112	.046	.163*	.086
PARCLASS	.021	.022	.008	.078	.056	-.013
HOURS	.026	.006	-.095	-.022	.000	-.009
MONEY	-.058	-.028	.050	-.004	-.087	-.025
OWNCAR	.077	.077	.052	.047	.070	-.004
OWNHOME	-.036	.055	.002	.049	-.059	-.049
ACESCAR	-.046	.033	.007	.042	.030	.049
GRADE	.051	-.046	.047	.103	.075	-.039
NUMBERD	-.037	.062	.072	.025	-.013	.020
NUMBERF	.228**	.312**	.232**	.300**	.306**	.335**
R-Square	.20	.36	.19	.23	.15	.23

```
*  = p < .05
** = p < .01
```

a job were more likely to engage in general delinquency and felony crimes when measured by incidence.

Gender and Relative Deprivation

The majority of delinquency research has been generated with male-only samples (Cernkovich and Giordano, 1979; Covington, 1985; Burton, 1991), and recent work on individualistic strain (revised strain) theory has been tested with males only (Agnew, 1985a, 1989). To assess whether relative deprivation is more salient for one gender group, we conducted separate regression analyses for females and males.

Table 4.3 includes the regression coefficients for the effects of relative deprivation and the control variables on female delinquency. Relative deprivation positively affected all forms of delinquency among females. Relative deprivation did not, however, statistically impact felony crimes. Age of the respondent, on the other hand, did statistically affect female felony crime, as well as prevalence of general delinquency. Owning a car statistically increased female prevalence of general delinquency and female incidence

Table 4.3

The Effects of Relative Deprivation and Control Variables on Delinquency—Females Only (Beta values reported)

	General Crime Scale (Inc.)	General Crime Scale (Prev.)	Drug Use Scale (Inc.)	Drug Use Scale (Prev.)	Felony Crime Scale (Inc.)	Felony Crime Scale (Prev.)
RELDEP	.238**	.318**	.152*	.207*	.090	.135
AGE	-.170	-.280*	-.068	-.064	-.345*	-.349*
RACE	.076	-.028	-.098	-.113	-.005	-.003
EMPLOY	.196	-.026	.010	-.073	.181	.017
PARCLASS	.141	.013	.047	.120	.104	-.084
HOURS	-.017	.043	-.094	.087	-.047	.030
MONEY	-.118	.030	.160	.066	-.062	-.022
OWNCAR	.120	.199*	.168*	.186*	.118	.129
OWNHOME	-.033	.013	-.030	.008	-.059	-.114
ACESCAR	.032	.144	.091	.063	.119	.158
GRADE	.081	.146	.071	.151	.239	.167
NUMBERD	.256**	.150*	.288**	.070	.065	.088
NUMBERF	-.025	.115	-.043	.060	.028	.059
R-Square	.23	.25	.23	.22	.12	.11

* = p < .05
** = p < .01

and prevalence of drug use. Further, the number of Ds received on the respondent's last report card was positively and significantly related to female general delinquency and incidence of drug use.

The results of our regression analyses for males is presented in Table 4.4. Relative deprivation positively and significantly affects all forms of delinquency except for incidence of felony crime. The relative deprivation measure was the most important predictor of prevalence of general delinquency for males. The number of Fs that respondents received on their last report cards was positively and significantly related to all measures of male delinquency. Alternatively, the number of Ds that respondents received on their last report cards negatively impacted incidence of general delinquency among males. Age of the respondent positively affected incidence of general delinquency and incidence of felony crime. The effect of being white was statistically related to prevalence of general delinquency and both measures of drug use. Finally, hours worked each week positively and significantly affected incidence of general delinquency.

Overall, relative deprivation affects general delinquency and drug use for both males and females. Relative deprivation affects the prevalence of felony crime among males but not for females. Generally, our regression models

Table 4.4
The Effects of Relative Deprivation and Control Variables on Delinquency—
Males Only (Beta values reported)

	General Crime Scale (Inc.)	General Crime Scale (Prev.)	Drug Use Scale (Inc.)	Drug Use Scale (Prev.)	Felony Crime Scale (Inc.)	Felony Crime Scale (Prev.)
RELDEP	.215*	.435**	.269**	.338**	.121	.272**
AGE	.209*	.157	.134	-.013	.232*	.149
RACE	-.060	-.211**	-.156*	-.176*	-.035	-.039
EMPLOY	.034	.140	.107	.091	.085	.120
PARCLASS	-.081	-.027	-.033	.033	-.019	.027
HOURS	.197*	.025	-.045	-.063	.179	.009
MONEY	-.091	-.044	.011	.000	-.120	-.020
OWNCAR	.048	-.023	-.020	-.051	-.050	-.130
OWNHOME	.048	.053	.022	.039	-.006	-.055
ACESCAR	-.123	-.044	-.055	.022	-.106	-.010
GRADE	.056	-.153	.028	.049	-.087	-.159
NUMBERD	-.217*	.063	-.031	.038	-.052	.043
NUMBERF	.316**	.411**	.307**	.375**	.536**	.463**
R-Square	.31	.43	.22	.28	.37	.31

```
*   = p < .05
**  = p < .01
```

account for more explained variance in male delinquency, with the exception of incidence of drug use. Therefore, relative deprivation may be more important in predicting delinquency among males, particularly more serious male crime. However, our results indicate that relative deprivation does not have a gender-specific impact on delinquency.

DISCUSSION

The individualistic measure of relative deprivation generated significant effects on all delinquency scales employed in this analysis. The results illustrate the usefulness of this conception of relative deprivation theory, which has been lacking in most previous studies assessing relative deprivation (for example, see Blau and Blau, 1982; Vold and Bernard, 1986; Burton, 1991; Burton and Cullen, 1993).

Of the control variables included in the analysis, race (nonwhite) demonstrated significant and inverse relationships to three delinquency measures and, thus, is consistent with previous empirical investigations of self-reported delinquency (see Elliott and Ageton, 1980). Additionally, gender (males) produced significant effects on the general delinquency scales. These findings are reflective of previous tests reporting that overall, males are more delinquent than females (see Elliott and Ageton, 1980; Canter, 1982; Kethinini, 1990; Burton, 1991).

To better understand the explanatory power of relative deprivation theory by gender, we found this measure of relative deprivation continued to produce significant relationships for most of the delinquency scales in the analyses. After regressing the relative deprivation and control variables onto the six delinquency measures, we found relative deprivation to be an important predictor for both male and female delinquency. Relative deprivation appears to be somewhat more important for predicting more serious delinquent acts among males.

No significant relationships were found for the Felony Crime scales. Relative deprivation did, however, significantly affect the Delinquency and Drug Use scales. Additionally, automobile ownership for females demonstrated significant effects for both incidence and prevalence of Drug Use scales. This finding suggests that females' possessing the means to escape parental controls and supervision promotes the opportunity for greater delinquent involvement (see Hagan et al., 1985).

CONCLUDING REMARKS

The gradual shift toward individual-level conceptions of strain theory has provided delinquency researchers with an alternative to traditional structural strain theory. With the emergence of "revised strain theory" (Agnew, 1985a, 1989) and the recent "general theory of strain" (Agnew, 1992), researchers now have the opportunity to employ an individualistic approach for investigating criminality and delinquent involvement from the strain perspective.

By focusing on the individual-level feelings of youths' "comparisons" of themselves against others in their reference group, we found support for this relative deprivation measure in predicting self-reported delinquent behaviors among middle-class youths. Moreover, our analysis indicated that the individual-level measure of relative deprivation was reliable and significantly predicted most forms of delinquency for this sample.

Furthermore, this individualistic conception of relative deprivation is capable of accounting for middle-class delinquency, since it measures individual-level feelings of deprivation rather than broad structural forces (e.g., inequality), which lead to feelings of deprivation as postulated by traditional strain theories (Box, 1981; Vold and Bernard, 1986).

Given our findings, coupled with the emerging trend of utilizing individual-level strain theories, we suggest that delinquency researchers continue to explore alternative conceptions of strain theory (Cole, 1975) in developing causal models of criminality. One researcher, Robert Agnew (1992), has taken this approach in developing his "general theory of strain" by focusing on the roots of stressful stimuli and individuals' restriction to valued goals. Moreover, several researchers are currently beginning to explore additional conceptions of individual-level relative (comparative) deprivation, along with its structural components, in an attempt to explain adult criminal involvement (Dunaway et al., 1992). This approach, we believe, enables researchers to fuse together traditional strain theories with the increasingly popular conceptions of individualistic strain models. In future study of crime and delinquency, this line of scholarly inquiry will promote the continued variability of the strain paradigm while satisfying the empirical demands of science and knowledge accumulation (Kuhn,, 1962). We hope this process will facilitate a merger of the old and the new.

5

Social Control, Family Structure, and Delinquency

JOSEPH H. RANKIN AND L. EDWARD WELLS

The increasing ideological appeal of "traditional family values" has been associated with renewed and widespread interest in the maintenance of the intact nuclear family. While frequently sympathetic, social science research has been more equivocal. Current research and juvenile policy support a range of widely discrepant conclusions regarding the significance of the so-called broken home as a causal factor in juvenile delinquency (see Rankin, 1983; Wells and Rankin, 1985, 1991). Some researchers and juvenile justice practitioners consider it a prime etiological factor (Gove and Crutchfield, 1982; Dornbusch et al., 1985). A number of others have reached a very different conclusion, arguing that its causal effects on delinquency are negligible (e.g., Rosen and Neilson, 1982; Van Voorhis et al., 1988). Despite these contradictions, there are a number of issues involving the influence of family conditions on which delinquency researchers do generally agree.

First, the type of data examined can affect the research results. Clinical studies and other research analyzing samples of questionable representativeness (e.g., arrest data) consistently demonstrate higher correlations between broken homes and delinquency than do studies analyzing self-report data (Herzog and Sudia, 1973; Datesman and Scarpitti, 1975; Johnson, 1986; Wells and Rankin, 1991). Second, family structure seems to have a selective, rather than a generalized, impact on delinquency, affecting mainly minor misconduct and rebellious or acting-out types of behaviors such as truancy, running away from home, and drug usage rather than serious forms of violence and predation (e.g., Cantor, 1982; Rankin, 1983; Wells and Rankin, 1985, 1991). Third, despite variations in samples and research methodologies, the bulk of the studies show a consistent but small correlation between broken homes and delinquency (Cantor, 1982; Rosen and Neilson, 1982; Rankin, 1983; Wells and Rankin, 1985, 1991; Johnson, 1986; Matsueda and Heimer, 1987). In sum, research does show that broken homes have an ostensible impact on juvenile delinquency, but the effects are not large and they seem to occur under limited conditions.

The central preoccupation of past research has been with questions specifying the *structure* of the family situation (e.g., number of parents absent, cause of parental absence, sex of the single parent, presence of a surrogate parent, age of the child). Although elaborate and multidimensional, such measures reflect only the physical composition of the household. They do not clarify the functional or interactional structures of the family that are integral to what seems to be conceptually meant by "broken homes" as a social condition (Wells and Rankin, 1986). From a theoretical standpoint, the significant question concerns not so much the absolute magnitude of this relationship as the intervening causal processes that connect broken homes to delinquent behavior. Although theoretical models relating broken homes to delinquency have been proposed (e.g., Wells and Rankin, 1986; Van Voorhis et al., 1988), empirical tests of these models are limited. Thus, the question of the intervening causal connections remains unresolved and ambiguous.

THEORETICAL MODELS

Instead of a simple direct effect of family structure on the likelihood of delinquency, a multistep causal sequence is usually proposed in which family structure operates *indirectly* on adolescent behaviors through its facilitative effects on family interactions. That is, the broken home precipitates certain interactional patterns between parents and children, specifically: poor communication, poor supervision, low attachment, and high conflict. In turn, these processes motivate or encourage delinquency. However, because different theoretical perspectives are possible, there is little agreement on the form and content of this intermediate step. Earlier analyses (Wells and Rankin, 1986; Rankin and Wells, 1987) identified four general theoretical perspectives on the broken-home-to-delinquency sequence, each distinguishing a different intervening causal dynamic between family structure and delinquency.

Socialization models focus on the family as the primary setting for social learning and personality development in early childhood. This developmental perspective depicts the important family dynamics as extending over a period of years—especially during the early, formative years of childhood and preadolescence. Any negative impact of structural changes in the family (e.g., divorce, parental absence) will be delayed and gradual rather than immediate and short-term.

Family crisis models focus on the family as an ongoing structure for overseeing daily conflicts and problems. Here, the family structure and delinquency relationship is viewed as a synchronous rather than a delayed process. Abrupt disruptions in family structure lead to temporary disturbances that induce stress, conflict, unhappiness, and antisocial behaviors. However, the change in family structure per se is not the key causal element; rather, factors such as parental conflict that precede the separation precipitate the crisis. Basically, the loss of a parent produces stress that is expressed in behaviors such as parental defiance, running away from home, or general ungovernability. Thus, this perspective predicts less serious, acting-out, or maladaptive misbehaviors that are likely to be a temporary rather than a long-term problem—being resolved as the family functionally adapts to the loss of the parent.

Social structure models focus on the family as a positioning mechanism for situating persons within larger social structures and institutions. This perspective focuses on the broken home as a socially and (especially) economically disadvantaged unit. For example, many families experience lower incomes as a result of the loss of a parent (usually the father) from the family unit. Less income may result in less material and economic consumption, a move to poorer housing facilities in a lower-class neighborhood, fewer educational opportunities, and more frequent associations with delinquent peers. Opportunities for success and goal-achievement are likely to be limited (Rankin and Wells, 1987). Thus, family structure itself does not cause delinquency; rather, it is a variable by which families (and their children) are sorted structurally into lower opportunity, higher risk situations.

Social control models focus on the family as the primary source of attachments, commitments, and disciplinary controls in adolescence. According to this model (e.g., Nye, 1958; Hirschi, 1969; Naroll, 1983), the family acts as a buffer against deviant influences by providing a source of basic ties and commitments to the conventional social order. The family furnishes a source of ongoing motivations to conform as well as normative definitions of culturally appropriate behaviors. The family also has an important coercive function; parental authority provides a strong mechanism for the supervision and punishment of children's behaviors. Thus, the properly functioning family keeps adolescents in line by motivating them to conform and out of trouble by restraining them from deviance. When family structure breaks down and adults are not available to perform the necessary parenting activities, the family loses its ability to motivate, supervise, and discipline its children (Wells and Rankin, 1986).

Among the various social control perspectives, Hirschi (1969) has provided the most explicit theory of the relationship between family and delinquency. The central focus of his theory is the inverse relationship between parent-child "bonds" (attachments) and delinquency. Positive parent-child bonds should result in fewer delinquent activities, since the child does not want to jeopardize these established relationships. However, a weak bond minimizes the child's sensitivity to parents' opinions, "freeing" the child to deviate in response to situational demands and peer encouragements. This parent-child bond can be strengthened along three dimensions: (1) parental supervision and discipline over their children's behaviors, (2) identification with or closeness to parents, and (3) intimacy of communication (Hirschi, 1969). On the other hand, parent-child conflict (i.e., the extent to which parents and their children argue or disagree with each other) can weaken this bond (Cernkovich and Giordano, 1979).

Within this perspective, a number of different factors could possibly explain the relationship between broken homes and delinquency, since parental absence could result in a loss of affection, lowered barriers to delinquent friendships, lowered commitment to academic goals, and/or loss of regulations, discipline, and general supervision over the child's behaviors. Reflecting the influence of Hirschi's model, the most common focus of study and discussion has been the loss-of-affection or loss-of-bonding factor. The presumed causal sequence is that family breakup (e.g., divorce or separation) negatively affects parent-child relationships (attachments or indirect controls), which in turn increases the likelihood of delinquency. A reduction in both the quality and quantity of contact with the noncustodial parent will weaken the child's relation with that parent. Moreover, the custodial parent's ability to maintain a positive relationship with her or his children may suffer for various reasons—for example, the sharply reduced amount of time the custodial parent now has to interact with the children (Peterson and Zill, 1986).

Hirschi (1969) proposed that attachment to one parent should be as effective in preventing delinquency as attachment to both parents. Thus, a broken home would have little or no effect on delinquency *as long as* the child had a strong bond to the custodial parent. Since the important consideration is whether any parent is *psychologically* present when delinquent opportunities arise, physical presence of both parents is not necessary to provide an effective buffer against delinquency. Hirschi's (1969) prediction contrasts sharply with other social control approaches. For example, Nye (1958) suggests that the general ability to supervise, discipline, and restrain children's behaviors (through "direct" controls) is substantially diminished in a single-parent household. Although the conceptual inconsistencies between Hirschi and Nye can be resolved through empirical research, the available evidence is sketchy and inconclusive, leaving it an open theoretical and empirical question.

Hirschi's theoretical perspective also suggests that the strength of the relation between parent-child attachment and delinquency is not sex-specific—that is, contingent on the sex of either the child or parent. As long as the strength of the bond is high, a boy raised only by his mother ought to be at no more risk than a boy raised by his father. This contrasts with most versions of the socialization perspective (especially those emphasizing sex-role modeling and identification), which assert that father absence has more negative effects on sons' behaviors than on daughters'. However, although some research has considered the differential effects of parental absence on boys and girls, the available evidence is sparse and clinically limited; it provides little clear support for this latter claim (see Rankin, 1983; Wells and Rankin, 1985, 1991).

PRIOR RESEARCH

Although socialization, family crisis, social structure, and social control perspectives are equally plausible theoretical models relating broken homes to delinquency, empirical tests have focused almost exclusively on the latter social control models. However, the difficulty has been that the intervening "control process" links between family structure and delinquency have not been well specified empirically (Blechman, 1982), especially in ways that family variables may interact. In keeping with a general preference for simple linear models, family structure and family process variables are most often examined separately as *competing* causes of adolescent misbehaviors. Few researchers have examined empirically the *interrelations* among these factors for the possibility of more complex causal contingencies and combinations.

Johnson (1986) examined the simultaneous impact of several family variables on self-reported delinquency among 734 high school sophomores in a large American city. He found virtually no bivariate relation between family structure (measured as a five-category typology) and self-reported delinquency, perhaps because his dependent measure *excluded* those self-reported behaviors usually found to be associated with broken homes (i.e., minor acts of delinquency and status offenses). Although white males with stepfathers did report significantly more delinquent behaviors than white males from intact homes, the size of this association remained largely unaffected by the introduction of several control variables, including attachments to both school and parents.

Hess and Camara (1979) examined the influence of divorce on children as a consequence of the quality of interaction among family members after the divorce. The negative effect of divorce on several outcome variables (including aggression) was only *partially* mitigated when the child maintained positive relationships with both the custodial and noncustodial parents. The child benefited less when a positive relation with only one parent was maintained. However, given Hess and Camara's (1979) small and highly unrepresentative sample, and an "aggression" index that is an inadequate proxy for delinquency, their conclusions seem inconclusive.

Peterson and Zill (1986) also focused on the role of parent-child relationships in mediating the effects of marital disruption. Based on an examination of a 1981 national sample of 1,400 children aged 12 to 16 (the same data analyzed in this chapter), Peterson and Zill found that positive relationships (attachments) with parents did mitigate the negative effects of marital disruption on a number of behaviors (e.g., depression/withdrawal, impulsivity/hyperactivity, and problems at school). However, this moderating influence was modest, diminishing the association between family structure and behavior problems only slightly. Like Hess and Camara (1979), Peterson and Zill's (1986) conclusions are uncertain, given that their dependent measures were (1) more indicative of general behavior problems than delinquent acts or even status offenses, and (2) based on reports of the parents "as characterizing the child" ("imputed" behaviors rather than the children's own self-reported "admitted" behaviors). The latter is especially problematic in that ratings by parents of their children's behaviors are likely to share with officially recorded statistics (e.g., arrests, court records) the problems of confounded measurement (see Wells and Rankin, 1986).

Dornbusch et al. (1985) examined a large and nationally representative sample of children (N = 6,710) 12 to 17 years of age to determine whether family decision-making styles could explain the relationship between broken homes and adolescent deviance. "Mother-only" families were compared with "intact" families on the extent to which the parents were perceived as exerting *direct* control over decisions concerning several adolescent issues. A "youth autonomy" family decision-making style (compared to "joint" and "parent alone" styles) was expected to contribute to a higher probability of delinquency in single-parent families. However, the relationship between broken homes and delinquency persisted even after statistical controls for several demographic variables (e.g., race and socioeconomic status [SES]). Interactions among the various independent measures were not statistically significant.

Using Hirschi's (1969) Richmond data in a test of differential association and social control theories, Matsueda and Heimer (1987) found that delinquent friends, attachments to parents (parental supervision) and peers, and belief in morality (definitions of delinquency) collectively mediated the entire effect of broken homes on delinquency. Specifically, they argued that broken homes weakened parental supervision, which in turn led to an increased number of delinquent friends and prodelinquent definitions; ultimately, this increased the probability of delinquent behaviors.

Matsueda and Heimer's (1987) research is unique as the only study to have totally "explained" the association between broken homes and delinquency by controlling for intervening factors. However, several methodological features of the study make this conclusion uncertain. First, the treatment of family structure as a dichotomy (broken versus intact homes) is too simplistic, given the varieties and complexities of nontraditional family structures (Rankin, 1983; Wells and Rankin, 1985). Second, the use of path analysis procedures precluded an examination of possible interactive and nonlinear effects, which other studies have reported (e.g., Wells and Rankin, 1988). Third, the use of a global delinquency index as a dependent variable ignores the prior research findings that broken homes appear to have a selective impact on different kinds of delinquent conduct, affecting minor delinquent behaviors more than serious misbehaviors.

Finally, Matsueda and Heimer's (1987) use of "peer delinquency" or "delinquent friends" as an explanatory variable is problematic. Gottfredson and Hirschi argued that their measure of "peer delinquency" (which purportedly mediates the broken homes and delinquency relationship) is really just another indicator of their dependent variable ("respondent delinquency"). That is, "the delinquency activities reported for friends are the same delinquent activities reported by the respondent himself" (Gottfredson and Hirschi, 1987: 598). The use of delinquent friends as a statistical control variable to "explain" the broken homes and delinquency relationship is dubious, due to the equivalence or collinearity of the dependent and control variables. Correspondingly, Warr and Stafford (1991: 863) argued that researchers "should distinguish between adolescents who are merely aware of their friends' behavior and those who have actually witnessed or participated in delinquency with their friends (i.e., as co-offenders)."

Only a handful of researchers have examined factors that mediate the relationship between family structure and delinquency. However, due to various methodological problems in this research, the analytical context of the broken home and delinquency relationship remains unresolved and ambiguous. Thus, the intent of our research is to develop more fully the mediating context of the broken homes and delinquency relationship within a social control framework. Many of the conceptual and procedural problems of prior research will be overcome by examining (1) the mediating effects of a wider range of social control factors (e.g., both direct and indirect controls), (2) the interrelations among these factors for the possibility of more complex causal contingencies (i.e., interactions), (3) several different types of self-reported delinquent behaviors (rather than one global index), and (4) several different types of broken homes (rather than dichotomizing family structure).

DATA AND METHODS

Sample

Our analyses are based on data from a sample of children (n = 1,377) in the United States interviewed as part of the 1981 National Survey of Children. The 1981 survey was administered as the second wave of a nationally representative longitudinal study designed primarily to focus on the effects of marital disruption on children (Moore et al., 1986); the first wave of data was collected in 1976. A five-year interval between the two waves was deemed too long for a panel study of the effects of family disruption, interaction, and control, especially when family conditions and children's perceptions of their parents can change relatively quickly. Thus, our focus is on the second of the two panel waves. This corresponds to the point in adolescence (12 to 16 years of age) at which delinquent activities are frequent and problematic, yet ostensibly still under family control and supervision.

Interviews were completed not only with the adolescents, but also with one of their parents and teachers when possible. Funding limitations precluded reinterviewing the entire 1976 sample of 2,279 children; budget restrictions also dictated that the 1981 interviews be conducted by telephone rather than by personal interviews. Nonetheless, statistical analyses of a random sample of personal interviews carried out in 1981 detected no discernible differences between the two interviewing styles (Furstenberg et al., 1983). For a full description of procedures on sampling and data collection, see Furstenberg et al. (1983), Moore et al. (1986), and Peterson and Zill (1986).

Operational Measures

Delinquency was measured by four separate indices, each reflecting distinct dimensions of juvenile misconduct. Division of specific items into the four scales was based on findings of prior methodological studies (Hindelang et al., 1981; Elliott and Huizinga, 1983), along with factor and item analyses of the specific items included in the National Survey of Children questionnaire (a fifth index of drug use was dropped owing to excessive missing scores because drug use questions were asked only of respondents fifteen years or older). All delinquency items refer to acts occurring within the year prior to the survey.

1. A *Delinquent Behavior* index was computed as the (unstandardized) sum of three self-report items covering acts of battery, vandalism, and shoplifting.
2. A *Status Offense* index was computed as the sum of three self-report items on truancy, curfew violation, and getting drunk.
3. A *Runaway* index combined both self-reports and parents' reports of runaway incidents.
4. An *Official Trouble* index combined self-reports of getting in trouble with school authorities and of being stopped by the police with parents' reports of their child getting into trouble at school.

Family Structure was initially measured as a multicategory variable, reflecting the number of natural parents present, which natural parents were present, and the presence of parent substitutes. The initial seven categories included both natural parents, natural mother alone, natural mother and stepfather, natural father alone, natural father and stepmother, adoptive parents, and "other." Based on frequencies and cross-tabulations with delinquency, this initial classification was reduced from seven to five categories by combining the two "natural mother" categories into one category and repeating this procedure for the two "natural father" categories. For some of the more complex analyses, categories of family structure were reduced to three by excluding cases where neither natural parent was present.

A number of family process factors were included to reflect differing aspects of the social control model. *Social control* was conceptually divided into "indirect control" (via attachments and identifications with parents) and "direct control" (via rule enforcement and discipline). Four variables were used to index indirect control mechanisms within the family. *Identification* with parents was measured by a combination of three items reflecting the strength of affective attachment between child and parent: feel close to parent, want to be like parent, and receive enough affection from parent. In two-parent families, the index was computed as the average of both parents' ratings. *Positive communication* was measured by three items covering the extent to which parents talked with the child about things, listened to the child's feelings and ideas, and accepted the child's input in family decisions. *Family activities* was a summary index of the frequency of seven activities the child's family might do together.

A distinct yet related dimension of indirect family control mechanisms is "Family Conflict and Stress" (Cernkovich and Giordano, 1987). This includes three variables: (1) an index of *Parent-child conflict* combined two items concerning frequency of child's arguments with parents; (2) *Parental stress* was measured by three items from the parents' questionnaire asking about parents' emotionality, frustration, and loss of self-control in dealing with their children; and (3) a general index of *Family life* was computed from seven items asking children how calm, relaxed, and happy (versus tense, frantic, and complicated) their family was.

Three more variables measured the "Direct Control" of juvenile misbehaviors through family rules, regulations, and discipline. *Supervision/regulation* was computed as a summary of eight items asking: (1) how much parents made explicit and consistent rules about their child's schoolwork, television-watching, dating, and general whereabouts; and (2) how closely parents checked on and kept track of the child's activities. *Punishment* was measured by two subindices (each based on three items): *inductive punishment* dealt with the use of approval, discussion, and withdrawal of privileges for discipline; *coercive punishment* measured the amount of parental yelling, threatening, and hitting behaviors.

Two variables measured the family's social and economic context. "Socioeconomic Status" was measured by a single eight-category measure of *family income*, and the family's "Social Environment" was measured by an index of *neighborhood quality* formed by combining the child's and parent's ratings of the desirability of their neighborhood "as a place to raise children." Sex, Race (nonminority, Black, or Hispanic), and Age (11–13 years, 14–16 years) were included as social-demographic variables.

Hypotheses

Beyond merely noting the degree of correlation between family structure and delinquent behavior, our aim is to move beyond simple bivariate descriptions and include additional social control (family process) variables and social contingencies in the analysis. Based on predictions and expectations derived from prior studies, we expect that: (1) the impact of family structure will be stronger on some types of delinquency than on others; specifically, its greatest effect should be on status offenses and less serious forms of juvenile misconduct; (2) the impact of family structure will be stronger for boys than for girls (due to loss of the male parent in most broken homes), greater for younger children than for older children (due to greater family dependence), and greater for families who live in lower socioeconomic conditions (due to greater social liabilities and fewer resources); and (3) the effects of family structure will be mediated by family process variables—reflecting loss of indirect and direct parental controls over their children.

Analytic Procedures

In multivariate analysis, an important difference exists between mediator and moderator effects. "Mediators" are variables that intervene between two events that are causally but distantly related. That is, mediators are more proximal causes of the dependent variables and serve to "explain" the effects of the initial causal variable. When mediators are included in a multivariate analysis, the association between the initial causal variables will decrease or disappear. Mediation does not mean that the initial association is spurious but rather that it is indirect.

In contrast, "moderators" are variables that interact with the causal variable to make its effects on the dependent variable conditional rather than independent and additive. A moderator can magnify, qualify, or mitigate the original causal relation, depending on its values and how it combines with other causal variables. In this sense, a moderator "elaborates" rather than explains the original causal relation.

Maintaining this distinction, our study used analysis-of-covariance procedures with interaction terms (accomplished via dummy variable regression) to test for nonadditive or complex effects. This allows for consideration of both mediating and moderating influences of social control variables on the link between family structure and delinquency.

RESULTS

Table 5.1 presents the summary statistics on the sample of respondents in the second wave of the National Survey of Children. It shows that the predominant family situation (55.5 percent) is an "intact" family (both natural parents present); almost half of the youths reside in an alternative ("broken") family arrangement—most commonly living with their natural mothers without a father replacement. As prior studies have shown, father absence is the most commonly occurring (33.8 percent) form of broken home (Natural Mother Alone and Natural Mother/Stepfather). Mother absence (with natural father present) is very infrequent, occurring in only 3 percent of the cases (Natural Father Alone and Natural Father/Stepmother). Table 5.1 also indicates that our sample is similar to population proportions on sex and age but has a slight oversampling of black respondents (constituting almost 24 percent of the sample).

The second step in our analyses examined bivariate patterns of association between the seven-category classification of family structure and the four indices of delinquent behavior. Since the independent variable is categoric while the dependent variable is numeric, we analyzed the data using a one-way ANOVA framework. The mean differences in delinquency between family categories are shown in Table 5.2. An overall F-statistic tested for reliable differences among the categories; an *eta* statistic (analogous to the "r" coefficient between numeric variables) measured the degree of association between family structure and delinquent behaviors. Supplemental post-hoc contrasts (Neuman-Keuls procedure) indicated which of the family structure categories were essentially equivalent in delinquency levels. These multiple contrasts indicated that nonintact families with the natural mother present were equivalent, regardless of whether the absent father had been replaced by a stepfather or other substitute. Thus, mother-only and mother/stepfather families were combined into one "father absent" category. The same pattern held for nonintact families in which the natural father was present; thus, father-only and father/stepmother families were combined into one "mother absent" category. This collapsing of categories resulted in a five-category family structure classification that was used in subsequent analyses.

The findings in Table 5.2 show the basic pattern of delinquency by family structure. Overall, mother-absent families (only the natural father is present) have significantly higher levels of delinquency than do father-absent or intact families. Replacement of the absent parent with a stepparent had no effect in regard to mean levels of delinquency. Rather, the important parental issue was *which* parent was absent. The impact of the other categories of family structure (i.e., adoptive parents and other living arrangements) was variable across different forms of delinquency. However, it is interesting to note that children from adoptive homes were *not* more likely than children from intact homes (both natural parents present) to commit delinquent offenses. In fact, adoptive families had slightly *lower* rates of delinquency on two indices (status offenses and official trouble), although the differences are not statistically significant (probably because of the extremely small number of

Table 5.1
Sample Characteristics of the 1981 National Survey of Children

Family Structure	Frequency	Per Cent
Both Parents Present	790	55.5
Natural Mother Alone	339	23.8
Natural Mother/Stepfather	142	10.0
Natural Father Alone	12	0.8
Natural Father/Stepmother	31	2.2
Adoptive Parents	28	2.0
Relatives' Home	33	2.3
Other	43	3.0
Missing Data	6	0.4
	1424	100

Sex		
Male	693	49.8
Female	699	50.2
	1392	100

Age		
11	134	9.4
12	261	18.8
13	268	19.3
14	259	18.6
15	275	19.8
16	195	14.0
	1392	100

Race		
Nonminority	1036	72.8
Black	337	23.7
Hispanic	38	2.7
Other	12	0.8
	1423	100

adoptive parent families in the sample—only 28). The lone exception to this pattern occurs for running away; adoptive homes had higher mean levels of running away from home by a statistically significant amount.

The family category labeled "other" also showed generally higher levels of delinquent acts; however, this category covered a variety of nontraditinal living arrangements; thus, it is substantively complex and too amorphous for consistent interpretation. In addition, the causal ordering between family structure and delinquency may be ambiguous (perhaps even reversed) for

Table 5.2

Mean Differences in Delinquent Behavior by Family Structure (total sample)

Delinquent Behaviors	Family Structure					Statistics
	Both Parents	Father Absent	Mother Absent	Adoptive Parents	Other	
Juvenile Delinquency	.53	.73	1.33	.71	1.14	F(4,1377)=6.9 Eta=.14[z]
Status Offenses	1.88	1.93	3.14	1.54	2.31	F(4,1377)=5.1 Eta=.12[z]
Official Trouble	.58	.84	.86	.36	1.24	F(4,1378)=5.1 Eta=.12[z]
Running Away	.09	.15	.30	.32	.26	F(4,1377)=5.0 Eta=.12[z]
N =	789	481	43	28	1384	

[z]$p < .001$

this family arrangement. Being placed in a foster or group home may be as much a consequence of delinquency as a cause of it. For these reasons, the "other" family arrangements category was excluded from subsequent analyses.

Table 5.2 also shows the variations in family structure effects across different forms of delinquency. While absolute rates of delinquency vary across indices (status offenses being the most frequent and running away the least frequent), the association between family structure and delinquency does not vary. The same pattern holds for all four indices, as indicated by the remarkably similar values among the *eta* coefficients (between .12 and .14). These levels of association match the sizes of coefficients usually found in large, self-report surveys (in the range between .05 and .15). However, the similarity of patterns across different measures of delinquent behavior is somewhat at odds with prior studies, which generally report that the association is stronger for status offenses and weaker for more serious forms of delinquency (e.g., Wells and Rankin, 1985, 1991; Van Voorhis et al., 1988). Thus, our first research hypothesis was not confirmed.

Next we examined whether the effects of family structure on juvenile deviance varied by different categories of youth. Specifically, the expectation is that the effect of family structure on delinquency will be different for boys and girls, black and white youths, and younger and older adolescents. As indicated earlier, prior research generally suggests important differences, but the available findings are inconsistent in regard to the direction of the differences. Our results do indicate that delinquency rates vary predictably by sex and age (i.e., males and older youths reporting significantly higher rates) although not significantly by race. However, the *association* between family structure and delinquency does not vary by these categories. The *eta* coefficients are similar for boys and girls, black and white youths, and younger and older adolescents. Although comparisons by race were complicated by very small cell sizes for black youths in two family categories, the patterns remained quite similar, nonetheless. None of the F-tests (to test for interactions between family structure and sex, race, and age) achieved statistical significance. Thus, our second hypothesis regarding broken home effects varying by age, sex, and race of children was not confirmed. The effects, while not large, are general rather than conditional.

The final step in our analysis examined the influence of social control (family process) variables in mediating or moderating the impact of family structure on delinquent behavior. Using dummy variable regression procedures, we tested for both mediator and moderator effects of our three sets of social control variables. Mediator effects were examined through a simple partialling procedure—that is, calculating whether the association between family structure and delinquency was still significant once social control variables were introduced. Delinquency was regressed on a set of social control variables entered into the regression equation as a block; next, the set of dummy variables for family structure (where intact family = omitted category) was added. The test for increase in R^2 with the added set of dummy variables provided a test of the independent (direct) effects of family structure. Moderator effects were analyzed by including a set of multiplicative interaction terms (for possible combinations of family structure and control variables). The R^2 change for these additional interaction terms provided a direct test of nonadditive "moderator" effects.

A summary of the tests for mediator and moderator effects is provided in Tables 5.3, 5.4, and 5.5 for Attachment (indirect control), Family Conflict and Stress (indirect control), and Discipline (direct control), respectively. Overall, these tables indicate that the effects of family structure on delinquency are mediated for some types of delinquency (i.e., status offenses and running away) but not for others (i.e., more serious forms of juvenile de-

Table 5.3
Effect Summary for Attachment Variables*

Delinquent Behaviors	Multiple R	F-Statistic(df)	P-Level
Juvenile Delinquency			
1) Attachment	.133		
2) + Family Structure	.152	3.14 (2,1138)	.04
3) + Interactions	.179	1.79 (6,1132)	.10
Status Offenses			
1) Attachment	.192		
2) + Family Structure	.194	0.54 (2,1138)	.60
3) + Interactions	.209	1.20 (6,1132)	.30
Official Trouble			
1) Attachment	.166		
2) + Family Structure	.183	3.60 (2,1138)	.03
3) + Interactions	.197	1.00 (6,1132)	.43
Running Away			
1) Attachment	.149		
2) + Family Structure	.161	2.08 (2,1138)	.13
3) + Interactions	.185	1.78 (6,1138)	.10

*Attachment Variables:

   Identification with Parents

   Positive Communication with Parents

   Family Activities Together

linquency and official trouble). These conclusions were consistent across all three sets of substantively different social control variables. Similar to earlier research by Hess and Camara (1979), Dornbusch et al. (1985), and Peterson and Zill (1986), our control variables contributed appreciably to explaining the relationship between family structure and delinquency, but they did not mediate *all* of the effects.

Table 5.4
Effect Summary for Family Conflict and Stress Variables*

Delinquent Behaviors	Multiple R	F-Statistic(df)	P-Level
Juvenile Delinquency			
1) Attachment	.152		
2) + Family Structure	.173	4.77 (2,1344)	.01
3) + Interactions	.191	1.50 (6,1338)	.18
Status Offenses			
1) Attachment	.249		
2) + Family Structure	.252	1.18 (2,1344)	.31
3) + Interactions	.260	1.00 (6,1338)	.43
Official Trouble			
1) Attachment	.201		
2) + Family Structure	.210	2.47 (2,1344)	.04
3) + Interactions	.231	2.20 (6,1339)	.09
Running Away			
1) Attachment	.154		
2) + Family Structure	.161	1.38 (2,1344)	.20
3) + Interactions	.170	0.71 (6,1338)	.65

*Family Conflict and Stress Variables:

　Parental Stress

　Parent-Child Conflict

　Family Life Rating

To check the possibility that it is a combination of all three sets of control factors jointly mediating the effect of family structure, an additional set of regressions constituting the most significant variables from each set of variables was analyzed. Together, these variables accounted for appreciably more variance in delinquency than any single set. However, the same pattern of mediation was observed for this regression. The effect of family structure

Table 5.5
Effect Summary for Discipline Variables*

Delinquent Behaviors	Multiple R	F-Statistic(df)	P-Level
<u>Juvenile Delinquency</u>			
1) Attachment	.169		
2) + Family Structure	.195	6.43 (2,1345)	.01
3) + Interactions	.201	0.56 (2,1339)	.76
<u>Status Offenses</u>			
1) Attachment	.141		
2) + Family Structure	.151	2.17 (2,1345)	.12
3) + Interactions	.161	0.66 (6,1339)	.69
<u>Official Trouble</u>			
1) Attachment	.172		
2) + Family Structure	.188	3.91 (2,1345)	.02
3) + Interactions	.200	1.09 (6,1339)	.37
<u>Running Away</u>			
1) Attachment	.083		
2) + Family Structure	.103	2.55 (2,1345)	.08
3) + Interactions	.111	0.37 (6,1339)	.90

[*]Direct Control Variables:

Regulation/Supervision

Inductive Punishment

Coercive Punishment

on more serious forms of delinquency (assault, theft, and vandalism) and for getting into official trouble (at school or with police) was still significant after controlling for the combined set of family process variables. Note, however, that the combined effects of family process variables were additive rather than interactive. The tests for interaction terms indicated no mod-

erator effects attributable to the social control variables; none of the statistical tests for interactions was significant.

DISCUSSION

Despite our use of a relatively large and representative national sample
of juveniles, more precise operational measures of both delinquency and
family structure, and the inclusion of a greater number and variety of social
process variables in the statistical analysis, our results suggest that social
control factors are only *partially* successful in explaining the correlation
between broken homes and delinquency. Whatever it is about nonintact
family structures that leads to increased delinquency, it is not entirely explained by the intervening social control processes of attachment, regulation
and discipline, and family conflict and stress.

Our results seem to confirm the findings of prior research. That is, we
found a modest but consistent association between family structure ("broken
homes") and juvenile delinquency—a correlation that holds across categories of sex, race, and age of the youths involved. In seeking to explicate
the causal content of this correlation, our analysis provided a more elaborate, multivariate view of the connection between family structure and
delinquency—particularly the family process variables that intervene between them. We focused mostly on mediating variables suggested by social
control theory, since this framework has been most explicitly developed
and studied in delinquency research. Thus, our results provide a pointed
test of control theory's ability to explain the impact of varying family conditions on juvenile delinquency and crime.

Our findings suggest that the social control model may be effective in
explaining the impact of broken homes for less serious forms of juvenile
misconduct—behaviors that might be described as "acting out," "rule testing," or "family-directed" delinquency. These include status offenses such
as curfew violations, truancy, running away, and fighting with parents.
When this form of delinquency is considered, the introduction of social
control factors into the regression equations reduced the associations between family structure and delinquency to statistically insignificant or negligible levels. This suggests that the family and delinquency correlations are
being "explained" by the control variables.

However, the social control variables do not fully account for the effect
of family structure on more serious forms of delinquency, including theft,
assault, vandalism, and getting in trouble with the authorities. For these
forms of delinquency, significant covariation remains even after all social
control variables have been included in the regression equations. These
results suggest a different causal dynamic involving etiological factors beyond parental attachment and supervision. Thus, while family conditions
may have an important impact on many forms of family-directed juvenile

deviance, these conditions may operate quite differently on delinquency that is more peer-oriented and occurs in settings independent of the family.

Our findings suggest at least two significant considerations for studying the family and delinquency relationship. First, they underscore the common caution against routinely and mechanically treating juvenile delinquency as a single homogeneous phenomenon that can be measured by a global index and explained by one general etiological model. While all forms of delinquency share a common legal attribute (i.e., they are subject to formal legal actions and labels), they differ considerably in their behavioral and social meanings. We lose far more information than we gain by combining and treating them a priori as interchangeable and equivalent.

Second, our findings suggest that the conventional social control model (mainly derived from Hirschi's earlier work) does not provide a full and general account for the effects of family conditions on juvenile delinquency. Family and delinquency analysis needs to move beyond the singular focus on social control that has dominated this area of research and consider more systematically other theoretical frameworks.

As noted earlier, far less research has focused on these other family and delinquency models. The predominant interest of social control explanations probably reflects a variety of considerations, including ideological and methodological as well as theoretical preferences. Conceptually, social control is presented as an integrated framework capable of encompassing and synthesizing a number of distinct theoretical models. It is also compatible with a wide range of ideological positions, especially more conservative perspectives widely favored in current discussions of delinquency policy. Methodologically, the social control model seems readily subject to empirical measurement and test, especially with broadly available survey data and conventional statistical analysis procedures.

In contrast, the causal dynamics of other theoretical approaches seem more complex and less directly testable with conventional delinquency data. Extended longitudinal research is required to test both the socialization and social structure approaches, since both are developmental perspectives suggesting that delinquent influences affect children at a very young age and then continue to influence them throughout childhood and later into adolescence. Both depict the impact of the family as lagged, indirect, and cumulative. This means that conventional statistical analysis, relying on atomistic linear coefficients, will not yield impressive estimates of family effects. In regard to social policy, any effects of social programs will also be delayed, diffused, and harder to detect and document. Indeed, the social structure approach suggests any corrective policies be aimed at a social context larger than the family unit itself, mainly toward the socioeconomic disadvantages often associated with nonintact nuclear families (a policy whose effects on juvenile crime are indirect and certain to be delayed).

Alternatively, future research might examine more fully the effects of the family crisis model on delinquency and juvenile misbehaviors. Since this model's view of the family and delinquency relationship is synchronous rather than delayed and cumulative, it does not require the methodological restriction of longitudinal data for its testing. Moreover, like social control, this model predicts less serious, maladaptive juvenile misbehaviors (rather than serious forms of delinquency) that are likely to be directed toward the parents themselves. Since this is exactly the kind of juvenile deviance most prior research has found to be associated with broken homes, this approach provides a plausible microsociological alternative for explaining the family dynamics of juvenile delinquency.

6

The Collective Reality of Crime: An Integrative Approach to the Causes and Consequences of the Criminal Event

FRANK SCHMALLEGER AND TED ALLEMAN

On July 22, 1991, a handcuffed man flagged down a police car in suburban Milwaukee (*USA Today*, 1991c). Officers soon learned that the man was Tracy Edwards, a thirty-two-year-old city resident. The story Edwards told soon led investigators to the apartment of a thirty-one-year-old loner by the name of Jeffrey Dahmer. Dahmer was quickly arrested, and a search of his apartment revealed the body parts of at least 11 people. In a confession to the police, Dahmer told of how he had repeatedly lured men to his apartment, murdered them, and dismembered their bodies. Soon police investigations implicated Dahmer in a ten-year killing spree that spanned several states and may have reached as far as Europe. Edwards, who had met Dahmer in a shopping mall, explained that he went to Dahmer's apartment because "he [Dahmer] seemed so normal" (*Fayetteville Observer-Times*, 1991a). Sadly, one of Dahmer's victims, a fifteen-year-old boy, had been discovered by police[1] dazed and bleeding. He was returned to Dahmer's apartment after police concluded that the situation involved nothing but a dispute between homosexual lovers.

Murder appears to occur with increasing frequency today. In late 1991 Texan Donald Leroy Evans admitted killing ten-year-old Beatrice Louise Routh (*USA Today*, 1991d). The young girl's homeless mother had given Evans permission to take Beatrice shopping. Soon after his capture, however, Evans (a parolee) confessed to sixty killings, and became a suspect in America's worst serial-killing case. His arrest came one month before Aileen Wuornos, whom investigators have called the "nation's first true female serial killer," was scheduled to be tried in Florida for killing seven men who had offered her rides, and two months before a gunman smashed a pickup truck through the front window of a Texas cafeteria and shot thirty-one lunch-goers to death.

Not all crimes involve violence. In August 1991, Stephen Blumberg of

Des Moines, Iowa, was sentenced in federal court to nearly six years in prison and fined $200,000 for the theft of more than 21,000 rare books from hundreds of libraries (*USA Today*, 1991a). Blumberg, whose interest in rare books began at yard sales and with searches in trash dumpsters, may have seen himself as involved in a messianic mission to preserve recorded history.

Also, August 1991 witnessed the unfolding of a huge financial scandal, with the potential to implicate the governments of many nations in the laundering of money for clandestine purposes. The multinational Bank of Credit and Commerce International (BCCI) was closed after investigators in a spate of countries indicted its leaders for fraudulent activities. Linked to BCCI were eighty-four-year-old Clark Clifford, chairman of First American Bankshares and former secretary of defense under Lyndon Johnson, and Robert Altman, Clifford's protégé and president of First American (*USA Today*, 1991b). Both men resigned their positions with First American Bankshares amid speculation that BCCI served as a financial conduit for subversive activities by the Central Intelligence Agency and Arab leaders.

These opening paragraphs provide a partial snapshot of crimes that were making the news during the fall of 1991. There were many others, including former Panamanian strongman Manuel Noriega's widely publicized trial on drug-running charges; and the conviction of a Houston mother charged with planning the kidnapping and murder of another woman because the two had daughters who were high-school cheerleading rivals (*Fayetteville Observer-Times*, 1991b). Tape-recorded conversations played at the trial of thirty-seven-year-old Wanda Webb Holloway appeared to reveal Ms. Holloway's plot to hire someone to murder Verna Heath, the thirty-eight-year-old mother of her daughter's antagonist. Following conviction, Holloway was sentenced to fifteen years in prison and fined $10,000.

Environmental crimes were also in the news, with people's sensitivity to such issues heightened by the Exxon Valdez disaster of a few years earlier, and the hundreds of still-burning oil-well fires in Kuwait that had been set by Iraqi leader Sadaam Hussein's retreating army during the 1991 Gulf War. Among efforts on the home front, Pennsylvania's Legislative Act 101, also known as the Municipal Waste Planning, Recycling and Waste Reduction Act, began to be actively enforced, but was cited by some as making "recycling criminals" out of uninformed members of the public, and as criminalizing the everyday routine activities of others (N. Wilson, 1991b).

From the crimes described above, what can we learn about their commonalities? At first glance there are so many differences between them that no common ground for analysis seems apparent. One thing we know, of course, is that criminal behavior encompasses a wide variety of behaviors. Because human beings are naturally curious, however, we would all like to know more. We would like to understand why crimes occur, what motivates people to commit them, how best to prevent them, and how to deal with offenders. What we need is a framework for dealing effectively with a vast array of offenses, all of which fall under the rubric of crime.

The analytical framework developed in this chapter is based not only on the idea that criminal activity is diversely created or caused, but that crime is also variously interpreted by the offender, the offended, and others. For example, a plethora of social interest groups—including criminal rights advocates, victim's assistance networks, and politically active organizations—all interpret law-breaking behavior from unique points of view. For this reason, we have chosen to apply the concept of social relativity to the study of criminality. Social relativity refers to the fact that social events are differently interpreted according to the cultural experiences and personal interests of the initiator, the recipient, or the observer of that behavior.

THE COLLECTIVE REALITY OF CRIME: AN INTEGRATIVE APPROACH

Figure 6.1 depicts the causes and consequences of crime in diagrammatic form. A glance at the figure shows that the criminal event is ultimately a consequence of the coming together of inputs provided by the offender, the victim, society, and the justice system.

The *offender* brings with him or her personal life experiences, a peculiar biology (insofar as he or she is a unique organism), personality, motivation, intent, values and beliefs, and various kinds of knowledge (some of which may be useful in the commission of crime). Recent research, for example, has tended to cement the link between child-rearing practices and criminality in later life. Joan McCord (1991), reporting on a thirty-year study of family relationships and crime, found that self-confident, nonpunitive, and affectionate mothers tend to insulate their male children from delinquency and, consequently, later criminal activity. Difficulties associated with the birthing process have also been linked to crime in adulthood (Kandel and Sarnoff, 1991). Birth trauma and negative familial relationships are but two of the literally thousands of kinds of experiences individuals will have. Whether or not the individual who undergoes trauma at birth and is deprived of positive maternal experiences will turn to crime is dependent on many other things, including his or her own mixture of other experiences and characteristics, the appearance of a suitable victim, a failure of the justice system to prevent crime, and the evolution of a social environment in which criminal behavior is somehow encouraged.

Like the offender, the *criminal justice system* also contributes to the criminal event, albeit unwillingly, through its failure to adequately identify and treat dangerous potential offenders, and via the early release of convicted criminals who later become repeat offenders. Prison itself may be a "school for crime," fostering anger against society, and a propensity for continued criminality in inmates who have been "turned out." Similarly, the failure

Figure 6.1
The Causes and Consequences of Crime

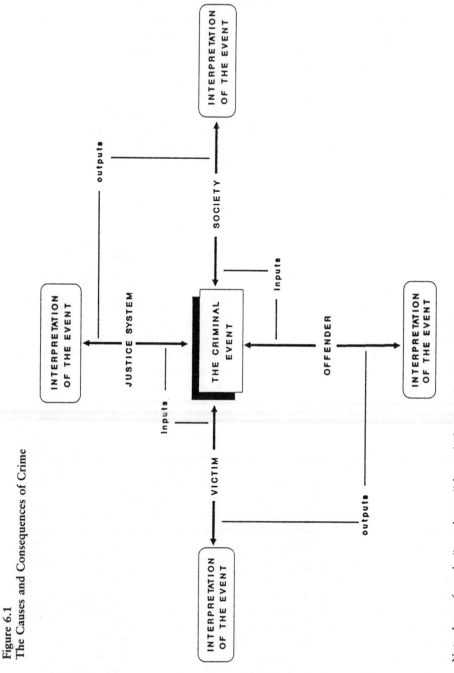

Note: Inputs form the "causal nexus" from which criminal activity arises. Outputs produce the social significance of crime.

of system-sponsored crime prevention programs, ranging from the patrol activities of local police departments to educational and diversionary programs intended to redirect budding offenders, all help set the stage for the criminal event. Of course, proper system response may help reduce crime. A recent study by Kohfeld and Sprague (1990) found that police response (especially arrest) could, under certain demographic conditions, dramatically reduce the incidence of criminal behavior. Additionally, Kohfeld and Sprague found that arrest constitutes communication to criminals in general, further enhancing the notion that inputs provided by the justice system enhance or reduce the likelihood of criminal occurrences.

Few crimes can occur without a *victim*. Sometimes the victim is just a passive participant in the crime, such as when innocent people have been killed by random gunfire on the streets outside their homes, or in instances of mass murder like the Texas cafeteria shooting mentioned at the beginning of this chapter. Even in such cases, however, the victim contributes his or her person to the event, which thereby increases the severity of the incident (i.e., the random shooting that injures no one may still be against the law, but it is a far less serious crime than a similar incident in which someone is killed). Sometimes, however, the victim contributes to his or her own victimization through the appearance of defenselessness (perhaps because of old age, drunkenness, disability, etc.), by failing to take appropriate defensive measures (leaving doors unlocked, forgetting to remove keys from a car's ignition, etc.), through an unwise display of wealth (flashing large-denomination bills in a public place), or simply by being in the wrong place at the proverbial wrong time (walking down a dark alley off of Times Square at 2:00 A.M.). In a recent study of Canadian victimization, Kennedy and Forde (1990) found that violent personal victimization is contingent on the exposure that comes from following certain life-styles. This was especially true, they found, for certain demographic groups, particularly young males. Victim-precipitated offenses, involving even greater victim participation in the initial stages of a criminal event, may take place when the soon-to-be victim instigates criminality in others (as in barroom fights, where the eventual victim may "ask for it" through insulting or rude behavior).

Finally, the *general public or society* contributes to the criminal event both formally and informally via a definition of particular situations and through the setting of public policy. Date rape, for example, may occur when a male concludes that his date "owes" him something for the money he has spent on her. That feeling, however inappropriate from the point of view of the victim and the justice system, probably has its roots in early learned experiences—including values communicated from television, the movies, and popular music—about the male's role under such circumstances. In other words, society, through the divergent values it places on people, property, and behavior under certain circumstances, may provide the valuative basis for some offenses. Similarly, we can identify other social roots of crime insofar as generic social conditions such as poverty, poor education, and discrimination can be said to contribute to criminal behavior. In addition, societal economics (i.e., free enterprise in the United States), which can shape the content of the mass media or the availability of public services, exercise a strong influence over behavior, criminal or otherwise. In a recent study of the availability of medical resources, especially quality hospital emergency services, Doerner (1988) found that serious assaults may become homicides where such resources are lacking, but that "homicides" can be effectively prevented via the effective utilization of capable medical technology. Hence, societal decisions on the distribution and placement of advanced medical support equipment and personnel can effectively lower homicide rates in selected geographic areas. In Doerner's (1988: 177) words, "the causes of homicide transcend the mere social world of the combatants." Additionally, the contributions society makes both to the background of the offender and victim and to the structure of the justice system, as well as the influences that each in turn has on the general social order, provide for a "feedback loop" implied in this view of crime (even though the loop is not shown in Figure 6.1 for fear of unnecessarily complicating it). Finally, society through its representatives contributes significantly to the criminal event by defining what forms of activity are criminal in the first place.

Examined together, all of the elements, experiences, and propensities brought to the criminal event by the offender, victim, society, and the justice system constitute what criminologists refer to as "situationally defined behavior" (or the "situation") that surrounds the impending event. Taken in concert these various aspects of the situation either give rise to the criminal event itself or they inhibit it. In a recent cross-national study of the situational characteristics of crime, LaFree and Birkbeck (1991: 73) defined the term *situation* as "the perceptive field of the individual at a given point in time." From our perspective, it is worthwhile to recognize that the situation surrounding a criminal event will be interpreted according to the perspective of the observer (i.e., whether she or he be the victim, the offender, etc.).

In an interesting and detailed study of the interpretive activity of criminal justice system personnel, for example, Gilsinan (1989) has documented what happens when callers reach the 911 dispatcher on police emergency lines. Since many prank calls as well as calls for information are made to 911 operators, the operator must judge the seriousness of every call that comes through. What the caller says was found to be only a small part of the informational cues the dispatcher seeks to interpret prior to assigning the call to a particular response (or nonresponse) category. Honest calls for help may go unanswered if the operator misinterprets the call. Hence, quite early on in the criminal event, the potential exists for a crucial representative of the justice system to misinterpret important cues, and to conclude that no crime is taking place.

Other interpretive activities are at least as significant. The justice system, taken as a whole, must decide guilt or innocence as well as attempt to deal effectively with convicted offenders. Victims must try to make sense of their victimization in such a way as to allow them to testify in court (if need be) and to pick up the pieces of crime-shattered lives. Offenders must come to terms with themselves, and decide whether to avoid prosecution (if escape, for example, is possible), accept blame, or deny responsibility. Whatever the outcome of these more narrowly focused interpretive activities, society—because of the cumulative impact of individual instances of criminal behavior—will also face tough decisions through its courts and law-making agencies. Societal-level decision making may revolve around the implementation of policies designed to stem future instances of criminal behavior, the revision of criminal codes, or the elimination of unpopular laws.

In sum, the perspective adopted here employs a double-barreled view of crime referring to both the multiplicity of causes and the continual interpretation and reinterpretation of social events and individual actors. This perspective has been variously termed "interpretive sociology," "phenomenological psychology," or "symbolic interactionism," depending on the subject matter to which it has been applied and on the scholarly era in which it has emerged. Accordingly, "crime" can be viewed as a dynamic phenomenon that arises out of the complex interrelationships between victim, offender, and the social order. We believe that the advantage of an integrated phenomenological perspective comes from examining and communicating the personal and social underpinnings as well as the consequences of crime. In the next section, the crime of rape is used to show how the study of any criminal event in particular can benefit from the integrative perspective advocated here.

A SYMBOLIC INTERACTIONIST VIEW OF DATE RAPE

During youth, when experiences are limited, hormones are active, and self-images are most vulnerable, sex can be an intense adventure. Some adolescents come out of their first sexual experience exhilarated, others depressed. Those individuals who hold strong desires for sex but lack opportunity often hang on every word of others who describe their adventures into the world of sexual intimacy. Fantasies, expectations, and desires built upon a biological base that splashes adolescence with sexual impulses. Whatever it may be, youthful sex is eventful, charging, and seldom forgotten.

Ironically, the idealized images of what sex is supposed to be like and the sound reality of what sex is rarely seem to match. For men, the sound or ideological construction of conquest, power, and unbridled satisfaction become synonymous with their emerging "manhood." For women, an ideology of intimacy, sharing, and thrilling exhilaration are expected outcomes of the penetration of their bodies. Pain, embarrassment, awkwardness, babies, or disease seldom slide into the background of the popular youthful depictions of sex.

Dwelling a bit on youthful sex and the images associated with it provides an important backdrop for understanding the crime of date rape. Date rape is multidimensional. Sexual urges and thoughts, being so intimately tied as they are to human biological drives, constitute a deep-felt source of behavioral incitements that not only motivate the rapist but also serve to place female victims in situations conducive to rape and other forms of sexual violence. The rapist brings to the event a constellation of images and expectations that seek reinforcement. Date rapists do not rape unless their actions appear, at least to themselves, as appropriate and justified. Victims of date rape, through their actions, can also bring to the social scene behaviors that, although inadvertent and unintentional, reinforce the perceptual view of the date rapist and, unfortunately, may serve to draw the potential date rapist to them. Sexuality, along with the imagery and perceptions associated with it, are central elements of the crime of date rape.

What goes through the mind of a rapist? How does a rapist view his victim? What experience does the rapist imagine his victim to be having as he may rip, tear, and penetrate her private parts? How can a rapist ignore the tears, fears, and protestations of his victim? How does a date rapist justify his behavior to himself and others who have knowledge of his violent propensities? How do rapists come to think the way they do? How are the thoughts and actions of date rapists different from other heterosexual males who do not rape?

Answers to questions such as these add to our knowledge of rape as a social phenomenon but the answers certainly do not form a complete picture. Rape, from a societal perspective, involves much more than the commission of the crime itself. The rapist and his victim, the law, the criminal justice response, the reaction of family, friends, and associates, as well as treatment by the media and the general public are all relevant to the social events we come to classify as rape. Why, for example, did it take until the early 1980s before the police began treating rape victims as though they were victims of real crime? And why were women who brought charges of rape to the police frequently interrogated, accused of encouraging the rape, questioned about their sex life, and generally humiliated by the criminal justice system? Why have rapists traditionally been accorded incredible leniency by the courts? Why was it that only in 1989 when Alabama removed the marital rape exemption clause from its laws that men in all 50 states could finally be accused of raping or sodomizing their wives? Questions such as these, based as they are on the actual behavior of police, prosecutors, judges, juries, legislators, and the general public, show rape to be a much wider social phenomenon than that behavior which takes place between the rapist and his victim. These questions also show the varying and changing degrees of legitimacy attributed to the act of rape.

An adequate theory of rape is one that takes into consideration all of the factors necessary to provide a complete explanation of the criminal event. The rapist, although commonly thought of in psychopathic or sociopathic terms, is typically more similar to nonrapist men and is actually a product of our androcentric and patriarchal culture. The victim, although certainly the unwilling recipient of the date rapist's misplaced aggression, anger, or sexual inadequacy, more often than not can be found to have been actively involved in the construction of events that led up to the violation of her body. The police, prosecutors, judges, jury members, as well as those concerned citizens who view rape from a more distant, less personal perspective also add their preconceptions of what rape is, how serious a crime it is, and how rapists and their victims should be treated. Rape as a social phenomenon is that complex whole that includes the interpretations of all of those who are either part of the criminal act itself or the social response that follows.

THEORIES OF RAPE

Traditional theories of rape can be divided into three categories (Hyde, 1982; Albin, 1977):

Victim Precipitated. This view of rape blames the victim. Rape, from this perspective, is the fault of the woman who purportedly provokes her own attack. By dressing or behaving provocatively, for example, the woman is seen as leading the rapist to the conclusion that she wanted to have sex with him. A woman who claims that she was raped is vulnerable to the counterclaim that she brought the rape on herself, especially if she had sexual relations with the rapist on previous occasions or demonstrated some kind of romantic intentions toward him prior to the rape by accompanying him on a date or to a private residence. According to this perspective, a woman who is perceived to have behaved "promiscuously" and is eventually raped is seen as having "asked for it" and "deserves what she gets."

Psychopathology of the Rapist. Rape, from this perspective, is the result of mental derangement. The rapist is seen as having some sort of "problem" and takes his anger or frustration out on women. A man who is sexually or socially inadequate rapes women to compensate for his own personal failures. Rape, therefore, is committed by people who are "sick."

Feminist Theories. Rape, according to feminist perspectives, is a weapon used by men to subordinate women and keep them in their place. Rape is seen as a natural part of patriarchal society in which men are socialized to dominate and control women. Violating and brutalizing women's bodies is one way in which men show women that they are the bosses. Feminist perspectives emphasize that rape is a crime of violence, not one of passion.

Each of the traditional explanations of rape limit themselves to particular points of view and, as a result, appeal to particular audiences. The view that rape is victim-precipitated, for example, places almost all blame on the woman and very little on the rapist. This view is particularly appealing to some groups of men who hold "macho" attitudes and assume sex to be a man's prerogative and a woman's responsibility. Implicit in this view is the belief that women should never tease men, unless they intend for sexual intercourse to follow. According to this perspective, men control sexual affairs and if women invite men to come on to them they must accept responsibility for all that may result. Such an outlook assumes sex to be a male-dominated arena and if females want to play the game they must abide by the male rules. The belief or view that women have the right to say "no" after a night of romantic dining and sexual outercourse (i.e., nonpenetrating sex) is basically at odds with this perspective.

The view that rapists are sick and maladjusted is equally as limiting. By treating rape as abnormal, this approach appears to explain much, but in light of the wealth of evidence that shows rape to be far from rare and rapists to be, on the whole, rather "normal," it really explains very little. There is little doubt that some rapists, especially those who beat, mutilate, or murder their victims, may suffer from severe social or psychological problems. But statistics show rape to be an event that is far more likely to take place in the living room than in a back alley, and most probably perpetrated by a boyfriend, relative, husband, or other acquaintance than by a stranger. In general, to explain rape as an instance of abnormality is to neglect the overwhelming reality that most instances of rape are committed by "normal" men.

The third type of explanation, the feminist view, sees rape as a vast "conspiracy" of men against women. Although feminist theories of rape—especially since the influential work of Susan Brownmiller in 1975—have provided a much-needed balance to the macho perspective that rape is the fault of the victim, they, too, can be one-sided in their approaches. If taken to an extreme, all men are potential rapists and rape is as much a political statement as it is a criminal act. Since feminist theories view social events from nonpatriarchal viewpoints, men are often portrayed as evil culprits and women as innocent victims. This view is certainly accurate in cases of stranger rape. Most rapes do, however, involve personal relationships or exchanges between the rapist and the victim. By downplaying gender, sexuality, and the symbolic interaction of rape, earlier and traditionally based feminist theories left out some important factors of rape.

In general, the three traditional theories of rape outlined above share the following limitations:

- Each theory presumes rape to be a particular kind of criminal act.
- Each theory assumes that a particular category of persons is responsible and culpable.
- Each theory takes the side of a particular group or class of persons.

By assuming that rape is always the fault of a particular class of persons, or that a particular kind of explanation is always best, traditional theories of rape oversimplify what is in reality a very complex subject. All rapists are not the same and all rapes are not committed for the same reasons. These traditional theories, to a great extent, prejudge events and introduce a degree of bias that is seldom supported by the facts of any particular case. By ignoring the circumstances surrounding the rape event—the who, what, where, why, and how of the crime—such one-dimensional theories are of little value in gaining an understanding of the factors responsible for specific instances of rape.

An adequate theory of rape is one that not only helps to explain specific criminal acts but also provides insight into the general statistics and trends associated with the crime. Why is it, for example, that lower-class males are more often convicted of rape? Why are certain ethnic or racial groups disproportionally involved in the crime of rape? Why are women who have been raped so hesitant to report the crime? Why has the criminal justice system been so insensitive to victims of rape? An adequate theory of rape should be able to provide answers to questions such as these.

In an attempt to forge a more adequate explanation of rape, it is necessary to look more closely at what we might term "normal" sex. Since rape in nearly all societies is a violation of the norms of sexual intimacy, we must first define what the rules are concerning sex. What is not surprising to those students of rape in the following sections is that the line between normal sex and rape appears to be very thin.

Normal Sex

Sex is a normal part of life. Erotic arousal is a biological fact in all cultures of the world. Although sexual drives and urges are highly variable from one individual to the next, sexual reactions are culturally standardized to a high degree (R. B. Taylor, 1973). In some cultures, for example, nudity is erotically interpreted, whereas in other cultures no particular sexual significance is assigned to the behavior of a man or woman who appears in public without clothing. In some cultures, women's breasts serve as objects of sexual orientation, whereas in others the lips or buttocks may be eroticized. In some cultures of the world, inflicting pain on the partner is a normal part of the sexual technique. The Apinaye women of South America, for example, have been observed biting off bits of their partner's eyebrows and noisily spitting them aside during love-making, whereas the Trukese women of the South Pacific will often poke a finger into the man's ear when they are highly aroused (Hyde, 1982). Or, take our own culture in which biting or sucking on the partner's neck to the point of leaving marks or scars is often viewed as a part of sexual technique, especially among sexually

Table 6.1
Social-Class Variations in the Sexual Behavior of Americans at the Time of the Kinsey Studies

	Educational Level		
	0-8 Years of Education, %	9-12 Years of Education, %	13 or more Years of Education,%
Males having premarital sex by age 20	83	75	44
Males having sex with a prostitute	80	61	35
Males having performed cunnilingus on their wives	4	15	45
Females who had never had an orgasm by the fifth year of marriage	28	17	15

Source: Drawn from Hyde (1982).

inexperienced adolescents. Although sexual behavior can be highly variable, especially from person to person, sexual regularities do exist within groups.

Studies of sexual norms have revealed that sexual attitudes and behaviors vary according to the gender, race, and class to which a person belongs. Attitudes relating to sex, dating, and date rape, for example, have been found to be strongly associated with gender, with males significantly more likely to hold attitudes condoning sexual violence as part of the courtship ritual. In examining the variable of race, blacks, in comparison to whites, report that males are expected to be aggressive in sexual activity (Dull and Giacopassi, 1987). Table 6.1 is of interest because it shows how level of education affected the sexual behavior of Americans several decades ago when this data was collected by prominent sex researcher Alfred Kinsey.

Notice in this data how having more education apparently reduced the likelihood of having premarital sex, reduced the likelihood of having sex with a prostitute, increased the use of cunnilingus in marriage, and, for women, reduced the likelihood of having an orgasm. What studies such as these suggest is that sexual behavior is learned behavior and is a reflection of the group into which one is socialized.

Peggy Sanday (1981), in what many consider to be a classic study of rape, furnishes insight into how the process of socialization serves to shape male behavior in the direction of rape. Remembering how powerful and influential social sanctions can be, especially when they shape behavior by undermining self-esteem, the following example of social control techniques is drawn from the literature to illustrate typical behavior in what Sanday terms a "rape prone" society:

Normal heterosexual intercourse between Gusii males and females is conceived as an act in which a man overcomes the resistance of a woman and causes her pain. When a bride is unable to walk after her wedding night, the groom is considered by his friends a "real man" and he is able to boast of his exploits, particularly if he has been able to make her cry. Older women contribute to the groom's desire to hurt his new wife. These women insult the groom, saying: "You are not strong, you can't do anything to our daughter. When you slept with her you didn't do it like a man. You have a small penis which can do nothing. You should grab our daughter and she should be hurt and scream—then you're a man" (quoted in LeVine, 1959).

We can only imagine how comments such as these serve to elevate the use of aggression and pain-inducing tactics in the lovemaking of the young boys of this rape-prone society. Interesting as these comments concerning other societies may be, are there like kinds of evidence that our own society is also rape-prone?

Of interest are studies of the idealized circumstances in which men and women in United States dream of having sex. It is well documented that the sexual fantasies of American males frequently involve situations in which they are powerful and aggressive and are engaged in impersonal sex (Hyde, 1982). But what about American women? Take a look at the following data that come from a study by Hariton (1973) in which married women reported the thoughts they typically had while having sexual intercourse with their husbands. The following were the seven most common themes in their fantasies, in order of frequency mentioned:

1. Thinking of an imaginary lover

2. Imagining being overpowered or forced to surrender

3. Pretending to be engaging in something that is wicked or forbidden

4. Imagining being in a different place, such as a car, a motel, a beach, or the woods

5. Reliving a previous sexual experience
6. Imaging themselves delighting many men
7. Imagining observing themselves or others having sex

Of the women who took part in this study, 65 percent reported having fantasies while having sex with their husbands. Notice in the list the frequency with which aspects of sexual "deviancy" occur: "thinking of an imaginary lover" (this is *adultery*), "imagining being overpowered or forced to surrender" (this is *rape*), "pretending to be engaging in something that is wicked or forbidden" (this is *sexual deviancy*), "imaging themselves delighting many men" (this is *group sex* or, if the sex is imagined to be forced, *gang rape*), "imagining observing themselves or others having sex" (this is *voyeurism*).

Among researchers, the role played by fantasy and imagination in the development of sexually aggressive behavior is becoming an increasingly important topic. There is little doubt that sexual fantasies are a source of self-stimulation, or autoeroticism (Hyde, 1982). And, although the dynamics of fantasy and its relation to sexual stimulation and performance is not entirely understood, it is clear that fantasies serve to excite and eroticize. Fantasies are dreams—dreams of ideal situations and ideal lovers. Fantasy allows a person to jump past the hurdles, rules, and limitations of the real world and enter a state in which personal needs are fulfilled completely. But, while fantasies do titillate, inspire, and even motivate some to realize their dreams, for most, fantasies are shaped, tempered, and often sublimated by the demands of the real world. To understand how, with whom, and under what circumstances people actually do engage in sex, it is necessary to go a step further and look at the ways in which fantasy is tempered by the behavioral and social demands of others.

Human Courtship Rituals

Sexual relationships are by their very nature participatory. By definition, sexual behavior is intimate behavior. Normal sex involves the intentional probing and exploration of the personal space of another. Sexual intimacy is a give-and-take in which private, deep-felt needs are satisfied through the mutual stroking and stimulation of a partner's erogenous zones, often with the aim of achieving sexual climax and orgasm. Throughout history, societies have imposed rules, barriers, and penalties on sexual behavior. For example, laws exist to define who is and who is not an appropriate sexual partner. Statutory rape is a criminal charge brought against a man who has sexual intercourse with a girl who is too young, even if the sex act was consensual. Incest laws are designed to prevent sex between persons who are closely related biologically. Adultery regulates consensual sex between a man and a woman who are married, but not to each other. Laws also exist to regulate sexual expression. Sodomy is the unlawful physical contact between the genitals of one person and the mouth or anus of another. Laws designed to prevent unanticipated sexual expression in public fall under the category of indecent exposure; and laws against prostitution are designed to prevent acts of sexual intimacy from taking place for illicit reasons. What is apparent from this list of criminal offenses is that sexual behavior, even when it involves the mutual consent of willing participants or when it harms no one, is a highly regulated form of social conduct.

While laws serve to regulate sex in the public sphere, human courtship rituals provide the ground rules that govern sexual behavior that takes place privately. And, unlike laws that attempt to deter certain behaviors from happening and then impose penalties on "deviant" actions that have already taken place, human courtship rituals impose controls on behavior as it happens. Courtship rituals serve both to bring to public scrutiny the private intentions and behavior of sexual participants as well as to regulate and control the private actions of lovers. Although participants are not generally aware that their most private acts of love are subject to social control, adherence to the courtship rituals of their society guarantees that their lovemaking falls within the boundaries of what is socially defined as "normal" and "legitimate."

Sexual relationships typically include a personal history. As two people meet, express through words and action a desire to be close, proceed through a progressive sequence of encounters and interactions to become intimate with one another, they embark on a privately constructed but eminently social courtship ritual. As their relationship becomes public knowledge, those who know the couple voice their approval or disapproval as to the legitimacy of the liaison, their opinion or advice as to how the relationship is proceeding, and, quite often, what socially desired objectives or goals should be sought after (e.g., go steady, live together, get engaged, marry, etc.). In a social sense, through personal feedback and the granting or withholding of support, courtship rituals serve to shape private sexual matters in the direction of social acceptability. In a personal sense, courtship rituals go even further by impacting directly the actual behavior that takes place between lovers.

Courtship rituals, as socially constructed models of idealized lovemaking and intimacy, provide the standard against which actual behaviors are measured. The pattern of courtship between a man and a woman is of fundamental importance because participation in courtship rituals determines (1) whether or not a person decides to have sex with a particular person, (2) the sequence of intimate actions that actually take place between sex partners, and (3) the subjective evaluations of the participants, during and after a relationship, as to whether the sexual encounter was good, bad, or somewhere in-between. By constructing the social expectations of intimacy, society has simultaneously constructed the difference between consensual (lovemaking) and forced sex (rape). By looking at sex from the participant's perspective we are able to see the ways in which courtship determines the legitimacy or the illegitimacy of any particular act of sexual intimacy.

Research reveals that there is a high level of agreement among both men and women as to the "proper" sequence of actions (stages) that normally take place in any sexual encounter (Brady and Levitt, 1965; Jemail and Geer, 1977). Generalizing from this research, the steps include:

1. kissing
2. kissing with tongue contact
3. his manipulating her breasts through her clothing
4. his touching her breasts under her clothing
5. hand and/or mouth stimulation of the genitals (singly or mutually)
6. sexual intercourse
7. orgasm

Several aspects of this sequence of behavior deserve mention. When asked, there was general agreement among the majority of those studied that each who had experienced one of the steps of intimacy described above had also experienced the preceding behaviors (Brady and Levitt, 1965). Each step, in fact, can be looked at as a decision point on which the partners decide whether or not to progress to the next stage of intimacy. The general expectation is that "going too fast" by jumping stages, or not heeding a partner's objection to stop at a particular stage, constitutes a breaking of the rules of intimacy. It is important to add that intimate actions such as those described above, particularly between people who first meet or who do not know each other well, normally do not just happen. In our culture, dating, dining, or at least conversing generally precede lovemaking. Part of the courting ritual is getting to know one another. This preliminary period may take hours or months, but once a man and a woman mutually acknowledge through their actions, gestures, and body language that they want to become intimate, a man's or woman's kissing, fondling, and undressing of their partner do fall within the realm of normalcy.

A CLASSIFICATION OF RAPE: "SEDUCTIVE, VIOLENT, AND HOSTILE"

In the preceding sections we have established the ground rules by which normal sex takes place. Generally, normal sex is driven by biological needs inborn to men and women that are shaped by social forces such as societal prescriptions and courtship rituals, and it is performed by willing participants in a socially acceptable manner. Overstepping the bounds set by courtship rituals constitutes what comes to be defined as sexual deviancy and, in the case of rape, criminal conduct. Research into the varied processes by which individuals distort or exaggerate the bounds of normalcy provides insight into why some men rape.

Rape has been traditionally divided into three major categories: (1) rape that is an outcome of a sexual encounter is termed seductive rape, (2) rape that involves a violent attack that is sexually motivated and is not an extension of courtship behavior is termed violent rape, and (3) rape that has little to do with sex but is an expression of hostility or aggression toward women is termed hostile rape.

In general, seductive rape is motivated by normal sexual drives, is perpetrated against a woman whom the man knows and/or has intimate access to, and is committed either because the woman "turns him on" or he thinks she owes him sexual favors. More often than not, seductive rape is an outgrowth of normal courting behavior. But, instead of adhering to the norms of sexual etiquette or heeding the desires of a partner to stop at a particular stage of intimacy, the seductive rapist aggressively forces or manipulates the woman into the unwanted act of copulation. Date or acquaintance rape serve as examples of this type of rape.

Violent rape involves an attack that is sexually motivated but is not an extension of courtship behavior. Three general types of rape fall within the general category of violent rape. First is the case of spousal rape in which a husband/cohabitator or former husband/cohabitator sexually assaults his wife/lover. This is often the result of anger, frustration, or inebriation. A primary component of this type of violent rape is the belief on the part of the husband/cohabitator that his wife/lover owes him sex whenever he chooses, even after they have separated. A second form of violent rape is impulse or opportunity rape where a man happens to be in a situation with a woman where he is able to exploit the woman sexually with little or no perceived cost to himself. A man who rapes a woman who happens to be home while he is burglarizing the house provides an example of this kind of violent rape. The third type of violent rape is compensatory rape and is committed by a man who is inept sexually and attacks a woman, usually a stranger, to prove his manhood and compensate for his lack of sexual prowess/self-esteem.

Hostile rape is an act of outright aggression against women and has little to do with the satisfaction of normal sexual urges. Since the dispositions and postures associated with normal sexual intercourse can also come to symbolize power, dominance, and status in interpersonal relations, hostile rape is committed for primarily antagonistic, status-seeking reasons, rather than sexual reasons per se. The rapist who viciously beats, degrades, and humiliates his victim, far beyond that necessary to gain compliance, is clearly manifesting frustration, hate, and animosity. Nevertheless, while hostile rape is sadistic behavior, it is usually perpetrated by a man who derives sexual satisfaction from this kind of aggression, and from inflicting pain and violence.

Rape is a form of criminal conduct that consists of more than just one set of behaviors or motives. Too often, rape as a form of criminality is oversimplified and evaluated solely in stereotypical terms. Many myths are associated with rape, and researchers have demonstrated that these myths provide ready-made rationalizations for stereotyping women and treating them as sexual objects. Burt (1980) defines rape myths as prejudicial, stereotyped, or false beliefs about rape, rape victims, and rapists. In the following section, we explore the ways in which rape is conditioned by diverse perceptions and/or interpretations that exist concerning the crime itself, and the treatment accorded those who are accused of rape as well as those who are victims of rape.

PERCEPTIONS OF RAPE AND THE CRIMINAL JUSTICE RESPONSE

Three major theories of rape were presented above. The essence of these traditional theories included the ideas that rape either is the fault of the victim (rape is victim-precipitated), rape is perpetrated by men who are abnormal (rapists are psychopaths), or rape is a weapon used by men to dominate and control women (men are sexual brutes). When compared with the kinds of rape that actually do take place, each of these theories can be shown to be overgeneralizations and built upon false assumptions about the intentions or motivations of rapists. However, while the three traditional theories of rape may not prove adequate as scientific explanations, they do serve to reinforce widely held beliefs in society that contribute in many significant ways to the generation, interpretation, and control of rape.

By its very social reality, rape is an ambiguous criminal event. Rapes usually occur in private settings and the only people who really know what actually happened are the rapist and his victim. For this reason, the police, prosecutors, judge and jury, reporters, as well as the general public must all interpret the event on the basis of secondhand, incomplete, and, at times, erroneous information. In such situations, popular theories of rape serve the purpose of socially reconstructing or typifying the event.

Typification is the process of using a preestablished framework for understanding and evaluating particular events (LaFree, 1989). Depending upon which theory of rape people subscribe to, the theory, as a social construction or typification, provides a ready-made explanation as to why rapes occur, how serious a crime rape is, what kinds of people rape, and what kinds of people are usually raped. Social typifications frame the criminal event by pulling in a preestablished set of perspectives and guidelines that are used to evaluate the truth or falsity of any particular charge of rape. Since social typifications, as generalized patterns of social thought, also reflect the societal values that are commonly held concerning women, sex, and sexual transgressions, it is beneficial to examine the ways in which the three prominent models have structured the ways in which rape, rapists, and rape victims are perceived.

It should be kept in mind that perception is a human process of seeing the world that brings to light specific aspects of a phenomenon while casting other dimensions or attributes into the shadows. What the three traditional theories of rape share in common is the assumption that rape is a social aberration. In other words, rape is typically perceived or constructed as a deviant form of human conduct; those held responsible for rape are viewed as women who should have acted differently, as men who were so depraved that they acted less than human, or as men who have resorted to any means necessary in order to maintain their dominance over women. By viewing rape as some kind of aberration from the norm, society overlooks the normality of sexual aggression. Moreover, by blaming rape on miscreants of one type or another, we avoid seeing ourselves and those around us as blameworthy in the sense that we have all participated in the social construction of "normal" and "deviant" sexual practices.

A position counter to this emphasis on deviancy and abnormality is one that recognizes rape as emerging out of normalcy. This alternative view of rape forces us to look at normal sex and recognize the extent to which male assertiveness and aggressiveness is part and parcel of what it means in this society to be sexually active. By focusing on "the rules of the game," it becomes clear that sexual conduct is both participatory (determined jointly through the actions of women as well as men), and structured (an accumulation and reflection of those behaviors that are repeated over and over in intimate settings). The different forms of rape, therefore, may be extensions rather than deviations from normality. Sex in society forms a continuum from which deviant and nondeviant forms emanate (see Figure 6.2).

Two important elements of classifying rape as extensions of normal sex deserve mention. First, notice in the figure how degrees of deviancy are determined by their lack of adherence to the rules of courtship. Seductive rape, for example, is forced sex that violates the rules of courtship, violent rape is forced sex that ignores the rules of courtship, and hostile rape is forced sex that disavows the rules of courtship. This depiction not only shows courtship to be the anchor by which aberrant forms are judged, but it also illustrates how the different manifestations of rape are but categories of deviancy that perceptually become more harmful as one moves progressively away from what is defined as sexual normalcy.

Second, it is important to note the reaction of the criminal justice system as rape progressively diverges from the standards set by sexual normalcy. Since seductive rape, perceptually and behaviorally, is viewed as an exaggeration of normal sexual practices, the criminal justice response demon-

Figure 6.2
A Typology of Heterosexual Rape

	- SEXUAL NORMALCY -		- SEXUAL DEVIANCY -	
	Normal Sex	Seductive Rape	Violent Rape	Hostile Rape
Degree of Deviancy	Conforming Behavior (Adherence To Courtship Ritual)	Forced Sex Through Violation Of The Rules Of Courtship	Forced Sex Without Regard To Courtship	Sexual Aggression Void of Sexual Connotation
Intimate Relationship Of Participants	Normal Intimate Behavior	Intimacy Is Forced & Without Consent of Both Parties	Intimacy Is Used By The Rapist To Express Rage; Victim Experiences Terror, Not Intimacy	Intimacy Is Absent & Replaced With Aggression & Terror
Usual Participants	Heterosexual Couple	Date, Relative, Known Associate	Husband & Wife; Ex-Husband & Wife; Boy-girlfriend; Strangers	Strangers
Reaction Of The Criminal Justice System	(None)	Suspicious/Cautions	Except For Marital Rape, Rapist Is treated As A Dangerous Criminal	Rapist Is Treated As A Dangerous Criminal
Impact On The Victim	There Is No Victim	Variable: Evidence of Deep Emotional & Psychological Problems	Event Can Be Deeply Traumatic; True Victimization Effects; Evidence of Life-Long Emotional Impact	Event is Deeply Traumatic;True Victimization Effects; Evidence of Life-Long Emotional Impact

Source: Derived from Classification Scheme of the Massachusetts Treatment Center as summarized in Curt R. Bartol, *Criminal Behavior: A Psychosocial Approach*, 3rd ed. (Englewood Clifis, NJ: Prentice-Hall, 1991).

strates much suspicion and caution in handling cases of this type. Seductive rape, involving that gray area where the difference between aggressive sex that is condoned as part of courtship and sexual aggression where sex is forced rather than participatory, is most ambiguous. This is part of the reason why victims of seductive rape typically find themselves subject to interrogation and investigation, purportedly until the system determines that they did not deviate from the rules of courtship. Conversely, the criminal justice system acts swiftly and harshly with violent and hostile rape cases where rapists are viewed as having clearly abridged the rules of courtship.

An alternative view of rape sees it as a violation or negation of the rules of courtship. This view sheds new light on many of the issues pertaining to rape, rapists, and rape victims. The following list of misperceptions questions the validity of continuing to view rape according to the three traditional constructions. Each misperception is documented in terms of the empirical evidence that suggests that an alternative view of rape is needed to explain the facts as they really are.

Misperception 1: Rape Is a Relatively Rare Event

Typified View. According to the U.S. Department of Justice, despite all their fearsome and brutal aspects, rape and attempted rape are relatively rare crimes. In fact, because of the relative infrequency of rape, it is difficult to collect enough information to analyze many aspects of the crime in detail (Bureau of Justice Statistics, 1985).

Alternative View. When seductive rape is taken into consideration, rape is a frequently committed criminal act. Surveys of young, male college students reveal that as many as one-third of these men fantasize about aggressively raping a woman, and over 50 percent fantasize about forcing a woman to have sex (Greendlinger and Byrne, 1987). Situations in which many male students report that they might rape are simply those in which they think they could get away with it (Malamuth, 1981; Briere, Malamuth, and Ceniti, 1981). In addition, research reported by Malamuth (1981) of anonymous self-report "sexual experience surveys" reveals that 23 percent of a sample of approximately 3,900 male college students said that they had actually been in a situation in which they became so sexually aroused that they could not stop themselves from having sexual intercourse even though the woman did not want to (Koss and Oros, 1980). Still another study found that 8 percent of a sample of nearly 3,000 college men outright admitted that they had actually raped or attempted to rape their dates (Koss, Gidycz, and Wisniewski, 1987).

There are at least two major reasons why rape is misperceived as being a relatively rare event: women who are raped are reluctant to report the crime to the police, and law enforcement agencies set up procedures that filter most cases of seductive rape from the system. Consider the following.

Based on a national sample of college students, nearly 30 percent of college women were victims of rape and virtually none of these women reported their rape to the police. According to this research on college women alone, the victimization rate for women is 3,800 per 100,000 as compared to the official rates of 65 to 75 per 100,000 (Koss, Gidycz, and Wisniewski, 1987). Most law-enforcement agencies are reluctant to prosecute any case of rape unless there exists substantial proof that the victim is telling the truth. According to surveys completed by the National Institute of Law Enforcement and Criminal Justice, most agencies required physical evidence that vaginal penetration occurred, over half also required physical evidence of both penetration and force, while another one-third required direct evidence of penetration, force, a weapon, and/or resistance by the victim (Chappell, 1977a and b). These procedures not only filter out of the system most cases of seductive rape in which deception, physical coercion, or drugs were used to commit the crime, but, according to this criteria, the only types of rapists who are prosecuted in any numbers are violent and hostile rapists.

Misperception 2: Many Rapes Are Victim-Precipitated

Typified View. Many women cause their own rape by dressing or behaving provocatively or by leading men on.

Alternative View. The idea that a woman can cause her own rape is logically inconsistent with the definition of rape as being a situation in which sex is forced against the will of the victim. No matter what the place, demeanor, or circumstance, a woman has the right to stop the sexual advance of a man. According to the law, it matters little how excited the man becomes, how much he is turned on by the woman, how provocatively she may act, or to what stage of intimacy "courtship" has advanced, when the woman unambiguously says "stop" the man must halt his sexual advance, otherwise, if penetration or sexual intercourse takes place beyond this point, it is rape.

Misperception 3: Real Rape Involves Violent Attack by a Stranger

Typified View. Any situation in which a woman is forced to have sex against her will is unfortunate, but the most devastating kind of sexual attack is one in which a stranger violently attacks his victim.

Alternative View. All forms of rape are equally tragic. However, by continuing to perpetrate the image that most rapes are committed by strangers, the enormity and immediacy of seductive rape is overlooked. Research focusing on college women indicates that between 85 and 96 percent of the victims knew their assailant (Mynatt and Allgeir, 1985). It is also not true that stranger rape is always the worse kind of rape experience. There is research that indicates that victims of acquaintance rape may actually experience the most severe adjustment problems. Because the woman is subsequently unable to trust other acquaintances, she begins to fear all acquaintances, thus producing devastating personal and social problems (Muehlenhard, Friedman, and Thomas, 1985).

Misperception 4: Rape Is a Violent Crime, Not a Crime of Passion

Typified View. Rape has nothing to do with sex. Since rape is a forced attack made against the will of the victim, all rape, by definition, is an act of violence.

Alternative View. Rape may not be a crime of passion, but many rapes are manifestations of sexuality. When seductive rape is taken into consideration, rapists are commonly young men who simply want to get laid. When young people combine alcohol, drugs, and intimacy, the cues as to whether or not intercourse is desired can become very ambiguous indeed. Granted, rape cannot be victim-precipitated in the sense that a woman causes her own rape, but rape can be victim-participated in the sense that women can voluntarily place themselves in vulnerable situations where they do lose control over the situation. As a result, a surprising number of young women experience unwanted and unplanned sexual activity while on a date (Dull and Giacopassi, 1987).

Misperception 5: All Rape Trials Are Judged According to the Same Standards

Typified View. Courts of law use the same criteria for judging the guilt or innocence of the accused.

Alternative View. Perception is a central element in cases involving rape and many kinds of extralegal considerations impact the decision-making process leading to a verdict. Consider the following evidence of the ways in which the preconceptions of rape, rapists, and rape victims held by jury members, judges, and law-enforcement personnel affect the legal process:

- Evidence exists that many individuals perceive acquaintance rape to be less serious and less "real" a crime than rapes involving strangers (Klemmark and Klemmark, 1976).

- When the victim was intoxicated, more responsibility for the rape was attributed to her (Richardson and Campbell, 1982).

- If the victim is physically attractive, subjective perceptions that an actual rape occurred shifts in favor of the victim (Seligman, Brickman, and Koulack, 1977).

- If the victim does not resist to the utmost of her capabilities, her charge of rape appears less credible (Clark and Lewis, 1977). [Additionally, if there is not clear resistance from beginning to end of the interaction, the victim is less likely to be believed (Cobb and Schaver, 1971)].

- Violent interaction is perceived less seriously when there is some suggestion of attraction in the victim-perpetrator relationship (Johnson and Jackson, 1988).

- Victims of rape tend to be blamed if it is perceived that they experienced sexual pleasure from the incident (McCaul et al., 1990).

- When comparing the attitudes toward women of police, rapists, rape-crisis counselors, and citizens, police officers' views of rape were more similar to the rapists' than they were to the counselors' and no significant differences were found between police and rapists on most dimensions (Field, 1978).

- In one study of the attitudes of judges, it was found that judges typify rape as being one of three types: (1) in cases of forcible rape committed by a stranger, the woman was perceived to be a "genuine victim"; (2) in cases where force and physical injury were less clear, the judges perceived cases of rape as "consensual intercourse"; or (3) "female vindictiveness," in which the woman was trying to get even (Bohmer, 1974).

CONCLUSIONS

Three sets of relations have been identified as being relevant aspects to the crime of rape: First rape, as a behavioral event, is highly variable and complex. A number of interrelating factors can result in the interpretation of rape, including an evaluation of just how far the victim-perpetrator interaction deviated from normal courting behavior. In general, the closer the interaction appears to approximate normal sex, the less likely it will be defined as an instance of rape.

Second, rape is as much a product of society as is any other relatively frequent, recurring social event. An adequate explanation must explore the extent to which rape is the product of normal patriarchal and capitalistic socialization processes. There is evidence that aggressive sex is socially acceptable in this society, thereby lessening the perceived seriousness and occurrence of seductive rape.

Third, due to the extent that popular constructions of rape influence the perceptual process, perception is a central variable for explaining rape and the societal reactions to the crime, its perpetrators, and its victims.

Nevertheless, popular perspectives on rape continue to be dominated by theories that see rape either as the fault of the victim, a product of a depraved mind, or an aspect of a male-dominated society that systematically victimizes women. As we have shown, rape is much more complicated than these one-dimensional theories suggest. There are not only different kinds of rape and different kinds of rapists, but the causes of these criminal events are more fundamentally integrated in the complex relations of character and social structure, and the consequences of rape in this illustration rely on the culturally responsive and biased law enforcement and juridical apparatuses.

Rape and the alleviation of rape remain as part and parcel of the socially constructed collective reality that not only fails to perceive most rapes, but that more often than not finds circumstances for the mitigation from legal guilt and for the reproduction of social rape.

7

A Neofunctionalist Model of Crime and Crime Control

THOMAS O'CONNOR

The influence of Talcott Parsons on criminology has not been overwhelming (Cullen, 1984). His most popular ideas were the youth culture concept (Parsons, 1942) and the compulsive masculinity thesis (Parsons, 1947). Both ideas generated considerable research and controversy (Vaz, 1967; Silverman and Dinitz, 1974; Naffin, 1985). His vicious cycle theory of deviance (Parsons, 1951: 249–61) made its way into the strain tradition, but sparked little outside interest or commentary (Smelser and Warner, 1976; Parsons and Gerstein, 1977). Almost entirely neglected except by integrationists (Bernard, 1989) was Parsonian action theory (Parsons and Shils, 1951; Parsons, 1951; Parsons, Bales, and Shils, 1953).

It is renewed critical interest in action theory that drives the neofunctionalist revival of Parsons' ideas. As Alexander (1985) points out, neofunctionalism bears only a family resemblance to the old functionalism. Gone is the teleology of explaining causes by effects. Gone is the tendency toward co-optation of other perspectives. The conservative ideology for which Parsons stood is no longer a burning issue. The revival, as Sciulli and Gerstein (1985) document, involves an interpretive reopening to the full range of Parsons' project (Hamilton, 1983) rather than the isolated works that drew heavy criticism (C. W. Mills, 1959; Giddens, 1968; Gouldner, 1970). Led by Alexander (1983), Munch (1987), and the recent attempt at consolidation by Colomy (1990), the neofunctionalist revival takes seriously the multidimensionality (Parsons, 1978) as well as the complexity of Parsons (1960; Parsons and Platt, 1973).

For present purposes of illustrating rather than testing neofunctionalism, the more manageable and familiar fourfold AGIL (Adaptation, Goal-Orientation, Integration, Latency) schema will be used. This theoretical device and the pattern variables constitute the essence of the tradition, although each instrument could stand alone (Munch, 1987). Previous work at operationalization (Dubin, 1960; Blau, 1962; Stouffer, 1962) suggests that the conceptual scheme provides a valid way to index a variety of meaningful acts, including crime and its control. It was decided to select terrorist acts and responses to them as the units of analysis because often the purpose of studying the former is to find civilized forms of the latter. The example chosen could just as well have been drugs (Sigler, 1987) or traditional violence (Wood, 1961), but the action components of terrorism seemed to fit well with the relational units (Dubin, 1969) of the neofunctional model. The data for analysis was kindly provided by Timothy Austin of Indiana University of Pennsylvania, who not only consented to the secondary analysis but served as an additional validity check.

Austin (1987, 1988, 1989, 1991; Austin and Ordona, 1980) has spent a decade doing intermittent fieldwork in the Philippines. From the beginning, he has been primarily interested in the individual and micro levels of explanation (Short, 1985). This has remained consistent as his topic shifted from dispute resolution to vigilantism to terrorism, although with the last, societal responses are given more consideration and results are organized around a natural disaster model. Lack of systematic crime statistics and researcher proclivity probably account equally for the absence of macro-level explanations in his work.

Related to this criticism is the charge of subjectivism (Groves and Lynch, 1990). Despite logicodeductive appearances, Austin's (1991) propositions are unverifiable and unfalsifiable. They are stated in terms of "tends to" and "fluctuates with," and there are no statements of direction or magnitude. This is because they depart sharply from a natural science model in which verifiable causal relationships are sought for purposes of prediction and control. Instead, this work is strongly in the tradition of interpretive theory, idiographic knowledge, hermeneutics, and the verstehen paradigm. Use of a preconceived conceptual model to aid interpretation is unscientific, and is an example of "abstracted empiricism" (C. W. Mills, 1959) if there is no theoretical specification of a structure prior to the use of the model for empirical inquiry. This treatise substitutes a neofunctionalist model to explain the same findings.

Instead of specifying structural or social system properties in advance, Austin (1989, 1991) simply describes the setting as a terror-prone region. Presumably, Lebanon and Northern Ireland demonstrate the same social system properties, but it is affirming the consequence to not ask how these regions came about. Parsons (1966, 1971) suggests and Currie (1985) concurs that the Philippines, like Mexico and Brazil, are comparable to the United States precisely because of the enhanced value of material competition. It then becomes significant to ask: What are the properties of these systems that would produce the same responses if individual occupants were interchangeable? Austin (1989) finds that habituated individuals are the

Figure 7.1
Results of Fieldwork on the Philippines

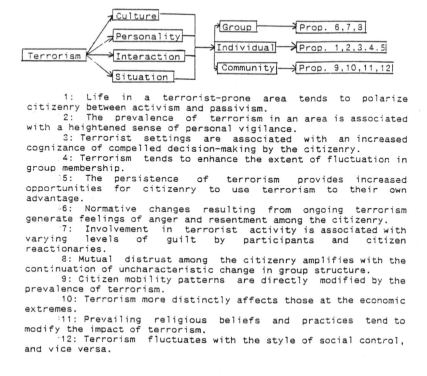

1: Life in a terrorist-prone area tends to polarize citizenry between activism and passivism.

2: The prevalence of terrorism in an area is associated with a heightened sense of personal vigilance.

3: Terrorist settings are associated with an increased cognizance of compelled decision-making by the citizenry.

4: Terrorism tends to enhance the extent of fluctuation in group membership.

5: The persistence of terrorism provides increased opportunities for citizenry to use terrorism to their own advantage.

6: Normative changes resulting from ongoing terrorism generate feelings of anger and resentment among the citizenry.

7: Involvement in terrorist activity is associated with varying levels of guilt by participants and citizen reactionaries.

8: Mutual distrust among the citizenry amplifies with the continuation of uncharacteristic change in group structure.

9: Citizen mobility patterns are directly modified by the prevalence of terrorism.

10: Terrorism more distinctly affects those at the economic extremes.

11: Prevailing religious beliefs and practices tend to modify the impact of terrorism.

12: Terrorism fluctuates with the style of social control, and vice versa.

most numerous in the data, and this finding alone would seem to negate the value of an individual typology and support an antinominalist ontology.

Austin's (1989, 1991) conceptual scheme and the theoretical propositions are as shown in Figure 7.1. The conceptual scheme is adapted from Bates and Harvey (1975) and the propositions are not axiomatic, but stratified by whether they are group-centered, person-centered, or institution-centered. Terrorism, in the model, is considered a constant stimulus. Culture, personality, interaction, and situation are called "axioms." Group, individual, and community refer to the scope, or level of explanation, at which the propositions apply. Each of the scopal factors and related propositions takes up the bulk of Austin's discussion, but these are not reviewed here since form, not content of the theory (Bernard, 1983), is more important at this point.

There is an epistemology implicit in treating terrorism as a constant. There is nothing wrong with trying to explain a variable by a constant; it is variables that do not do well at explaining constants, as long as one is trying to get at some law-like trend (Marsh, 1967). Since the essential part of the definition of terrorism involves purposive change in the social order (Gibbs, 1989), it can be conceived of as social action that always involves attributes of the actor, whether motive or intent. Terrorist acts are social acts, and like responses to terrorism, there must be some universal moral-normative regulation, or social order, to which action is oriented. This is an episte- mology of analytical realism as opposed to philosophical idealism. It pre- sumes that there are conceptual schemes that give meaningful order to experience, and that thinking always adds to the world. Munch (1987), a neofunctionalist, has identified this epistemology as the "Kantian core" of Parsons' synthesis, and it involves no separation of knower from known.

What law-like trends are to be sought? Parsons (1966) sought to explain nothing less than the evolution of societies. Neofunctionalists like Alexander (1985) have focused upon differentiation, defined as the process of increase or decrease in the number of structurally distinct and functionally specialized roles and collectivities in societies. Criminologists have generally sought after master trends, like modernization (Shelley, 1981; Wolf, 1981), claim- ing modern societies are soft targets for terrorism, or universal collective values (Newman, 1976) like competition (Leavitt, 1990). The important question, which is even implicit in fear of crime studies (Garofalo and Laub, 1978), is: What are the long-term effects of living with a constant shock or disturbance to the social order? This is what Wilkins (1965) called tolerance for unusualness. What follows is an alternative scheme that addresses these questions.

A CONCEPTUAL MODEL

There are three features of the neofunctionalist perspective that deserve attention: (1) A society can be modeled in terms of solidarity, crime rates and control mechanisms, feedback loops, and terrorism as an extraordinary event in the external environment of the system. (2) What are called "ax- ioms" in the previous model are better conceived of as functionally specific subcomponents of a system—that is, the Parsonian *AGIL* schema. (3) Prop- ositions can be recast in terms of pattern variables, which were designed for comparative use, and should interrelate the new propositions in more axiomatic form. The model of society is shown in Figure 7.2. *E* is the exogenous factor, terrorism, which as an extraordinary event directly im- pacts solidarity (*S*), the basis of society. Solidarity explains crime rates (*CR*), which, in turn, leads to crime conrtol (*CC*), which reinforces solidarity. Crime control often increases crime rates, thus a positive feedback loop exists between them. Crime control often decreases solidarity, thus a neg- ative feedback loop exists between them.

Figure 7.3 shows the subcomponents of a social system. *A* (adaptation) refers to those functions dealing with relations to the external environment. *G* (goal-orientation) deals with leadership qualities such as those found in

Figure 7.2
Consensus Model of Society

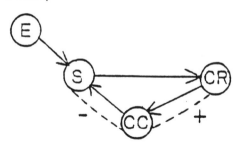

Source: Adapted from Hawkes (1975) and Liska (1987)

Figure 7.3
Parsonian Four-Function Paradigm

A (Milieu)	G (Personality)
I (Structure)	L (Culture)

personalities or political and economic institutions. *I* (integration) refers to stable patterns of interaction. *L* (latency, or pattern maintenance) deals with ideas or institutions such as religion that help the subcomponents to work together smoothly. "Axioms" in the previous model relate directly to this schema. "Situation" refers to *A* (adaptation), the material atmosphere or physical configuration of a place, and will be relabeled "Milieu." "Personality" refers to a number of intrapsychic processes, and will not be relabeled. "Interaction" refers to the collective basis for social relations, and will be relabeled "Structure." "Culture" refers to the ideational basis for social relations, and will not be relabeled.

The pattern variables are described in Figure 7.4 and will be discussed later.

EXPANDED THEORETICAL PROPOSITIONS

Turning to Austin's original twelve propositions, two of them can be discarded as having to do with secular or nonsocial developments. Proposition 1 can be eliminated because its claim to an active/passive polarization process is based almost entirely on the availability of newspapers and radios. While the impact of such technology makes for interesting criminological study, it is not relevant in the present analysis. The notion of active and

Figure 7.4
Parsonian Pattern Variables

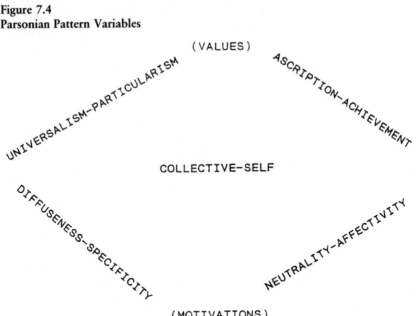

(VALUES)

UNIVERSALISM-PARTICULARISM

ASCRIPTION-ACHIEVEMENT

COLLECTIVE-SELF

DIFFUSENESS-SPECIFICITY

NEUTRALITY-AFFECTIVITY

(MOTIVATIONS)

passive mentality, however, is incorporated in other propositions, specifically those dealing with the personality subsystem. Similarly, Proposition 5
deals with availability of firearms and can be eliminated because it, too,
deals with technology. Although this particular proposition has the workings
of an imitative learning theory of terrorism, it is used primarily as a remnant
of the initial researcher's interest in dispute resolution. Having cut these
two out, there are ten propositions left to fit into the *AGIL* schema.

Propositions 10 and 12 fit into the A-cell. Their key elements, respectively,
are poverty and urbanity, both elements of societal adaptation to the external environment. The main findings are that the poorest regions become
targets for terrorist efforts at conversion, and that urban areas, with their
predominantly formal controls, are also more frequent targets. The main
qualitative finding, however, is Proposition 2, which can also be fitted into
the A-cell. Austin (1991) finds that Filipinos have attained a tradition of
community vigilance. They avoid certain target areas, make escape plans,
and often go to sleep at night with shooting in the distance. While this
finding certainly has cultural and personal ramifications, it more properly
belongs in the A-cell because, congruent with indigent and urban conditions,
it affirms an holistic understanding of the situation, material atmosphere,
or milieu as a "climate of nervousness." The A-cell will be so labeled with
ramifications into other subsystems as indicated in Figure 7.5.

Propositions 6 and 7 fit into the G-cell. Their key elements are the emo-

Figure 7.5
A-Cell Subcomponent

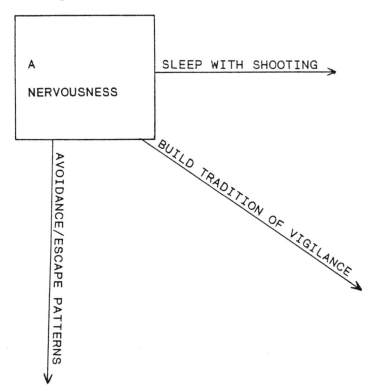

tions of anger and guilt. The main findings are outrage at groups forcing sociocultural change and a mood of embarrassment or shame in the region. Austin (1991) describes social ridicule and office intrigues centering upon ideological differences. While only hints of a modal personality are offered here, when combined with notions about passive polar types (who are a majority), habituation, and vigilance, a profile can be reached. This personality would be one with a timid disposition, a passive mentality, and emotional hyperreaction at times. The G-cell is, then, characterized by explosiveness and will be so labeled along with subsystem interconnections as indicated in Figure 7.6.

Propositions 4, 8, and 9 fit into the I-cell. Their key elements are, respectively, repressed interaction, shifting allegiances, and restricted geographical movements. The main findings for Proposition 4 are fearfulness of strangers, avoidance of marketplaces, and alteration in friendships or flux in group memberships because of allegiances. For Proposition 8, loss of trust, a sense of suspicion, of being infiltrated, less distinctive barrios,

Figure 7.6
G-Cell Subcomponent

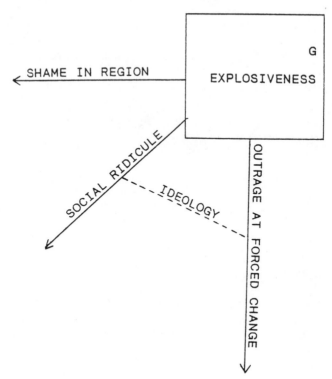

and double-agent roles are the main findings. Proposition 9 finds reduced immigration, tourism, and economic investment, as well as a "brain drain" condition where professionals and intellectuals leave for safer places. Here can be found numerous linkages with other subsystems, but it is more difficult to characterize this particular component. The closest quality aptly describing social interaction appears to be suspiciousness, since this covers elements from all three propositions and is likely the chief sanctioning mechanism across class lines and modes of organization, whether formal or informal. The I-cell will, therefore, be labeled with suspiciousness and connections to other subsystems as indicated in Figure 7.7.

Propositions 3 and 11 fit into the L-cell. Their key elements are compulsion and diversity. The main findings are that the wearing of uniforms and badges forces a change from traditional patterns of filial piety to compelled decision making, and that religiously diverse areas are frequent terrorist targets. Austin (1991) finds young Filipinos coerced to change from traditional family beliefs, and he introduces the interesting notion of "purity" to explain terror-free regions. Apparently, these purer areas existed

Figure 7.7
I-Cell Subcomponent

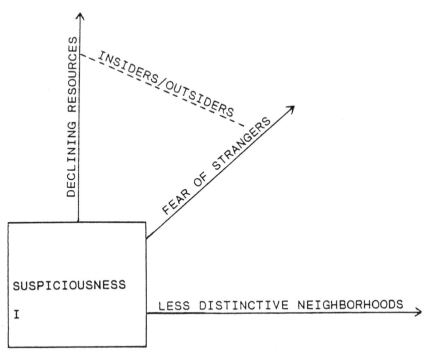

prior to the impact of terrorism, and targeting should not be confused with impacting. The common factor between compulsion replacing traditional authority and encroaching impurity is authoritarianism, a willingness to let pattern maintenance be handled by powerful, opportunistic leaders. The L-cell is characterized by this and ramifies into other subsystems as indicated in Figure 7.8.

Putting the subsystems together produces a system as shown in Figure 7.9 for the Philippines, with ramification patterns as indicated in Figure 7.10.

While a discussion of the composite and its ramification patterns would be interesting at this point, it must wait until analysis is completed by additional consideration of the pattern variables. Drawing upon our composite of Philippine society, the polar end of each pattern variable that best represents each subcomponent is represented in Figure 7.11. Values and motivations are listed as endpoints to illustrate the links between roles and personalities.

Looking at subsystem ramifications in Philippine society in terms of these polar ends, certain additional patterns appear to describe and predict how

Figure 7.8
L-Cell Subcomponent

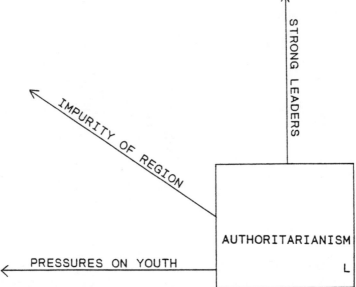

Figure 7.9
System Composite

A nervousness	G explosiveness
suspiciousness I	authoritarianism L

system shock interpenetrates throughout the whole system. These processes are diagrammed in Figure 7.12.

The pattern variables are defined as complete polar alternatives of possible orientation selection (Parsons, 1951: 58–67). *Neutrality-affectivity* refers to the satisfaction or renunciation of immediate gratification. Every society must make a choice between expressiveness or discipline. Filipino society, particularly culture, has been characterized by affectivity, because motivations and attitudes appear to be organized around cathetic, emotional, or expressive orientations toward social objects.

Self-collectivity orientation refers to long-term interests and whether these are private or shared. Roles, of course, mix these, and this pattern variable

Figure 7.10
Ramification Patterns

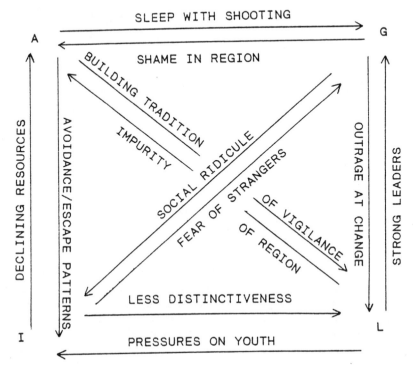

Figure 7.11
Composite Patterns

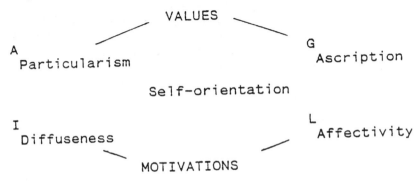

Figure 7.12
Interpenetration Patterns

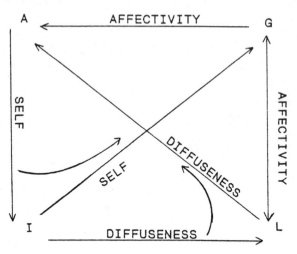

fits into the "middle" of societal components, since it basically serves regulative and integrative functions. Filipino society has been characterized by a self-orientation because personal survival is most prominantly at stake.

Universalism-particularism refers to normative standards by which action is evaluated. Universalism is primarily cognitive since reference is made to universal morality. Particularism is primarily appreciative, such as "I must try to help my neighbor." Particularism best characterizes Filipino society because not only is membership based on this, but appreciation appears to take precedence over cognition in the determination of standards.

Ascription-achievement refers to the "modality" or focus on social objects. Achievement focus is on role performance, and ascriptive focus is on qualities, or attributes of actors. Filipino society, especially the personality subsector, appears to fall into this latter category.

Diffuseness-specificity refers to scope of interests, or the determination of relevance. In diffuse societies, like the Phillipines, the burden of proof is on outsiders to prove the irrelevance of any action. Filipino shame in their region is a prime example of diffuseness.

Certain properties of interaction between pattern variables are already well known (Parsons, Bales, and Shils, 1953). First of all, deviance follows a *LIGA* sequence while social control follows an *AGIL* sequence. Links between universalism-particularism (a value component) and diffuseness-specificity (a motivational component) are what explains the origin of deviance in the inherent tension buildup that must be released. Since Filipino society is diffuse rather than specific, however, one would expect little deviance, because reinforcement schedules are not based on specific likes or dislikes about an actor's motivations. The link between ascription-achievement (a value component) and neutrality-affectivity (a motivational component) is what explains social control. One would expect to find much social control in the Philippines, regardless of the extent of deviance, because ascription means qualitative assessment of the whole person and is reinforced by cultural support for affective expression. Social ridicule is a prime example of the social control expected.

Further, Alexander (1987) has identified the key to unraveling Parsons' conceptual scheme as a matter of role sequencing. This is similar to the deviance and social control sequences described earlier, but it is also referred to as interchanging or interpenetrating by Munch (1987, 1988). Certain known patterns exist (Alexander, 1987) with regard to education (an L-A-G sequence), power (an A-I-L sequence), and voting behavior (a G-I interchange). We are interested in determining the sequences that best describe the impact of terrorism upon a society like the Philippines.

FORMAL NEOFUNCTIONAL PROPOSITIONS

Six propositions, stated in terms of their interchanging or sequencing, will be presented. It is assumed that terrorism affects the whole social system, that it directly impacts on social solidarity, and that the subsystem components interact by producing outputs that are inputs for other specific components. In turn, this process of interpenetration best explains societal return to equilibrium, and the impact of terrorism.

Proposition 1: The Particularistic-Ascriptive Value Pattern. Parsons (1951: 198–200) discussed this type as, historically, being artistic societies, and in more contemporary terms, being the Spanish-American pattern. This particular pattern, or the A-G interchange, is what determines value-orientation in a society. This pattern is claimed to be a result of the impact of terrorism. Filipinos react passively (ascription) and respond by appealing to kinship or community ties (particularism). The resulting combination of pattern variables means that a kind of indifference to social issues is taking effect. Work and morality are seen as necessary evils, and integration is by symbols of power from the cultural component. Government is looked upon simply as insurance against instability, and authority is sometimes welcomed as a stability factor. Such societies, then, become prime candidates for the appearance of dictatorships.

Proposition 2: The Diffuse-Affective Motivational Pattern, or the I-L Interchange. This pattern means that the impact of terrorism has consequences for the socialization practices of a society, or the preparation of personalities for placement in the social structure. Holding constant the normal ambivalence of adolescence, diffuseness means that generalized erotic interests are channeled into affective cultural standards for expression.

The result is that people are motivated in a way that "automatically" results in the formation of families. Strict family morality becomes a substitute for personal security needs. Parsons (1951), in his chapter on social change, identified this as the "instinctual" basis for families, and said that it is especially pronounced in revolutionary times where a "regression" to basic needs takes place. This pattern can also be identified as a basis for the adaptive functions of terrorism for a society undergoing social change.

Proposition 3: The A-I-G Sequence. This pattern of particularism-diffuseness-ascription explains the impact of terrorism on norms in a society. It is driven by the "middle" pattern variable of self-orientation, which is created as an output of the A-cell, fed into the I-cell, and ends up as input for the G-cell. Looking back at the ramification patterns for our system composite, it can be seen that avoidance/escape patterns are the initial output of the A-cell and are mediated by the I-cell into fear of strangers, which inputs into the personality subsystem. The impact of terrorism is where a flight mechanism is converted to norms based on insider/outsider distinctions. When we looked specifically at the ramifications for the I-cell, the mediating variable in this case, we found that there was an indirect connection between two of the outputs—fear of strangers and declining resources. The former extends even to economic investors who could help the region. This connection is the insider/outsider distinction and represents the creation of norms, which are one way the system adjusts.

Proposition 4: The I-L-A Sequence. This pattern of diffuseness-affectivity-particularism explains the impact of terrorism on roles in a society. It is driven mainly by the pattern variable of diffuseness, which involves the specification of scope, or relevance, of social roles. Less distinctiveness is the output of the I-cell into the L-cell, which, in turn, outputs impurity into the A-cell. As roles become more diffuse owing to the impact of terrorism, the perception of less distinctiveness in one's neighborhood is generalized into a perception of less distinctiveness, and even shame, in one's region. This not only forces the L-cell to send a need for strong leaders to the personality subsystem, but puts enormous pressure on youths to be all things to all people. The whole system reacts by expanding the relevance, or scope, of existing roles to the point where each role satisfies a wide range of interests. Role stress and conflict are avoided because the society is not achievement-oriented, and evaluation is not on performance of roles, but the affective qualities, or statuses, of occupants of roles.

Proposition 5: The L-G-A Sequence. This pattern of affectivity-ascription-particularism explains the impact of terrorism on the motivational structure of a society. Disregarding socialization concerns, the immediate impact of an affectivity concern in a culture sends an output of need for strong personalities to the G-cell, which, mediated by explosiveness, sends a variety of emotions to other subsystems. The most important of these may be the input of shame in region to the A-cell. This converts what may be a potentially dangerous message to the G-cell into a more diffuse, and rather harmless, emotion directed at the adaptive structures of the society. The G-cell is able to do this because it sends a countermessage of outrage back into the L-cell and vents social ridicule across to another subsystem. The result is almost a perfect balance of personalities expressing outrage at forced change and, at the same time, wanting desparately to bring about some change to deal with the causes of shame. When we looked specifically at the ramifications of the G-cell, we saw that there was an indirect ideological connection between outrage and social ridicule. This is significant because there is no connection between shame in region and ideology. Instead, an impact of terrorism is to destroy whatever emotional energy is available to tie ideology into adaptive social change. Instead, the self-orientation of society places motivational power in personalities, not collectivities, and social ridicule is the result based on the false pretense of ideology. Energy that appears to be expended uselessly serves the purpose of restraining the impact of terrorism by channeling ideological concerns into other concerns than purposive social change.

Proposition 6: The L-G Interchange. This pattern of affectivity-ascription is basically the relationship between culture and personality. When we looked at the subsystem ramifications, we found a reciprocal relationship between the L- and G-cells. Culture expresses demands and personalities express outrage. This is the main link between value and motivational orientations. Role expectations and need dispositions are synchronized by the impact of terrorism, and, for this reason, there is no disjunction that can result in deviant behavior despite all the mutual outrage. The complementarity of expectations represents a process of institutionalization, where the impact of terrorism results in indifference, habituation, or passivity, but these qualities are the result of reciprocal demands for immediate gratification. There is little renunciation of gratification, thus fewer restrictions upon deviance. An impact of extraordinary events is wider tolerance for more ordinary events. There is, however, the general expectation that people be gratified, so life becomes a measure of obtaining simple pleasures. The modal personality in this kind of culture is one who may express discontent on the surface, but deeply feels "spiritually" at peace with one's existence.

DISCUSSION AND CONCLUSIONS

The value of a neofunctionalist analysis should be apparent in the wider generalizability and comparability of the expanded propositions obtained. There are, indeed, many more insights to be gained from elaborating the model further. One can potentially predict the causes (exogenous shock) and control (equilibrium) of terrorism with a fair amount of precision, and propositions can be derived about the impact of terrorism that are, if not axiomatic, certainly complete and follow logically from the utility of prior theoretical specification. Advantages include the possibility of integration with other theories because of multidimensionality—for example, everything from biology to theology. Parsons' ideas are more compatible with Marx and Weber than Durkheim and Merton (Black, 1976). Rather than give tacit approval, for example, to social problems by finding functions, neofunctionalism seems to be useful in identifying points of intervention, sequences, and interchanges. Neofunctionalism rounds out the criminological repertoire by adding a pluralistic consensus theory to existing typologies.

Terrorism is a very complex phenomenon, involving, as it often does, political and religious conflicts. It seems reasonable that neofunctionalist analysis would be perfectly capable of handling these complex macrostructures and perhaps even the problem of urban, international terrorism in the world economy (Bassiouni, 1975). One unanswered question is the issue of "soft targets." The particularistic-ascription-oriented society studied here is certainly more prepared to absorb the impact of terrorism. What is needed is study on the contrasting case of a universalistic-achievement-oriented society. There is, indeed, much work to do in learning about macro-level responses. The neofunctionalist model provides another way to study society, law, justice, legitimacy, and order, as well as crime and its control, without losing the connectiveness between these phenomena. Because this tradition, or "literature," is not widely known by most researchers, the present analysis was intended only to be a sample. It remains to be seen if the neofunctionalist revival will continue by inspiring further theoretical and empirical work.

Part II

Critical Criminology

8

Confronting the Agenda of Authority: Critical Criminology, Anarchism, and Urban Graffiti

JEFF FERRELL

Critical criminologists in the United States today work within a swirl of confounding circumstances. These are the emerging circumstances of injustice and inequality: the domination of social and cultural life by a consortium of privileged opportunists and reactionary thugs; the aggressive disenfranchisement of city kids, poor folks, and people of color from the practice of everyday life; and the careful and continuous centralization of legal, political, and economic authority. Whether teaching and counseling their students, investigating new forms of crime and criminalization, or participating in public debate, critical criminologists encounter an environment shaped by enforced inequality and, with it, increasing intolerance. Willingly or not, as they go about the work of criminology, they confront the agenda of authority.

In fighting back against an increasingly authoritarian social order, critical criminologists can productively draw on an intellectual and political orientation particularly well-suited to the task: anarchism. Anarchist perspectives help reveal the various shapes of authority, and they are especially useful in accounting for the many manifestations of legal and political authority in contemporary society. Equally important, they help uncover the various forms that resistance to this authority may take. As Tifft (1979; Tifft and Sullivan, 1980), Pepinsky (1978, 1991; Pepinsky and Jesilow, 1984; Pepinsky and Quinney, 1991), and others have begun to show, anarchist orientations can thus inform and enliven critical criminology; they can serve not as some rigid corrective, nor competing paradigm, but as analytic sparks within an already lively alternative criminology.

As a concept regularly misused, "anarchism" bears a bit of explanation. Anarchism can be defined by its opposition to—or perhaps more accurately, defiance of—authority. In contrast to other progressive orientations, anarchism opposes not a particular configuration of power and authority but all hierarchical systems of domination. Significantly, this domination resides in structures of knowledge, perception, and understanding. Authority operates not only through prison cells and poverty, but by constructing and defending epistemologies of universality and truth. Anarchism attacks these hierarchies of credibility (Becker, 1967) and seeks to undermine the mythologies of certainty and truth on which they are built. In their place, anarchism offers a new sort of epistemic and aesthetic pluralism. Accompanying this fragmented and decentered pluralism is ambiguity—an ambiguity that celebrates multiple interpretations and styles, and embraces particularity and disorder.[1]

The social arrangements of anarchism follow from this unraveling of authority and its epistemic structures. Anarchism supposes a delicate, negotiated balance of collectivity and diversity, a tolerant community of autonomous persons and groups. In place of centralized power and authority, anarchism calls on an ongoing process of collective negotiation as a means of problem solving. Anarchism thus operates less as a concrete ideology than an inherently social, and communal, process. And if anarchism is a social process, it is a direct, spontaneous, and funny one, as well. From Emma Goldman to the Industrial Workers of the World, from early twentieth-century Russian anarchy to the late twentieth-century punk scene, anarchists have replaced "representative" systems with "direct action" in the situations of daily life. To keep this process of direct action fluid, anarchists incorporate into it large doses of spontaneity and improvization. To further avoid rigidity and encrustation, anarchists turn to humor. Humor protects against taking our own social processes too seriously, against mistaking human constructions for immutable forces. At the same time, it creates room for these processes by undercutting the aura of legitimacy that legal, political, and economic authorities so carefully construct.[2]

As we blend this anarchist orientation into critical criminology, a variety of foci can be imagined. Certainly, such an integrated approach would critique the encrustation of human relationships in structures of legal authority. Kropotkin (1975: 30), for example, found the law's "distinctive trait to be immobility, a tendency to crystallize what should be modified and developed day by day." Tifft (1979: 397, 398; see Tifft and Sullivan, 1980) therefore argues that "justice must be warm, must be living... face to face justice," and advocates "needs-based," retrospective justice in place of current rights-based prospective systems. Pepinsky and Jesilow (1984: 10, 133) argue similarly that we must move from the current criminal justice system, which serves as a "state-protection racket," to more direct, informal networks of "cross-cutting ties" within communities.

This perspective on crime and justice also emphasizes that if law and legality are worth preserving at all, their mission must be radically altered; instead of protecting property, privilege, and the state, as they now do, they must be made to insure tolerance and protect diversity. Tifft (1979: 397) contends that a move to needs-based, retrospective justice would be beneficial, because it would encourage "tolerance of ambiguity, acknowledgement of alternative meanings (and reality systems), and respect for diversity." Kevin Ryan and I (Ryan and Ferrell, 1986: 193) have likewise argued that an antiauthoritarian vision of justice "would entail respect for alternative interpretations of reality and alternative realities. But, further, it would require opposition to any attempt to destroy, suppress, or impose particular realities." To this we might add, as does Tifft, that anarchist justice would also allow for, and even encourage, unresolved ambiguities of meaning and identity now forcefully resolved by the rule of law.[3]

Though these sorts of insights certainly set the context, the following discussion takes a somewhat different direction. It develops out of my ongoing research into urban graffiti and the campaigns by legal, political, and economic authorities to suppress it (Ferrell, 1993). This research has, over the past four years or so, incorporated extensive field research and participant observation with the graffiti underground in Denver, Colorado, and close scrutiny of Denver's lengthy antigraffiti campaign. It has also largely focused on "hip hop" graffiti as practiced in Denver and other cities. Originating out of the black neighborhood cultures of New York City in the early and mid–1970s, "hip hop" denotes a set of cultural practices that includes rap music, break dancing, and graffiti writing. Unlike street gang graffiti, this hip hop graffiti is organized not around issues of territoriality and control, but around the stylistic imperatives of graffiti "writers" who produce complex systems of street imagery and design. As this style of graffiti writing has spread in the last two decades to cities throughout the United States, Europe, and beyond, it has come to define not only the practice of graffiti writing, but the practical concerns of those who campaign against it (see Castleman, 1982; Cooper and Chalfant, 1984; Hager, 1984; Chalfant and Prigoff, 1987; Lachmann, 1988). Contemporary hip hop graffiti and the response to it can thus highlight for critical, anarchist criminologists the social and cultural politics of criminality and criminalization, and the possibilities for research and activism around this issue.

To get at this politics of criminality, critical, anarchist criminology must begin by integrating approaches to crime traditionally categorized as "political/economic" and "interactionist." As the case of graffiti writing will show, we cannot understand the nature of crime without understanding both its immediate construction out of social interaction and its larger construction through processes of political and economic authority. Moreover, "both" is not enough. That is, we must not only use each perspective, but also find ways to integrate them in our research and analysis.

In discussing the development of alternative criminology in Britain in the late 1960s, Cohen (1988: 68) has spoken of the "adoption of a structurally and politically informed version of labeling theory." Turned another way, this approach might be thought of as an analysis of authority and power, which looks for their presence in the daily situations of criminality. In whatever configuration, this dialectic between situations and structures of criminality, between the style and substance of crime, lays the foundation for a critical, anarchist criminology.

If we understand political/economic domination and inequality to be causes, or at least primary contexts, of crime, we can also understand that these are mediated and expressed through the situational dynamics, the symbolism and style, of criminal events. To speak of a criminal "event," then, is to talk about the acts and actions of the criminals, the unfolding interactional dynamics of the crime (both between the "criminals" and among the criminals and victims), and the patterns of inequality and injustice embedded in the thoughts, words, and actions of those involved. In a criminal event, as in other moments of everyday life, structures of authority, social class, and ethnicity intertwine with situational decisions, personal style, and symbolic references. Thus, while we cannot make sense of crime without analyzing structures of inequality, we cannot make sense of crime by only analyzing these structures, either. The meaning and aesthetics of criminal events interlock with the political economy of criminality.[4]

Graffiti writing embodies this dialectic between structures and situations of crime. The writing of graffiti in Denver and elsewhere unfolds within systems of legal and economic domination, systems that guarantee unequal access to private property and cultural resources. These systems are in turn utilized and managed by those who expand political/economic authority by criminalizing graffiti writing. But while these factors set the context for graffiti writing, they do not define the writing itself. They alone cannot explain the subtle ways in which writers appropriate and subvert pop culture imagery and draw on hip hop culture—itself an elegant and elaborate response to political/economic and ethnic domination. They cannot predict the "adrenalin rush" that graffiti's illegality generates for its writers, or the many ways in which criminalization in fact amplifies and reconstructs the writing of graffiti. These details of graffiti writing—these intersections of politics and interpersonal style, of criminalization and criminal event—can only be explained from inside the writing itself.

This dialectic means that critical criminologists must look up and down at the same time—that is, we must pay attention to the subtleties of legal and political authority, the nuances of lived criminal events, and the interconnections between the two. To speak of this as looking up and down does not imply, of course, reverence toward those above nor disrespect for those designated as below. Quite the opposite; such a perspective incorporates a fundamental insight of critical, anarchist analysis—that modern societies are structured into hierarchies of authority and power—and attacks these hierarchies and those who ride atop them. When critical criminology looks up, then, it is with a different eye than when it looks down and around. As critical criminologists look up at authority, they must do so disrespectfully—that is, they must engage in a "vast operation of decon-secration" (Guerin, 1970: 13). When they look down and around at the lived experience of criminality, they must do so respectfully—not with re-spect for any and all criminal acts, but for the possibilities of meaning that are embedded in them.[5]

DISMANTLING AUTHORITY

The disrespectful gaze that critical criminology turns upwards toward authority will, it is hoped, serve to dismantle its legal and political config-urations. To dismantle is to engage in two related processes, both of which are appropriate to a critical, anarchist criminology. The first involves strip-ping away—dismantling—that which covers or conceals. As seen previously, epistemologies of certainty and truth form the mantle of authority; they present authority as a reasonable and legitimate medium for making sense of the world, and in so doing conceal its abuses. And this authoritarian artifice is nowhere better developed than within the law. Increasingly, po-litical, economic, and cultural authorities hide behind the law; and the inequity of the law is itself concealed behind mythologies of truth and justice.

A critical, anarchist epistemology can tear away these mythologies, ex-posing the inherent inequities they are designed to conceal. In particular, critical, anarchist criminology is well suited to investigate the fundamental mythologies of the legal process—that, for example, legal rules and social facts exist exterior to those who utilize them, and can thus be apprehended objectively—and to document the specific manner in which the powerful create these rules and facts in their interest (see Ryan and Ferrell, 1986). This investigation, it should be noted, is not an exercise in philosophy, but sociology. It requires the very sort of integrated approach noted previously, whereby critical, anarchist criminologists take a political/economic per-spective into the courtroom and the street to observe the interactional dy-namics between cops, judges, lawyers, and criminals. This process of epistemic demystification in turn leads to a larger project: revealing that the "justice" by which the legal system defines itself is in fact a facade for an elaborate system of institutionalized injustice. Critical criminology must demonstrate, in case after case, the difference between justice and law.

The dismantling of authority's concealments also necessitates paying at-tention to the many covers under which authority operates. Legal and po-litical authority certainly does permeate the dynamics of the courtroom, the street dealings of police officers, and the operations of the prison. But this authority pervades other areas of social and cultural life as well. Graffiti writing and the response to it highlight the aesthetics of this authority, and thus its presence in clean walls and carefully planned and controlled "public" space. Kropotkin (1975: 27) reminds us that "the ferule of a law . . . regulates every event in our life—our birth, our education, our development, our love, our friendship." The scope of legal and political authority is such, then, that critical criminologists must pay attention not just to prisons, courtrooms, and other traditional concerns of criminology, but to each moment of social life—to people renting houses, making love, negotiating divorces, drinking beer, visiting art galleries, and otherwise getting on with their daily lives. Each of these events forms an appropriate domain for criminology; in each is embedded various, subtle dimensions of legal/political authority, and therefore the potential for legal conflict, criminalization, and institutional labeling. Dismantling legal and political authority requires unpacking the various social circumstances in which it is hidden.

Dismantling the law in this way—uncovering the myths and circumstances behind which it is concealed—creates the possibility for a second sort of dismantling, as well: taking apart the law as a means of tearing it down. As critical criminologists make visible pervasive legal mythologies—and thereby expose the inequitable intrusion of legal authority into every area of social and cultural life—they contribute to a more general disrespect for law and authority. Through their own activist scholarship, and in conjunction with other progressive individuals and groups, they raise the possibility of unraveling the law's legitimacy. As they engage, for example, in "newsmaking criminology" (Barak, 1988) by investigating and publicly confronting criminalization campaigns, unchecked white-collar crime, and crusading politicians, they not only stand up to particular public abuses, but also tear down the hierarchy of credibility on which such abuses are predicated.

Denver's War on Graffiti

Especially in those cases likely to receive media attention or otherwise be made public, critical criminologists can productively draw on a basic anarchist strategy: making fun of authority. In Denver's "war on graffiti," the Denver police department set up a special bicycle squad to look for graffiti vandals, in broad daylight. At a local gallery opening, Denver police "arrested" an album containing photographs of graffiti murals, took it to police headquarters to be photographed, and later claimed that their photographs of it reflected a summer of "collecting intelligence information" (Garnaas, 1988: 1) on graffiti. Robin Pfeiffenberger, the Education Coordinator for the city agency charged with stopping graffiti, took her antigraffiti "Clean Team" to local elementary schools, with Robin playing the part of a graffiti-covered wall. The *Denver Post* dutifully helped kick off a 1988 clampdown on graffiti by running a photograph of a particularly troublesome graffiti mural—still conspicuously visible from a main downtown viaduct three years later. And a local weekly that same year labeled graffiti the "Worst Trash Problem" for Denver. When noted publicly, these and other instances are of course good for a laugh; but because they are laughable, they are also instructive. They teach memorable lessons about the absurdity of authority, and provide opportunities for undermining the legitimacy of law and its proprietors. And as they accumulate, they make the authorities out to be the dangerous fools that they are.[6]

As they act to ridicule and unravel authority, critical criminologists will unavoidably encounter, and must actively oppose, "those in the upper levels of the social structure" who work to criminalize more and more of our social life—that is, they must confront "moral entrepreneurs" (Becker, 1963: 147, 149). Although often laughable in their blundering intensity, the campaigns of moral entrepreneurs cannot be ignored or discounted, since they stand in direct conflict with the progressive goals of critical criminology. While critical criminologists attempt to dismantle the machinery of law, moral entrepreneurs work to create new laws and new crimes; while critical criminologists work to undercut legal authority, moral entrepreneurs expand the scope, structure, and legitimacy of legality. Kropotkin (1975: 30) noted that there existed

a race of law-makers legislating without knowing what their laws are about.... legislating at random in all directions, but never forgetting the penalties to be meted out to ragamuffins, the prison and the galleys, which are to be the portion of men a thousand times less immoral than these legislators themselves.

Today, these legislators work with evangelists, right-wing interest groups, media consultants, and other moral entrepreneurs as they continue to expand legal control in all directions.

The "wars on graffiti" that moral entrepreneurs wage in Denver and other cities exemplify this egregious expansion of legal and political authority. Increasingly coordinated by groups like the National Graffiti Information Network—an organization of political and corporate elites that disseminates information, develops legislation, engineers "sting" operations, and pressures those supporting graffiti-style art—these campaigns aggressively criminalize graffiti writing. Promoted in part to deflect attention from an attempted mayoral recall, Denver's antigraffiti campaign has, like the campaigns in other cities, underwritten political opportunism with the money and support of the local business community. And it has utilized this confluence of political and economic power to alter the practice and perception of graffiti writing.

In criminalizing graffiti, Denver's campaigners have moved to reorient the perspectives of police officers and judges, and to expand and coordinate the antigraffiti operations of the criminal justice system. Campaigners have worked directly with the chief of police and other top officials, and have conducted "roll call training" with police officers. As a result, the police department has incorporated new enforcement procedures—which the chief of police characterized publicly as an attempt to save Denver from a "nightmare of painted obscenities and satanic symbols" (Briggs, 1989: B2)—and increased arrests. Those arrested have in turn been "streamlined" under selected courts and judges, who themselves have been instructed to "make this stick and not just slap them on the hands" (Purser, 1990). Along with jail time, punishment regularly includes participation in a supervised graffiti clean-up program—a sort of "degradation ceremony" (Garfinkel, 1956; see S. Cohen, 1972/1980; Cosgrove, 1984) designed to humiliate and publicly disgrace convicted writers.

In addition, the campaign has developed a "Graffiti Stoppers" program—whose business-funded cash awards for information on graffiti have promoted incidents of vigilante entrepreneurship—and an "Adopt-A-Spot" program in which citizens volunteer to clean and paint over graffiti. As noted previously, campaigners have also moved into local schools, where they "educate" children as to the evils of graffiti. And beyond educating school children, police officers, and judges, the campaign has carefully created "moral panic" (Cohen, 1972/1980) in an attempt to reconfigure the public's perception of graffiti writing and graffiti writers. Repeatedly employing precisely derogatory images of graffiti "vandalism" as a social and environmental menace spreading out of control, and graffiti "vandals" as violent psychopaths who attack, rob, and even "rape" their victims, campaigners have constructed a sort of epistemic clampdown, a paradigm of fear and condemnation that undergirds their narrower strategies of criminalization.

Moral Entrepreneurs, Youth, and Resistance

The Denver case and the many others like it emphasize that opposition to moral entrepreneurs and their campaigns of moral panic may now constitute the primary project of critical criminology. Moral campaigns operate as well-planned exercises not only in criminalization, but in victimization and blame, deflecting the public gaze from those in authority and toward those least able to counter it. As part of this process, they create an ideological context in which legal and political authority can be widely expanded, and resistance to that authority legitimately suppressed. At their most successful, these campaigns thus approach the worst form of authoritarian domination: a hegemonic state in which alternatives literally become "unreasonable," or even "unthinkable." Legal and political authorities fight the "wars" of late capitalist society—the "war on graffiti," the "war on drugs," the "war on gangs"—not only against individuals and groups, but against the possibility of resistance.

These various "wars" share strategies of legal manipulation and control, and together draw on sophisticated ideological machines designed to reconstruct the meaning of everyday activities. Significantly, they for the most part also share a pool of potential villains: the young. The war on graffiti interlocks with the wars on gangs, on drugs, and on other "social problems" in that all serve to focus a broad-ranging clampdown on a youthful population. In Denver, for example, the antigraffiti campaign has been paralleled by well-publicized campaigns against youth gangs and youthful "cruising." A 1989 state law "concerning the war on gangs and gang-related crimes" (Session Laws, 1989)—which also incorporates harsh antigraffiti provisions—has been supplemented in the Denver area by a variety of control strategies. Denver schools have "outlawed gang colors, insignia, hand signals and other indications of membership... in a new policy called 'Zero Gang Tolerance' " (Bailey, 1990: 8). Suburban communities have also passed strict antigang laws, and a popular local amusement park has even inaugurated "a tougher policy on excluding known gang members or people wearing obviously gang-related clothing and paraphernalia" (Ensslin, 1991: 6). The City of Denver has also passed an ordinance regulating car stereo volume, and initiated a clampdown on the primarily Hispanic kids who cruise West 38th Avenue, a local thoroughfare, on weekend nights. The combination of these two control strategies resulted, on a typical spring weekend in 1991, not only in a maze of barricades and police officers, but in 293 traffic tickets and 18 arrests along the avenue (see Flynn, 1990; *Rocky Mountain News*, 1991: 16; Soto, 1991).

The politics of this organized assault on the young incorporates the same sort of dialectic already seen, between the interactional foreground of crime and the political economy of criminalization. Writing graffiti, cruising the avenue with a pump-up-the-jam stereo, "gangbanging"—these are not only particularly youthful forms of crime, but particularly stylish ones as well. And if we look at other contemporary and historical examples, we find the same pattern: the deviant and criminal identities associated closely with youth—zoot suiters, pachucos and pachucas, skinheads, rude boys, punks— are also the identities that exhibit the sharpest concern with aesthetics and style. Clearly, the social construction of youth in our culture is such that young people and their subcultures accelerate the development of distinctive styles of crime and deviance, of an aesthetically rich criminal foreground. In the context of shoplifting and other youthful "sneaky thrills," Katz (1988: 73, 76–77) suggests that this has to do with the interplay of private and public identity, and "personal esthetic triumph." Whatever its individual origins, this confluence of youth and style points to the fact that "acceptable" youth cultures—those organized around music and fashion, for example— and "deviant" youth subcultures exist not as distinct alternatives, but along a continuum of stylized social marginality and alternative meaning.

The coincidence of youth, style, and crime develops therefore out of the politics of youth, out of the relative powerlessness and marginality of the young, and out of the particulars of their resistance to this. The political economy of this coincidence reveals a two-pronged assault. While entrepreneurs of mass consumption and commodified style profit from some aspects of stylized youth subcultures—through record and video sales, fan magazines, and fashions appropriated and resold—moral entrepreneurs profit from others. Corporate entrepreneurs attempt to reconstruct the stylistic resistance of the young as a commodity, and to sell it back to them; moral entrepreneurs—their aesthetic of authority offended by the loud exuberance, the sheer audacity of youthful style—work to reconstruct it as crime. The evolution of hip hop reveals this double bind. Developed by inner-city, minority kids as a multifaceted alternative style, hip hop has been appropriated in some cases into mainstream commercial culture, and in other cases has come under legal and political attack. Thus while pseudo-emcees now rap for McDonald's commercials, 2LiveCrew, Ice-T, and assorted graffiti writers dodge police harassment and jail time. On the one side stands the velvet glove of commercialism, on the other the chain-mailed fist of the law; and in the middle, a kid with a tape deck and a can of Krylon.

In attacking legal and political authority, critical, anarchist criminologists must be willing to confront the moral entrepreneurs of the moment, and to push for decriminalization and other strategies that can begin to dismantle some of the repressive legal machinery left over from past entrepreneurial campaigns. But critical criminologists must also be ready to comfort the victims of past and present moral panics—that is, to side with young people and the often unpopular responses they make to the authority under which they are placed. In this process of standing up to moral entrepreneurs and defending the young against them, critical criminologists of whatever age would do well to remember that kids are really OK.[7]

PAYING ATTENTION TO CRIME AND RESISTANCE

This process of siding with the young, and looking beyond politically constructed stereotypes of them to see possibilities of meaning and resistance in their actions, points to the broader approach critical criminologists can take when they look down and around to focus on the lived experience of criminality. At its most basic, this approach embodies the notion that it is worth our while to pay attention to the particular dynamics of interaction, meaning, and style that evolve in events labeled as "criminal." Critical criminologists cannot begin their work by setting themselves up as authorities on crime and presorting people and events into theoretically convenient categories: political or apolitical, constructive or destructive, innovative or conformist. Instead, they must begin with attentiveness to and respect for the various lived experiences of those they study, with immersion in the realities of writing graffiti, shoplifting, gang fighting, and stealing cars. Such is the politics of paying attention.

The grounded inquiry employed here draws not only on anarchist commitments to epistemic pluralism and social process, but on recent developments in areas as disparate as U.S. sociology, British cultural studies, postmodern social theory, and feminist theory. Although certainly not reducible to a single theme, these emerging analytic orientations cluster around some central ideas: the texture of everyday life—the popular culture of people, groups, and events—matters. The choices made and styles adopted within everyday life are profoundly political. Situated language, symbolism, and meaning stand therefore as definitive components of social life, inexorably intertwined with the economic and political structures of society.[8]

These perspectives confirm what we have already seen: paying attention to the foreground of criminality reveals not only the nuances of situated experience, but the presence of legal, political, and economic authority in that experience. And as anarchist perspectives can highlight, it is not only authority that is played out in the experience of crime, but various forms of resistance to it as well. Paying attention to moments of criminality, then, means appreciating also the possibilities of resistance carried within them.

These possibilities will of course develop differently within different criminal events—more so in some than others, and not at all in crimes that reproduce the violence of present authoritarian arrangements.[9] Critical, anarchist criminologists should by no means feel compelled to discover moments of resistance in all crimes because they find them in some. Still, an anarchic critical criminology is particularly well-suited to appreciate the plural and eclectic forms that resistance to authority can take. In the same way that anarchism embraces a plurality of life choices, critical, anarchist criminology can affirm the plurality of resistances embedded in social events and identities that those in power define as criminal. Breaking curfew or breaking windows, doing drugs or getting drunk, shoplifting jewelry or hotwiring cars, riding with outlaw motorcyclists or cruising the boulevard—none of these should be reified and afforded unquestioned respect, but all should be respected, and investigated, for their possibilities. When critical criminologists pay attention to such forms of criminality, they may find that these forms embody orientations that get outside the boundaries of authority, even if in ways that are sometimes badly compromised. They may discover shapes and styles of resistance that others ignore (see Hall and Jefferson, 1976; Hebdige, 1979; Atlanta and Alexander, 1989; Sholle, 1990; J. C. Scott, 1990).[10]

Youthful adventures in crime—vandalism, theft, shoplifting—exemplify these possibilities. Shoplifting, for example, certainly has to do with the creation of needs, the structuring of consumption, and the commodification of desire under late capitalism. Yet these societal processes alone cannot explain the particular, situational dynamic of shoplifting. The event of shoplifting has a "magical" (Katz, 1988: 54) quality about it that often develops independently of any overt need on the part of the shoplifter for the shoplifted items. For the shoplifter, the event unfolds as a sort of thrilling and sensually gratifying game, a dramatic and illicit adventure. This magically empowering adventure is, of course, tangled up with the illicit acquisition of late capitalist consumer goods; but it is tangled in a particularly revealing

fashion. Shoplifting embraces and undermines capitalist culture and, simultaneously, reinforces and resists the constraints of legal authority. Our
understanding of crime, capitalism, and resistance is thus enriched by paying
attention to the particular contours of shoplifting.[11]

When we pay attention in this way to graffiti writing, we find its many
nuances pointing in a direction we have already seen: toward an anarchist
resistance to authority. The "adrenalin rush" of graffiti writing—the moment of illicit pleasure that emerges from the intersection of creativity and
illegality—signifies a resistance experienced as much in the pit of the stomach
as in the head (see Lyng, 1990). Guerin (1970: 13) asserts that "anarchism
can be described first and foremost as a visceral revolt," and graffiti writing
certainly constitutes visceral resistance to the constraints of private property,
law, and corporate art. Engaging in "direct action" against these authorities,
graffiti writers together celebrate their insubordination in spray paint and
felt-tip marker, and in the pleasure and excitement of doing graffiti. And
this forbidden pleasure in turn reveals as much about authority, and resistance to it, as the moments of intellectual clarity gained from a close reading
of Karl Marx and Friedrich Engels' *The German Ideology* (1846).

That the pleasures of graffiti writing result not only from its illegality,
but from the collective creativity of the writers, confirms its meaning as a
form of anarchist resistance. Working together, graffiti writers construct an
alternative, streetwise aesthetic that subverts the prepackaged imagery of
the culture industry and city hall. Playing with their own images and designs,
appropriating and reconfiguring pop culture icons, they engage in a process
of cultural resistance enlivened by beauty and style. If Emma Goldman
taught us that a revolution without dancing is not worth attending, graffiti
writing confirms that resistance without creativity—resistance as a sort of
analytic, intellectualized machinery of opposition—may not be worth the
trouble. Without the spark of playful creativity, resistance becomes another
drudgery, reproducing in its seriousness the structures of authority it seeks
to undermine. The imaginative play, the irreverent humor, of graffiti writing
and other anarchist enterprises defines their existence outside the usual
boundaries of intellectual and emotional control.[12]

As with more violent forms of anarchist resistance, graffiti writing is also
notable for the sudden and mysterious manner in which it appears. If graffiti
writing escapes the uninspired seriousness of conventional politics, it escapes
the scheduled tyranny of deadlines and datebooks as well. This detail of
graffiti writing—that writers do graffiti in the middle of the night, when
and if they feel like it—carries two sorts of political meaning. It pulls the
writers outside the world of daily work, insures that graffiti writing will
not itself become a sort of routinized labor, and thus further locates graffiti
writing outside conventional channels of authority and control.[13] This spontaneity also contributes to the threat that graffiti writing poses to those in
authority. Denver City Council President Cathy Donahue complained to

the 1990 Metro Wide Graffiti Summit (1990): "It is illegal to deface somebody's property, but the problem became that no one ever sees them. And
people have tried to catch [them]. . . . I've seen acres of graffiti and I have
never, ever seen anybody put it on." Her comments of course recall the
lamentations of other authorities faced with episodes of "undisciplined"
guerrilla warfare and popular insurgency, as well they might. As a form of
aesthetic guerrilla warfare, graffiti writing resembles the resistance waged
by Makhno and his anarchist fighters during and after the Russian revolution: "When cornered, the Makhnovists would bury their weapons, make
their way singly back to their villages, and take up work in the fields,
awaiting the next signal to unearth a new cache of arms and spring up again
in an unexpected quarter" (Avrich, 1973: 23).

Any characterization of graffiti writing as "guerrilla warfare," though,
must be balanced against another essential detail of its production: its vulnerability. As seen previously, antigraffiti entrepreneurs take care to portray
graffiti writers as forcing their images on defenseless victims in a series of
violent assaults. The lived experience of graffiti writing, though, shows this
assertion to be false in two ways. First, graffiti writers paint not on people,
but on property; if their painting embodies disrespect, it is not for individuals, but for the sanctity of private (and "public") walls and fences. Only
in a social order that systematically confuses persons and property could
moral entrepreneurs hope to confuse graffiti writing with assault. Second,
when faced with graffiti on their property, the majority of homeowners—
and certainly large corporations and cities—have ample ability to erase the
offending images and symbols. With access to financial and technological
resources far greater than those of the writers, property owners can wipe
out in minutes graffiti that may have taken hours to produce.[14]

Rather than forcing their art on helpless victims, then, graffiti writers in
fact produce art in and of the urban community. This graffiti art is vulnerable
to direct public response in ways that city-administered "public" art is not;
and its images intrude on the public with far less impunity than those of
the television commercial and the roadside billboard. In fact, unlike the
administrators of commercial and "public" art, graffiti writers make no
claims as to protecting, preserving, or profiting from their public art. They
own and control their art less than they simply expose it to public appreciation (or condemnation). As Eye Six, one of Denver's graffiti "kings,"
says: "In that respect, it's probably the dumbest crime you can get involved
in. Not only are you in danger of getting thrown in jail and getting fined
and such, you don't get any money out of it at all" (Ferrell, 1990: 10).[15]

Because of this, conflicts over graffiti writing are susceptible to the sort
of direct, street-level resolution essential to anarchist social relations. Conflicts among the writers themselves are played out in the stylized dynamics
of the subculture. Property owners and city governments can resort to the
censorship of the sandblaster—with, of course, the possibility that the writ-

ers will return to paint again the clean wall. And, as has happened in Denver, this interplay may eventually result in some agreement or compromise between writers and property owners. While these are not perfectly harmonious processes of community negotiation—partly because they originate in inequalities of privilege and power—they can at least keep the resolution of conflict in the hands of the participants, and outside the authoritarian entanglements of the law. Interestingly, the vulnerability of graffiti writing to these direct processes is mirrored in other forms of street art and entertainment. Noting the "eccentric, anarchistic nature of the busker," Parks (1990: 8; also see Tifft, 1979: 399) argues that "minstrel buskers remain public property. They are accountable daily to the people. They are naked, vulnerable, and open to judgement every time out. . . . This closeness to hand-to-mouth existence is what expunges the tyranny of the pop show and by example strengthens resistance to it."

The contrast between graffiti art and the "art" of the corporation and the government, and the link between graffiti writing, busking, and other forms of anarchist entertainment, both point to a final dimension of graffiti writing as anarchist resistance. Graffiti writing breaks the hegemonic hold of corporate/governmental style over the urban environment and the situations of daily life. For the participants, graffiti writing disrupts the lived experience of mass culture, the passivity of mediated consumption. As Eye Six says,

Your average person is just subservient to whatever is thrown up. Whatever building is built, whatever billboard is put up—whatever. They just sit on their asses; they pretty much go with the flow like all sheep do. . . . At least we act on our feelings. We don't just sit around and doodle in our houses, we go out and get paint (Ferrell, 1990: 10).

For the commuter and the office worker, graffiti provides a series of mysterious, ambiguous images—and some of the few available public images not bought and paid for by corporate art programs, city governments, or National Endowment for the Arts grants. Graffiti resists not only authority, but the aesthetics of authority as well.[16]

CONCLUSION

Appreciating graffiti writing as a form of anarchist resistance, then, does not require romanticizing the process of doing graffiti, nor ignoring graffiti's social and cultural contexts. In fact, a sense of graffiti writing as resistance develops from quite the opposite direction: from paying close attention to the lived politics of its production. Created out of the direct, collective action of young writers, graffiti survives as a playful resistance to a prefabricated culture, a resistance as disrespectful of legal and political boundaries as it is of the private and public property through which they are enforced. It exists as a public art outside the control of public authorities, an alternative style outside the circle of corporate style and consumption. It illuminates the city, but sporadically, less a series of lasting monuments than evocative moments, vulnerable to the give and take of the street. Ultimately, it stands as a sort of decentralized and decentered insurbordination, a mysterious resistance to conformity and control, a stylish counterpunch to the belly of authority.

In this sense, graffiti writing and critical, anarchistic criminology occupy common ground. Both construct innovative alternatives to increasingly authoritarian arrangements, alternatives that violate the vacancy of a centralized social and cultural life. Both empower those whom the caretakers of economic and political control would condemn, and in so doing begin to reveal the various shapes that resistance may take. And both, at their best, confront and disrupt the agenda of authority.

NOTES

1. Anarchism thus opposes Churchill and Stalin, Reagan and Gorbachev, Bush and Hussein alike, to the extent that all function as "authority figures," as embodiments of appropriated power and meaning.

For more on epistemic pluralism and ambiguity, see, for example, Feyerabend (1975) and The Second January Group (1986). Postmodernism—an orientation that, at its best, shares much with anarchism—also embodies this sense. York (1980: 211) notes that "whatever [the development of postmodernism] was, it was 'ambivalent' and 'ambiguous.' " A number of other writers on postmodernism—Jencks (1977), Baudrillard (1985), Jameson (1985)—use the term "schizophrenia" to denote this condition of multiple, ambiguous meanings.

2. May (1989) in fact characterizes anarchism in terms of its opposition to "representation." For more on the uses of "direct action" and humor by the Industrial Workers of the World and their affiliate, the Brotherhood of Timber Workers, see, for example, Ferrell (1991), Ferrell and Ryan (1985).

3. On tolerance, see also Pepinsky and Jesilow (1984: 134–138). Labeling theory teaches us that situations and interactions carry multiple, ambiguous meanings, until such time as they come to be categorized and labeled by authorities as "criminal" or "deviant." The notion of anarchist justice presumes that the authorities would be removed from this privileged role, thus leaving the ambiguities tolerated and unresolved, or placing their resolution in the hands of an egalitarian community. And in this sense, perhaps the law needs not to be altered, but destroyed (see Kropotkin, 1975: 30–31).

4. This sense of an integrated political economic/interactionist approach also points to the incongruity between progressive criminologies and positivist methodologies. The methods and epistemologies of positivist or "structural" criminologies—the dislocated number sets that crossmatch crime's background factors in an attempt to measure criminality "objectively"—obscure not only the interactional process through which crime is constructed, but its political content as well. To

ignore the foreground of criminality in favor of an analysis of political or economic structures is, ironically, to miss the very meaning of these structures in the reality of crime. On this, see, for example, Becker (1963), Polsky (1969), Hall and Jefferson (1976), Cosgrove (1984).

5. This argument for different approaches to "studying up" and "studying down" is based on the work of Marcuse (1965), and on Sagarin's (1973) application of Marcuse's work. Both contend that, given the vast inequalities of status and power in modern society, quite different approaches are justified in dealing with those at the top and those at the bottom. See also Becker (1967).

6. This argument draws not only on anarchist strategies, but on Sjoberg and Miller's (1973: 139) contention that researchers must work the momentary breaches and gaps in otherwise impenetrable structures of power. See Ferrell (1993) for more on the Denver incidents.

7. Or, as Earl Kelley (1962) argued some thirty years ago,

Our young people are all right when we get them. If all is not well with them, it is due to what has happened to them in an adult-managed world. . . . Let us try: Acceptance of all of our young as worthy, valuable, uniquely blessed with some gifts. . . . Involving youth in what is to be undertaken. . . . Cooperation and democracy in the place of authoritarianism.

For more on the politics of youth, see, for example, Cohen (1972/1980), Hall and Jefferson (1976), Greenberg (1977), Hebdige (1979), Brake (1980), Schwendinger and Schwendinger (1985). Pepinsky and Jesilow (1984: 139) note that youthful energy is often reacted to as "pathological."

Interestingly, criminologists who argue that youth and crime are highly correlated often fail to see the construction of this correlation by (old) authorities. And given this politics of youth, it seems clear that youth must be considered a social/political category along the lines of gender, class, and ethnicity.

8. For a sense of the rediscovery of cultural concerns in sociology, see, for example, R. A. Peterson (1990), Becker and McCall (1990). Angela McRobbie's work (see, for example, 1980, 1986, 1989) offers a remarkable blend of feminist, postmodern, and cultural studies perspectives on these issues. For other British cultural studies and postmodern perspectives, see, for example, Cohen (1972/1980), Hall and Jefferson (1976), Hebdige (1979), Foster (1985), and Chambers (1986). The work of the Frankfurt School, of course, laid much of the groundwork for any politics of culture.

9. Rape stands as an example of a crime where any trace of political resistance or rebellion on the part of the perpetrator is obliterated by the crime's perpetuation of violent, hierarchical arrangements. Thus, for example, Eldridge Cleaver's (1968: 25–26) "insurrectionary" raping of white women "as a matter of principle" surely promoted not insurrection, but the continued domination of both women and ethnic minorities by white males—that is, the very "system of values" it was designed to violate.

10. Such forms of criminality seem, at the very least, to slip for a moment the constraints of capitalist consumption and legality, to violate the mandate that we "consume quietly and die." As Hunter Thompson (1966: 333) wrote in regard to the Hell's Angels,

they are reconciled to being losers. But instead of losing quietly, one by one, they have banded together with a mindless kind of loyalty and moved outside the framework, for good or ill.

...One night about halfway through one of their weekly meetings I thought of [Wobbly organizer] Joe Hill.... [The Angels'] reactions to the world they live in are rooted in the same kind of anarchic, para-legal sense of conviction that brought the armed wrath of the Establishment down on the Wobblies.

As the Left realists would remind us, paying attention to criminal events also means paying close attention to the actual, lived effects of these events on their victims. As we do so, though, we must distinguish between crimes against corporations and the state—shoplifting from chain stores, spraying graffiti on "public" property—and crimes that further victimize women, the poor, and other relatively powerless groups. Again, paying attention to the nuances of distinct criminal events—rather than, for example, lumping all acts of "theft" together—is critical. For more on the situated rationality of criminal events, see Katz (1988). And in this regard, Michel Foucault (in Simon, 1991: 31) tells the following story about Jean Genet's experience in prison:

just as Genet was about to be handcuffed to another prisoner, the latter asked the guard, "Who is this guy you're handcuffing me to?" and the guard replied: "It's a thief." The other prisoner stiffened at that point and said, "No, I'm a political prisoner, I'm a Communist, I won't be handcuffed with a thief." And Genet said to me that from that day on, with regard to all forms of political movements and actions that we have known in France, he has had not merely a distrust, but a certain contempt....

11. Shoplifting thus embodies both an immersion in commodity culture, and a misshapen but powerful resistance to its rules. But what if everyone shoplifted? Indeed, to what extent would systematic shoplifting constitute a collective resistance to capitalism? This sort of analysis thus moves beyond Robert K. Merton to consider the politics of deviant or criminal "innovation."

12. See Hebdige (1979), Atlanta and Alexander (1989), Ferrell (1991). Interestingly, in a discussion of people's remaking of mass culture into popular culture, Fiske (1991: 5–6) argues similarly that

one has to look for the origins of evasion or resistance in the specific social circumstances of those who do this remaking.... The main gain is pleasure and a sense of self-control, or at least control over some of the conditions of one's existence... popular pleasures are socially located and organized by the subordinate.... Popular pleasures are often much more located in the body, in the physical, they are much more vulgar.

13. This distaste for scheduling also creates problems in writers' doing paid "signpainting" for others. Becker (1963: 97, 117) likewise notes jazz musicians' nocturnal schedules as contributing to their deviant careers. See also Melbin (1987) on the conflicts between "nighttimers" and "daytimers."

14. Denver antigraffiti activists proudly announced to the 1990 Metro Wide Graffiti Summit that, with newly available equipment, they could remove graffiti far faster than writers could put it up (see Gottlieb, 1990: 6B).

15. Chalfant and Prigoff (1987: 10) also note the irony of graffiti's "imposition" on others in their discussion of "3D," a British graffiti writer:

To the objection that writers are forcing their art on a public that has had no say in the matter, 3D answers that people are quite powerless in any case to do anything about the esthetics of their surroundings: "In the city you don't get any say in what they build. You get some architect that does crappy glass buildings or gray buildings. No one comes up and says, 'We're building this, do you like it? Here's the drawings, we'll take a poll.' So why should I have to explain what I do? I live in the city, I am a citizen."

16. On the corporate control of "public" environments, see Schiller (1989). Pink, a female graffiti writer in New York City, says "Graffiti means 'I'm here'. . . . People think ghetto children should be seen and not heard, that we're supposed to be born and die in the ghetto. They want to snub us, but they can't" (Mizrahi, 1981: 20; see Atlanta and Alexander, 1989: 167–168).

9

Young People, Culture, and the Construction of Crime: Doing Wrong versus Doing Crime

MIKE PRESDEE

In the early 1990s, the spectacle of young people rioting on the streets of England had focused all sections of the community on the causes of crime. For example, in the summer of 1991 in Oxford and the North East of England, and most recently in the industrial city of Coventry, there were youth riots. At these times almost every conceivable theory was rehearsed, trotted out, and paraded around the country as possible explanations for the transgressions of youth, ranging from the then Home Secretary Kenneth Baker's statements that these were "evil crimes" committed by "evil people," to the Archbishop of Canterbury's view that poverty and inequality were substantial factors in youth crime. This debate has been mirrored in the United States after the spring 1992 Los Angeles riots, by then Vice-President Dan Quayle who clearly stated that the cause was "directly related to the breakdown of family structure, personal responsibility and social order" (*Manchester Guardian*, May 21, 1992). In other words, reflecting the moral crusaders of the nineteenth century, what we have in both England and the United States is a moral rather than economic problem. Within this sterile debate, both sides set about searching on the one hand for somebody who is not poor but riots, somebody who is poor but doesn't, and on the other hand that only the poor or dispossessed do.

The popular press, as always eager to promote the evilness of people as a central behavioral concept, have added their suggestions to future policy and show how they are still deeply embedded in hereditary concepts: "We sell contraceptives to the third world because the poor there cannot feed themselves. Perhaps we should just send food to them and *ship the condoms into our worst estates*" (*London Evening Standard*, September 12, 1991).

Criminologists too have taken up their positions along the structure/agency—civilized/savage—mind/nature continuum. Yet there has been little debate about how cultural practices might have been crucially important in the events of the summer of 1991 in England. Indeed it seems almost unbelievable that when one of the major problems has been the misuse of cars by young men, there has been no discussion about the cultural practices of working-class young men as they relate to space and the city, and no debate about masculinity; while in the offense of smashing into shops by using cars there has been no debate about the place of consumerism in British society. The theft of automobiles holds an appeal for young working-class men because of a culture that stems from their position in the class structure. The offense itself is in a sense "made necessary" by the inequalities of urban living such as the lack of transport, or even the lack of shelter of the homeless.

The act of so-called joyriding is aptly named, being rich in excitement and a dramatic break from the boredom of being wageless and wealthless in a consumer society. The skills needed to steal a car—which car to steal, how to gain entry, and how to start an engine without a key—all emanate from the culture of male working-class life (White, 1990). Even so, there has long been a respectable strand within criminology that has addressed the importance of the examination of cultural practices, discourses, and sites by developing more the idea of transgression, doing wrong, rather than simply doing crime (Foucault, 1977).

That is, it is not enough to equate only poverty and class with "official" crime, which effectively centers poverty as the main cause of crime. At the same time, however, we can observe that the structuring of criminal law around the cultural practices of specific groups makes being a member of that group a crime. So in that sense it becomes a crime to be working-class, young, and poor and therefore we should not be overly surprised to find that "official" criminal law is reflected in "official" criminal statistics. But if we make the object of our study the realm of cultural practices (or the personal resolution of structure and agency or of the savage and the civilized), then we can discard the notion of "doing crime" for the notion of "doing wrong," without in any way devaluing the effects of poverty.

Next we should examine, as Taylor has already begun to do, what effects the deregulation of economies, on a global scale, have had on populations who have suffered an increase in the regulation of their everyday lives (I. Taylor, 1990; White, 1990). Or as Katz (1988) has pointed out, it is rather the social economic situation (structure) that prepares the way, while sensuality (agency) creates the coup de grace. The end product in the 1990s has been an escalation of riots on the streets.

The task for criminologists is to mend the fracture of subject from society and examine how we both push to the limits our existing social behaviors, which in turn create new limits that allow for new social action, new orders, and, importantly, new disorders. As Foucault (1977) suggests, transgressions belong in a place where the question is the "limit" rather than the "identity" of a culture. It is these same limits that are pushed in the "edgework" discussed by Mugford and O'Malley (see their Chapter 10 in this volume) when analyzing the work of Lyng (1990).

At the heart of the process of pushing at the limits is the notion of resistance and challenge, and at the heart of challenge is excitement. If we put together the regulation of boundaries with the desire and excitement to break them, then we are left with an examination of the history of the creation of boundaries coupled with the emotion of desire. At this historical time we are confronted with a developed system of production, distribution, and consumption that relies almost entirely on a system of regulation over workers mixed with the desire to consume—what we might call the self-destructive cocktail of capitalism. This self-destruction is now being acted out on the streets by the youth of England (and the United States).

Under the imperatives of liberalism all emotions become repressed except for excitement. All, with the exception of tears, of the body's products become simply unmentionable in decent society (Greenblatt, 1982). Desire, excitement, and doing wrong become essential ingredients in a consumer, commodity culture. Like the nineteenth-century British fairs, which were thought to destroy the character of all who visited them, so the modern fair—the marketplace—becomes the site of transgression. It is the market-place that becomes a carnivalesque site of pleasure and, in the same way that the carnival has always been part of the celebration and calendar of systems of production and consumption, now it becomes a permanent and almost daily part of modern life. The carnival of consumption challenges the very system of commodity production and becomes an important site of doing wrong (Stallybrass and White, 1986).

THE SHOPPING CENTER

For young people the seductive world of commodities is often the world of their first transgressions. They correctly perceive a common desire to possess, to have, to consume. What they become aware of is the Veblian nature of conspicuous consumption "writ large." What Baudrillard (1988) described as style through acquisition, which instead of being applied only to the "leisured classes" can now be applied to all, irrespective of class or income. We are now what we consume. Consumption becomes a central cultural activity, which by its nature has a short shelf life and needs to be continually reproduced. We cannot consume only one day in twenty, we must consume, we must desire commodities all the time. New excitements and desires become an essential part of everyday life. Excitement under these conditions becomes a commodity to be bought, sold, and consumed like all other objects. And it is this excitement that is at the heart of disorder.

But a consumerism that neither satisfies the desire it perceptionally constructs nor satisfies the social situation of its participants is futile. Personal change as a result of consumerism is only perceived in terms of the importance that ownership carries. What it portends to offer the consumer is an escape from the realities of working life. But this escape—the comfort of the home, the car, video, television, and travel—is only ever momentary and dependent on the money available to participate in the images and dreams. This is indeed a culture that literally "plays at life" and where transgression, doing wrong, can become a leisure activity in itself. Not that leisure becomes a crime, but that crime itself takes on the characteristics of leisure. It is the challenge of the carnival that rears its head here.

For young people, especially the unemployed, there has been a continuing congregating within the modern shopping centers, the cathedrals of consumption (Presdee, 1985). At the mall—where desires are created and fulfilled and the production of commodities, the very activity from which the unemployed are barred, is itself celebrated on the altar of consumerism—young people push back the limits imposed upon them. In the big hyperstores of modernity we are faced with hyperspace and hyperconsumption. We become literally lost in space with no outside meaning (Jameson, 1984). Young people, cut off from normal consumer power, invade the space of those with consumer power. They have become the "space invaders" of the 1990s, lost in a world of dislocation and excitement; a space where they should not be. Modern consumerism demands that they look, touch, and take, or appropriate. This is a culture that plays at life, where the marketplace becomes like the pleasure pier of the seaside resorts, the site of pleasure, leisure, desire and, most important, a place for pushing back limits. It has all the characteristics of carnival: repugnance yet fascination; power, desire, and disorder; where all, irrespective of wealth or morality, join in a world upside down. But most of all it is a world of doing wrong. It would seem that what we experience, or need to experience, in a world based on mind and rationality is the coming closer to the realms of desire and excitement, which we must deny ourselves in a civilized rather than savage society. This is what Katz (1988) has described as the "delight of being deviant." It is a transient, ephemeral, yet sublime experience that, like all seductions, needs to be played with and experienced again and again. In this way carnival, popular dissent, and riot become part of the fabric of fun.

YOUNG PEOPLES' EXPLANATIONS OF DOING WRONG

During research, I've collected accounts of doing wrong by many young people (myself included). During early 1992 I specifically worked with two groups of young people. The first group was in a school in Ramsgate, England, and is unusual in that it has no children of professional families; it is totally working-class in composition (in an area of between 16 and 30 percent unemployment), where few of the young people leave school for permanent, well-paid work. Since 1980 there have been 232 children from this school reported for potential criminal offenses. The second group was the entire first-year intake of Occupational Therapists at Christ Church College undertaking a Bachelor of Science degree, almost all of whom have high levels of successful schooling and originate from predominantly middle-class families, or are in a process of upward mobility.

A similar task was given to both groups. They were asked to write, if they wanted to, about an episode where they did wrong, when they knew they were doing wrong. Apart from differences in spelling, grammar, and structure, the contents of the accounts were remarkably the same. There were no students, either from school or from college, who had not done something that they regarded as wrong. In almost all cases emotions were central to the process and the subjects' assessment was that what they had done was not criminal to them, even when they had come in contact with the criminal justice system. There was, importantly, no difference in the enormity of the crimes committed. Between them they ranged from truancy to shoplifting, joyriding to receiving stolen goods, from drug dealing to arson, and from fraud to harboring criminals. Indeed when the accounts were shuffled, the origins of the accounts could not be decided on content alone. The common ground was the ambivalent sense of excitement, and the promise of freedom to be found in the sublime experience of success. Excerpts from these accounts are from Presdee (1992).

On Stealing Time

I can't clearly remember all that I did, or that it was a particularly enjoyable alternative to school, only that I wasn't at school, I had escaped, I was free. Between the restrictions of home and the rules of school, this was my time, stolen time, when I would shout angrily and pointlessly at the big hawthorn hedges surrounding the playing fields near the railway lines. I would stand on the bridge and scream at the express trains as they passed underneath, their noise drowning out my desperation, silencing me, and for a moment I became invisible in the white smoke that engulfed me. In that moment I was free, nothing existed; I was no more. I always felt a tremendous relief after truanting as if all the tensions and anxiety of life had left me and I became calm again and able to rejoin the world of the clock.

Once the teacher was in full flow we crawled under the curtain. Once under the curtain you had a feeling of excitement, making you want to laugh. After going once you felt a sense of achievement . . . the kick from getting there and back [to the classroom] made you want to go more.

One morning me and my sister were walking down the road on the way to school and for some reason I ran away to the other end of the road and on to the shops in town. I didn't do anything there, I just wanted to get away from school.

Another time I sat in a tree all day—I was not going to school—I did not want to go to school. That's where I stayed—in a tree.

I skived down the market on a Friday afternoon. I left school happy. When I got down the market I felt as if everyone was watching me and I felt very nervous. I couldn't wait to get home. When I looked at my watch at 3:30 it gave me a great feeling that I had got away with it.

On Stealing Travel

We all had dodgy train tickets purchased off a friend who used to work for British Rail. We were very nervous but at the same time there was a sense of excitement. It was an exhausting journey emotionally.

We decided to stay on the train at Faversham and on to London and spent it in the toilet. I remember feeling afraid ... but wanting more than anything for the feeling of excitement to continue.

It was terrifying for me but not enough to want to stop ... it felt like near freedom for the first time.

On Stealing Objects

I made a conscious decision that on my next visit to the shops I would shoplift. I remember feeling sick in the shop and fumbling a bar of chocolate into my pocket. ... I can also remember the feeling that it was not really me doing the deed, but that instead I was simply looking down on the scene.

I stole a brown halter neck tee shirt top. Not only had I "done it" but what a prize! I felt ... very proud and pleased with myself.

I nicked a Mars bar and a Marathon bar. I felt scared and people walked past me. But when it was all over I felt great, that I could do it all over again! I felt brilliant!

I was short of money so I devised a way of taking some fags [cigarettes] from the supermarket where I worked. I knew what I was doing was wrong yet the thrill of working it out seemed to override the fear and the knowledge of the wrong. I actually managed to get away with it. ... I did enjoy doing the job and enjoyed telling some of my mates who thought it was great.

Somewhere, sometime, I started to steal; from my father, the paper shop, the church collection, Woolworths, Ron next door. Suddenly, it seemed, I was aware of "wanting" and of being "without" as advertising and consumerism began to be part of my life. ... I wanted to possess: to be a consumer, to own, to escape into the world of the object. Possessing was visual; everyone could see that you were what you owned—toys, clothes, school uniform, sports gear, food, even haircuts. ... Most of my newly acquired wealth went on food: chocolate bars, crisps, doughnuts, and presents for the family. I bought the things that families who had to have priorities should never be seen with, luxuries that you could consume without thinking, without guilt; the excesses of life that tell you that you have no need to have priorities; that you have an excess.

On Doing Wrong

I went into the students' union and was meant to pay £1 (one pound British) for a disco. I handed the girl a £5 note and she gave me 5 one pound coins back.... With slight excitement and anxiety I rushed into the disco.... After a few minutes when I realized that she wasn't going to find me I felt really happy that I had managed to get in free.

I decided I'd like to try it once (just smoking stuff)... when she got some gear... we set about finding a suitable spot. We decided on a common. She drove there and proceeded to give me a step-by-step lesson on how to skin up. People kept walking past and I was very conscious of the fact that I was about to indulge in something illegal.

I changed a C− on my report card to a C+... although I felt vaguely guilty afterwards.... I felt euphoric at having succeeded at the deception!

One subject, having been trusted to use a teacher's office, stole blu-tack from the teachers' desk to put up "distasteful" magazine cuttings. She could have asked for it and she was allowed in the office, but

as I did it the adrenalin began to flow, and a few seconds after I'd left I saw him go into the office. That only improved the thrill of it... the whole incident was just one big joke because I'd been so close to getting caught—and he carried on trusting and respecting me.

And on an illicit affair:

It was a secret relationship. It was exciting to be living a secret life.... It was the excitement of the "secret" that gave us energy... we both knew it was wrong.... I knew it was wrong from the beginning but the realization of that gave it the excitement for me to try for more.

These accounts of doing wrong show a sensitive reflection on the processes involved. Indeed in most cases they are very vivid accounts, complex stories remembered down to minute details. These are important happenings in their lives. Although in many cases they are legal transgressions, they are, for the subjects, connected with freedom and an escape into the realms of unrealness. The driving force is excitement, the notion of guilt heightens the sensations, and pushing to the limits provides the thrill. In many of these accounts the sensations that are consumed emanate from the "soil of everyday life" (Lefebvre, 1971) and the episodes take on the appearance of entertainment, of the carnival.

Indeed, while Britain continues to debate the horrors of estate violence, young people continue to enjoy the media's version of real crime as entertainment. By now, we are used to enjoying television programs that look at real everyday crimes and ask us to help solve them. "Crime Watch" is one U.K. program that rates highly. However, BBC's Radio One breakfast show has turned this on its head and, through the Simon Mayo show, asks listeners to send in stories of things they have done wrong. If the "posse" likes them you get forgiven, if not you may still get a "true confessions" book. Here "doing wrong" becomes the entertainment. In less than one year, Simon Mayo has had over 5,000 confessions. Of those that are actually broadcast, arson, divorce, torture, cruelty, infidelity, and obscenity are just some of the topics that have been covered (Mayo, 1991). "Imagine what gets thrown out!"

During the 1992 Olympics, Britain's athletes were invited to make their own "confessions," which predictably involved events such as throwing bricks through pub windows rather than drug abuse. After only a short period of listening to the program, the wrongdoings mount up. Misuse of computer information, reckless driving, assault, fraud—all events that could easily be classified as crimes. Yet here in this medium they are entertainment, experiences that excite, that we can all relate to. No longer is the actor needed to produce fiction. Here is real crime, to enjoy and laugh along with. Of the people who questioned his motivation, Mayo (1991) simply stated: "Actually I told them...I fear all we are doing is having fun."

The grotesque of the carnival reasserts itself and is made available to all groups, all ages, and all classes through the public airwaves—a veritable carnival of the air. There is then a price that has been paid, across society, for the ever-increasing regulatory process that is held over and against people that masquerades as the civilizing process—that is, the loss of emotions. Now in an historical period that needs to create, as an integral part of its economic organizations, desire and excitement on a huge scale, we become again acquainted with what we were previously denied—public forms of passion. The quest for happiness now becomes the general state. We can only achieve happiness and freedom through excitement. Doing wrong can produce for us, "at no cost," that same transient feeling.

For the debate in the United Kingdom to move forward, young people's common culture will need to be once again reevaluated. Young people's common culture involves the way they invest with meaning both their spaces and social practices. The creation of culture is essential to the very survival of their identity. It is, and involves, what Willis (1990) calls necessary work. Young people are involved in the daily remaking of their world through their culture. Their cultural practices are predicated on the production and pursuit of pleasure and excitement. These parts of their common culture have been appropriated and commodified and the "best things in life" are no longer free:

I did wrong, right from the start. There at the start, when rules are first brought to bear on us, and we start to learn about control; who the controllers are and what's being controlled. The first lesson was in how to control ourselves; how to control our bodily functions; how to use a potty and when; bringing together both a sense of time and place. Just after meals—last thing at night—once a day. "A time and place for everything." This early form of self-oppression was something I never really conquered until I was ten.

Those policymakers in charge of our cities are going in the wrong direction if they see the course of modern disorder embedded in moral degeneration. In the postmodern city, excitement and meaningless dissent may well be an integral part of a consumer culture that both releases and relies on an emotion it cannot survive without. The postmodern city may ultimately contain the seeds of its own destruction.

10

Crime, Excitement, and Modernity

PAT O'MALLEY AND STEPHEN MUGFORD

This chapter explores aspects of the relationship between criminal action and emotional states—in particular, extreme emotional feelings such as excitement. It takes seriously the need to rescue agency in the explanation of criminal action by providing a phenomenological account of the moral, sensual, and emotional attractions of crime (rather than assuming a narrowly rational choice approach), without merely reverting to the limited models provided by interactionism and labeling theory during the 1960s and early 1970s. Accordingly, this chapter will commence with an analysis of the elements of Jack Katz's account of moral transcendence, and of related theorizing. From this springboard we will consider the implications of situating Katz's account within a broader historical context.

Katz's *The Seductions of Crime: The Moral and Sensual Attractions of Doing Evil* (1988) has struck a very responsive chord among criminologists and sociologists of deviance. Perhaps, as exemplified by Goode (1990; see also Newman, 1990), much of this response could be attributed to the hope that here might be the foundations for a novel paradigm to enliven a field that has seen better days. Perhaps also it is the Nietzschian character of the work that renders it compatible with currently popular postmodern, anti-materialist theorizing. Certainly, Katz manifests considerable hostility toward simplistic materialisms (although his wrath is reserved for Mertonian rather than Marxist versions), and it is clear that the realm of subjective experience—moral, emotional, and sensual—is where he locates the crucial foundations for understanding crime. Thus, in discussing the array of crimes with which the book is to be concerned, from petty pilfering through the violence of "street elites" to "righteous slaughter"—Katz argues that "central to all these experiences in deviance is a member of the family of moral emotions: humiliation, righteousness, arrogance, ridicule, cynicism, defilement, and vengeance. In each the attraction that proves to be most fundamentally compelling is that of overcoming a personal challenge to moral-not-material existence" (p. 9).

As will be made clear later in this chapter, Katz is not denying the importance of the material order. Rather his intention is to understand the complex ways in which material existence is related to criminal action via human experience. His rejection of Mertonian strain theory, for example, is directed primarily at its failure to link background to action via an understanding of the criminal experience. Indeed, most criminology either ignores this linkage, leaving a "black box" in the center of the enterprise, or by default provides a simplistic rational choice theory that in Katz's view can explain none of the vitality, emotionality, and excitement so evident in much criminal action. Moreover, Katz argues that attention paid to the experiential level often renders established structural accounts implausible. Thus in relation to his analysis of the offenses committed by non-Anglo "street elites," Katz argues that although these groups are usually found in working-class and slum areas, it is not anomie or urban poverty that generate crimes of this kind. Rather, when attention is paid to emotional and moral dimensions, what emerges as crucial is the experience of humiliation in this specific social "structural" context, the vital feature of which is the existence "in the generational background, of a culture humbled at the prospect of entering modern, rationalized society . . . this humbled background, by way of juxtaposition, elicits and makes sense of the postures of arrogant domination" (Katz, 1988: 12).

As this passage begins to suggest, Katz not only is arguing that rational choice models are inappropriate for explaining much crime, but that other forms of experience provide models more in keeping with the vitality of criminal offenders. He is also making the claim that much crime is to be understood as an array of reactions against mundane, secular rationality and against the (especially modern) forms of social setting in which they are inextricably implicated. But here we move slightly ahead of our argument, for we wish later to claim that these observations require a close attention to historicity, which is not fully developed in *The Seductions of Crime*, nor in the work of those such as Lyng (1990) who have recently begun to explore similar models with respect to leisure pursuits. Before moving on to these matters we must first map out the elements of Katz's "theory of moral self-transcendence," which is intended to displace the "black box" and rational choice theory as the phenomenological mainspring of much criminality.

CRIME, RATIONALITY, AND TRANSCENDENCE

As the passage quoted earlier indicates, the attraction or seduction of crime is to be understood at the emotional or moral level, rather than as seduction by merely sensational or material pleasures. In many contexts the seductiveness of criminal action is that it provides relief or escape in emotionally critical situations. Consider in this respect Katz's (pp. 312–313) discussion of the central role of humiliation in the array of crimes his work considers:

Running across these experiences of criminality is a process juxtaposed in one manner or another against humiliation. In committing a righteous slaughter, the impassioned assailant takes humiliation and turns it into rage. . . . The badass, with searing purposiveness, tries to scare humiliation off; . . . young vandals and shoplifters innovate games with risks of humiliation, running along the edge of shame for its exciting reverberations. Fashioned as street elites, young men square off against the increasingly humiliating social restrictions of childhood by mythologizing differences with other groups of young men.

Each of these reactions is understood by Katz to involve the process of moral transcendence as a means of resolving an intolerable moral condition. The seduction of crime for the impassioned killer, for example, appears in the sense that the killer is unable to imagine the possibility of moving out of the immediate situation back to his or her ordinary mundane relationships with any degree of self-respect. In order to transcend this situation, the would-be killer, through the practice of "righteous slaughter," leaps at the opportunity to embody some everlasting, universal form of good (p. 314). How then is the transcendent experience generated?

Transcendence appears to involve crossing (or at the very least "playing with") a threshold or limit between being in and out of rational control in order to experience the self in the grip of emotional or moral forces. These emotional states involve experiences unavailable to the rational consciousness in the mundane world and that therefore register as extraordinary their emotional intensity providing, literally, an excitement of experience similar in kind with those cathartic episodes often associated with religious, sexual, or deviant experiences.

Yet because rationality cannot overcome itself, it is reliant on the manipulation of the material or social environment to generate the conditions for excitement. In a sense, rationality manages situations in order to generate mood-changing states, thereby to effect changes in the balance of rational and emotional control. Thus the transcendent process is closely related to issues of control and loss of control, and to the pleasures that are thereby generated, the pleasures that are an essential part of seduction. This may be made a little more clear by examining Katz's claim that rage is one of the key emotional vehicles that transports the individual from the experience of humiliation into criminal action. To begin with, humiliation is constructed as a painful awareness of a mundane future; a keenly sensitive awareness that once I extricate myself from the present situation, I will still not be able to escape the degradation.

The mundane and the degrading cue in the experience of humiliation and among the array of responses are righteousness and rage. These are plausible responses to humiliation precisely because they provide "a blindness to the temporal boundaries of existence," they take us out of time, and thus they provide an escape from the sociotemporal trap of humiliation: "rage is mercifully blind to the future" because it "focuses consciousness on the here and now" (pp. 30–31). This is rage's transcendence and its seduction: it is "soothing" and a "great comfort." Katz maintains that rage moves toward the experience of time suspended, and that this is the "spiritual beauty of rage."

In this transcendence of time is also to be found the "deaf," "blind," and "inarticulate" transcendence of reason, as rage blots out all other experience including the experiences basic to calculative rationality. Rage is "sophisticated incompetence . . . deaf in the sense of being indifferent to reasoned argument" (pp. 30–31). This also is a feature of related reactions to humiliation such as emerge in the ways of the "badass" and "street elites." Thus the "ultimate source of the seductive fascination with being a badass is that of transcending rationality," a state achieved by the badass because he "threatens to dominate all experience, stimulating a focus of consciousness so intense as to obliterate experientially or to transcend any awareness of boundaries between the situation 'here' and any other situation 'there.' "

In one way or another, all of Katz's actors are involved in the same project, albeit that their situations and solutions vary greatly. In all cases, emotionality is managed in order to resist or evade the consequences of confronting an intolerable situation generated by a confrontation with rationality, understood as "the modern moral competence to adjust the self to situationally specific expectations"(p. 112). Even in the most trivial of the crimes Katz investigates, in which the transports of rage and indignation are not present, he sees individuals who refuse to come to terms with the expectations implicit in mundane rationality. In considering "sneaky thrills" (most especially shoplifting), the key conception of transcendence is related to the attempt to overcome, rather than come to terms with, the boredom endemic to the routine nature of modern life. Shoplifting creates transcendence through "the emotional power of this thrill" (p. 77), itself generated by flirtation with the risk of humiliation in detection and capture. But what is the transcendent nature of the thrill? Katz argues that it lies in the fundamental differences between experience in worldly activities and in various alternative "worlds," including, for example, films, dreams, jokes, laughter, and so on. Experience in the mundane worlds of practical reality is also confined by time, space, and social boundaries. Dreams, fantasies, and similar experiences do not defer to such limitations. Thus for Katz (p. 77) the parallel is drawn between the dreamer who "suspends the focus of his consciousness on the historical time and the geopolitical space he is in, and the socially bounded process of sleeping and dreaming that he is going through."

In short, whether we are considering major or minor crimes in Katz's theory, the key is the process of transcendence. Its seductive power is in the contrast between an intolerable mundane reality in which the actors find themselves, and the altered state of consciousness produced by moving up to, flirting with, and sometimes crossing the boundaries between rational and emotional control, between order and chaos.

EDGEWORK: CONTROL, PLEASURE, AND CONSCIOUSNESS

Parallels between Katz's discussion of the seductions of crime and Lyng's (1990) recent work exploring the concept of "edgework" invite close comparisons. Edgework activities

involve a clearly observable threat to one's physical or mental well-being or one's sense of an ordered existence. The archetypal edgework experience is one in which the individual's failure to meet the challenge at hand will result in death or at the very least debilitating injury...[involving] the ability to maintain control over a situation that verges on complete chaos, a situation most people would regard as entirely uncontrollable (Lyng, 1990: 858–859).

Now the first thing to note is that Lyng's individuals keep in control whereas some of Katz's conditions (e.g., rage) involve a contrived loss of control. Edgework involves "the commitment to get as close as possible to the edge without going over it" (Lyng, 1990: 862). Also in apparent contrast to the more extreme of Katz criminals, who seek passionate transcendence through the deliberate subordination of the self to objective forces, "participants in virtually all types of edgework claim that the experience produces a sense of 'self-realization', 'self actualization', or 'self determination' " (p. 860). The badass on the other hand seeks a managed loss of control for "the person most fearsomely beyond social control is the one who does not appear quite in control of himself because his soul is rooted in what to us is chaos" (Katz, 1988: 261).

Initially, then, there appear to be quite major differences, especially when contrasting edgeworkers with criminals driven by rage (although, as we have seen, even the more "evil" of Katz's criminals still are seen as "playing with the line" between control and loss of control). Nevertheless, there are many parallels. As with Katz's work, there is in Lyng's a great stress on the emotionality involved and on its key role in producing altered consciousness. Moreover, both Katz's and Lyng's actors are attempting to subject themselves to extreme experiences in order to generate mood changes as a form of resistance or escape from the mundane. Thus, for example, initially the strongest feeling in edgework is fear, "but as one moves to the final phases of the experience, fear gives way to a sense of exhilaration and omnipotence" (Lyng, 1990: 860). As with Katz's criminals, the stress for Lyng is the edgeworkers' transcending of the mundane time/space context: "as they approach the edge . . . edgeworkers not only are oblivious to extraneous environmental factors, but they also lose their ability to gauge the passage of time in the usual fashion" (p. 861).

Likewise a common report is "the sense of the edgework experience as a kind of 'hyper reality' . . . more real than the circumstances of day-to-day existence" (p. 861). It seems that edgeworkers don't seek to immerse themselves in chaos in the way of the badass, however, for "what they seek is the chance to exercise skill in negotiating a challenge rather than turn their fate over to the role of the dice" (p. 863). But it is nevertheless the emotional experiences produced at the *edge* of chaos that they seek. "Edgework involves the extreme state . . . [of] 'anxiety-producing chaos.' "

Thus it would appear that we arrive at two closely related accounts of transcendental experiences. The experiences and actions can be thought of as existing at the extremes of a continuum. The continuum expresses a range of techniques for the production of passionate experience: of consciousness-alteration generated by extreme emotional experiences. At one end of the continuum, lying close to the world of mundane, bourgeois rationality, are Katz's sneaky thrill-seekers. These seek to escape the mundane order of things by exposing themselves to risk of humiliation. Next along the line are the street elites who court danger and trouble to transcend their structurally induced humiliation; further along still lie Lyng's edgeworkers who expose themselves to risk of death and injury. All of these attempt to manage such situations in order to stimulate emotional reactions through the *achievement* of control at the limits of (physical or social) survival. The badass and righteous murderer appear at the distant pole of the continuum, "over" the edge in a managed transcendence into chaos.

Even so, sneaky thrill-seekers, edgeworkers, and badass robbers all share a refusal of the mundane, rational, calculative world and seek to escape through a *joy in survival* whether at the edge of chaos or, like the badass, deep in its bosom. In this respect we might well feel that what ties these people together is more important than what differentiates them.

To the extent that this is true, Katz's Nietzschean fascination with evil, with the moral superman, places too narrow constraints upon analysis. What "evildoers" have in common with morally and legally legitimate edgeworkers is that they sweep aside the rational constraints of modern Western culture in order to achieve emotional transcendence via the effects of strong (moral, emotional, and sensual) sensations. The aim of Katz's criminals is "to transcend the control of the system" (1988: 231). Lyng (1990: 878) likewise explores the implication that it is the mundane order of modern alienation that is the trigger to his edgeworkers:

The experience of self in edgework, then, is the direct antithesis of that under conditions of alienation and reification. If life under such circumstances leads to an oversocialized self in which numerous institutional "me's" are present but ego is absent, ego calls out the anarchic self. Simply put, people feel self-actualized when they experience a sense of direct personal authorship in their actions, when their behavior is not coerced by the normative or structural constraints of their social environment.

The parallels between Katz and Lyng may be stronger than their differences, raising a pertinent question about Katz's work: namely, to what extent is his work a theory of crime *as* crime? We suggest (and the suggestion informs much of what we say below) that his work is read best as a general account of the attractions of exciting and transcending activity, focused down to explain particular types of crime. That is, the transcendent characteristics of the acts are more crucial than their criminality (see Stallybrass and White, 1986).

Emotions, the Self, and the Modern World

Katz's analysis suggests that the seductions of crime are less to do with "pleasure" in any simple sense of enjoyment than with emotionality, with thanatos as much as with eros. Lyng likewise is concerned with eros and thanatos, with the powerful, exciting sensations generated by fear and a consciousness of chaos. While both writers clearly are intrigued by the seductive powers of negative emotional states, they tend to accept the pursuit of pleasure (in this sense of seeking strong sensations) as a given, transhistorical characteristic of humans. Put simply, when writers like Katz or Lyng deal with transcendence, they already presume that there is something to be transcended, whatever the motivation for that transcendence may be.

What then is transcended? In broad terms, the answer is straightforward: it is the division, central to modern culture, between body and mind, emotion and reason, chaos and order. Further, it is the privileging of mind, reason, and order over body, emotion, and chaos. The question that follows is fairly obvious. Is this division between two polar opposites a feature of all social orders, or is it possible that it arises only in historically specific contexts? Katz and Lyng are both aware that the answer must be the latter, yet they frequently overlook this and reason as if the process of transcendence were ubiquitous to the human condition. Our view tends to emphasize much more strongly the historical location of the division and the explanation of how the division is best understood. One distinct possibility, as Colin Campbell (1983, 1987) argues, is that its foundations emerge out of the nineteenth-century Romantic reaction against the routine, oppressive, and materialist nature of modern industrial existence.

Romanticism centered upon an immanentist doctrine of the individual as an infinite reservoir of possibilities constrained by social fetters, and linked this to an antirational conception of experiential knowledge—for example, of "feeling as a way of knowing" (Campbell, 1983: 286–287). Out of this, Campbell (p. 287) suggests that

> what Romantics did was to redefine the doctrine of individualism and the associated idea of improvement or advancement. Instead of individuals improving themselves in this world through hard work, discipline and self-denial they substituted the idea of individuals "expressing" or "realizing" themselves through exposure to powerful feelings and by means of many and varied intense experiences. . . . the self is conceived of as an immanent indwelling spirit, identified with powerful feelings and imaginings, such a spirit requires expression through release and the overthrow of constraints, necessarily imposing as a duty the pursuit of exciting, pleasurable and stimulating experiences.

In this account we see many of the ideas worked upon by Lyng and Katz. Most especially we see the dialectics of rational consciousness and emotional control, and the relationship of these to the conception of an inner self-yearning to be realized or released from a constraining mundane reality by emotionally transcendent experience. With this in mind, it would appear that the perceptions of Katz's and Lyng's subjects (or at least those authors' interpretations of them) express a Romantic theory of human nature that has a very definite historical biography. But Campbell (1987: 60–73) has more to offer our understanding of Lyng's and Katz's work, for he suggests that, corresponding to the above doctrine, Romanticism constructed a specifically modern form of hedonism.

First, it is argued that the modern form of hedonism primarily involves emotional rather than (as in premodern hedonism) physical sensations. The particular attraction of emotion is that it "produces a range of physiological changes in human beings which for sheer stimulative power generally exceed anything generated by sensory experience alone" (Campbell, 1987: 70). It is for this reason also that for Katz emotional transcendence ultimately is "seductive," and why (as noted earlier) the seduction of emotionality is distinct from simplistic conceptions of pleasure as associated only with positive sensations and emotions. As Campbell argues (1987: 70), and an interesting parallel may be drawn with Barthes (1972), it is

> certainly not the case that some emotions, such as gratitude or love, are pleasant, while others, such as grief or fear, are not, for there are no emotions from which pleasure cannot be obtained. Indeed, since the so-called "negative" emotions often

evoke stronger feelings than others, they actually provide a greater potential for pleasure.

In turn, in the Romantic view, if individuals are to achieve self "realization" through powerful feelings, then they must cultivate a capacity for emotional control,

by which is meant not simply self-discipline, but rather a capacity for the deliberate cultivation of an emotion, especially in the absence of any "naturally occurring" stimulus, and although this is in part a corollary of the power to suppress feeling, it also transcends it (Campbell, 1987: 71).

Evidently we are looking at processes that also are at the heart of the transcendent projects investigated by Katz and Lyng, but Campbell suggests that this idea of controlled emotionality is specifically modern. Campbell (1987: 73) points out that "it is typically the case that in pre-modern cultures emotions are seen as inherent in aspects of reality, from whence they exert their influence over humans." The idea of humans managing their emotionality emerges with what Max Weber described as the disenchantment of the world. For Campbell (1987: 72),

a significant corollary of disenchantment was the accompanying process of de-emotionalization such that the environment was no longer seen as the primary source of feelings but as a "neutral" sphere governed by impersonal laws which . . . did not, in themselves, determine feelings. A natural consequence of this fundamental shift in world-view was that emotions were re-located within individuals, as states which emanated from some internal source.

Thought of in slightly different terminology, it is clear also that the separation of reason from emotion, the identification of the former with the intellect and the latter with the body (carnality) was a crucial element of the Enlightenment project. Stephen Toulmin (1990: 114–116), for example, takes as one of the key assumptions that formed the modern world-view the identification of emotions as being within the body, and therefore as base and to be subordinated to reason. Culturally constructed in this fashion, emotions become controllable or manageable. Indeed, the idea is that they must be controlled, "individual human beings were expected to execute their life projects without letting themselves be 'carried away' by their feelings" (Toulmin, 1990: 163). Simultaneously, this aspect of the emergence of modernity brought into being both the expectations against which Katz's criminals react (rational management of the self) and at the same time clarified the cultural alternative. Reason became calculative reason, and while the emotions were thus to become beyond reason or outside of reason, they were all that is not calculative (the resonance with Katz's account here is deafening). Resistances and reactions henceforward are always likely to be shaped by this very fact. Once reason has been delineated and established as real, then both what is being escaped from and "where" the escape will be to are already discursively structured. Katz's people are not original innovators of experience, they escape down a track created for them by modernity, pioneered by the Romantics. We are now perhaps in a better position to locate the historicity of Katz's and Lyng's theory, although we will elaborate the matter further in the latter part of this chapter.

We may locate the process of transcendence as peculiarly modern for three specific reasons. First, as Katz and Lyng frequently suggest, the disenchantment of the modern world generates the routinized, despiritualized world of calculative rationality, and an attendant order of time, space, and sociality to which Romanticism, edgework, and crime (of the kind discussed by Katz) are transcendent responses. Second is that this same process separated out a world of the emotions, and delineated in such a fashion that it appears (to actors) as the natural "alternative," the "other," to be resorted to by those seeking to escape from, to resist, or to transcend mundane, modern rationality. Third, the cultural conditions for controlling the emotions in the fashion implied by Katz did not always exist, but are themselves of comparatively recent construction, These, too, emerge out of the disenchantment of the modern, rationalized age, a disenchantment expressed forcefully by the Romantic movement. They assume a culturally specific model of emotional and personal transformation that may not have been available in the premodern era. Moral transcendence begins to appear, ironically, both as necessitated and made possible by the conditions of modernity. Yet this account, and especially aspects of it based on Campbell, is not without its problems for our analysis. Can we accept that control of the emotions is peculiarly modern, that premodern people were not in some way in control of their emotions, or that control of emotions follows automatically from the disenchantment of the world? We might also ask how far there is a (dis)continuity between the "self" of the premodern and the modern ages.

Civilizing the Self and Its Consequences

It has been suggested that in Katz's account, "moral self-transcendence" as a phenomenological process in the modern world is a response to the specific collision between actors' sense of themselves and mundane rationality, understood as the cultural expectations of a modern moral competence to adjust the self to situationally specific expectations. In response to this our line of thinking leads to a simple question: Was premodern life different in this respect? One answer may be found in Norbert Elias' (1982) investigations into the "civilizing" process.

Elias' work allows us to proceed with a very important question explicitly recognized by Katz: namely, how far is the kind of moral self-transcendence that is the core of his theory something that is only conceivable for the modern self? To put this very crudely, Elias' work suggests that confronted by humiliation, the medieval person may very well have reacted with slaughter, violence, and rage, but without involving him or herself in a process of moral self-transcendence. Similar behavioral reactions to humiliation, boredom, and so on may have involved a different set of experiences and "mental" operations, for in Elias' view the civilizing process involves processes that direct the psychological predisposition of individuals away from what would now be thought of as "excesses" of rage, anger, violence, swings of mood, and extremes of action.

Elias suggests that as societies become more functionally differentiated, and as physical violence is increasingly monopolized by central powers, networks of peaceful interdependence expand their coverage and close their mesh. In such contexts, as Durkheim might agree, integration restrains individuals:

The more threatened is the social existence of the individual who gives way to spontaneous impulses and emotions, the greater is the social advantage of those able to moderate their affects, and the more strongly is each individual constrained from an early age to take account of the effects of his own or other people's actions on a whole series of links on the social chain (Elias, 1982: 236).

The result is the rational, mundane order that provides the boundaries that Katz's actors seek to transcend, that provides the social expectation that individuals should monitor and calibrate their actions to suit the conditions rather than "allowing" free rein to passion. This emerging social environment forces people "to restrain their own violence through foresight or reflection; in other words it imposes on people a greater or lesser degree of self-control or more precisely "a more *dispassionate* social control" (Elias, 1982: 239, emphasis added). More than this, the civilizing process is argued to produce such rationality in conjunction with many other rationalities that now tend to be taken for granted. The "moderation of spontaneous emotions, the tempering of affects, the extension of mental space beyond the moment into the past and future, the habit of connecting events in terms of chains of cause and effect" are all taken by Elias to be aspects of the same transformation of conduct that emerges with the two key aspects of modernity—the monopolization of physical violence, and lengthening of the chains of social action and interdependence (Elias, 1982: 237).

In this we see the emergence of the rationality that Katz relates to moral transcendence, which creates both the moral crisis of the self and the necessity for a transcending project. Only in a society where there exist effective barriers to spontaneous expression of emotional extremes will a process of moral self-transcendence be called for. Moreover, Elias (p. 238) argues that the self in premodern situations will be distinctly different from the "modern self":

To the social structure of this [premodern] society with its extreme polarization, its continuous uncertainties, corresponds the structure of the individuals who form it and of their conduct. Just as in the relations between man and man danger arises more abruptly, the possibility of victory or liberation more suddenly and incalculably before the individual, so he is also thrown more frequently and directly between pleasure and pain.

Or again,

The personality . . . is incomparably more ready and accustomed to leap with un-diminishing intensity from one extreme to the other, and slight impressions, un-controllable associations are often enough to produce these immense fluctuations . . . [With civilization] . . . the fluctuations and affects do not disappear, but are mod-erated. The peaks and abysses are smaller, the changes less abrupt (p. 239).

In this new rationalized world, the individual must embark on the process of transcendence noted by Katz, because these bounds, not there in pre-modern society, have to be overcome. Moreover, as noted earlier, we must take note of a second possible explanation for some phenomena dealt with in Katz's work, and hinted at in his explanation. This second possibility concerns resistance and refusal.

If, as Elias argues, the "civilizing process" starts in particular locations (such as court society) and then spreads as social conditions favor it, it follows that at any one moment in time uncivilized behavior will be more prevalent—and hence the dominance of emotional control, of reason, and of calculation will be more obvious—in some social locations than others. The variation in civilization will be apparent by class, by gender, by place, and by race, with powerful groups and places (upper class, male, metro-politan, white) seeming more civilized than others (lower class, female, peripheral, black). Urban racial ghettoes, for example, may appear less civilized than rich, white suburbs. In such locations, we might suppose, the refusal to employ rationally controlled modes of behavior, to value instead expressivity and spontaneity, may be refusal from outside the dominant culture rather than an attempt at transcendence from within it.

Such reasoning is politically risky, for it appears to reconceptualize some behavior only at the cost of racism. Is not the next step, one might suppose, to begin explaining black music or success in sports as being due to a "natural sense of rhythm"? And does not this suggestion that some behavior is less civilized open up a justification of continued exploitation? Such charges are, however, constructed from within a modern discourse that is the true heir of the Enlightenment project. Privileging calculative reason above all else, it cannot but construe a reference to its opposite as an insult. If one prefers to argue, as we do, that different discourses, voices, and organizations are valid and equally meritorious to the dominant ones, the line of argument we propose neither insults the ghetto dweller nor provides any justification for denying those in the ghetto the citizenship rights they rarely receive. Our argument opens up the possibility that one may not need to explain certain types of action as merely relative, since the experience of some people may be that, not embroiled in mundane modernity, they have no alienation to transcend.

We do not suggest that this possibility should be pursued to the exclusion of transcendence. Rather, our concrete suggestions would be that the contradictory location of ghetto dwellers and others, partly in and partly out of modernity, would mean that both explanations bite, in complementary ways, on the phenomena to be explained. We also seek to avoid any latter-day romanticism about deviance. To begin moving to the opposite extreme, to praise the deviant for spontaneity and authenticity, risks the absurdities of earlier deviance theorists with their naive and romantic championing of deviant-as-class-hero. The specialist treatment that Elias offers us on this topic is thus enhanced if we widen our view to include other approaches, well-established in the sociological mainstream, which bear on the nature of modern selfhood. What we offer below, of course, is a schematic account of several well-known and interconnected themes, focused on the deceptively simple question, "What is it about modernity that makes excitement important to the self?"

Modernity, Excitement, and the Self

There are several competitors for an answer to our question that supplement the arguments about mind/body dualism and the growth of modern hedonism (Toulmin/Campbell), and about the changing nature of "civilization" (Elias). On close examination, these other approaches are more complementary than contradictory. Among the main additional candidates for explaining the dilemma of the modern self, and the way that excitement is relevant to that dilemma, are alienation, clock time, and commodification. Let us examine these in turn.

Alienation. In this context we refer to alienation in a fairly strict, Marxist sense rather than as a generalized sense of angst in modernity. By alienation we refer to that condition in which the sale of labor for wages alienates the seller from the labor process and from the product. In such circumstances, one can sensibly argue, the worker feels real only in and through leisure. Yet leisure is increasingly commodified and subject to what Simmel (1950) called neurasthenia. That is, each new thrill eventually palls, requiring therefore bigger and bigger thrills to excite the jaded palate. Hence, by a relatively simple route alienation can be connected to the search for excitement.

But this far from exhausts the bite of the concept on this topic, for alienation is not merely a general condition of the capital/wage labor nexus. New forms of alienation develop as the nature of labor changes. Central to our discussion here is the work of Hochschild (1983). Focusing in particular

on airline hostesses, Hochschild deals with the effects on workers and relations between workers and customers when the emotional expression of
the worker becomes not a resource unselfconsciously drawn upon in the
course of work but rather something that the company actively sells as a
commodity:

The emotion management that sustains the smile on Delta airlines competes with
the emotion management that upholds the smile on United and TWA. What was
once a private act of emotion management is sold now as labor in public-contact
jobs.

What was once a privately negotiated rule of feeling or display is now set by the
company's Standard Practices Division. Emotional exchanges that were once idiosyncratic and escapable are now standardized and unavoidable. Exchanges that were
rare in private life become common in commercial life.... All in all, a private emotional system has been subordinated to commercial logic, and it has been changed
by it.

It does not take capitalism to turn feelings into a commodity or to turn our capacity
for managing feelings into an instrument, and so it has organized it more efficiently
and pushed it further. And perhaps it does take a capitalist sort of incentive to
connect emotional labor to competition and advertise a "sincere" smile, train workers to produce such a smile, and then forge a link between this activity and corporate
profit (Hochschild, 1983: 185–186).

What follows from this "commercialization of human feeling"? Hochschild identifies three stances that workers adopt toward work, each with
an attendant risk. The first stance is when the worker identifies too strongly
with work, risking burnout. The second is when the worker clearly separates
herself from the job and avoids burnout, but here the risk is that she may
feel guilty for making this distinction and criticize herself for insincerity.
The third stance occurs when the worker separates herself from her act but
does not feel guilty, for her work seems to require a conscious performance
of roles. In the last case, the risk is estrangement and cynicism (Hochschild,
1983: 187). This type of alienation is increasing in modern society with its
greater emphasis on service occupations. When the problem of the "real
me" is not a problem only for the audience but also for the actor, we have
what has been called a crisis of authenticity:

To pursue authenticity as an ideal, as something that must be achieved, is to be self-
consciously paradoxical. But those who seek authenticity insist that this paradox is
built into the structure of the world they live in. This world, they say, represses,
alienates, divides, denies, destroys the self. To be oneself in such a world is not a
tautology but a *problem* (L. Berman, quoted in Hochschild, 1983: 190).

A connection of these processes to problems identified by Nietzsche and
to postmodernist writers ought also to be suggested at this point:

In *Spurs*, Derrida discerns in Nietzsche a metaphysics of appearance, in which Being only exists in and through its masks. On this view, there is no Being as such, no truth of man or indeed of woman. In reality as in Nietzsche's own text, there are only interpretations or "appearances." Baudrillard extends this idea of a world of appearances or simulacra into the realm of sociological description, arguing that the real has given way to the hyperreal, where the referents of previous culture and politics are maintained only in simulated form. *Everything takes place at the level of images, the only level remaining in the post modern world* (Patton, forthcoming: 2–3, emphasis added).

The hyperreality that Baudrillard (1983) identifies (and, in our view, somewhat exaggerates) can be seen as the institutional complement of the sense of alienation experienced as a result of modern work (although this is not the road that Baudrillard treads). The connection of these factors to our question about selves and motives should now be evident. As the crisis of self is accelerated by the process of commercializing human emotional labor and the real increasingly subverted by the hyperreal, a possible transcendent route for the individual lies in adopting pursuits that, by their excess and danger, stir powerful emotions that recreate and reassure oneself of oneself. At the same time, the subversive nature of the world of images should be noted, for there is always the possibility that the flight toward extreme behavior, especially criminal behavior, could be dimly connected (in the motivation of the actor) to the possibility that such action will create notoriety. For example, the well-known process by which soccer hooligans or street demonstrators in Northern Ireland increase their violence when TV cameras arrive suggests that a desire to see oneself on TV—that is, to live in the hyperreal world—adds to the excitement of deviant action, a perverse version of Andy Warhol's famous aphorism that in modern life everyone is (in)famous for fifteen minutes.

Clock Time. Closely connected to the type of alienation to which we have referred, but not absolutely reducible to it, is the issue of clock time and the artificial division of time between work and leisure. In modern life, time, as Giddens (1981) elaborates, becomes a commodity. The commodification of time means that time develops a "double existence," typical of every commodity. A more "natural" sense of time as lived experience is paralleled, in modern culture, by a sense of time as pure or "formless duration" and the latter sense comes to be seen as the more fundamental meaning of time. As Giddens emphasizes, in this respect, time is indeed like money, for it seems to be the measure (or value of) all things. Similarly, time is disconnected from the material existence, and appears as real and objective. Like money it is expressed in a universal and public mode and like money this appearance of objectivity is deceptive. The commodification of time is at the heart of major transformations of daily life, from the structure and experience of work to the organization of leisure and the private domain (Giddens, 1981: 130–131). There are many results of this transformation:

The major consequence, according to Eliade, is the "fall into time." No longer having the sense of living in a cyclical time, pertaining to the realm of the sacred, modern man finds himself alone, without his gods, confronted by the never-ending but final passing of time. The fall into time, says Eliade, begins with the desacralization of work; it is only in modern societies that man feels himself to be a prisoner of his environment, since he can no longer escape from time. And because he cannot "kill" time during his working hours—that is to say while he enjoys his true identity—he attempts to "get away from time" during his free time; *hence the stupefying number of forms of entertainment invented by modern civilizations. In other words the situation is precisely the opposite of that found in traditional societies where "entertainment" does not exist,* since any responsible task takes one "away from time" (Provonost, 1986: 9–10, emphasis added).

With the division of time comes the necessity to switch between times, a demand that is linked to the problems noted above by Hochschild. Gusfield (1987) and Mintz (1985) have both discussed time switches in relation to the consumption of alcohol and to tea and coffee drinking. Food and drink, especially drinks that contain psychotropic drugs, provide rapid transitions in mood state that at once parallel *and* symbolize the rapid transitions between work and leisure, production and consumption. This switching from one state to another, and the fact that biochemical assistance to such switching becomes intertwined with social rituals designed to promote it, is directly connected to the commodification of time and the process of desacralization described by Giddens and by Eliade. When time has a social unity, there is no work/leisure divide to cross either practically or psychically. In Dayak society, for example, religious observance, joking, chatter, eating, and drinking rice wine are all as much a part of working in the rice fields as are the labor activities themselves (Helliwell, 1990). In contemporary work sites, all of these sorts of activities are subject to social control attempts to eliminate them. Transcendence, then, is aided by consumption. And, of course, where drugs are concerned, the more powerful and exciting they are, the more rapidly and effectively they may effect the change of mood. A powerful illegal drug may achieve marked mood alterations and in doing so incorporates both a socially sanctioned method (commodity consumption) and a rebellious instance (illicit pleasure) that may enhance the excitement.

Since the experience of the self is intimately rooted in the sense of time, processes of commodification and desacralization have profound effects. Among them is the tendency to establish novelty and excitement, in the form of "entertainment," as routes to authenticity. Hence an examination of time offers a second answer to our question.

Commodification. We have already mentioned the impact of commercial life, but here we focus directly upon it. In a capitalist money economy there is a tendency for all areas of life to be drawn, progressively, into the commodity form. We have discussed the impact of this when the commodity is labor, but of course there are also effects on social relations caused by the creation, circulation, and sale of the myriad of inanimate commodities. Again, the contours of this process are well established, but there are some key points worth drawing out and Haug (1986) and Ewen (1988) offer germane analyses.

Haug draws particular attention to the fact that the development of a market introduces a radical and increasing separation between use value and exchange value as the majority of people enter one market as sellers only (of labor) and other markets as buyers only (of consumer goods). In such circumstances, the appearance of goods becomes the only way that their apparent value can be estimated, driving forward a process in which image and appearance gradually become the mainstays of commerce (the process that Baudrillard claims has gone much further still). Ewen deals with the way that the process of commodification has now resulted in a world in which style (its adoption, rejection, and so forth) has become a central feature of a modern consumerist culture:

In American society today—where "image management has become a lucrative business and a matter-of-fact necessity in commerce, industry, politics and inter-personal relationships—style has ripened into an intrinsic and influential form of *information*. In countless aspects of life, the powers of appearance have come to overshadow, or to shape, the way we comprehend matters of substance.... As a form of information (or dis-information) style places us on slippery and dangerous ground. Where style has become a visible world of memorable "facts," easily as appended to a facade to almost anything, it has emerged as a powerful element of what Herbert Marcuse once described as "the closing of the universe of discourse." As style increasingly becomes ubiquitous, other ways of knowing, alternative ways of seeing, become scarce.... Most notably, as the evanescent becomes increasingly "real," reality becomes increasingly evanescent (Ewen, 1988: 259–262).

Seabrook (1988) offers a glimpse of such struggles, of the attempt to invest meaning and excitement into a style of leisure and consumption, when he discusses the make-believe world of the Western cowboys where "Dusty and Jim," an otherwise prosaic English couple, spend as much time as they can:

We have to have the right clothes whichever group we belong to.... All our colors have to be right, no zips or buttons, just hooks and eyes. We get our inspirations from pictures, books in the library. We were at a Civil War wedding last weekend. [And she takes out a picture of an English country church, with the guard of honor dressed in Southern Civil War uniform, grey and red, with swords raised. The bride is in crinolines, with garlands looped around the hem of her dress.] *After that though, we have to come back to reality for a time. What is reality, though? It makes life very dull. We live for the next meeting, the next show.*

We call each other by our Western names. We're known as the Wild Bunch....

There's Vegas and Carolina, Palomino, Wishbone.... At the wedding last weekend, his name was Blue, hers was Belle. They never found out each other's real names until they came to get married—David and Sue. We travel in convoy to wherever the show is, communicate with other over the CB. *It makes life very exciting. The only trouble is, you have to come down to earth at the end of it* (Seabrook, 1988: 98–101, emphasis added).

Here, then, is another linked answer to our question. As commodification proceeds apace, the world becomes dominated by style, by appearance, by simulacra. In such a world, the self becomes swallowed in consumerism, but that consumerism is ultimately rather hollow and unsatisfying. The pursuit of selfhood may involve seeking liberation through consumption by indulging in more extreme forms of experience, but in so doing one risks mere conformity to a consumerist imperative. The three themes that we have dealt with in this section intersect with the earlier themes concerning hedonism and civilization, to produce the following, ironic dilemma. Within modern cultures there is a steady and increasing pressure toward emotionally exciting activities, including leisure activities, as a source of transcendence and authenticity with which to offset the suffocation of an overcontrolled, alienated existence within the mundane reality of modern life. Yet, precisely because of the success of the Enlightenment project in privileging reason over emotion, mind over body, and control over spontaneity, such activities are suspect even before they are engaged in. To abandon calculative rationality in modernity is intrinsically questionable and disreputable, which is why skydivers and others who execute edgework continually run the risk of being written off by mainstream culture as "crazy."

Excitement and Gender: Do Girls Just Want to Have Fun?

Before turning to our last task, connecting this line of reasoning to the question of how it impacts on criminology theory, we turn our attention to an issue previously touched on but not confronted—namely, the issue of gender. In a recent critique of Lyng, Miller (1991: 1531) suggests that his "examples throughout are of risky behaviors that are prototypically male: piloting experimental aircraft, mountain climbing, car racing, engaging in combat, and high stakes dealing in business." Miller goes on to outline how it is in her view that this uneven distribution of examples exemplifies a bias in the heart of Lyng's work. This is an important point, for most of the examples that Katz, too, draws upon are of crimes in which the distribution of offenses and of offenders is similarly skewed. Is it possible, then, that the theoretical enterprise of which our work is part is a partial account (applicable more to men than to women) masquerading as a general account for all people? We think not, and in claiming that make three major points. First, the core of Miller's critique is that Lyng concentrates too much on the world of work and its impact; on what we see as his productivism. What, she asks, of those who do not enter the world of paid work on a regular basis, a category that includes many women as well as both sexes among various racial and ethnic minorities? As to whether the critique applies fully to Lyng's argument we eschew comment here, but the general point that Miller makes must be almost incontrovertible. The gender insensitivity that was dominant until recently in disciplines like sociology, and which remains common today in the bastions of "hard" research, is traditionally connected to a strong productivist stance. This privileges some areas as central and important (work, the city, politics, social control, social stratification) while downplaying other areas as soft and peripheral (leisure, the home, family relations, child rearing). Nonetheless, our emphasis on consumption, on leisure, and activities that are frequently seen as "private" or "personal" removes us, we contend, from this productivist bias. For this reason the general processes of change that we discuss impact on the full range of people in our society, albeit with varied degree depending on their initial location within the social order.

The second point, concerning Miller's critique, is that she provides material that powerfully enhances our own argument (and which, incidentally, Lyng acknowledges and which, he suggests, expands the range of scope of the edgework concept rather than undermining it). Consider, for example, the following point:

These women [that Miller studied] engage in elaborate plans to ensure the success of their "missions," they speak of those who are successful in maneuvering the dangers of the streets and coming home unscathed as "having the wisdom," they attribute death or injury to the fact that the person in question "just didn't have it in her blood," and they ridicule "square girls" for not knowing what "putting one over" feels like. To be able to "push the edge" while high is an even greater rush, but those who cannot do so because they are too "strung out" are to be avoided (Miller, 1991: 1533).

What this (and other accounts of women's agentive activity in a variety of settings) reveals is that, despite dominant gender stereotypes, the attraction of excitement is not confined to one gender, even if some elements of the repertoire of excitement may be gender typed. Lyng (1991) clearly acknowledges in his response to Miller that women do seek excitement and that he intends his analysis to apply across gender (and class) lines, even if his own primary research work focused (not surprisingly) on groups to which he, as a white, middle-class man had access.

This brings us to the third point. We seek, in our general argument that expands on the thrust taken by Katz and Lyng, to identify a central set of processes leading toward a particular end point—that being the special status of excitement and emotional arousal in contemporary society. In developing this line of reasoning, we are explicit that the dynamics of those processes have different impacts on different categories of people, but that, overall, the general effect remains the same. Moreover, we see a strong trend toward a globalizing homogenization of culture, driven by the globalization of trading and production, of mass media links, and of consumer goods. As Mennell (1985) rightly argues in respect to foodstuffs, consumer patterns involve a decrease in *contrast* combined with an increase in *variety*. Our argument is that this trend is not confined to foods, but is characteristic of consumption and leisure pursuits generally.

It follows that, insofar as selfhood is constructed on the basis of consumption, the impact on gender roles will be, at least at some levels, toward "androgynous" repertoires. This is not to say that such androgyny is currently the dominant state of affairs. That would be absurd, and would ignore the extent to which conventional images of gender difference are emphasized in marketing some products. Rather it is to argue that this is the direction in which consumerism is taking us (see also Bryson, 1989). A wide variety of evidence, much of it still fragmentary or anecdotal, supports such a view. For example, F. M. Cancian's *Love in America* (1987) discusses the extent to which an androgynous model of interdependence is replacing older styles, concluding that instead of looking back to traditional gender roles or way ahead to the distant possibility of revolutionary change, we should recognize and cultivate this positive development in American styles of love. Some of the changes in this trend involve the "feminization" of traditional male roles, evident in discourse ranging from caring partners/fathers to the burgeoning market for male fashions and cosmetics. Others involve alterations in traditional female roles, including such diverse phenomena as advertisements that offer explicit instruction to female viewers as to how to gaze at male bodies in the open fashion that men have gazed at women, through to women choosing to engage in specifically male sporting pursuits because of the excitement. In short, on this third point we argue that while many of the examples that Katz and Lyng concentrate on are more masculine, the emphasis on excitement in modern culture involves both sexes, that despite double standards and the extra jeopardy that women face in sexual relations, increasingly the attitude that girls just want to have fun identifies a key element of women's motivations.

IMPLICATIONS FOR CRIMINOLOGY

Katz and Lyng are quite explicitly concerned with the late twentieth century and may take the historicity of their models as a side issue, so one may ask whether our attempt to locate their work in a wider historical context is important. We suggest that the significance of the arguments outlined above relates to realizing the promise of a phenomenological approach for providing new directions in theorizing about crimes and other social phenomena. As noted, other commentators have looked for this promise in Katz and come away disappointed, but we suggest that the work *does* provide the promise of new theoretical development. It does so not simply because of its insistence on the importance of a phenomenological understanding of crime, for this is nothing new. Rather, we suggest that its importance lies in the use of a contextualized phenomenology in order to locate deviant actions in specific forms of experience. In the exploration of transcendence, as we have tried to show in our reference to the work of Campbell and Elias, *Seductions of Crime* points the way toward linking criminal actions with novel ways of thinking and theorizing about taken-for-granted elements of social existence. For example, *pleasure* has appeared in traditional criminologies as a more or less "obvious" explanatory variable (Mugford and O'Malley, 1991). While criminologists may have exercised themselves over the question of why certain types of people are prone to a "short-run hedonism," the category and experience of pleasure upon which it is built appeared to need no investigation. Katz's work leads us to move beyond this superficiality. A phenomenology of pleasure may be linked to social and historical theories of pleasure, an area of considerable and radical development in recent years.

It should be made clear that we are not holding out any brief for the return of the naive or idealist phenomenologies of 1960s interactionism and labeling theory. While we entertain doubts about the Nietzschean undertones of Katz's work, nevertheless it does manifest a direct concern with the foundation of experience in material existence (without that implying any narrowly productivist framework). Such promise can be realized by connecting abstract general arguments to concrete matters of differential access to resources and experiences. As a consequence of the inequality of resources in society, some of the ways of transcending mundane life are more open to some groups of people than to others. Skydiving, for example, may offer a transcendent experience, but it is unlikely to be available to many young black members of the urban underclass. Crack, on the other hand, may provide a similarly transcending experience (which is only more "artificial" on a very narrow reading of artifice), but unlike skydiving is available to all, rich or poor. Moreover, the poor, perhaps more than any others in modernity, are faced with lives in which meaninglessness and the destruction of the self are ever-present possibilities. For this reason they have less to lose if they choose to prefer short-term (and relatively certain) pleasure and excitement over long-term (and uncertain) calculative rationality (compare Light, 1977). It is important to stress such points in order to avoid that type of pitfall identified by Ehrenreich (1989: 5), in which the experience of one class is conflated with the experience of all classes:

We are told, periodically, that "Americans" are becoming more self-involved, materialistic, spineless, or whatever when actually only a sub-group of Americans is meant: people who are more likely to be white collar professionals...than ma-chinists or sales clerks. Usually, this limitation goes without mention; for in our culture the...middle class is taken as a social norm...from which every other group...is ultimately a kind of deviation.

Here we come full circle, for the relevance of Katz to an historically contextualized phenomenology of the attractions of crime is seen at its fullest when linked with a Mertonian analysis of structured opportunity. As we noted at the outset, a close reading of Katz shows him to be hostile not to the Mertonian project, but to the Mertonian project devoid of those links that connect opportunity and meaning. In this way Katz bridges the gap between agency and structure, between a 1960s phenomenology that got excited about meanings of actions, but did so in an historical and structural vacuum, and that of mainstream criminology, which comprehended the structure of opportunity, but then slid, via a black box assumption, toward a premature closure of explanation.

Furthermore, when linked to a more historical perspective, a range of phenomena now becomes intelligible. For example, as Kellner (1990: 143) argues, "seduction is always evil...in the philosophical tradition, seduction is traditionally taken as the realm of artifice and appearance, versus that of nature and reality." We are now in a better position to locate the way that seduction and criminal activity intersect. The more that a world of emotion and excitement is set off against a mundane and controlled world of everyday work and responsibility, the more the promise of the former can be used to subvert the latter in a classically seductive way.

Indeed, it is at this point that we can recall the significance of transgression (Stallybrass and White, 1986). As these authors indicate, the more that there are efforts to map out a world of morality and permissibility and the more the impermissible is repressed, the more perversely attractive it becomes and the more that liminal zones (space-time locations where the impermissible occurs) become covertly valued and pursued. So it is that red-light districts, especially during the darker hours (compare Melbin, 1978) become places of disreputable pleasure in which otherwise reputable people dabble, reproducing the divisions that lie at the heart of modern culture while playing with the (moral) edge between them. And, of course, insofar as liminal zones are also places where minorities live, the very liminality enhances and sup-ports the way of life within a deviant context.

This raises the familiar point that the deviant and the reputable are inex-tricably intertwined, that the right side of the tracks can exist only in contrast to the wrong side of the tracks. And, in turn, that links to our earlier concern with how one explains motivations within, for example, urban, racial ghet-toes. To the complexities of resistance and transcendence we need to add the fact that certain modes of thinking, acting, and experiencing are differ-ently adapted to different locations. That is, if reputable society views as impermissible certain ways of being, the effect is not to remove those ways of being, but more usually to restrict their operation to moments of deviance and to liminal zones. To live in such a liminal zone is, therefore, to be exposed to the possibility that locally dominant modes of being are modes of "otherness," of deviance—defined, constructed, and cathected by the dominant and reputable groups. In such a case motivations toward action may include conformity to a local, liminal culture as much as transcendence or resistance. The modern, rational rejection of certain modes of thinking or acting, connected to the moral discourse of permissibility, provides the basis upon which we can construct ideas of seduction. Once one has defined as proper and normal the primacy of rationality and control, and certain places, people and activities as reputable, one must reject as deceptive, seductive, and improper their opposites: for example, the realm of pleasures and emotions. Yet in so doing, that world becomes all the more attractive.

11

Gender and Justice: Feminist Contributions to Criminology

SUSAN CAULFIELD AND NANCY WONDERS

Within feminist theory considerable attention has been given to what is termed the "decentering" of feminism (Gagnier, 1990). Central to this notion of the decentering of feminism is the claim that feminist theories, like all other theories, are historically contingent—that is, they reflect constructions of reality that are shaped by time and place, rather than universal truths. Consequently, some feminists currently argue that *a* feminist perspective does not and cannot exist (Gelsthorpe and Morris, 1990). From their point of view, many voices sing the song of feminism, and the voices are definitely not in harmony.

Within the criminological literature, as well, there is a tendency to focus on differences within feminism and the fragmented and multiple perspectives that it offers. Although we believe that the focus on divisions within feminism provides important information to those interested in the history of feminist thought, we feel that it also tends to minimize the amount of agreement between feminists, and, more important, the contributions of feminism to the academic enterprise.

In this chapter we outline several key contributions that have been made by feminist theorists. Although we acknowledge that differences exist within feminism, we choose to focus here on the commonalities within feminist thought—the widely shared beliefs and contributions that are too often overlooked. While others are highlighting the lack of harmony among feminists, we prefer to focus on the common song they are trying to sing— however haltingly, however sharp or out of tune, however loudly the audience tells them all to be quiet. It is our contention that these contributions have already begun to influence criminology in lasting ways, and that they hold the greatest promise for those who wish to integrate feminist concerns into their work.

Ultimately, our exploration of the commonalities within feminism reveals two points about the relationship between feminism and criminology. First, we offer the bad news that feminism has often been ignored and misunderstood by criminologists and, thus, much of the usefulness of feminist theory has been overlooked or neglected within the discipline. Second, we offer the good news that some recent research projects do offer embers of hope with which to fan the flames of feminism within criminology.

In this chapter, we outline five major contributions that have been made by feminist scholarship and practice. We describe both the impact and the potential impact of these contributions on criminology. As we explore these key contributions, we will identify numerous research projects that exemplify the way that feminism can alter how criminologists conduct their work. Indeed, as we point out, some scholars are contributing to the feminist enterprise without consciously naming their work "feminist." In that sense, the impact of feminism has been much greater than many might imagine. Throughout the chapter, emphasis will be placed on the need for criminologists to employ a broader conception of feminism than has previously been used. It is our hope that the suggestions and insights provided in this chapter will both inform and inspire others to consider the promise of a criminology that is feminist in orientation.

FEMINIST CONTRIBUTIONS

Given the shortage of explicit scholarly attention to feminism within criminology, it seems clear that for many criminologists, feminism is seen as peripheral to the field, "girl-stuff," or a theoretical nonissue once "sex" has been added to their equations. Few journal articles in the United States have attempted to make feminism clear and relevant to the field, but two recent pieces are noteworthy. Both Simpson (1989) and Daly and Chesney-Lind (1988) explore the current state of feminism within criminology. Their views of feminism are similar and not unlike our own. From Simpson's (1989: 606) point of view, feminism is "both a world view and a social movement that encompasses assumptions and beliefs about the origins and consequences of gendered social organization as well as strategic directions and actions for social change." Similarly, Daly and Chesney-Lind (1988: 502) call feminism "a set of theories about women's oppression and a set of strategies for social change."

Both articles make important contributions to criminology by outlining different perspectives within feminism and linking the various perspectives to important concerns within the field. In that regard, both Simpson and Daly and Chesney-Lind emphasize the divisions within feminism. Daly and Chesney-Lind, in their appendix, discuss the core elements of "traditional," "liberal," "Marxist," "radical," and "socialist" feminism. Simpson, on the other hand, examines "liberal," "socialist" (which includes "Marxist"), "radical," and "women of color" feminism.

A needed complement to their work, however, is a more detailed articulation of the shared assumptions that guide feminism, and the important contributions that feminism has offered. The five contributions of feminist scholarship that we describe, which can help to guide research and practice within criminology, are:

1. The focus on *gender* as a central organizing principle for contemporary life
2. The importance of *power* in shaping social relations
3. Sensitivity to the way that the social *context* shapes human relations
4. The recognition that all social reality must be understood as a *process*, and the development of methods that take this into account
5. The commitment to *social change* as a critical part of feminist scholarship and practice

These contributions represent conceptual tools with which to understand the social world. As we will point out, these contributions have begun to alter the way that some criminologists conduct their scholarship and live their lives. We believe that the insights drawn from these contributions, and current criminological research that exemplifies them, can help to improve the field immeasurably.

Gender

At the heart of much feminist scholarship is the assumption that gender is a central organizing principle of contemporary life, shaping human interactions in every sphere, including within the criminal justice system. Many people object to feminism because they believe that the perspective represents a narrow focus on women. Importantly, this belief represents a fundamental misunderstanding of feminism, and it has minimized the impact that feminism has had on criminology. However, some criminologists are integrating gender concerns into their work, and doing so has made all the difference in their analysis.

Despite the admonition that "you can't just add women and stir," many scholars believe they are feminists because they add women into their analysis. But, in fact, feminism has urged us to go beyond dichotomies (male/ female, objective/subjective, etc.) to explore the relations between categories and social world. Contrary to popular conceptions, it has been women, particularly women of color, who have refused to be reduced to single "variables" and who have pointed out the distortion that such oversimplification creates for understanding society. Feminism does not call for an exclusive focus on women; instead, it suggests that we ought to be concerned with the social construction of difference, particularly the construction of masculinity and femininity as meaningful social categories.

The distinction between "sex" and "gender" has a long history within feminist theory. For feminists, sex has typically referred to the biological differences that are socially determined to be appropriate for distinguishing between women and men, while "gender" refers to the social construction of behavior and attitudes considered appropriate for individuals of a particular sex (Sargent, 1984). Sex is conceived of as a dichotomy (female/male) while gender is a continuum (ranging from very feminine to very masculine). Thus, women *become* "gendered," which in our society means they are socialized to take on feminine characteristics, but they are *born* female. This distinction, common in the feminist literature, has been lost on many criminologists. The proliferation of articles with "gender" in the title should be encouraging, but a large number of those articles completely ignore issues related to gender; instead, they add "sex" into their equations and use the term "gender" synonymously with "sex" to describe their findings (see, for example, LaGrange and Ferraro, 1989). As Flax (1990: 40) states: "a fundamental goal of feminist theory is (and ought to be) to analyze gender relations: how gender relations are constituted and experienced and how we think or, equally important, do not think about them."

While we welcome more research that looks at differences between women and men, there are three problems that we wish to highlight with this research. First, in many projects that make "sex" synonymous with "gender," the real interest of the researcher seems to be to investigate women. Menkel-Meadow and Seidman Diamond (1991: 222) describe the problem with this lack of clarity when they write that "there is danger that, once operationalized, gender becomes a not too subtle code word for 'woman'—that is, the 'gender' problem is the women problem, just as the 'race' problem is the black problem, as if whites had no race." There is, of course, a need for more research exploring women's lives, but it is frustrating that so much of the research that is aimed at understanding women does so only in contrast to men. Men are the standard to which women are compared and from whom they are assessed to be "different."

Second, research that focuses exclusively on sex differences may actually be misleading. Much of the best work in criminology today looks at the gendering of the social world and its impact on crime and justice issues. We will describe some of that work in a moment, but wish to mention here that this research often concludes that a narrow focus on sex may overlook the way that people are dealt with differently because of gender, especially because of assumptions about appropriate sex-role behavior.

Third, the failure to address gender explicitly tends to legitimize the meaning we attach to biological sex. When "female" and "male" are entered into an equation and used to explain phenomena, embedded in the research are a host of unexplored assumptions about what those terms *mean*. Recently postmodern feminists have challenged the distinction between sex and gender, arguing that sex only has meaning *because* the world is gendered

(Flax, 1989; Gagnier, 1990). Regardless of which position is taken on the relationship between sex and gender, the clear implication of all feminist work is that the meaning attached to any difference is socially constructed. Thus, researchers who employ conceptions of difference have an obligation to explore the assumptions they make about the difference, as well as how the construction of that difference matters in their own research.

A deeper understanding of the way that social life is gendered is both critical and central to the concerns of criminology (Morris and Gelsthorpe, 1991; Daly and Chesney-Lind, 1988). Others have already highlighted some of the ways that gender is linked to the most pressing issues within contemporary criminology (Daly and Chesney-Lind, 1988; Simpson, 1989). Daly and Chesney-Lind point to two problems related to gender and crime that have the potential to transform the discipline if they are resolved. The first is the "generalizability problem," which suggests that theories based on male behavior may not be generalizable either to women or, we would add, to all men. In fact, the more we learn about the way that sex and gender shape people's experiences within the criminal justice system, the more the theoretical basis of current criminological theory is called into question (Leonard, 1982). Two lessons that can be learned from the lack of generalizability of most contemporary theories are, first, that universal theories of crime and social control are probably unattainable, and, second, that current theorists would be wise to temper the breadth of their claims and offer greater explanation of the contingent nature of their assertions.

The second issue Daly and Chesney-Lind (1988) discuss is the "gender ratio problem," which emphasizes the need for research that helps to explain why women are less involved in crime—and, importantly, why men are more involved. The gender ratio problem best highlights the central place that "gender" must have in criminological analysis. Let us explain.

It is true that to date feminism has brought to criminology a deeper understanding of *women's* lives. Research has been conducted on female offending (Carlen, 1988; Chesney-Lind, 1986; Miller, 1986), on women's victimization (Gordon and Riger, 1991; Tifft and Markham, 1991), and on women's experiences as professionals within the criminal justice system (Jurik, 1985; S. Martin, 1980). Much of this research is significant because it attempts to create an understanding of women's experiences that is not simply in contrast to men's. We believe, however, that much feminist work remains to be done that would explore the relationship of gender to *male* offending, victimization, and professional experiences. After all, if men are more likely to be involved in criminal behavior, perhaps we should be focusing on what it means to be a male in this society. Edwards (1989: 165–166) sees a pattern to this contradiction: "Although males are the chosen subjects of study in the overwhelming majority of cases, maleness or masculinity are hardly ever mentioned as a possibly significant variable." We should make it clear that we are not suggesting that there has been too little research on men—that would be patently absurd—but we do wish to note that there is a noticeable absence of research on masculinity and criminal justice issues from a feminist perspective.

Despite this oversight, several recent research projects within criminology have used the concept of gender constructively to better understand the social world. These projects highlight the difference that it makes to go beyond "sex" to look at characteristics that represent the gendering of our culture. For example, Daly (1987, 1989), in her research on sentencing, found that both women and men received more lenient sentences if they were the primary caretakers of dependent children. As she points out, researchers that look only for "sex" differences would discover that women are treated more leniently, but would not uncover the relationship between sex roles and sentencing practices. If caring for dependent children is the salient variable in sentencing decisions, then looking only at the "sex" of the offender may hide the way that the gendering of the social world shapes judges' perception. Another example is offered by Kruttschnitt (1984), where she argues that all women are not treated the same within the judicial system. Women whose offenses conform to appropriate sex-role stereotypes (such as shoplifting) are dealt with more leniently relative to men, than are women who engage in offenses considered to violate sex role stereotypes (e.g., robbery). In other words, some women are more "respectable" than others, and more deserving of leniency.

In general, this research illustrates that the way the social world is gendered may shape responses within the criminal justice system. It also suggests that our explanations of crime, criminal justice processing, and correctional strategies may be enriched by greater attention to gender issues.

Power

Feminism has also sensitized us to the importance of power in shaping social life. Of course, many other theoretical perspectives have also emphasized power, but feminism's legacy has been to emphasize the relationship between patriarchy and the power to define reality. As Minow (1990: 380) suggests,

by naming the power of naming, feminist work explores the relationship between observer and observed. By exposing the assignment of difference based on a limited norm, feminists have made vivid the interactions between theory and context, parts and wholes. Feminist work shows the power of connections, alongside distinctions, and welcomes the sometimes frightening recognition of our mutual implication in what we study and in one another.

Mainstream criminology has always had difficulty incorporating power into its analysis. Despite the rise of conflict and critical theory, criminology has found it difficult to move beyond a relatively rigid belief in traditional science as the road to truth. Yet, as Foucault's (1980) work indicates, we must always be attentive to the interconnections between knowledge and power. The assumptions of objective, value-free research are "positivist" assumptions from a man-made and male-dominated field of social science research. As Acker, Barry, and Esseveld (1983: 140) state, "research is embedded in a definite social relationship in which there is a power differential in favor of the knower who assumes the power to define in the process of the research."

The failure of the discipline to adequately address gender is partly related to the relative power of different voices within the field. As Daly and Chesney-Lind (1988: 518) note, it is important to realize that "the dimensions of a major criminological problem—the place of men and women in theories of crime—cannot be separated from a problem for the sociology of knowledge—the place of men and of women in *constructing theory and conducting research*" (emphasis added).

Once we appreciate that those with power use their power to define reality from their vantage point, much of what we think we know about the world becomes suspect. However, our recognition that reality is socially constructed need not be seen as problematic. Many feminists stress the value of ambiguity in theories and research that attempt to understand the social world (Fraser and Nicholson, 1990; Minow, 1990). They acknowledge and embrace the fact that feminist theory, like all other theories, is particularistic, biased, and limiting. From this perspective, *all* theories represent particular standpoints, and in every theory some standpoints are likely to be better represented than others. Indeed, "a search for a defining theme of the whole or a feminist viewpoint may require the suppression of the important and discomforting voices of persons with experiences unlike our own" (Flax, 1990: 48). Because this is so, the creation of theories that represent different standpoints is a critical part of reshaping knowledge and power relations. As Minow (1990: 376) writes:

the perspective of those who are labeled "different" may offer an important challenge to those who imposed the label, but it is a corrective lens, another partial view, not the absolute truth. It is the complexity of our reciprocal realities and the conflict between the realities that constitute us which we need to understand.

Some feminists suggest that the ambiguity in feminist theory is actually a more realistic representation of the world. Harding (1986: 164), for instance, writes that

coherent theories in an obviously incoherent world are either silly and uninteresting or oppressive and problematic, depending upon the degree of hegemony they manage to achieve. Coherent theories in an apparently coherent world are even more dangerous, for the world is always more complex than such unfortunately hegemonous theories can grasp.

Although feminism does not offer a universal theory, or a grand theory that comprehensively explains the relationship between power and social life, it does provide us with tools for better appreciating the power that shapes most people's lives. As Smart (1989: 68) notes, "feminist analysis increasingly falls into the category of 'deconstruction,' which challenges naturalistic, overgeneralized and abstract assumptions about the social world. Feminist work has a growing affinity with the idea of analyzing the micro-politics of power, and the everyday oppression of women which are invisible to the grand theorist."

Several research projects within criminology have illustrated the critical importance of power relations for research within our field. Some work has focused on the relationship between power and the ability to define the meaning of crimes and harm. For example, much work has been conducted on the redefinition of victimization, and the acts that contribute to that victimization. Because of feminist analysis, two of the most frequent victimizations for women—rape and battering—have begun to be understood in terms of the structural position of women in society. Rape, which had previously been considered to be an act of sex (brought on by the seductive wiles, or dress, of the woman), was finally seen to be an act linked to power, control, and domination. Crucial to expanding this definition were the works of Brownmiller (1975), Griffin (1971), and Russell (1982). A reanalysis of battering also occurred that questioned the ancient assumption that the home was a "sacred place" and therefore beyond the purview of the police. It also challenged the assumption that a man had the right to control "his property" (see, e.g., Straus, Gelles, and Steinmetz, 1980; D. Martin, 1976).

Feminist research in criminology has also addressed other manifestations of power. Power is not only exercised through the definitional process or through brute force. In fact, perhaps the most significant exercise of power over women is through "soft" social control mechanisms, such as domestic ties, the division of the social world into private and public domains, patriarchal authority, the creation of ideology, and through popular culture (see, e.g., Heidensohn, 1986). Socialization to acceptable gender roles through cultural institutions (such as the family, schools, and media) goes a long way toward controlling women in U.S. culture (Morris and Gelsthorpe, 1991). Research has been conducted that links gender socialization into sex-appropriate roles affects the processing of women within the criminal justice system. As several studies have shown (Heidensohn, 1987; Kruttschnitt and Green, 1984; Rosenblum, 1990), women are processed differently than men, in part depending upon the extent to which their offenses deviate from "appropriate" female behavior. Further, some researchers have focused on the way that ideology shapes conceptions of appropriate behavior. For example, researchers such as Tifft and Markham (1991) have analyzed the critical similarities between beliefs that allow men to batter women and those that permit the state to go to war against (batter) other countries.

An emerging area of research explores the extent to which the state participates in the gendering of law and the differential treatment accorded women under the law. In our previous work (Caulfield and Wonders, 1992), we emphasize the relationship between state power and violence against women. We stress the critical role the state plays in sanctioning violence against women through its failure to pass and enforce laws limiting violence, particularly violence toward women. We call the state's role in supporting patriarchy and fostering violence against women a form of "political crime." We do so, because naming the state's complicity in the violence "crime" recognizes the power of words and ideas to shape our understanding of reality.

Power is also central to our understanding of what the discipline of criminology is and can be. Throughout the history of the field there have been competing theories and explanations of crime and criminal justice, but some explanations have had greater hold on the discipline than others, and some ways of understanding the world, such as positivism, have had greater hegemony. Feminists do not seek to replace one hegemony with another. Rather, they offer a different vantage point from which to participate actively in the dialogue about what the discipline should be. Perhaps most important, they argue that "as we make audible the struggles over which version of reality will secure power, we disrupt the silence of one perspective, imposed as if universal" (Minow, 1990: 389).

Context

Another key contribution of feminist scholarship to criminology is the sensitivity within feminist theory to the way that the social context shapes events and our understanding of them. There is a tendency in mainstream criminological work to attempt to categorize the world. Hence the use of such categories as "white" or "black," "male" or "female," "underclass" or "middle class." Feminist scholars have problematized these classifications and have urged others to consider what these categories mean relative to real human lives; to recognize that the characteristics of peoples' lives do not operate singularly.

As Anthias and Yuval-Davis (1983) note, even "sisterhood" is a myth, since not all women are the same. While early feminist theory tended to generalize about women's experiences, contemporary theorists are much more interested in celebrating human difference (hooks [Watkins] 1990; Minow, 1990). The critical issue for feminism today is how to understand the relationship between the social context and the many varieties of human experience. As Stacey and Thorne (1985: 307–308) point out, "reducing social life to a series of measurable variables diminishes the sense of the whole that is crucial to theoretical understanding of social, including gender, relationships."

To talk about the context of human lives means to recognize that people are never just one characteristic at a time. Women are never just "women"; they are also rich or poor, dark or light, working at home, working at a job, or working the streets. Spelman (1988: 166) warns us in succinct fashion:

If we assume there are differences among women, but at the same time they are all the same as women, and if we assume the woman part is what we know from looking at the case of white middle-class women, then we appear to be talking only about white middle-class women. This is how white middle-class privilege is maintained even as we purport to recognize the importance of women's differences.

Simpson (1989) directs this concern toward criminology when she mentions the possibility that theories of female crime may be theories of white female crime, since the causes of crime may differ by race. She writes that "more quantitative research is needed on minority groups other than blacks . . . to establish a better knowledge base, but qualitative studies that probe culture and subjective differences between women of color and whites are also essential" (p. 619).

In addition to research that explores the rich context of individual lives by analyzing the multiple social locations that people hold, feminists also encourage research that takes into account the way that structural and institutional forces shape individual lives. As we have said, women are never just women; but, furthermore, the fact of their femaleness may be more or less salient depending upon the particular institutional and structural context. A woman appearing in a courtroom dominated by women may have a different experience than one appearing in a courtroom dominated by men. Women in communities that have disproportionate numbers of women in single-headed households may have different experiences as offenders and victims than their sisters in other communities.

At least two recent research projects (Myers and Talarico, 1987; Wonders, 1990) have explored the way that the institutional and structural context shapes experiences within the criminal justice system. Both projects discovered that efforts to explore discrimination within the criminal justice system are likely to be misleading unless contextual factors—such as prior court decision making, urbanization and inequality within the community, and related variables—are taken into account.

In sum, feminism provides us with a more holistic perspective that encourages researchers to take seriously the way that the larger structural, institutional, and individual contexts shape human lives. While we can try to analyze crime and justice issues apart from these contexts, we run the risk of distorting reality for the sake of analytical simplicity. It is our belief that we are likely to learn far more about the contemporary world by developing theoretical and methodological strategies that help us to appreciate and investigate this complexity, rather than minimize it.

Process

Further contributions of feminism include the recognition that all social reality must be understood as a process, and that this understanding requires the development of methods that take this into account. As Mies (1991: 63) writes, "while dominant science views things as static, dualistically ahistorical, mechanical, and additive, feminist science, which has not lost sight of its political goal, strives for a new view of the whole societal constellation in which things appear as historical, contradictory, linked to each other, and capable of being changed." Feminist scholarship has, by and large, been more reflexive than mainstream scholarship. "By reflexivity, we mean the tendency of feminists to reflect upon, examine critically, and explore analytically the nature of the research process" (Fonow and Cook, 1991: 2).

The recognition that the social world is dynamic has required feminist scholars to develop and utilize methodological techniques that are sensitive to the transitory nature of social reality. "Feminist theory reveals and contributes to the growing uncertainty within Western intellectual circles about the appropriate grounding and methods for explaining and interpreting human experience" (Flax, 1990: 40–41). Criticisms of mainstream methods "range from charges of bias in selecting research topics and interpreting results to rejecting rationality and objectivity as purely male products" (Simpson, 1989: 609). In addition, as we have already suggested, with traditional methods, human "subjects" tend to become fragmented and disembodied during analysis.

For some, feminist research methods are in marked contrast to traditional positivistic methods. According to Simpson (1989: 609), "feminist methods are necessarily subjectivist, transdisciplinary, nonhierarchical, and empowering." Qualitative research methods have come to be viewed by many as the hallmark of feminist research. Participant-observation, ethnographies, life histories, interpretive methodologies, and other similar techniques have been employed by feminist researchers in order to reveal parts of the social world that remain hidden by more traditional techniques (Carlen, 1983; Lugones and Spelman, 1983; Stanley and Wise, 1983; Westokott, 1979). Some maintain that in order to "see" the experiences of women, "feminist women must deliberately and courageously integrate . . . their own experiences of oppression and discrimination . . . into the research process" (Miles, 1983, as cited in Simpson, 1989: 609). In general, many feminists prefer qualitative methods, not because they can more accurately uncover scientific "truths" and generalizations, but because they are better able to consider reality as a process—always changing, always in the process of being constituted. Mies (1991: 67) puts it this way:

My criticism of quantifying methods is not directed against every form of statistics but at its claim to have a monopoly on accurately describing the world.... The difference between quantitative and qualitative methods lies, in my view, in the fact that the qualitative methods, despite ideological distortion, do not break living connections in the way that quantitative methods do.

The growing utilization of qualitative research strategies within criminology reveals the lasting impact that feminism has had on criminology. While much research that has employed qualitative methods is not explicitly feminist (e.g., Wheeler et al., 1988), feminism has helped to create a climate that legitimizes the use of such methods. Some qualitative projects have revealed important information about the criminal justice process that would have been overlooked using only traditional quantitative methods. Traditional quantitative approaches tend to present the research process as orderly and logical, but this "hygienic" approach is misleading (Stanley and Wise, 1983). The techniques that feminist researchers employ may appear less "hygienic," but they better represent the dynamic realities that shape human experience.

An excellent example of feminist criminological research that employs alternative methods is work conducted in Great Britain by Carlen (1988). Rather than imposing a rigid format on the subjects of her research, she conducted ethnographic analysis, using interviews to understand women's involvement in crime. What she discovered was that for some women, there was simply no incentive to conform to law. In the face of poverty, sexism, and racism, some women got to the point where they felt they had nothing to lose, and everything to gain by engaging in criminal activity. Carlen (1988: 12) goes further to link these women's behavior to the larger structure: "The implicit logic...of their law-breaking was similar to that of many corporate criminals: that the competitive ethos embodied in Thatcherite capitalism had created conditions implicitly licensing them to get what they could by any means necessary." The qualitative methods used were far better able to get at the diversity and richness of responses regarding the motives guiding women's behavior than traditional quantitative methods would have been.

While feminists' focus on qualitative methodological strategies is an important contribution to criminological research, we believe that the feminist legacy is actually broader than any particular method might suggest. As other recent feminist scholars have pointed out, feminism represents a way of thinking and acting in the world, more than a particular method of studying it (see, for example, Harding, 1987; Yllo, 1988). Harding describes just this when she writes that "feminist researchers use just about any and all of the methods, in this concrete sense of the term, that traditional androcentric researchers have used. Of course, precisely how they carry out these methods of evidence gathering is often strikingly different" (p. 2).

Some feminists do employ quantitative research methods, but they typically try to conduct quantitative research somewhat differently, with greater emphasis on variables that attempt to reflect the complexity and dynamic nature of the social world (for examples, see Daly, 1987, 1989; Wonders, 1990). As some authors suggest (see, for example, Morris and Gelsthorpe, 1991), the concern is not so much the quantification itself, but quantification of a simplistic or insensitive nature. Perhaps the best research strategy is one that matches the method to the issue to be explored, and that mixes quantitative and qualitative methods to capture reality (see Wheeler et al., 1988 for a nice mix of methodological strategies).

Feminism does not mandate a particular topic of study, but it does suggest a reflexivity with respect to the way that research is conducted. Thus, to be a feminist researcher does not require that researchers desert their current research agendas and begin studying women. On the contrary, while we still have a lot to learn about women's lives and their relationship to criminal justice, we also need more scholars who are able to apply a feminist perspective to traditional areas of concern. What we have pointed out in this section is that conducting feminist research involves developing strategies that begin to capture the dynamic and fluid nature of human history and existence. If, as M. K. Harris (1987: 27) suggests, "conventional approaches ... provide little promise for a significantly better future," then attention to alternative methodologies is paramount.

As we discuss alternative methodological strategies, we wish to emphasize that it is not helpful to foster methodological narrowness in a complex social world. If criminology is going to become more "feminist," it is likely to do so in an incremental fashion. That means that the tools used to reshape the discipline must be viewed as acceptable to a large proportion of the discipline (Morris and Gelsthorpe, 1991). Attempts to replace one rigid methodological strategy with another can only result in failure to make progress. As Morris and Gelsthorpe put it: "to promote separatism is self-defeating in this context because it would mean the perpetuation of traditional methodologies and conventional knowledge boundaries, and it is these which feminist perspectives seek to challenge" (p. 22).

Social Change

A final contribution of feminism that we think is especially noteworthy is the emphasis on social change as a critical part of feminist scholarship and practice. Again, feminism is not alone in linking theory to action, but their charge that "the personal is political" challenges scholars to create social change, not just in the political back room, the boardroom and the classroom, but also in the living room. There are several targets for change that have been discussed by feminists and that have potential for transforming criminology and justice in America.

The first, and the most recognized, is the need for research to be linked to particular policy outcomes. For many feminists, the point of studying the world is to change it (something they share with scholars from the critical perspective). Within criminology, several feminist research projects have been explicitly linked to efforts to change criminal justice in light of new information on the ways that gender, power, social context, and process issues shape criminal justice outcomes. Of particular importance are studies that have focused on victimization. Much of the work on rape and battering, for example, was conducted in order to change criminal justice response to these events. The existence of domestic violence shelters and sexual assault specialists on police forces are just two manifestations of the success of this link between scholarship and political action.

Law, as a form of public policy, has also been a target of feminist action within criminology. Some believe that attempting to change law is futile, since the effort itself helps to legitimize law, which is viewed as hierarchical and, therefore, inherently oppressive. "Yet law remains a site of struggle. While it is the case that law does not hold the key to unlock patriarchy, it provides the forum for articulating alternative visions and accounts" (Smart, 1989: 88). While the long-term objective, for some, might include the elimination of law, those who are harmed *today* need to be protected, by whatever means are currently available.

A second area of action for feminists is in the area of education. Throughout the academy, feminists have been engaged in efforts to transform the curriculum to be more inclusive of diverse perspectives. While it is true that within criminology some of the contributions of feminism have begun to affect scholarship, these contributions have rarely filtered into criminal justice curriculums. While many Criminal Justice departments have a course on "Women and the Criminal Justice System," which does represent progress from our point of view, these courses have several problems (see, e.g., Wonders and Caulfield, 1993). Two that are especially important are, first, that there is no guarantee that these courses will offer a "feminist" perspective, and second, even when they are taught from a feminist perspective they tend to reinforce the idea that feminism is a "women's" issue. Ultimately, these courses have too often served to provide a justification for the exclusion of feminist concerns from other courses. Yet, teaching about the relationship of feminism to criminology is one of the key tools we have for integrating feminist concerns and research strategies into the discipline.

Teaching feminism within criminology has several important implications for the field. First, it creates an atmosphere that is more tolerant and encouraging of alternative viewpoints. Interestingly, Pepinsky (1989) found that introducing students to feminist perspectives in a seminar not only allowed women to celebrate their connectedness and peacemaking side, but had the added effect of "feminizing" men; that is, it allowed men to explore alternative methods of dispute resolution, and to openly discuss problems with existing methods. As N. Wilson (1991a) has noted, if women are traditionally thought to resolve disputes through nonviolent means, then the lack of attention to women's lives is tacit acceptance of male strategies of resolving disputes. A second consequence of feminism's integration into the criminology classroom is that attention to sex and gender issues is likely to make the discipline more welcoming for female students. Since women are often marginalized from working within the criminal justice system when it is portrayed as a male-dominated institution, describing the impact of gender on the field of criminal justice can help to make the discipline accessible to a greater variety of people. And increasing the number of women within the field of criminology may herald other changes as well. For, "not only should there be female police; but there should also be room for women's perspective on what policing should be" (N. Wilson, 1991a: 91). While police work traditionally has been associated with men, there is nothing inherently masculine about social control. Analysis of environments that are all female, or where social control is engaged in by women—such as convents, sororities, elementary school systems, and families—would provide examples of alternative social control strategies that might hold promise for the field of criminal justice (N. Wilson, 1991a).

Integrating feminism into the curriculum goes beyond adding women and feminism as topics of study; it also includes utilizing a feminist pedagogy for teaching, which embodies the principles of democracy and sensitivity to others (Schniedewind, 1983: 271). Feminist teachers "make the gendered subjectivities of themselves and their students part of the texts they teach. And at the same time, they ground a critical inquiry in a deep respect for their students' lives and cultural values" (Weiler, 1988: 149). Feminist pedagogies empower students to see their own experiences as valid, their own opinions worth expressing. Thus, discussion is a technique more consistent with feminist pedagogy than is the traditional hierarchical lecture. In general, feminist teachers tend to employ teaching methods that permit students to critically engage the material by reflecting on their own lives (Maher, 1984). We believe that feminist pedagogy is particularly useful for teaching crime and justice issues because these issues are so often deeply personal to our students. Feminist pedagogy values the experiences that students have had as offenders, workers, and as victims of crime and it gives our students permission to believe that justice should be about them.

A third focus for social change emerges from the contention that the personal is political. Change must also come from within. As Pepinsky (1989) points out, a feminist perspective has implications for personal growth. In addressing the linkages between the personal and the political, Pepinsky notes that structural change cannot occur unless change first occurs within individuals. If exposure to feminist-oriented perspectives can bring about change in individuals, such as cause them to question violent response tactics versus nonviolent mediation, then they have the potential to influence policy, with the ultimate capability of changing the current structure and its institutions.

Accepting that the "personal is political" goes beyond the academy and into the personal lives of feminist scholars. Most feminist scholars find it difficult to restrict their change strategies exclusively to the "ivory towers" of the academy. A critical dimension of feminism is commitment to change in our own lives and in our communities. As M. K. Harris (1987: 31) tells us, "feminist belief that the personal is political means that core values must be lived and acted upon in both public and private arenas." Furthermore, as N. Wilson (1991a) notes, we must provide models if we hope to change the existing system. Within our communities, there are already numerous models in existence that demonstrate that social change is possible (e.g. shelters, rape crisis centers, police policies). Many feminist criminologists are nurturing these organizations through volunteer activity, at the same time that they are attempting to create new organizations that address other unmet needs. In addition, some feminists are encouraging renewed political activity directed at the state, arguing that local community responses are functioning as a pressure valve, permitting the federal government simply to ignore problems that directly affect huge segments of the population, such as domestic violence (Dobash and Dobash, 1992). Finally, for many feminist criminologists, change begins within their own interpersonal relationships. Reducing conflict, fostering communication, and eliminating corporal punishment from our homes and violence from our relationships are all part of making the personal political, and are also part of creating a better and more just world for us all.

FEMINISM AND CRIMINOLOGY

To say that you are a feminist usually evokes preconceived notions of identity, role or behavior.... you are popularly assumed to be an aggressive, man-hating and banner-waving *woman*. To say that you are adopting a feminist perspective in an academic discipline or a feminist methodology in research usually leads to puzzlement, claims that there is no such thing or accusations of bias, one-sidedness, over-involvement and the like (Morris and Gelsthorpe, 1991: 3–4; emphasis added).

Along with Morris and Gelsthorpe, we believe that these charges are misguided and fundamentally misunderstand the feminist enterprise.

In this chapter we have outlined several of the key contributions feminism has made to social research and to criminology. We have argued that feminism has encouraged a focus on gender as a critical element of social life in the contemporary period. Feminism has also emphasized the importance of power and the larger social context in shaping our understanding of reality and human experience. Feminism has offered us tools for analyzing the dynamic nature of social reality: to see human existence—reality itself—as a continuously unfolding process. In addition, feminism has emphasized the importance of social change as a critical focus and a necessary outcome of scholarship and practice.

It is important to note that what we prescribe here is not a "feminist criminology," but a criminology that is "feminist-oriented." This is an important difference. As we have pointed out, and others have noted (Daly and Chesney-Lind, 1988; Gelsthorpe and Morris, 1988), a feminist criminology does not exist—nor is it likely to. Just as there are different criminologies, there are different feminisms; it follows, then, that there are different feminist perspectives within criminology (Gelsthorpe and Morris, 1988; Morris and Gelsthorpe, 1991). But there are lessons to be learned from feminism, not as a unitary theory, but as a set of perspectives that have made several shared contributions.

In order to achieve the vision of a criminology that is truly feminist, it will be necessary, borrowing from Cain (1989, 1990) and Morris and Gelsthorpe (1991), to "transgress" traditional criminology. This transgression, or "going beyond the boundaries," must occur at a number of levels and across a number of areas covered within criminology. We hope that our discussion of feminist contributions has provided new tools and new perspectives that criminologists can employ to achieve this end.

We are keenly aware that the development of a criminology that is feminist-oriented is an on-going process. We know that we cannot afford to dismiss the works of the past, for they have helped to create the present and the future. Nor do we suggest a simple or narrow vision for what is to come. Instead, we offer our thoughts about the promise of feminism for criminology, and we celebrate the fact that feminism has already moved us appreciably closer to a more just world.

12

Law, Ideology, and Subjectivity: A Semiotic Perspective on Crime and Justice

DRAGAN MILOVANOVIC

Critical theoretical thought about law-finding has been conspicuously absent in the sociology of law literature. Much investigation has been of a descriptive nature. In this chapter we wish to focus on a critically informed, psychoanalytic semiotic approach to law and justice-rendering (law-finding). It is our contention that descriptive as well as formalist investigations, although, perhaps initially, a necessary component of a full-fledged critical examination, fall short of providing an explanation of the mechanisms and architectonics for such phenomena as hegemony, reification, and repression. The task before us is to provide the rudiments of a perspective that also attempts to restore subjectivity to a position of centrality in any investigation of repressive practices. We must question the notion developed in the West of the Cartesian subject: a unitary and plenary *I*; and the self-centered, determining *individual*. This illusory conception of the coherent, stable, and determining individual is indeed a functional requirement of the capitalist mode of production, manifest in an explicit form in the notion of the juridic subject.

In the following sections we will describe the notion of a linguistic co-ordinate system (LCS); the idea of juridicolinguistic production and circulation; the three interrelated axes of the semiotic grid and their effects on reality construction; the interaction between system and inter- and intra-psychic generated semiosis; the idea of subjectivity as an effect of insertion in a multitude of subject-positions to which one *both* temporarily accepts as the spatiotemporal coordinate for social action and to which one reacts; and how hegemony is maintained in the social formation. We will focus on storytelling at the trial stage where the imaginary intersects with the discursive.

Figure 12.1
Signs and Signifying Chains (Lacan's version)

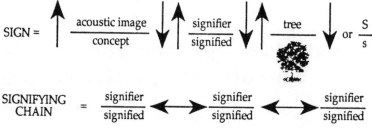

LINGUISTIC COORDINATE SYSTEMS

The notion of a linguistic coordinate system is an amalgamation of concepts derived from the various views in discourse analysis that have developed in recent years. LCSs can be envisioned as bounded spheres of sedimented, differentiated, and systematized signifying practices. We will argue later that a person situates her- or himself (or is inserted) within these LCSs that offer subject-positions. To communicate is to situate oneself within these bounded spheres, and to borrow from the available linguistic forms. That is, one must take a position as a signifier, an *I* in discourse. But prestructured subject-positions are pervasive and this is not without effect. Rationality, logic, *reason*, and so forth are constituted within these domains (see Milovanovic, 1986, 1992). Subjectivity, too, is constituted here.

LCSs are composed of signs. Saussure (1966) has argued that the sign connects an acoustic (sound) image with a concept (see also Lacan, 1977: 149–154; Borch-Jacobsen, 1991: 169–196). The acoustic image is a psychical trace of the sound—the representation of the word. Thus, the acoustic image may be termed the signifier; the concept, on the other hand, is the signified. The particular value of the sign is constituted by its particular location and relationship to all other elements in the sentence or utterance (signifying chain). These relationships are depicted in Figure 12.1. Semiotic production (semiosis) can be defined as the linking of a signifier to a specific signified. (Note: Lacan's 1977 version is depicted here.)

Elsewhere we have identified several LCSs (Milovanovic, 1986, 1988, 1992). For our purposes we will focus on the dominant, juridic, pluralistic, and oppositional forms. The dominant LCS can be envisioned as that ubiquitous signifying practice that the ideological state apparatuses (the sphere of superstructural practices) seeks to perpetuate—by way of the school, the media, the family; it is synchronized, diachronically, with the logic of capital (see also Laclau and Mouffe, 1985). The juridic LCS is that discourse which is produced, policed, and sustained by the judiciary. Law schools indoctrinate the neophyte law student with the appropriate (pertinent) discourse, which will be the relevant medium by and through which storytelling in the courtroom is constructed (see also Goodrich: 1984, 1990; Kennedy, 1982; Granfield and Koenig, 1990; Bourdieu, 1987). To do law, one quickly finds out, is to situate oneself within (or be situated in, inserted in) this bounded sphere of signifying practices. As Bourdieu (1987: 831) has noted: "entry into the juridical field implies the tacit acceptance of the field's fundamental law ... which requires that, within the field, conflicts can only be resolved *juridically*—that is according to the rules and conventions of the field itself." Doing law, then, requires a "complete translation of all of the aspects of the controversy ... [in order to] institute the controversy *as a lawsuit*, as a juridical problem that can become the object of juridically regulated debate" (p. 832).

Pluralistic LCSs can be envisioned as reflecting the idiosyncratic accentuations of the multifarious groups within a social formation. Overlap exists between their accentuations and the dominant LCS's accentuations. As Volosinov (1986: 23) has informed us, the sign is but the occasion for the intersection of differently oriented accents. Thus we can speak of the social *multiaccentuality* of the sign (p. 23). Finally, we can identify the oppositional LCS. Here linguistic forms—signs—render the social formation a critical accentuation. Put in another way, the signified is infused with excluded voices seeking expression. The signifieds resonate deeply in the psychic structure, bringing forth in an articulate form the asymmetrical propensities of a repressive capitalist mode of production. Persons, situating themselves within this discourse, have available for use critical tools for self-reflection, critical analysis, and codifications that render the given generated hegemonic myths of the capitalist mode of production a destabilizing accentuation. Needless to say, the hegemonic group will attempt to give the multiaccentual nature of the sign a uniaccentuality (Volosinov, 1986: 23–24), one consistent with the internal dynamics of capital logic.

The trial represents the occasion in which a clash of alternative constructions of reality takes place. It is "a struggle in which differing, indeed antagonistic world-views confront each other. Each, with its individual authority, seeks general recognition and thereby its own self-realization" (Bourdieu, 1987: 837). Clients, however, are disempowered from the onset of the battle when deferring to the expertise of their mouthpieces, lawyers. It is the state's version of truth or understanding that ultimately prevails, and hence the symbolic field is repeatedly created anew.

SPHERE OF JURIDICOSEMIOTIC PRODUCTION AND CIRCULATION

We have said that two levels of semiotic production can be isolated: at the level of system (structure) and at the level of the intra- and intersubjective. First, as to the system level, we are guided by Marx (recall his distinction between commodity production and circulation) in distinguishing two spheres connected with an LCS. The sphere of juridicolinguistic production finds its locus within higher courts (state appeals courts, state supreme courts, U.S. appeals courts, U.S. Supreme Court). It is here where the drama of the uniaccentuating of the ideological sign unfolds. Words such as *mens rea, willingly, knowingly, voluntarily,* and so forth, undergo precise codification. The higher courts render signs that are consistent with the formulations formed within given ideological structures. Once these are established they then become the elements constitutive of the sphere of circulation. To do law is to situate oneself within this loci. Any differences with dominantly codified linguistic structures are quickly neutralized in practice. The pragmatics of the court assure that heretics will be at a minimum, and, where they do exist, ample machinery will quickly be mobilized for their eradication (see Milovanovic, 1988; Milovanovic and Thomas, 1989; Bannister and Milovanovic, 1990).

In advanced (or state-regulated) capitalism, the higher courts are evermore active in intervening in the social formation to stave off crises tendencies (Habermas, 1975, 1984; Friedrichs, 1980; Milovanovic, 1987: 276–278). Hence, the balancing-interest approach will assure the codification of primordial sense data beneficial to hegemonic group interests. What constitutes a constitutionally protected interest is itself a juridic construct, overdetermined by the political economy. Especially conspicuous is the focal point of semiotic production by the higher courts on the sphere of commodity circulation (here we include the dynamics of the fetishism of the commodity and of the worker as seller of his or her labor power, and with it the logic of equivalence-effects), rather than on the sphere of commodity production (the hierarchically organized structure of the workplace). Hence this politically directed glance of attention effectively heads off alternative sedimentations of accentuations reflecting a hierarchical, exploitive, and repressive workplace and potentially liberating emerging forms. Put another way, the courts give idealized expression to phenomenal forms—appearance of equality, individuality, proprietorship—emanating from the sphere of circulation (the logic of equivalence) rather than to the hierarchical and repressive dimensions found in the sphere of production. Indeed, the latter is beyond incrimination.

SPHERE OF INTRAPSYCHIC AND INTERSUBJECTIVE SEMIOTIC PRODUCTION

The second level of semiotic production can be isolated as the intrapsychic/intersubjective instance. We have spelled out above that it is the higher court structure that uniaccentuates the ideological sign. To stay with this, however, is to be overly formalistic if not deterministic. Early semioticians such as Saussure (1966), and theoreticians more recently such as Jacobson (1971: 69–96), Metz (1982: 174–196), Silverman (1983: 87–125), and Lacan (1977: 146–175) have specified different axes that coordinate language's sedimentation and usage. It is to the Lacanian revisionism of Freud that we look for guidance. A plethora of semiotic research has surfaced, oriented around his suggestive, if not almost inaccessible, works.

To understand the interaction between an LCS and persons situated (inserted) within its domain and the subsequent effects (i.e., reality construction, the constitution of subjectivity), we must first grapple with the axes (sometimes referred to as tropes) identified to be constitutive of signifying practices—reflecting the interaction between signifiers and signifieds—and hence subjectivity. We will refer to these interpenetrating axes as the semiotic grid (see Figure 12.2, later in this chapter). To begin with, we may identify the axes of paradigm-syntagm, condensation-displacement, and metaphor-metonymy. Although there are similarities among the three axes, the differences are of considerable import. For our purposes, rather than following the topography of the early Freudian model, we posit the importance of Metz's idea of degrees of secondarization. Secondarization and linguistification can be defined as the process by which primordial sense data (mnemic traces, thing-presentations) undergo linguistic structuration (word-presentations) through the binding of excitatory (psychical) energy, the end result of which is the attaining of a concrete form in the word, utterance, or sentence. The affective and sensory intensities are harnessed (stasis), thus producing meaning (signifier-signified chains). Put in another way, free, unbounded psychical energy is bound in quiescent states in signifier-signified formations, providing an energized field in which thought can be activated. Semiotic production at the intra/interpsychic level entails an overdetermination emanating from the interactive effects among practices in the semiotic grid. We must, however, also look to the subject, the stand-in, activated by desire (in discourse, the grammatical subject), the *I* of these linguistic forms. We turn now to the three axes that are constitutive of a semiotic grid within which legal reality (the "what happened?") as well as subjectivity is created.

Paradigm-Syntagm Semiotic Axis

Ferdinand de Saussure, in his posthumously published book *Course de Linguistique Generale* (1966), has identified the paradigm-syntagm axis in terms of selection and combination (alternatively we may speak of choice and ordering, substitution and contextuality, etc.). For discourse (the domain of *parole*) to take place, certain linguistic forms must be chosen from some range available (the domain of *langue*, acting more as referents), which then must be arranged in some definite order; to be meaningful, words cannot be placed randomly in a linear-oriented sentence structure. Paradigm is the vertical axis along which words are clustered by their similarity or differences (comparability—Metz, 1982: 188–189). Saussure has noted that words chosen from the paradigm axis enjoy a relationship with numerous others that have some associative connection (e.g., warm-hot-boiling; duress-willingly; entrapment-intent; standards of proof in law: suspicion, reasonable suspicion, probable cause, clear and convincing, beyond a reasonable doubt). Other paradigmatic sets might include words with the same prefix or suffix—here some common nuclei exist: willingly-unwillingly, voluntarily-involuntarily. This delimited field provides us with a range of options from which we may select. Any word that helps to define the value of another within this axis is hence paradigmatically related to it. Thus paradigmatic sets must either diverge or converge to establish differences. All that is necessary is that some implied comparison exists.

The syntagm axis (or the horizontal axis), on the other hand, reflects the process of word placement in a sentence, in a chain of signifying practices. It represents the actual speech chain. For example, consider the prosecutor eliciting evidence during direct examination. What she or he attempts is to pose questions to the witness, the answers to which, it is hoped, will elicit responses that, in a temporary constructed imaginary space, jurors will fill in a plausible flow of events that ostensibly or self-evidently lead to the commission of the crime, a picture consistent with the creator's (lawyer's). Much like the director of cinema, what is being constructed is an imaginary space within which the event is situated. The hope is to contextualize the event in a spatiotemporal frame, within commonsensical understandings of motivations for behavior, in order that inferences will be made by jurors that this is how and why such and such happened. During direct- and cross-examination, where an attempt is being made to suggest the right answer without raising objections and having them sustained by the judge as "leading the witness," the lawyer reassembles previously introduced information in a new order, followed by the question, "Isn't that true?" in an attempt to construe, for the jurors, "what happened?" The words chosen (paradigm) and their ordering in a particular statement (syntagm) are meant to arouse in the jurors' minds a plausible picture of "what happened?" However, absent from this emerging picture are contextualizing factors (verbal and nonverbal) that in fact are determinants, or are contributors. We merely stress the point here that the notion of contiguity—the ordering of the elements of the statement—is central in storytelling in the courtroom. Shifting a noun or verb from one part of the sentence to another will dramatically alter the message (i.e., arousing, for example, an objection from the opposing lawyer as "directing the witness"). Within the psychoanalytic semiotic perspective of which we here give the bare outlines, this axis has effects at the preconscious-conscious levels. Or to put it in another way, in the Freudian/Lacanian model, it typifies secondary processes.

Condensation-Displacement Semiotic Axis

This second axis is consistent with the Freudian topography (accepted but much less discussed in the Lacanian construct). Again, rather than one or the other we have degrees. Both phenomena reside more in primary logic and the unconscious sphere. Condensation is the process by which over-determined wishes (desires), which are disallowed from consciousness by the censor (by which we understand as diachronically constituted by political and economic determinants), are given a representation in manifest signi-fiers. This allows certain discharges of psychical energy. These signifiers, then, must be traced to their latent signifieds. Displacement involves the transfer of excitatory energy from unacceptable objects onto acceptable ones. Concrete examples of the work of condensation and displacement, Freud tells us, can be found in parapraxes, neuroses, and hysterical symp-toms. Consider one example he uses, pointing out their joint effects: "he treated me famillionairely," which is clearly a condensation of the words millionaire and familiarly. Condensation effects can also be found induced by the filmic state (Metz, 1982: 104–128). "The filmic situation brings with it certain elements of motor inhibition, and it is in this respect a kind of sleep in miniature, a waking sleep" (p. 116). In other words, some regression occurs due to a reduced critical attentiveness. A passive viewer (or reader, listener) is more at the mercy of primary processes.

Metaphor-Metonymy Semiotic Axis

This axis, according to Silverman (1983: 110), mediates/facilitates be-tween the axes of metaphor-metonymy and condensation-displacement (see also Lemaire, 1977: 199–205). Jacobson (1971), Lacan (1977), Metz (1982), and Silverman (1983) have argued for its significance in the interplay of signifier, signified, and in the degrees of secondarization manifested. Other theorists (Manning, 1979; Morgan, 1980, 1983; Barley, 1983) have made abundant use of this axis, although neglecting the other two and their interactive effects, in their investigations of reality construction in organi-zational settings.

Metaphor is the centering in an imaginary space of similar objects. As a general rule, in this sphere there exists one word for another. It is the bringing of two signifieds under one signifier. Morgan (1983: 602) has said that "metaphor turns imagination in ways that forge an equivalence between separate elements of experience ... metaphor creates meaning by understanding one phenomenon through another in a way that encourages us to understand what is common to both." It is a "form of creative expres-sion which relies upon constructive falsehood as a means of liberating the imagination" (Morgan, 1980: 612). Or, said in even another way, it is a way of "seeing things *as if* they were something else" (Manning, 1979: 661).

Consider Barley's (1983: 402–407) example of "the ship plows the sea." Similarity is established between plowshares and the ship's bow; both cut furrows over the surfaces they traverse. But ploughs and ships' bows are in separate domains, one in the agricultural, the other in the nautical domain. Or consider the statement: "She's a real dynamo." Here we have reference to technology, a machine, and to an energetic person. This machine metaphor underlies much organizational theory (Taylorism survives in metaphors!) where human beings are valued for their instrumental abilities (hence the criteria by which a worker is judged in his or her performance centers on the utilitarian schema of means-ends and purposive rationality). Indeed, metaphor is a structuring mechanism: it structures our thoughts, perceptions, and actions. In the cinema context, consider, for example, a presentation of an image of breaking waves or the leaping of flames to imply an outpouring of passion (Metz, 1982: 185). Or consider the 1988 U.S. presidential campaign. The Bush media ideologists presented a shot in which inmates were seen as entering a revolving door and returning back. This metaphor was directed toward his opponent in the campaign.

Metonymy is the replacement of the whole by its part. It is "the whole ... reduced to and represented in terms of constituent elements" (Morgan, 1983: 602). Manning (1979: 661) adds: "it works through the mechanism of reduction, with the adduced parts being linked in some fashion with some explicated force which causes their identified patterning." Consider, for example, the word *Bordeaux*. More likely one immediately associates wine (the signified) with it rather than the place it is produced. Or consider the inventor Guillotine of that death machine (see Metz, 1982: 154). Or consider some conversational use such as *thirty sails* to refer to thirty boats, or one hundred dollars per head rather than per person, or reference to the *crown* when really referring to the king. Or, finally, focusing on the court, think in terms of the prosecutor presenting peripheral evidence, bits and pieces of evidence, in his or her attempt to elicit a flow of events in the jurors' minds that will lead to a conclusion that this part/piece of evidence stands for or indicates a bigger and complete picture. The clearest example, objectified in law, is the case of having possession of burglary tools (in other words a possessory act), which is a crime.

In the Lacanian construct the metaphor-metonymy axis cannot be assigned to the primary or secondary process, rather it is more part of the Symbolic order. We add that the content of metaphors and the metonymic can only be understood materialistically; that is, a particular mode of production, with its existent level of technology and the political economic structure that manufactures ideology, supplies core materials to be used in the construction of metaphors and metonymies (for example, machine metaphors).

Figure 12.2
Semiotic Grid

Conscious Plane	Paradigm	Syntagm
↕	Metaphor	Metonymy
Unconscious Plane	Condensation	Displacement

Interactive Effects: The Semiotic Grid

We must now be precise as to how these semiotic axes interact. Figure 12.2 represents the semiotic grid out of which ideal types can be posited. What distinguishes the paradigm-syntagm axis from the metaphor-metonymy axis is that whereas the former is constituted by the internal laws of discourse (i.e., grammar) the latter makes reference to something real or imaginary outside of discourse itself (Metz, 1982: 188). For Metz's project, the cinema text was the focus. For us, we are interested in how semiotic production takes place in storytelling in the courtroom. That is, how does a story get constructed with given elements? We are suggesting, then, that a story undergoes a construction process. However, during juridicosemiotic production, a fixed range of core signifiers and their appropriate signifieds have already been established. These limit the form of discursive syntactical expression, while creating in the referent, manifest and latent signifieds that on one level are always already diachronically situated in technological and ideological spatiotemporal coordinates. Within an imaginary space, images emanating from the Other (for Lacan, the unconscious as a repository of floating signifiers) and its constitutive metaphorical and metonymical signifying practices are given temporary coherence within a narrowly circumscribed spatiotemporal frame, in the process fixing a conception of reality. Within the juridic field, the very concept of crime and the process of adjudication—with its focus on proving the existence of individual criminal intent and the commission of the act—narrowly circumscribe the semiotic grid in use. Only a limited accentuation of wider contextual factors takes place during law-finding practices, hence contributing to the ideology of an autonomous, determining individual, rather than to the idea of the human being situated within diverse and often contradictory semantic domains and their effects.

Subjects within the judicial arena must, therefore, consider:

• The sedimented legalistic paradigm: "What words can I choose (from a limited inventory with uniaccentuated signifieds) in constructing a story which is favorable to my client?"

- Syntagm: "How can I ask a question to elicit a desired response which will not be stricken as, for example, 'leading the witness' "; in other words: "How do I pose the question that is syntactically correct, legalistically speaking that is?"

- Metaphor: "How do I construct an imaginary space within which the juror will willingly insert her- or himself, and thus be bounded, unbeknowingly, by its implied logic?"

- Metonymy: "How to focus a line of questioning on a particular element in a story that stands for, or is seen as logically connected to, a greater whole—that is, how can the part lead the audience (jurors) into constructing the whole through cogitation over the parts?"

For example, the prosecutor strives to re-create metaphorically the system of metonymical signs that are normally assumed as indices of criminal activity and mind. Put in another way, she or he attempts to induce a shift in semantic domains from one of law-abider to one of lawbreaker. Storytelling inevitably presents the jurors with gaps, with unexplained spaces, that need to be negotiated. The process of suture (examined further below) functions in such a way as to create a stable, coherent, and logical sequence in the story's linear progression, and, in the process, reaffirms the dominant social order while giving an imaginary unity to the subject.

In sum, we envision the semiotic grid as being given specific articulation by the higher courts and as being functionally connected with the internal logic of capital, mitigated somewhat by oppositional struggles.

The Efficacious Signifier

Contrary to Saussure's schematic depicting the signified over the signifier, Lacan's model posits the primacy of the signifier (see Figure 12.1). In fact his much-celebrated statement has it that a "signifier is that which represents the subject for another signifier" (1977: 287, 298, 316; 1981: 198–199, 207, 218–219, 236; see also Lee, 1990: 72–81; Borch-Jacobsen, 1991: 169–196; Smith, 1988: 71–77; Pecheux, 1982: 188–190; Silverman, 1983: 172–173). This is Lacan's way of saying that subjectivity is the effect of signifying practices.

In the Lacanian framework, speech can be understood in terms of a periodic knotting, much like the button fastening upholstery to a chair. This puts a stop, a punctuation (an arresting) to the perpetual flow of signifieds under the signifier, producing an anchoring point, a join, the end result of which gives a temporary fixity to meaning (Lacan, 1977: 154, 160, 303–320; see also Lemaire, 1977: 40, 101–102, 116–117; Laclau and Mouffe, 1985). The unconscious, the discourse of the Other—constituted primarily by its two central mechanisms of metaphor and metonymy, for Lacan, a locus where only signifiers circulate, not meaning—periodically imparts (manifests) gaps and divisions between signifiers, which is perceived as a lack, an absence, to which the subject responds with the activation of desire. The subject is temporarily materialized as a stand-in by this suturing process. During this moment of lack, perceived as absence, an interplay between the Imaginary (the sphere of imaginary identifications of self and other) and the Symbolic (the sphere of language) transpires, assuring that a resolution will manifest itself in the direction of an imaginary unity, resulting in the appearance of a Cartesian determining subject. The result is the appearance of lack-of-lack, a plentitude. Thus the subject is temporarily closed off from the unconscious, producing a momentarily coherent, unified speaking-being (Lacan's *l'etre parlant*), the *I*, which now participates in the production of meaning at the cost of being.

The Lacanian subject appears in discourse as a negativity. Drawing from Kojeve's (1980) lectures on Hegel, it is said that the naming of a thing constitutes the murder of the thing (pp. 140–141; Lacan, 1977: 104; Borch-Jacobsen, 1991: 169–196). Say *dog* and it appears in its absence. Say the words *Chicago Bears* and a team of football players appears, present in their absence. It is a manifesting of an absence. Similarly the subject that speaks in language abolishes itself there. To say I in discourse (the subject of speech, the grammatical subject), is to negate the subject of the enunciation. It is to present the subject in his or her absence. The subject of the enunciation disappears while manifesting itself in the subject of speech.

Desire is awakened continuously at the initiation of absence. As MacCabe has said (1985: 127): "Desire is the passage along the metonymy of signifiers and it is in those moments when the signifier is no longer under the domination of the signified that desire speaks: that 'it' talks there where 'I' have lost control." The result of the dialectical interplay between the different instances and its effects leads us to picture "the individual as a set of overlapping and contradictory practices which produce a plurality of contradictory subjects" (p. 153).

In sum, we are persuaded that manifest signifiers with their temporarily stabilized signifieds are effects of the interplay of the three semiotic axes we have explored above. Importantly for the Lacanian model, suture takes place between the Imaginary and the Symbolic, constituting a temporary unitary subject. Lacan, however, misses the effects of ideological structures. The Imaginary and the Symbolic in our model are through and through ideological. It is by way of a materialistic critique of the mode of production and its effects in the social formation that we can convincingly argue about the wherewithal of subjectivity.

Extraverbal Context

A statement on semiotic production would be incomplete unless we also add the determinant of the extraverbal context. In other words, an utterance must be situated historically (diachronically) in time and space. Consider such utterances as "So!" or "Hm," or "Yes!" (Bakhtin cited in Todorov, 1984: 42). Or consider the expression "Ah . . . coming." Clearly in itself little meaning is attached to the utterance outside of a context of its enunciation. Imagine, for example, that some people are waiting for a bus. No one will state "The bus for which we are waiting is coming" but rather just "coming," or applying Vygotsky's (1962: 199) example to contemporary Western society, "Ah . . . coming." Hence the extraverbal context of interlocutors consists of (1) their "common spatial purview"—that is, what is directly visible to the interlocutors, the Real in Lacan's framework; (2) their "common knowledge and understanding of the situation"—in the courtroom context, what one thinks it is that takes place; and (3) their "common evaluation" of the particular situation (Volosinov, 1986: 99; see also Medvedev and Bakhtin, 1978: 122).

These concrete and specific historical contexts are occasions for the generation of themes—unique, unitary, indivisible, unreproducible thematic wholes (Volosinov, 1986: 100)—that seek expression in the form of the word or an utterance. Meaning can only be established through an active mutual orientation of each of the interlocutors in a particular context (Bakhtin, 1986: 68). It is through and through an intersubjective phenomenon.

Interlocutors, then, find themselves faced with a particular LCS within which they must insert themselves in order to communicate, in order to be understood. Language provides the interlocutors with words: (1) that have dictionary meanings, empty forms—and hence, on their face, these appear as neutral with potentialities; (2) that become, in dialogue, populated with the other's intentions, values, and accentuations—they appear, that is, with a voice, embodiments of themes; and (3) that become subject to an appropriation, an accentuation of the word, expressing or reflecting a particular interlocutor's theme (Bakhtin, 1986: 88). The utterance, then, is determined, in part, by (1) the referential and semantic exhaustiveness—the extent to which the theme is allowed full expression in that particular sphere of life, (2) the speech plan—interlocutors actively imagine what the other wishes to say in determining the relationships of the unfolding utterances; and (3) the choice(?) of a particular LCS (speech genre) (Bakhtin, 1986: 77–78). Taking these three aspects we may say that the generated utterance's connection to a particular subjective theme can be ranged along a dimension of congruency, from very restrictive to very enabling. Courtroom storytelling, for example, finds itself in a restrictive domain. The themes of defendants are never fully expressed in their concrete contexts. Nor can defendants smoothly insert themselves within the new speech genres to present their version of "what happened?" in plausible ways. This frustration often manifests itself in terms of what Goffman (1967: 113–136) calls alienation from interaction. More important, in courtroom storytelling, the polyvocal nature of discourse and the plurality of LCSs in a social formation is both denied and replaced by a unitary, decontextualized, and static juridic LCS of relevance.

Semiotic production, then, at the intrapsychic and intersubjective level, can be studied in terms of the interaction of these different levels. The capitalist semiotic grid is a pervasive disciplinary mechanism, producing the individual of docility and utility as its primal effect (see also Foucault, 1977, 1980). The thesis of the colonization of the lifeworld (Habermas, 1984) is augmented by a systematic arresting, a punctuation of the perpetual sliding of signifieds under the signifiers congruent with system imperatives of domination and exploitation. This is mitigated by (1) periodic political economic legitimation crises engendering a temporary loosening of these binds, and their recoupling by such juridic mechanisms as interest balancing (Milovanovic, 1987), and by (2) oppositional struggles.

NEXUS

Let us summarize and give some precise examples of where our analysis has led. Lawyers have a monopoly over the use of juridic linguistic tools that are used in the construction of reality in law-finding practices. As Bourdieu (1987: 835) has argued, "legal qualifications comprise a specific power that allows control of entry into the juridical field by deciding which conflicts deserve entry, and determining the specific form in which they must be clothed to be constituted as properly legal arguments." Lawyers construct stories. Stories are organizational devices for presenting believable (plausible) chains of events (B. Jackson, 1991).

Applying film theory to lawyers' attempted presentations of a coherent, logical story, we may say that "the image of a scene, a sequence, of a whole creation, exists not as something fixed and ready-made. It has to arise, to unfold before the senses of the spectator [juror]" (Eisenstein, 1975: 18). That is, "the series of ideas is built up in the perception and consciousness into a whole image, storing up the separate elements" (p. 17). Jurors are not in a normal *visee* (orientation of consciousness). Rather the requirement of jurying is that one place oneself in a particular visee: an attributional visee. Hence, presuming this, lawyers attempt to construct a story that may be understood on a number of levels, much like a film director in the attempt to direct the audience (the viewers) to draw definite inferences from the juxtaposition of shots in syntagmatic clusters with their activated referential signified clusters.

A heightened degree of creativity will be of a premium in trials where only circumstantial evidence exists; here the prosecutor no doubt will attempt to create an imaginary space where opportunity, motivation, and capability are constructed so that the juror will fill in the inferential to create a composite picture of "what happened?" in line with the theme of the prosecutor. Put in another way, here a semantic domain will be induced in the imagination of the jurors where a metonymical system of expressions will include indices of opportunity, motivation, and capability. Eisenstein (1975: 30–31) has stated it well:

Before the inner vision, before the perception of the creator [here lawyers], hovers a given image, emotionally embodying his theme. The task that confronts him is to transform this image into a few basic *partial representations* which, in their combination and juxtaposition, shall evoke in the consciousness and feelings of the spectator, reader, or auditor [here, jurors], that same initial general image which originally hovered before the creative artists.

Since jurors, too, normally situate themselves in taken-for-granted stances (the normal visee), they must now, if we may use Husserl's (1975) term, place themselves in a judgmental position, an *epoche*: Could things happen the way this lawyer is implying? Jurors situate themselves in the subject-position that is preconstructed. Their heightened inquisitiveness to story elements localizes them between the interplay of the Symbolic (here, the language of the courts) and the Imaginary. In the latter, jurors actively construct an imaginary identification with an ego-ideal, the reasonable man in law, which then becomes the basis of comparison, of identification. The assumed *I* is distinguished from the *you* of the defendant in relation to the ideological construct of the juridic subject in law. This tension tends toward a resolution of the "what happened?" Each side (the prosecutor's and the defense counsel's) attempts to construct jurors as spoken subjects. In other words, by an identification with the respectively induced imaginary constructs—along a spatiotemporal frame (implying causality, responsibility, capability, motivation, or lack thereof)—a stable conception of reality and subjectivity is sought. Often, in the process, the intervening signifying chains recede from consciousness and only the beginning and end of the whole process are perceived (see also Eisenstein, 1975: 15). In this complex process, gaps will exist as lawyers elicit elements being used to construct the believ-ability of the story. Jurors, then, must confront these gaps by filling in the logical connections between story elements. We understand, too, that the juror is faced with at least two competing constructions of reality.

The process of suture is such that an interplay between the Symbolic (language) and the Imaginary (the specular) takes place in which subjects attempt to fill in gaps in the story being presented; this is always subject, however, to the interplay and effects of the available elements within the semiotic grid we established above. We can see very quickly that the LCS in which jurors, lawyers, and judges find themselves inserted narrow the available elements (signifiers with their circumscribed static signifieds) that can be appropriated for use. Argumentation—bounded syntactically, par-adigmatically, metaphorically, and metonymically—is always already restricted by a politically overdetermined constructive process.

Elements from an alternative LCS—that is, of an oppositional variety (most clearly expressed in political trials), are denied entrance into this arena. Or, at best, only a few elements are allowed. Hence the clash between the oppositional and juridic LCSs, where fewer semiotic forms from the former are articulated than from the latter, militates against telling convincing (plausible) stories that are politically constituted. What is perpetuated is a form of symbolic violence (Bourdieu, 1987: 850; Goodrich, 1990; Lecercle, 1990) in which dominant juridic understandings are continuously written over oppositional readings; Leviathan stands ready and willing to take up arms against those in opposition.

In sum, each of the opposing lawyers in a trial attempts to creatively breakup his or her initially conceptualized theme into linguistic representations, guided predominantly by the paradigm-syntagm semiotic axis, with the purpose of bringing to life a story that will be experienced by the jurors in an identical manner. What we emphasize is that for even the politically motivated lawyer who attempts to bring a politically contextualized story into the trial, a series of censors (i.e., objections raised, with the judge sustaining; renderings by the judge of nonjusticiability, etc.) will be activated, which assure that an alternative and coherent oppositional story will not unfold (see also Milovanovic, 1988; 1992; Milovanovic and Thomas, 1989; Bannister and Milovanovic, 1990).

So far we have stayed within a formalistic presentation. It is now time to turn to the agent of signifying practices.

SUBJECTIVITY

Two competing conceptions of the person are currently in vogue in the literature. Descartes' *cogito ergo sum* (I think, therefore I am) represents a view given centrality with the development of the capitalist mode of production in the seventeenth and eighteenth centuries and more generally of modernist society in the aftermath of post-Renaissance thought. This Cartesian conception has it that man/woman is determining rather than determined, that man/woman is unified, stable, and is the active, rational, and free producer of discourse and action. It assumes a knowledgeable, determining subject as an a priori. In distinction is the dualistic model that Lacanian analysis offers. Man/woman is not totally determining, rather is more determined; is subject to the forces stemming not only from conscious states but from the effects of unconscious processes. Descartes' conception is replaced by Lacan's (1977: 166): "I think where I am not, therefore I am where I do not think." Rather than situating a person only within a stream of consciousness, this approach situates him or her more in a stream of signifying practices.

Here we will try to resituate the contemporary debate within psychoanalytic semiotics, drawing from the critical Marxist tradition as well as recent

Figure 12.3
Schema L

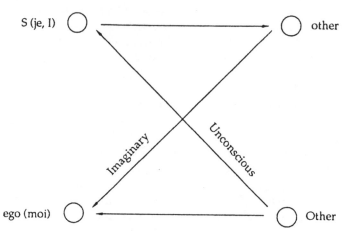

cinema theory. We must rescue subjectivity from the abyss that has befallen it. The human being is not only a creature of rational thought and action but also one who is the locus of drives, wishes, desires, emotions, loves, and feelings—simple as it may sound, these often are neglected in scientific inquiries of man/woman. Resituating the focus of debate may provide more beneficial vistas in the analysis of the contemporary malaise of man/woman—that is, may lead to a better understanding of the wherewithal of her/his contemporary existential plight of loss of meaning and freedom.

The Freudian model has rightfully been criticized for its exclusive intra-psychic emphasis. It is to Lacan's Hegelian inspired analysis that we turn for additional elements in our approach. He situates the person within an intra- and intersubjective frame, particularly focusing on the effects of the interplay of language and the Imaginary. Hence his development of the idea of the Symbolic, Real, and Imaginary is useful.

Lacan has it that the Symbolic represents culture and language. The Imaginary represents the initial outcome of the mirror stage of development where the child (6–18 months of age) sees itself in the mirror for the first time and constructs an imaginary unity, an ideal image of its fragmented, uncoordinated existence. This primordial specular image henceforth remains ever-present in the person's everyday constitution of self. The Real signifies the organic, the biological, that which is beyond knowledge. It is these three orders that have a prominent effect on subjectivity. Figure 12.3 depicts Schema L, the Lacanian quadripartite subject (Lacan, 1977: 193–194; 1981; 243; see, also Ragland-Sullivan, 1986: 2; Lemaire, 1977: 237–238).

Briefly, the *S* stands for the *I*, the subject of discourse. The *moi* is the ego, an imaginary construct, having taken on an original form during the mirror stage of development. The *other* represents the other interlocutor, the thou (the *tu*) who is the object of desire and recognition. The *Other* (and Lacan gives it many meanings) represents language, the locus of the signifier, the unconscious, "the locus in which is constituted the I who speaks with him who hears," the "place where it thinks: another scene" (Lacan cited in Lemaire, 1977: 157). For Lacan the subject is stretched over all four corners. Trying to pinpoint its precise location is much like the classic physicist's abortive attempts in trying to define the electron in terms of an objective existence in some point in space. In the Lacanian quaternary construct, the *ego-other* axis is further defined in terms of imaginary relations of identification and attraction made explicit in the need for recognition. The *S-Other* axis is much like Hegel's and Kojeve's stipulated master-slave relationship, with the Other being the master. In the *S-Other* axis, the symbolic/unconscious axis, the *I* of discourse (the *I* as signifier), is the subject of speech, the effect of the Other, of signifying practices.

It is by speaking to the image (myth) of the other, by exteriorizing-alienating itself that the subject represents itself as an object in discourse and hence through the mediation of the other develops self-consciousness. Hence, in the Lacanian schema, desire exists for the other; for recognition, judgment, and love. The subject then seeks the recognition of the other; it is through his or her recognition and judgment that it understands itself. Thus, "the function of speech is not to inform but to evoke [the response, the recognition of the other]" (Lacan, 1977: 86; Ragland-Sullivan, 1986: 219). The *moi*, the ego, then, is evanescent, elusive, kaleidoscopic; on the other hand, the *I* of discourse seeks to accommodate itself to the ego's ideals, while assimilating itself to the cultural normative order, in the process, providing a temporary sense of unity (see also Ragland-Sullivan, 1986: 43). The subject is caught in the dialectical interplay of these subject-object relations.

Of course, in the Lacanian schema, rather lacking is the notion of ideological impositions; cultural mediation is only implied (with the exception of his seminars of 1969–70: see Lacan, 1991; Milovanovic, 1992). In other words, the mirror that is so central to the Lacanian framework is most often devoid of the effects of manipulative ideological practices. To ground his otherwise cogent argument concerning subjectivity we must introduce a materialistically derived ideological framework. We seek guidance from Althusser (1971: 164–165), whose much-celebrated statement has it that

all ideology represents in its necessarily imaginary distortions not the existing relations of production (and the other relations that derive from them), but above all the (imaginary) relationship of individuals to the relations of production and the relations that derive from them. What is represented in ideology is therefore not the system of real relations which govern the existence of individuals, but the imaginary relations of those individuals to the real relations in which they live.

Here Althusser uses two terms germane to Lacan's analysis—imaginary, real—and only implies the symbolic. Although some distortion of Lacanian terms is taking place, we need not be too quick to abandon the overall thrust of Althusser's insights. The Imaginary, then, indeed is the sphere in which the specular is central in the constitution of unitary ego-ideals, but it is always already aided (constituted) by ideological state apparatuses such as the media, school system, family, legal structures. Just as in the carnival mirror—which by simple manipulation of the mechanism, the apparatus, the mirror—distorted images are reflected to the viewer. This Imaginary sphere is through and through ideological, always unevenly reflecting (predominantly) the particular constructs of hegemonic group interest. Oppositional struggles will attempt to provide their specular constructs consistent with their subversive ideals. And this, too, is an arena of struggle (Laclau and Mouffe, 1985; Henry and Milovanovic, 1991; Milovanovic, 1992). Apart from rightfully being critiqued for having an overly deterministic emphasis (i.e., the individual is only a functional support of structures), Althusser's model also lacks a sophisticated understanding of subjectivity and particularly its inseparability from language. Here we turn to Benveniste (1971).

It is Benveniste's thesis that when we speak of subjectivity, we must distinguish between two levels. First, we have the subject of enunciation (*le subject de l'enonciation*)—the speaking subject, the speaker, writer; the producer of the discursive chain; the maker of a statement; that with which the discoursing subject identifies (the discursive elements)—in the cinema model, the act of constructing a sequence of images that speak; the domain of the Real. Second, we have the subject of *ennonce* (*le sujet de l'enonce*)—the subject of speech, or the subject of the utterance; what is said, written; the *I* as signifier; the grammatical subject; the statement—in the cinema model, the level of fiction. Hence we have the speaking subject and the subject of the utterance or speech. These are two separate spheres. In fact it is precisely during suture that the subject stands in as signifier, as an *I*—the subject of speech—that gives him or her access to the Symbolic order. Here, entrance into language is correlated with the appearance of subjectivity. The *I* is a stand-in for an absent subject.

Consider Lacan's example (1981: 139) of the different spheres at play reflected in the statement: "I am lying." Or consider Smith's (1988: 76) "I choose." Clearly, two planes are being evoked: even though related, one cannot simultaneously be meaningfully in both. Hence, the speaking subject belongs to the realm of the Real. However, it attains subjectivity or self-knowledge only by way of signifying practices—the domain of the Symbolic (Silverman, 1983: 196). To apprehend one—the speaking subject—is to effect an aphanisis (a fading) of the other—the subject of speech (Lacan, 1981: 211–213, 218). By this, we, with Lacan, imply that meaning is created at the cost of being, and being at the cost of meaning (Lacan, 1981: 211, 218; Smith, 1988: 73; Silverman, 1983: 170–172, 200). The two subjects, in other words, are never reducible to each other; they are forever separated by the barrier of the real and the symbolic, of reality and signification, of being and meaning. Signifiers are only activated and given form in discourse and hence need a subject who will fill in the signifieds and who will also identify with the most important signifier, the *I* (Benveniste, 1971: 218; Silverman, 1983: 197; Borch-Jacobsen, 1991: 169–196). For Benveniste it is not possible to isolate subjectivity from discourse or language from subjectivity. The pronouns *I* and *you*, as signifiers, are only capable of signifying in discourse itself. The "I refers to the act of individual discourse in which it is pronounced, and by this it designates the speaker" (Benveniste, 1971: 226).

Thus, for Benveniste, *I* as a signifier only takes on form and substance in discourse. At the level of *langue*, words such as *I*, *you*, *here*, *there*, *then*, *when*, and verb tenses have no meaning outside their use in a particular discourse—that is, outside their situatedness in syntagmatic clusters and the mobilized referential axis (signifieds). *You*, *here*, *there*, *then*, and verb tenses only take meaning (in relational terms), are filled-in, in signifying practices where the inserted *I* is subject.

We add here that for the juror the same process takes place. The juror identifies as the subject of speech; ideally for the prosecutor, she or he becomes a spoken subject—one that identifies completely with the story being presented ("I see it as the prosecutor sees it"). The imaginary that the prosecutor seeks to construct is that space within which subjectivity, the juror's, is being constituted.

Further, imaginary constructs are produced elsewhere, constructs with which a person must engage in an asymmetrical dialogue, a monologue if you will, and, hence, for example, in cinema theory the viewer is spoken as subject. We need to examine this. Two concepts have been provided in recent literature—one from cinema theory, the other from a Marxist critique of the mode of production—which specify the mechanisms by which the viewer is spoken in such a way that the subject is given the illusion of continuity and stability, a neo-Cartesian mirror, well in accord with the logic of capital. These are *suture* and *interpellation*.

The notion of suture, likened to a stitching as in a surgical joining (see Heath, 1981: 13, 52), was first used by Lacan. He states that it is "a conjunction of the imaginary and the symbolic" (1981: 118). It functions to produce an imaginary coherent *I* in discourse (Smith, 1988: 75). During moments of separation, or gaps in its existential field, which the subject perceives as a lack, an absence, what Lacan calls a *manque-à-être* (a lack-in-being), desire is activated and the subject fills in, sutures this existential lack by presenting itself as a stand-in, an imaginary function. What is construed, in other words, is an imaginary plenitude, a lack-of-lack. This imaginary function gives a unity, a coherence necessary for language. This is the speaking subject, now translated into the *I* in a discourse (i.e., the imaginary construct of the reasonable man in law, the juridic subject with formal rights). The *I* as speaker, as the creator of the discursive chain, appears temporarily and episodically congruent with the *I* as the grammatical subject, the subject of speech. This whole process is such that the subject is temporarily closed off from the effects of the unconscious. It perceives itself as one: the speaking subject and the subject of speech appear as identical.

Smith (1988: 76) has well stated the point: "suture is the mechanism by which the 'subject' is closed off from the unconscious, or the unconscious is closed off from the *subject*, in the effort to produce a coherent representation for the *I* which may engage in the production of meaning (that is, may engage at the level of *signs*)." Silverman (1983: 231) has stated it in yet another way: it is "the process whereby the inadequacy of the subject's position is exposed in order to facilitate (i.e., create the desire for) new insertions into cultural discourse which promises to make good that lack." In sum, in the act of speaking, writing, or viewing cinema, as well as in the case of the jury audience listening to lawyers presenting facts, or elements of a story, the *I* is both alienated from its twofold character while simultaneously disavowing that very alienation and, in the process, giving meaning to its existence.

The notion of suture developed by Lacan and advanced by cinema theorists, however, is still missing an ideological component. What overcomes this omission is the mechanisms of interpellation. The notion of interpellation has been developed by Althusser, who defines it as a form of hailing. He states that "ideology 'acts' or 'functions' in such a way that it 'recruits' subjects among the individuals ... or 'transforms' the individuals into subjects" (Althusser, 1971: 174). He likens it to a cop hailing someone by "Hey, you there!" By the very 180-degree turn of the person hailed he becomes a subject. Put in another way, by this very recognition one has inserted oneself in a particular discourse as subject. Implied, of course, is that the speaking and spoken subject are separate entities to begin with. The point being here that subjectivity is only activated in discourse (and with it, the paradigmatic-syntagmatic clusters associated with the attendant subject-positions—that is, it is activated by being inserted in an ongoing signifying system, an LCS that preexists the person.

Althusser's position on the effects of interpellation, by itself, is in danger of resurrecting "the philosophical subject, coherent and homogeneous, into a Lacanian schema which has as its explicit aim the subversion of that subject" (MacCabe, 1985: 109). Pecheux's (1982) attempted refinement of Althusser's argument, which poses the idea that the subject is trapped in discursive formations, with its determining elements of the preconstructed subject-positions and the attendant support-effects, provides, as MacCabe (1985: 107–108) has concisely analyzed, an overly rigid frame that is hard pressed to explain ideological struggles and transcendence. Better here is

MacCabe's resolution that subject-positions are constantly undermined and threatened by language and the eruption of desire (p. 108). It is at this instance that alternative readings of reality may materialize and subversive ideologies gain ascendancies. We agree with MacCabe that this provides the starting point for our investigation of ideological struggles. Hence, we build on Smith's (1988: xxxv) definition of subjectivity: "the conglomeration of positions, subject-positions,...into which a person is called momentarily by the discourses and the world that he/she inhabits," and state that subjectivity is the conglomeration of positions, subject-positions into which a person is called momentarily by the LCS and the world that she or he inhabits and to which she or he reacts. This overcomes the deficiencies of Althusser's deterministic definition. We see as a necessary element for a coherent subversive ideology to develop the necessity of an alternative oppositional LCS in which, if only momentarily, the subject may insert her- or himself to construct an alternative conception of reality, of what is and what may be (Milovanovic, 1992). Hegemonic groups will do all in their power to rechannel, subvert, repress or co-opt this incipient, internecine development.

CONCLUSION

In sum, Lacan's schema L (see Figure 12.3) can be constructively augmented by a critical materialistic analysis. The Subject-Other axis, a Symbolic/unconscious axis, is the domain in which subject-positions (i.e., the juridic subject, criminal conceptions) are established by the dominant and juridic LCSs and where the spoken subject is constituted. The semiotic grid, synchronically and diachronically linked with capital logic, already limits the process by which reality is constructed. The hegemonic arresting (punctuation) of the sliding phenomena circumscribes semiotic and hence speech production. The juridic subject (the bearer of abstract, formal rights), a creation of the capitalist mode of production, is a constitutive element of legitimation. The legal subject becomes an active participant in producing and reproducing dominant relations and justifying ideologies. The ego-other axis, an Imaginary relation, is structured by such processes as commodity fetishism, both directly or indirectly. The perception (myth) of the other and of self is manipulated by ideological state apparatuses that convey images of self-determining, autonomous individuals. The I-thou relation where genuine personhood is found by way of the mediation of the other is torn asunder, replaced by manipulated images, reflected in the everyday mirror employed. The specular, indeed, provides the illusory images of certainty, unity, and freedom.

13

Crime, Criminology, and Human Rights: Toward an Understanding of State Criminality

GREGG BARAK

State criminality or the harm illegally or legally organized and inflicted up-on people by their own governments or the governments of others have skimpily but increasingly been documented by social scientists/criminolo-gists (Schwendinger and Schwendinger, 1970; Block and Chambliss, 1981; Falk, 1988a; Block, 1989; Chambliss, 1989; Luyt, 1989; P. Scott, 1989; Zwerman, 1989; and Barak, 1991b). Nevertheless, it is still safe to argue that after some twenty years of recognizing state criminality as a concept, little progress has been made in either precisely specifying what the various forms of "state criminality" are, or in analyzing such case studies as those that present themselves, for example, before the United Nations Human Rights Commission. In other words, despite the many mass-mediated dis-cussions of these "crimes against humanity" as found in publications like *Newsweek*, *Time*, and *The Wall Street Journal*, or in those more critically oriented discussions as found in such publications as *Mother Jones*, *The Nation*, and *In These Times*, one still observes a scarcity of scholarship by criminologists on this topic. Until such time as this scarcity is removed, or until such time as there is serious development in the study of state crimi-nality, there will remain significant gaps in the study of crime and of state and social control.

More specifically, the relationship between state criminality and social control requires recognition by criminologists that we, too, play a role in not only defining the boundaries of the discipline, but also in helping to create what constitutes "crime" in the real world. It is important, therefore, that as critical criminologists, we develop ways of communicating progres-sive perspectives on crime and social justice to popular audiences (Barak, 1988). It is my further contention that the study of state criminality must become central to the study of crime and social control, if we are to develop a Left realist critical criminology that is capable of intersecting with the common sense social reality of crime and violence. Efforts at developing an understanding of these relationships have been occurring for the past couple of decades. Beginning in the late 1960s and early 1970s, revisionist historians and critical sociologists alike were starting to focus attention on the inter-relationships between the modern state and the various systems of social control (Cohen and Scull, 1985).

Out of this work there has reemerged the macro or classical nineteenth-century sociohistorical interest in the importance of the connections between questions of order, authority, power, legitimization, hegemony, organization, and change. These questions of social control have gone well beyond the micro or predominant twentieth-century questions that merely created various typologies of the means and processes involved in the socialization of conformity. The abandonment of a social-psychological perspective on a social control divorced from the history and politics of individual, group, and class struggles, and the preference for a social control grounded in the interplay of cultural production, ideological construction, and political economy, has served to resurrect the role of the state as central to each of these areas of social control.

It was precisely these macropolitical and -economic relations, ignored by traditional or positivist criminology during most of the twentieth century, that have historically limited the scope of the field to the study of the criminal behavior of the powerless. Gradually, however, over the past fifty years there has been an expansion over the "acceptable" boundaries of criminological focus to include the criminal behavior of the powerful, beginning with the professional, white-collar, organized, and, most recently, corporate criminals. During this shifting in criminological paradigms, the establishment of a critical criminology reunited the study of the state with the study of crime that had previously been separated by positivist criminology. Although progress has been made in describing the integral connections between class, race, gender, crime, social control, and the state, very little light has been shed on understanding the role and the development of state-organized criminality in the reproduction of the crimes of both the powerful and the powerless. Before such an understanding can come about, there must first be a development of state criminality and its legitimation within the field of criminology.

TOWARD AN UNDERSTANDING OF STATE CRIMINALITY

Is it not an ultimate contradiction that the state has been both a crime-regulating and crime-generating institution? That is to say, the state through its formal and informal policies not only engages in crime control, but also engages in the development of crime, its own and others. As a criminogenic institution, the state not only violates the rights of individuals, but it contributes to the production of other forms of criminality as well. From the perspective of critical criminology, these injuries or harms ("crimes") may or may not violate law per se.

The criminological journey toward the development of a criminology of state criminality will not be accomplished without resistance from both inside and outside the boundaries of academic criminology. Simply put, there are a number of disciplinary biases and political obstacles to overcome. To begin with, the study of state criminality is problematic because the very concept itself is controversial. This is due, in part, to the debate over whether or not one should define "crime" in terms other than the law codes of individual nations.

Traditional criminology has always ascribed to the legalistic state definition of crime, investigation, and analysis confined to legally proscribed behavior and its control (Schwendinger and Schwendinger, 1970; Platt, 1974; Michalowski, 1985). Outside of the conventional confines of criminology have been those acts such as imperialism, exploitation, racism, and sexism, or those acts not typically prosecuted such as tax-evasion, consumer fraud, government corruption, and state violence. Critical criminology, accordingly, has not confined itself to studying legally defined crime. Utilizing other definitions such as crimes against humanity or politically defined crime, critical criminology has studied harmful and injurious behavior that may or may not be sanctioned by particular nation-states' definitions of illegality, but that are recognized in the "higher" criteria established in various international treaties, covenants, or laws. Therefore, for the purposes of this discussion, crimes by and of the state, like those crimes against the state, may be viewed similarly as involving exploits of both a violent and nonviolent nature. They may, in fact, involve violations of the same established legal relations or prohibitions, including but not limited to such behaviors as murder, rape, espionage, cover-up, burglary, illegal wiretapping, illegal break-in, disinformation, kidnapping, theft, assassination, terrorism, secrecy, unaccountability, corruption, exporting arms and importing drugs illegally, obstruction of justice, perjury, deception, fraud, and conspiracy. In addition, state criminality may include the more general transgression of both domestic and international laws, not to mention the more subtle institutional relations or behaviors that cause social injury such as the bankrupting and the destroying of whole economies or the violation of universally shared notions of fundamental human rights.

These critical definitions of crime that have opened up the scope of "criminality" have certainly not as yet been adapted by conventional criminologists nor even been considered by the general public. In fact, both Leftists and Rightists, inside and outside of criminology, have found such conceptualizations of crime to be unreal, unnatural, idealistic, impractical, or irrelevant. The point, however, is that for those critical criminologists who think otherwise, the time is long past due for the serious development of the substantive areas of state criminality. Through this type of critical development within criminology there stands the possibility of transforming the very nature of the study of criminality from the individual to the political.

In order to carry out such a criminological agenda, investigators cannot be deterred in their study of state criminality by the lack or failure of the state to adjudicate itself or its agents as criminals. After all, just because it has been the case that states have chosen to ignore, dismiss, or downplay their own criminality, it does not follow that we criminologists should do the same. Similarly, criminologists should extricate themselves from the trap of viewing state crimes within the old political double standard: treating the phenomenon as though it involves the behavior of certain designated bad guy states and not the behavior of so-called good guy states.

For example, the case of terrorism presents much theoretical, strategic, and ideological work to be done. Scholarly interest in this area, especially as conducted by students of criminology and criminal justice, has been highly focused or selected on some but not all terrorist acts. This selectivity refers not only to countries emphasized and neglected, but to the various forms of terrorism committed. By most legally defined or state-based notions of terrorism, the typically incorporated crimes include those "retail" terrorist acts committed by groups or individuals against agents or symbolic representatives of a real or imaginary enemy state. Typically omitted from most discussions are those "wholesale" acts of terrorism waged by state-supported networks against various independence or national revolutionary movements (Chomsky and Herman, 1979; Herman, 1982).

Or what about the role of covert and overt aid in the domestic affairs of developing nations, especially in trying to effect the outcomes of elections? It used to be, in the glory days of the American empire, that neither the president, the Congress, nor the people considered whether we had a right to intervene in the domestic affairs of another nation. U.S. aid in those days, mostly covert, "was routine, and so pervasive as to be immune to political criticism" (Weinstein, 1989: 14). But with respect to the practicalities, if not the underlying principles, U.S. foreign policies are now beginning to be publicly questioned. At the same time, however, for example, the Bush administration during its first year in office attempted to redefine the term *assassination* in an effort to circumvent President Ford's 1975 executive order formally banning U.S. assassinations of foreign officials. According to a recent "memorandum of law," the original order has not been changed, only watered down to exclude the possibility of assassination without premeditation (Wright, 1989: 1C). Whatever the state finally decides about these "murders," elections, and other forms of covert and overt intervention, criminologists should not be precluded from exploring and examining these actions as state crimes against humanity.

Like the study of corporate crime, the study of state crime is problematic because it involves examining behaviors engaged in by agents and organizations that are both socially and politically acceptable (Clinard and Yeager,

1980; Ermann and Lundman, 1982). Access to studying the politically powerful, especially with respect to deviant behavior, has always been difficult. While both corporate and state criminality have the potential for undermining the very stability of the system that the corporate-state strives to protect, it is the latter crimes by the state that pose the greater threat to the political legitimation of the system as a whole. State criminality, in other words, provides the type of inherent contradictions that simultaneously challenge the prevailing political ideology yet accommodate the same behavior in the name of greater common interests or national security. The political repression or governmental crimes committed against the Chinese demonstrators in 1989 was an excellent example of this point. To label and to study such behavior as criminal was to participate in a delegitimation of the Chinese state; one can well imagine the consequences for any Chinese criminologist who would have attempted to examine this form of state criminality.

Analysis of state criminality is further complicated because it involves not only the overlapping activities of "criminal" and "noncriminal" organizations, but also because it involves the study of state-supported corruption and violence, which never can be totally separated from individual acts of criminality and terrorism as each is somehow related to the inequitable distribution of economic wealth and legal-juridical privileges. Concerning the former set of relationships, Block (1986: 59) summarized the situation nicely when he argued that traditionally organized crime and state-organized crime are inseparable in many cases because "organized crime has been and continues to be inextricably linked to transnational political movements and to that segment of the American political establishment known as the espionage community or more aptly, the transnational police force." He further concluded that this kind of interplay between organized and state criminality results in the situation where

it may very well be the case that certain political assassinations or other intelligence moves may be done not in the interests of foreign policy carried out by hired goons and thugs, but rather in the interest of drug smugglers and international gamblers carried out by their clients in the intelligence services (p. 76).

As for the connections between individual criminality and state criminality, Dieterich (1986: 50) has argued, for example, that the material debasement of the "majority of the Latin American peoples is an inevitable consequence of the current capitalist accumulation model" and the physical and psychological submission of these peoples "into a state of apathy and fear is a functional prerequisite for that accumulation model." On the U.S. domestic front, Henry (in Barak, 1991b) has already demonstrated the relationship between a "free market" economy and street criminality as both are tied to policies of omission and marginality and to the viability of informal economic activity as an alternative response to legitimate work. Therefore, the ability of criminology to recognize not only the criminal content and the criminogenic nature of various forms of state intervention into the affairs of other countries, but also the criminality and the crime-producing influences of domestic policies of noninterventionist omission, becomes a necessary prerequisite for the development of the serious study of state crimes.

In sum, the development of a criminology of state criminality requires that criminologists move way beyond the rather one-dimensional media portrayals and political discourse associated with the selectively chosen crime by the state. In order to establish a criminology of the structural and etiological reasons (causes) of state criminality, criminologists and other legal and political scientists must first present the kinds of conceptual frameworks that not only incorporate the full array of state crimes, but that can aid us in understanding the relative harm and injury inflicted by the behaviors and policies of nation-states.

STATE CRIMINALITY AND THE U.S. EXPERIENCE

It should be pointed out that state criminality is not indigenous or symptomatic of any particular socioeconomic formation, including precapitalist, capitalist, or socialist. As far back as the fifth century A.D., for example, state criminality had been acknowledged in the course of realizing that the actions of pirate bands were essentially the same as those actions of states and empires. That is to say, both pirates and empires had the capacity to seize property by force or violence. The only real difference between the two was the scale of their endeavors and the success of pre-states or empires to impose a justifying rhetoric or ideology for their theft of land, property, and people (Jenkins, 1988; Chambliss, 1989). In the contemporary world, of course, regardless of the particular socioeconomic and state formation, crimes by and of the state can be found globally. In other words, historically it has been the case that both democratic and undemocratic regimes have engaged in state criminality. It may very well be the case that political repression and state crime have less to do with the democratic nature of the government per se, and more to do with the power of a particular state regime such as the United States or the former USSR.

A glance at the "democratic" history of the United States reveals the patterned actions of state criminality. Whether we are discussing the nineteenth-century crimes of the U.S. government that were in violation of the fundamental rights of Native and African American peoples, or we are examining those state crimes that have violated the legal and civil rights of workers, minorities, and dissidents over the past century, the evidence clearly demonstrates that these crimes were not accidental or due to some kind of negligence. On the contrary, those state actions engaged in and/or the consequences of the policies of a developing political economy were the outcome of premeditated and intentional decisions. In fact, some of these "crimes against humanity," such as slavery, were in full compliance with the supreme laws of the land.

In light of these historical realities, the student of twentieth-century U.S. state criminality, for example, when studying the role of the Federal Bureau of Investigation (FBI) as a formal institution of social control, should strive for an integration of the dual-sided nature of state "crime-fighting" and "political-policing." The Palmer Raids and the Red Scare of 1919, the McCarthyism of the early 1950s, and the counterinsurgency campaigns of the late 1960s and early 1970s used against those citizens protesting the involvement of the United States in Southeast Asia reveal a domestic history of extraordinary political repression or state criminality against those who have seriously challenged or posed any kind of threat to the status quo (Glick, 1989). Such activities, covert and overt, have not been limited to domestic enemies alone, but have included foreign political enemies as well. Since it was established in the late 1940s, the Central Intelligence Agency (CIA) has had a rather consistent history of supporting repressive dictators in such countries as Cuba, Iran, the Philippines, Nicaragua, Brazil, South Korea, and Argentina, and of overthrowing or destabilizing democratically elected governments in Guatemala, Chile, Jamaica, and Nicaragua—to name only a few (Bodenheimer and Gould, 1989). Here again, as with the domestic state crimes, these international state crimes would appear to select their victims in response to the needs of laissez-faire or the free market economy, consistent with the real or perceived needs of capitalist accumulation.

What these domestic and international examples of state crime have shared in common has been their ongoing series of legal and illegal clandestine operations used against those politically labeled deviants. Within the United States, the FBI's Cointelpro (counterintelligence programs) of the 1960s and 1970s used against the Black Panther Party for Self-Defense, the antiwar movement, and the American Indian Movement included a variety of illegal and unconstitutional techniques to delegitimate or to otherwise criminalize lawful organizations (Churchill and Wall, 1988). These state crimes have involved such everyday illegal activities as surveilling, burglarizing, and tampering with the mail. In addition, there have been the more exotic forms of state criminality such as employing propaganda to smear progressive organizations, or sending out disruptive *agents provocateurs* (Wolfe, 1973; U.S. Congress, 1976; Caute, 1978; and Churchill and Wall, 1988).

The study of state criminality, more so than the study of any other form of criminality, is by definition a highly politicized undertaking. In other words, the study of state crimes cannot be separated from the emotionally charged landscape of a changing political economy, which involves, among other things, the study of law, power, and ideology as well as the study of public policy, foreign and domestic. A case in point is the study of terrorism where one person's "terrorist" has been another person's "freedom fighter." For example, with respect to U.S.-supported state terrorism, it should be recognized that such forms of state criminality as the involvement in systemic counterrevolutionary warfare, proinsurgency, or interventionism are responsible for all kinds of human casualties. The tens of thousands of lost lives and an even larger number of permanently injured citizens of Latin American countries, over the past few decades, reveals just some of the harm done by the international state criminality. I refer specifically to the illegal detentions and the mass torturing, murdering, and kidnapping by U.S.-trained secret police and militia in such countries as Guatemala and El Salvador (Nelson-Pallmeyer, 1989).

This kind of U.S. state-engaged criminality—or what has otherwise euphemistically been referred to by the military, the U.S. State Department, and the mass media as "low-intensity" conflict or warfare—has been virtually ignored by students of governmental or organizational crime. Such state policies have been designed "not only to defend the U.S. empire against the rising challenges from the poor but also to conceal from U.S. citizens the unpleasant consequences of empire" (Nelson-Pallmeyer, 1989: 2). These low-intensity activities have involved an unprecedented degree of coordination among the White House, the National Security Council, the Central Intelligence Agency, the State Department, the Agency for International Development, conservative private aid groups, and a semiprivate network of drug-runners, arms merchants, and assassins (Nelson-Pallmeyer, 1989). The "secret" crimes of low–intensity conflict have strived to integrate the more traditional military, political, economic, and psychological aspects of warfare with the more modern, technological aspects of mass communications, private consumption, and social control. Such interventionism, for example, into the affairs of Nicaragua eventually wore the people down and contributed to the defeat of the Sandanistas in the elections of 1990.

The study of U.S. state criminality not only should include those "proactive" crimes of the state, at home or abroad, such as the Iran-Contra affair and the subsequent behaviors of the Contras and Sandinistas or the recent invasion of Panama, but it should also include the crimes by state "omission," such as the denial of the fundamental right to work for an adequate income or the right to be permanently free of homelessness in a society as rich as the United States. With respect to the former crimes by the state, the syndicated columnist David Broder has drawn out important parallels between Oliver North and Manuel Noriega. In response to an editorial that appeared in *The Wall Street Journal* shortly after General Noriega and his people stole the results of the May 1989 election in Panama, Broder (1989) maintained that the correct lesson to learn was the one concerning U.S. hypocrisy in relationship to Noriega in particular and to the crimes against the people of Nicaragua in general. He wrote:

When the executive branch of the U.S. government evades laws passed by Congress, when it brushes aside the verdict of the World Court on its illegal mining of Nicaraguan harbors, then it cannot be surprised when the head [Noriega] of a client government decides to ignore the election returns (p. 2B).

With respect to the crimes of omission, it is precisely those state domestic and economic policies of noninterventionism and deregulation that have combined not only to deny people of their basic human needs, but that have also helped to contribute to the production of the more traditional forms of criminality (Henry, in Barak, 1991b; Barak, 1991a).

In the context of human rights for the people of both developed and developing countries, therefore, it is my contention that the study of state criminality should be connected to those struggles that have historically attempted to expand the notions of fundamental justice for all. In the next section, I will attempt to show the linkages between crime, criminology, and human rights and the worldwide effort of the United Nations Human Rights Commission to challenge some of the more commonly experienced state crimes against humanity.

THE POLITICS OF HUMAN RIGHTS VIOLATIONS

The politics of struggling for worldwide social justice and the politics of condemning the human rights abuses of nation-states by such organizations as Amnesty International or the United Nations Human Rights Commission (UNHRC) will not put an end to the global spectacle of human rights violations and to the suffering of millions of people any time in the near future. More likely, the politics of condemning human rights violations will continue to "heat up" as the strength of the various geographical blocs continues to increase. Most recently, for example, regional blocs involving nations from Latin America, Africa, and the Middle East have begun to "rival" the blocs of the two superpowers and the older European nations. For example, at the 1990 UNHRC meetings in Geneva, resolutions were passed against the human rights abuses of the Israeli resettlement of Soviet Jews in the Occupied Territories and the U.S. invasion of Panama. At the same time, the Commission rejected a loosening of the sanctions on South Africa. China, however, despite the massacre at Tiananmen Square, managed to escape an official sanction from UNHRC. Also escaping sanction were the 1989 human rights abuses that occurred in such other countries as Guatemala, Iraq, Sri Lanka, Cambodia, and the Philippines. What effect the current democratic revolutions in Eastern Europe and the former Soviet Union will have on the centuries-old struggle for social justice is still too early to discern.

The problem in studying the politics of human rights violations cannot be separated from the problem of studying state criminality because they are both related to the basic issue of confronting the fundamental and irreconcilable differences between empire and social justice. Countries that have lived under the "sphere of influence" of the former USSR or the United States have experienced various forms of exploitation and domination. Neither superpower has been very likely to admit to its own crimes against humanity. In fact, both countries have gone to great lengths to rationalize and justify their politically necessary behavior. Through propaganda and disinformation efforts, each of the superpowers has attempted to suppress or to put a noble label around their seamy and contradictory behavior as they have been in conflict with the professed ideals of each country.

The principles for addressing human rights abuses globally have been evolving at least since the French and American revolutions. Today the means for addressing these violations include the shaping of world opinion and the holding of nation-states accountable to edicts of international law, to global treaties and declarations, and to universal concepts of human rights—in short, supporting those worldwide efforts aimed at achieving self-determination and independent development for all peoples on the earth. The role of the United States in the domestic and international affairs of developing nations serves as an example. Since 1945, U.S.-dominated foreign interventions in places like Africa and Asia have certainly served more as deterrents than facilitators of the materialization of human rights for Third World people. And for the past two decades, of all governments in the West, it has been the United States that has most consistently opposed the realization of the right of self-determinism by the peoples of developing nations. As Falk (1989) has argued, it comes as no surprise, therefore, that the United States has been the nation consistently portrayed as an implacable foe of the rights of people. This hegemonic resistance by the United States places both ideological and physical obstacles in the way of maximizing human rights worldwide.

When it has come to the ratification of the major multilateral human rights agreements or instruments, the United States has one of the very worst records among Western liberal democracies. By refusing to sign and recognize these various documents, the United States has, at least indirectly, contributed to the worldwide abuse of human rights. For example, it was not until 1988 that the United States finally ratified the Prevention and Punishment of the Crime of Genocide, which was opened for signature in 1948. As of 1989 the United States had still failed to ratify such human rights documents as the Convention on the Reduction of Statelessness (1961), the International Convention on the Elimination of All Forms of Racial Discrimination (1965), the American Convention on Human Rights (1965), the International Covenant on Economic, Social and Cultural Rights (1966), the International Covenant on Civil and Political Rights (1966), the International Convention on the Suppression and Punishment of the Crime of Apartheid (1973), and the Convention on the Elimination of All Forms of Discrimination Against Women (1979).

Naturally, signing and enforcing any of the documents that have identified and attempted to delegitimate those public and private policies, domestic and foreign, that have helped to reproduce crimes against humanity have often been correctly viewed as impediments to capital accumulation. This is true whether we are discussing developed or developing nations. With regard to the post–1945 construction of a U.S. foreign policy based on isolationism and interventionism, the international recognition of "human rights" as legally binding would certainly help to alter the philosophy of a leadership that has never truly "trusted law or morality or international institutions as the basis for maintaining international security" (Falk, 1988b: 4). Grounded in the failures of Wilsonian idealism and the interwar diplomacy, U.S. post-World War II diplomacy, policy, and ideology has always been based on the belief that the way to peace (and "democracy") was through superior military power and the contradictory preparation for war as the only basis for peace. Perhaps, in light of the current thawing of the Cold War, and in response to the Soviet Union, the United States may be "forced" to rethink its policies, for example, on low-intensity conflict.

The mere rejection of low-intensity conflict as business as usual or its recognition as a form of state criminality vis-a-vis the internationalization of human rights law, would, in effect, outlaw such behaviors as counterrevolutionary terrorism and structural violence that afflict the poor and underdeveloped peoples of the world. Accordingly, Falk (1989: 68) has stressed that "the rights of peoples can be undertaken at its deepest level as a counter-terrorist code of rights and duties, especially directed against state terrorism of the sort associated with foreign policies of leading imperial governments." More generally, resisting all forms of state criminality is no simple enterprise as it calls for challenging the prevailing ideologies of militarism, nationalism, and regionalism. The struggle for world peace, social justice, and the reduction in the crimes of and by the state also necessitates, on the one side, a decreasing role of the national police apparatuses and, on the other side, an increasing role of multilateral cooperation among nations. To put it simply, this utopian world vision requires that peoples of the global community understand that "no problem we face, not the nuclear one, not the ecological one, not the economic one, can possibly be handled, even addressed, on a unilateral national basis" (Ellsberg, 1988: 18).

Nevertheless, some people have argued that it is simply naive to believe that these kinds of agreements are going to eliminate the state criminality of human rights abuses. After all, as they say, these agreements have no teeth. Others, however, have argued that it is just as naive to dismiss these efforts simply because of the politicalization of the process itself. In other words, since the end of World War II the struggle for social justice in general and the work of the UNHRC in particular has minimally functioned to successfully "establish norms and goals for the international community. The growing consensus on an expanded definition of fundamental human rights can be linked to the existence of U.N. covenants and the efforts of the Commission" (T. Allen, 1990: 12).

Karel Vasak, former UNESCO legal advisor, has called on nation-states worldwide to sign on to what has been termed the "third generation of rights," which goes further in its attempts than the first and second generation of rights did in their attempts to maximize the realization of human rights for all people of the world. Each generation of politically evolved human rights violations have been the product of different historical struggles waged by people without rights to obtain them. With each passing historical period, there has been the expansion of both the notions associated with fundamental rights and with respect to whom those rights pertained.

The first generation of rights have been referred to as "negative rights" in that they have called for restraint from the state. These rights were derived from the American and French revolutions and the struggle to gain liberty from arbitrary state action. These rights can be found in the Civil and Political Rights of the International Bill of Rights. The second generation of rights have been referred to as "positive rights" in that they have required affirmative action on the part of the state. These rights can be found in the economic, social, and cultural rights of the International Bill of Rights. They emerged from the experiences of the Soviet Union and they also resonate in the welfare state policies of the West.

Finally, the third generation of rights have called for international cooperation. These rights are currently evolving out of the condition of global interdependence confronting the earth today. For example, in 1990, UNHRC members introduced a resolution that encouraged an expanding role for the world body in defining the relationship among technology, development, and the ecological integrity of the planet. The UNHRC resolution, while not recommending any action at this time, has gone on record to say "that the preservation of life-sustaining ecosystems under conditions of rapid scientific and technological development is of vital importance to the protection of the human species and the promotion of human rights" (Quoted in Allen, 1990: 13). Such a resolution, of course, recognizes that human rights obligations can no longer be satisfied within the boundaries of individual nations. Therefore, the rights of people independent of states are required not only for a reduction in state-organized violence and the maintenance of world peace, but for the protection of the environment and for a massive scale of global development (Crawford, 1988).

Putting human rights into practice by all types of universal agreements reached by both state and nonstate representatives is certainly one of the prerequisites for a reduction in all forms of state criminality, especially the more blatant forms often ignored by even the most "democratic" of nations like the United States. The argument here is that recognition of these critical relationships by criminology and the adoption of basic human rights obligations as part and parcel of a progressive criminological practice are absolutely essential for the establishment of a criminology of state criminality. Moreover, without the legitimation of the study of state criminality both inside and outside of our academic discipline, criminology will remain captive of the prevailing social and moral contexts of legally defined state crime.

CONCLUSION

This chapter has implicitly argued that state criminality is ubiquitous. It has also been explicitly argued that state criminality is victim-producing and criminogenic. Consequently, crimes by and of the state are responsible for much of the global crime, injury, harm, violence, and injustice. Historically, it has been suggested that we are in the emerging period of the third generation of rights as evidenced by various declarations and the expanding movement or struggle on behalf of universal human rights. Accordingly, I have contended that the time has come for criminologists to actually devote serious time to the study of state-organized crime.

If such work is finally emerging, then the lag in time between the introduction of the concept "state" to the field of criminology and the actual practice of studying state criminality may be roughly parallel to the time lag between the introduction of white-collar/corporate crime as a concept and the actual practice of studying this form of criminality. That is to say, it took some two decades after Sutherland first introduced "white-collar crime" before criminologists were seriously engaged in studying the crimes of the "privately" powerful. It now appears that it may have also taken about two decades between the time when radical criminologists of the late 1960s first introduced the concept of state criminality to the discipline, and the time when criminologists finally began to seriously examine the crimes of the "publicly" powerful.

To reiterate, whether the study of state criminality involves the detailed investigation of agents or organizations violating the rights of its own citizens, or whether it involves the examination of interstate terrorism, or whether it involves exploring the patterned interaction between the two, analysis requires that criminologists and others appreciate the two-sided and often hypocritical nature of this form of political deviance. A case in point would demand the unraveling of the connections between the U.S. savings and loan (S&L) scandal and the involvement of known CIA agents and members of organized crime. Of course, with respect to these S&L state-organized thefts, what laid the foundation or groundwork was the federal deregulation of the S&L industry passed into law by a bipartisan Congress during Ronald Reagan's first term as president. Without this change in the legal structure and in the policies controlling the operations of the individual savings and loans, there would not have been the institutionalized opportunity for the biggest theft in U.S. history—a theft that is currently being estimated, at a cost to the Americans taxpayers, of something on the order of $500 billion to $1 trillion (Reeves, 1990).

Moreover, with respect to the study of state criminality and crime in general, both the S&L thefts and the S&L bailouts as well as the deregulation itself cannot be divorced from the underlying changes in the political economy that were creating economic dilemmas that deregulation sought to obviate. Failure to develop such macro-level analyses and criminological constructs of the crimes of the powerful typically results in very unsatisfying and highly reductionist analyses about individual greed and organizational survival divorced from the political economy itself. Such contemporary analyses, which are perhaps better than no analyses at all, may help explain to some degree why it has often been the case that these allegedly unacceptable behaviors can be so easily swept under the political and criminological carpets.

In *Revolutionaries and Functionaries: The Dual Face of Terrorism*, Falk (1988a) has underscored this point with respect to state terrorism in particular. He has argued persuasively that unless there is the development of both objective and neutral scholarship and action, then the chances are strong that the study and transformation of political violence and state criminality will fall victim to the often-employed double standard of justice. This kind of victimization can come about by the scientific and uncritical acceptance of the language and discourse used to describe politically deviant global behavior. As criminologists, therefore, not only should we be involved in the process of demystifying political deviance, but we should also be on the lookout for all forms of state criminality brought about by antidemocratic and repressive forces, whether they operate at home or abroad.

I know there are skeptical criminologists out there, consisting of both the sympathetic Left and the adversarial Right, who question not only the value of a criminology of state criminality, but also of an expanded definition of "criminality" in the first place. These criminologists and others have asked me, for instance, what kinds of contributions can criminologists make to the study of crimes by and of the state that the other social scientists and even journalists could not make? Let me briefly respond to each of these concerns.

Regarding the appropriateness of a criminology of state criminality and the expanded definition of crime: First, I believe that both are consistent with the more critical trends in criminology as represented traditionally by arguments advanced by Thorsten Sellin and Edwin Sutherland in the 1930s and 1940s, and more recently by the radical arguments advanced by William Chambliss, Richard Quinney, Anthony Platt, and others beginning in 1970 with Herman and Julia Schwendinger's classic statement: "Defenders of

Order or Guardians of Human Rights?" Second, as I have argued throughout this chapter and elsewhere, the serious study of the systems of exploitation, including the state and its policies as a crime-producing institution, have yet to be considered, especially as these are related to the processes of both victimization and criminalization.

As for the critical contributions that I believe could be made by the scientific study of state criminality as opposed to the traditionally "noncriminological" study of crime by the other social scientists, or by those treatments of the mass mediated or even the alternatively mediated discussions of crime by journalists, they appear to me to be self-evident. As students of the convergence of crime, law, justice, control, politics, and change, criminologists are in the unique position of having a focus on the interaction of the dynamics of these properties as they have shaped the development of crime, criminology, and social control. Bringing this kind of "special" knowledge to the study of state criminality presupposes having undergone the type of demystification of crime and justice not typically experienced by either social scientists in general or journalists in particular. And I would argue that while this will vary by degree, it is still equally true of bourgeois or critical social scientists and of mainstream or alternative journalists.

In the end, if criminology does not become engaged in the serious study of crimes by and of the state, then this omission will not only have stood in the way of criminology providing the complete picture of crime, but it will have been partially responsible for the reproduction of the ongoing criminalization and victimization of people around the globe. Stated differently, the lines of inquiry pertaining to the theoretical questions posed by the crimes of the powerful and by the relationships between social control and social justice require that the examination of state criminality be central to this whole area of investigation. Finally, to confront state criminality as a legitimate enemy of civil society is to join the struggle for universal human rights and social justice.

References

Acker, Joan, Kate Barry, and Johanna Esseveld. 1983. "Objectivity and truth: Problems in doing feminist research." In Mary Margaret Fonow and Judith A. Cook (Eds.), *Beyond Methodology: Feminist Scholarship as Lived Research*. Bloomington: Indiana University Press.

Agnew, R. 1984. "Goal achievement and delinquency." *Sociology and Social Research*, 68: 435–451.

———. 1985a. "A revised strain theory of delinquency." *Social Forces*, 64: 151–164.

———. 1985b. "Social control theory and delinquency: A longitudinal test." *Criminology*, 23: 47–61.

———. 1987. "On testing strain theories." *Journal of Research in Crime and Delinquency*, 24: 281–286.

———. 1989. "A longitudinal test on the revised strain theory." *Journal of Quantitative Criminology*, 5: 373–388.

———. 1991. "Strain and subcultural crime theories." In J. F. Shelley (Ed.), *Criminology: A Contemporary Handbook*. Belmont, CA: Wadsworth.

———. 1992. "Foundation for a general strain theory of crime and delinquency." *Criminology*, 30: 47–86.

Ainsworth, M. P. 1982. "Attachment, retrospect, and prospect." In C. M. Parkes and J. Stevenson (Eds.), *The place of attachment in human behavior*. London: Tavistock.

Akers, R. 1985. *Deviant Behavior: A Social Learning Approach*, 3rd ed. Belmont, CA: Wadsworth.

Akers, R. L., M. D. Krohn, L. Lanze-Kaduce, and M. Radosevich. 1974. "Social learning and deviant behavior: A special test of a general theory." *American Sociological Review*, 44: 636–655.

Albin, Rochelle S. 1977. "Psychological studies of rape." *Signs*, 3: 423–435.

Alexander, J. 1983. *Theoretical Logic in Sociology*, Volume 4: *The Modern Reconstruction of Classical Thought: Talcott Parsons*. Berkeley: University of California Press.

———. (Ed.) 1985. *Neofunctionalism*. Beverly Hills, CA: Sage Publications.

———. 1987. *Twenty Lectures: Sociological Theory Since World War II*. New York: Columbia University Press.

Allen, L. 1992. "Sexual orientation and the size of the anterior commissure in the brain." Proceedings of the National Academy of Sciences, Vol. 89.

Allen, Terry. 1990. "The politics of human rights." *In These Times*, April 25–May 1, 12–13.

Althusser, L. 1971. *Lenin and Philosophy*. New York: Monthly Review Press.

Anthias, Floya and Nira Yuval-Davis. 1983. "Contextualizing feminism—gender, ethnic and class divisions." *Feminist Review*, 15: 62–77.

Anzai, Y. and H. A. Simon. 1979. "The theory of learning by doing." *Psychological Review*, 89: 124–140.

Arendt, R., F. L. Cove, and A. L. Sroufe. 1979. "Continuity of individual adaptation from infancy to kindergarten: A predictive study of ego-resiliency and curiosity in preschoolers." *Child Development*, 50: 950–959.

Atlanta C., and G. Alexander. 1989. "Wild style: Graffiti painting." In Angela McRobbie (Ed.), *Zoot Suits and Second-Hand Dresses*. Houndmills, UK: Macmillan, 156–168.

Austin, T. 1987. "Conceptual confusion among rural Filipinos in adapting to modern procedures of amicable settlement." *International Journal of Comparative and Applied Criminal Justice*, 11, 2: 241–250.

———. 1988. "Fieldnotes on the vigilante movement in Mindanao: A mix of self-help and formal policing networks." *International Journal of Comparative and Applied Criminal Justice*, 12, 2: 205–217.

———. 1989. "Living on the edge: The impact of terrorism upon Philippine villagers." *International Journal of Offender Therapy and Comparative Criminology*, 33, 1: 103–119.

———. 1991. "Toward a theory on the impact of terrorism: The Philippine scenario." *International Journal of Comparative and Applied Criminal Justice*, 15, 1: 33–48.

Austin, T. and F. Ordona. 1980. "Barangay justice." *CLSU Scientific Journal*, 1: 19–28.

Avrich, Paul. 1973. *The Anarchists in the Russian Revolution*. Ithaca, NY: Cornell University Press.

Bailey, J. 1990. *The Serenity Principle*. San Francisco: Harper and Row.

Bailey, J., K. Blevens, and C. Heath. 1988. "Early results: A six-year post-hoc neocognitive psychotherapy." Paper presented at the Seventh Annual Conference on the Psychology of Mind, Coral Gables, FL.

Bailey, Karen. 1990. "Schools target gang colors." *Rocky Mountain News*, October 10, 8, 11.

Bakhtin, M. 1986. *Speech Genres and Other Late Essays*, C. Emerson and M. Holquist (Eds.). Austin: University of Texas Press.

Bandura, A. 1977. "Self-efficacy: Towards a unifying theory of behavior change." *Psychological Review*, 84: 191–215.

———. 1989. "Human agency in social cognitive theory." *American Psychologist*, 44: 1175–1184.

————. 1991. "Self-regulation of motivation through anticipatory and self-relative mechanisms." In R. Dienstbier (Ed.), *Nebraska Symposium on Motivation: Perspectives on Motivation.* Lincoln: University of Nebraska Press.

Bannister, S. and D. Milovanovic. 1990. "The necessity defense, substantive justice and oppositional linguistic praxis." *International Journal of the Sociology of Law*, 18: 179–198.

Barak, Gregg. 1988. "Newsmaking criminology: Reflections on the media, intellectuals, and crime." *Justice Quarterly*, 5, 4: 565–587.

————. 1991a. *Gimme Shelter: A Social History of Homelessness in Contemporary America.* New York: Praeger.

————. (Ed.). 1991b. *Crimes by the Capitalist State: An Introduction to State Criminality.* Albany: State University of New York Press.

Barley, S. 1983. "Semiotics and the study of occupational and organizational cultures." *Administrative Science Quarterly*, 28: 393–413.

Barthes, R. 1972. *The Pleasure of the Text.* New York: Spectrum.

Bassiouni, M. 1975. *International Terrorism and Political Crimes.* Springfield, IL: Charles Thomas.

Bates, F. and C. Harvey. 1975. *The Structure of Social Systems.* New York: Gardner.

Baudrillard, J. 1983. *Simulations.* New York: Semiotext.

————. 1985. "The ecstasy of communication." In R. Foster (Ed.), *Postmodern Culture.* London: Pluto Press, 126–134.

————. 1988. *America.* London: Verso.

Baumrind, D. 1985. "Familial antecedents of adolescent drug use: A developmental perspective." *National Institute on Drug Abuse Research Monograph Service*, 56.

Baylor, G. W. and J. Gason, Jr. 1974. "An informative processing theory in aspects of the development of weight seriation in children." *Cognitive Psychology*, 6: 1–40.

Beck, A. T. 1970. "Cognitive therapy: Nature and relation to behavior therapy." *Behavior Therapy*, 1: 184–200.

Becker, Howard S. 1963. *Outsiders: Studies in the Sociology of Deviance.* New York: The Free Press.

————. 1967. "Whose side are we on?" *Social Problems*, 14 (Winter): 239–247.

Becker, Howard S. and Michael McCall (Eds.). 1990. *Symbolic Interaction and Cultural Studies.* Chicago: University of Chicago Press.

Benedikt, M. 1891. *Anatomical Studies Upon Brains of Criminals.* New York: DaCapo Press.

Benveniste, E. 1971. *Problems in General Linguistics.* Coral Gables, FL: University of Miami Press.

Bernard, T. 1983. *The Consensus-Conflict Debate.* New York: Columbia University Press.

————. 1987. "Testing structural strain theories." *Journal of Research in Crime and Delinquency*, 24: 262–280.

————. 1989. "A theoretical approach to integration." In S. Messner, M. Krohn and A. Lista (Eds.), *Theoretical Integration in the Study of Deviance and Crime.* Albany: State University of New York Press, 137–159.

Black, M. (Ed.). 1976. *The Social Theories of Talcott Parsons.* Carbondale: Southern Illinois University Press.

Blau, P. 1962. "Operationalizing a conceptual scheme: The universalism-particularism pattern variable." *American Sociological Review*, 27: 159–169.

Blau, P. and J. Blau. 1982. "The cost of inequality: Metropolitan structure and violent crime." *American Sociological Review*, 47: 114–129.

Blechman, Elaine, 1982. "Are children with one parent at psychological risk? A methodological review." *Journal of Marriage and the Family*, 44 (February): 179–195.

Block, Alan. 1986. "A modern marriage of convenience: A collaboration between organized crime and U.S. intelligence." In Robert J. Kelley (Ed.), *Organized Crime: A Global Perspective*. Totowa, NJ: Rowman and Littlefield.

———. 1989. "Violence, corruption, and clientelism: The assassination of Jesus de Galindez, 1956." *Social Justice*, 16, 2: 64–88.

Block, Alan and William Chambliss. 1981. *Organizing Crime*. New York: Elsevier.

Block, J., S. Keyes, and G. Block. 1986. *Longitudinally Foretelling Drug Usage in Adolescence: Early Childhood Personality and Environmental Precursors.* Berkeley: University of California, Institute of Human Development.

Blumer, H. 1969. *Symbolic Interactionism: Perspective and Method.* Englewood Cliffs, NJ: Prentice-Hall.

Bodenheimer, Thomas and Robert Gould. 1989. *Rollback! Right-wing Power in U.S. Foreign Policy.* Boston: South End Press.

Bohmer, Carol. 1974. "Judicial attitudes toward rape victims." *Judicature*, 57: 303–307.

Borch-Jacobsen, M. 1991. *Lacan: The Absolute Master.* Stanford, CA: Stanford University Press.

Bordua, D. J. 1958–59. "Juvenile delinquency and 'anomie': An attempt at replication." *Social Problems*, 6: 230–238.

Bourdieu, P. 1987. "The force of law: Toward a sociology of the juridical field." *The Hastings Law Journal*, 38: 814–853.

Box, S. 1981. *Deviance, Reality, and Society.* New York: Holt, Rinehart, and Winston.

Brady, J. P. and E. E. Levitt. 1965. "The scalability of sexual experiences." *Psychological Record*, 15: 275–279.

Brake, Mike. 1980. *The Sociology of Youth Culture and Youth Subcultures.* London: Routledge and Kegan Paul.

Brennan, P. and S. Mednick. 1990a. "Reply to Walters and White: Heredity and crime." *Criminology*, 28: 657–662.

Briere, J., N. Malamuth, and J. Ceniti. 1981. "Self-assessed rape proclivity: Attitudinal and sexual correlates." Paper presented at APA meeting, Los Angeles.

Briggs, Bill. 1989. "Writings on the wall: Cops OK graffiti scrub-down." *Denver Post*, January 25, B2.

Broder, David. 1989. "Lawlessness at home invites defiance." *The Montgomery Advertiser and The Alabama Journal*, May 14.

Brownmiller, Susan. 1975. *Against Our Will: Men, Women and Rape.* New York: Simon and Schuster.

Bryson, L. 1989. "The proletarianization of women: Gender justice in Australia?" *Social Justice: A Journal of Conflict, Crime and World Order*, 16: 87–102.

Bureau of Justice Statistics. 1985. "The crime of rape." NCJ–96777, 3/85, Rockville, MD: Justice Statistics Clearinghouse.

Burger, P. L. and T. Luckman. 1966. *The Social Construction of Reality*. Garden City, NY: Doubleday.

Burns, D. D. 1980. *Feeling Good*. New York: Morrow.

Bursik, R. J. Jr. and J. Webb. 1982. "Community change and patterns of delinquency." *American Journal of Sociology*, 88, 1: 24–42.

Burt, M. R. 1980. "Cultural myths and supports for rape." *Journal of Personality and Social Psychology*, 38: 217–230.

Burton, V. S. 1991. "Explaining adult criminality: Testing strain, differential association, and control theories." Unpublished Dissertation, University of Cincinnati.

Burton, V. S. and F. T. Cullen. 1993. "The empirical status of strain theory." *Journal of Crime and Justice*, forthcoming.

Burton, V. S., F. T. Cullen, and B. G. Link. 1989. "Strain, control, and differential association theories: Assessing the evidence." Paper presented at the 1989 Midwestern Criminal Justice Association annual meetings, Chicago.

Cain, Maureen. 1989. *Growing Up Good*. London: Sage Publications.

———. 1990. "Toward transgression: New directions in feminist criminology." *International Journal of the Sociology of Law*, 18: 1–18.

Campbell, Colin. 1983. "Romanticism and the consumer ethic: Intimations of a Weber-style thesis." *Sociological Analysis*, 44: 279–296.

———. 1987. *The Romantic Ethic and the Spirit of Modern Consumerism*, 1st ed. Oxford: Basil Blackwell.

Cancian, F. M. 1987. *Love in America: Gender and Self-development*. Cambridge: Cambridge University Press.

Cantor, Rachelle. 1982. "Family correlates of male and female delinquency." *Criminology*, 20, 2: 149–167.

Carlen, Pat. 1983. *Women's Imprisonment: A Study in Social Control*. London: Routledge and Kegan Paul.

———. 1988. *Women, Crime and Poverty*. Philadelphia: Open University Press.

Carlson, E. T., J. L. Wollock, and P. S. Noel. 1981. *Benjamin Rush's Lectures on the Mind*. Philadelphia: American Philosophical Society.

Carver, C. S. and M. F. Schier. 1990. "Origins and functions of positive and negative affect: A control-process view." *Psychological Review*, 97, 1: 19–35.

Castleman, Craig. 1982. *Getting Up: Subway Graffiti in New York*. Cambridge, MA: MIT Press.

Caulfield, Susan L. and Nancy A. Wonders. 1992. "Personal AND political: Violence against women and the role of the state." In Ken Tunnell (Ed.), *Political Crime in Contemporary America*. New York: Garland Publishing.

Caute, David. 1978. *The Great Fear: The Anti-Communist Purge Under Truman and Eisenhower*. New York: Simon and Schuster.

Cermack, L. S. and F. M. Craik (Eds.). 1979. *Levels of Processing in Human Memory*. New York: Wiley.

Cernkovich, S. N. and P. Giordano. 1979. "Delinquency, opportunity, and gender." *Journal of Criminal Law and Criminology*, 70: 145–151.

Chalfant, Henry and James Prigoff. 1987. *Spraycan Art*. London: Thames and Hudson.

Chambers, Iain. 1986. *Popular Culture: The Metropolitan Experience*. London: Methuen.

Chambliss, William. 1989. "State-organized crime." *Criminology*, 27, 2: 183–208.

Chandler, M. J. 1973. "Egocentrism and antisocial behavior: The assessment and training of role-taking and referential communications skills in institutionalized emotionally disturbed children." *Developmental Psychology*, 9: 326–337.

Chappell, D. 1977a. "Forcible rape: A national survey of the response by police" (LEAA). Washington, DC: U.S. Government Printing Office.

———. 1977b. "Forcible rape: A national survey of the response by prosecutors" (LEAA). Washington, DC: U.S. Government Printing Office.

Chesney-Lind, Meda. 1986. "Women and crime: The female offender." *Signs*, 12, 1: 78–96.

Chester, C. R. 1976. "Perceived relative deprivation as a cause of property crime." *Crime and Delinquency*, 22: 17–30.

Chilton, R. J. 1964. "Continuity in delinquency area research: A comparison of studies for Baltimore, Detroit, and Indianapolis." *American Sociological Review*, l29: 71–83.

Chomsky, N. 1989. "A review of verbal behavior by B. F. Skinner." *Language*, 35: 26–58.

Chomsky, Noam and Edward S. Herman. 1979. *The Washington Connection and Third World Fascism*. Boston: South End Press.

Churchill, Ward and Jim Vander Hall. 1988. *Agents of Repression: The FBI's Secret Wars Against The Black Panther Party and The American Indian Movement*. Boston: South End Press.

Cippolone, A. 1986. *Research, Program and Policy Trends in Dropout Prevention: A National Perspective*. Cambridge, MA: Education Matters, Inc.

Clark, L. and D. Lewis. 1977. *Rape: The Price of Coercive Sexuality*. Toronto: The Women's Press.

Clayton, R. R. and H. L. Voss. 1981. *Young Men and Drugs in Manhattan: A Causal Analysis*. Rockville, MD: National Institute on Drug Abuse.

Cleaver, Eldridge. 1968. *Soul on Ice*. New York: Dell.

Clinard, Marshall and Peter Yeager. 1980. *Corporate Crime*. New York: The Free Press.

Cloward, R. and L. Ohlin. 1960. *Delinquency and Opportunity: A Theory of Delinquent Gangs*. New York: Free Press.

Cobb, K. and N. Schaver. 1971. "Michigan criminal assault law." In D. Chappel, R. Geis, and G. Geis (Eds.), *Forcible Rape: The Crime, the Victim, and the Offender*. New York: Columbia University Press.

Cohen, A. 1955. *Delinquent Boys: The Culture of the Gang*. New York: The Free Press.

Cohen, Stanley. 1972/1980. *Folk Devils and Moral Panics: The Creation of the Mods and Rockers*. New York: St. Martin's Press.

Cohen, Stanley and Andrew Scull (Eds.). 1985. *Social Control and the State*. Oxford: Basil Blackwell.

Cole, S. 1975. "The growth of scientific knowledge: Theories of deviance as a case study." In Lewis A. Coser (Ed.), *The Idea of Social Structure: Papers in Honor of Robert K. Merton*. New York: Harcourt, Brace, Jovanovich, 175–220.

Collins, R. 1986. "Is 1980s sociology in the doldrums?" *American Journal of Sociology*, 91: 1336–1355.

Colomy, P. 1990. *Functionalist Sociology and Neofunctionalist Sociology*. New York: Edward Elgar.

Conger, R. D. 1976. "Social control and social learning models of delinquent behavior: A synthesis." *Criminology*, 14: 17–40.

Coombs, J. and W. W. Cooley. 1986. "Dropouts: In high school and after high school." *American Educational Research Journal*, 5: 343–363.

Cooper, Martha and Henry Chalfant. 1984. *Subway Art*. London: Thames and Hudson.

Cosgrove, Stuart. 1984. "The zoot-suit and style warfare." *Radical America*, 18: 38–51.

Covington, J. 1985. "Gender differences in criminality among heroin users." *Journals of Research in Crime and Delinquency*, 22: 329–353.

Crawford, James. 1988. *The Rights of Peoples*. Oxford: Oxford University Press.

Cressey, D. 1979. "Fifty years of criminology: From sociological theory to political control." *Pacific Sociological Review*, 22: 457–480.

Crystal, A. and R. Shuford. 1988. "The efficacy of a neocognitive approach to positive psychological change: A preliminary study in an outpatient setting." Paper presented at the Seventh Annual Conference on the Psychology of Mind, Coral Gables, FL.

Cullen, F. T. 1984. *Rethinking Crime and Deviance Theory: The Emergence of a Structural Tradition*. Totawa, NJ: Rowman and Allanheld.

———. 1988. "Were Cloward and Ohlin strain theorists?" *Journal of Research in Crime and Delinquency*, 25: 214–241.

Currie, E. 1985. *Confronting Crime: An American Challenge*. New York: Pantheon.

Daly, Kathleen. 1987. "Discrimination in the criminal courts: Family, gender, and the problem of equal treatment." *Social Forces*, 66, 1: 152–175.

———. 1989. "Neither conflict nor labeling nor paternalism will suffice: Intersections of race, ethnicity, gender and family in criminal court decisions." *Crime and Delinquency*, 35, 1: 136–168.

Daly, Kathleen and Meda Chesney-Lind. 1988. "Feminism and criminology." *Justice Quarterly*, 5, 4: 497–538.

Datesman, Susan and Frank Scarpitti. 1975. "Female delinquency and broken homes." *Criminology*, 13, 1: 33–55.

Deci, E. L. and R. M. Ryan. 1991. "A motivational approach to self: Integration in personality." In R. Dienstbier (Ed.), *Nebraska Symposium on Motivation*, Vol. 38: *Perspectives on Motivation*. Lincoln: University of Nebraska Press.

Dieterich, Heinz. 1986. "Enforced disappearances and corruption in Latin America." *Crime and Social Justice*, No. 25.

Dobash, R. Emerson and Russell P. Dobash. 1992. *Women, Violence and Social Change*. New York: Routledge.

Dodge, K. A. 1986. "A social information processing model of social competence in children." In M. Perlmutter (Ed.), *Cognitive Perspectives on Children's Social and Behavioral Development*, Minnesota Symposia on Child Psychology. Hillsdale, NJ: Lawrence Erlbaum Associates.

Dodge, K. A. and C. M. Frame. 1982. "Social-cognitive biases and deficits in aggressive boys. *Child Development*, 53: 620–635.

Dodge, K. A., R. M. Murphy, and K. Buchsbaum. 1984. "The assessment of intention and discrimination cues in children: Implications for developmental psychopathology." *Child Development*, 55: 163–173.

Doerner, William. 1988. "The impact of medical resources on criminally induced lethality: A further examination." *Criminology*, 26, 1: 171–177.

Dornbusch, Sanford, J. Merrill Carlsmith, Steven Bushwall, Philip Ritter, Herbert Leiderman, Albert Hastorf, and Ruth Gross. 1985. "Single parents, extended households, and the control of adolescents." *Child Development*, 56, 2: 326–341.

Drahms, A. 1900. *The Criminal*. New York: Macmillan.

Dubin, R. 1960. "Parsons' actor: Continuities in social theory." *American Sociological Review*, 25: 457–466.

———. 1969. *Theory Building*. New York: The Free Press.

Dull, Thomas and David Giacopassi. 1987. "Demographic correlates of sexual and dating attitudes." *Criminal Justice and Behavior*, 14, 2: 175–193.

Dunaway, R. G., F. T. Cullen, V. S. Burton, and T. D. Evans. 1992. "Specifying the class/crime relationship by social context: A test of the relative deprivation hypothesis." Paper presented at the 1992 American Society of Criminology Annual Meetings, New Orleans.

Dunham, R. and G. Alpert. 1987. "Keeping juvenile delinquents in school: A prediction model." *Adolescence*, 22, 85: 45–58.

Edwards, Anne R. 1989. "Sex/gender, sexism and criminal justice: Some theoretical considerations." *International Journal of the Sociology of Law*, 17: 165–184.

Ehrenreich, B. 1989. *Fear of Falling. The Inner Life of the Middle Class*. New York: Harper Perennial.

Eisenstein, S. 1975. *The Film Sense*. New York: Harcourt Brace Jovanovich.

Ekstrom, R. B., M. E. Gortz, J. M. Pollack, and D. A. Rock. 1986. "Who drops out of school and why? Findings from a national study." *Teachers College Record*, 87, 3: 356–373.

Elias, N. 1982. *The Civilising Process*. Vol. 1: *The History of Manners*. Oxford: Basil Blackwell.

Elliot, D. S. and S. Ageton. 1980. "Reconciling race and class differences in self-reported and official estimates of delinquency." *American Sociological Review*, 45: 95–110.

Elliot, D. S., S. S. Ageton, D. Huizinga, B. A. Knowles, and R. J. Canter. 1983. *The Prevalence and Incidence of Delinquency Behavior: 1976–1980, The National Youth Survey Report No. 26*. Boulder, CO: C/A Publications.

Elliot, Delbert and David Huizinga. 1983. "Social class and delinquent behavior in a national youth panel." *Criminology*, 21 (May): 149–177.

Elliot, D., and D. Huizinga. 1984. *The Relationship Between Delinquent Behavior and Abnormal Problems*. Research Conference on Juvenile Offenders with Serious Drug, Alcohol, and Mental Health Problems. Boulder, CO: Behavioral Research Institute.

Elliot, D. S., D. Huizinga, and S. Ageton. 1985. *Explaining Delinquency and Drug Use*. Beverly Hills, CA: Sage.

Elliot, D. S. and H. Voss. 1974. *Delinquency and Dropout*. Lexington, MA: D. C. Heath.

Ellis, A. 1962. *Reason and Emotion in Psychotherapy*. Secaucus, NJ: Lyle Stuart.

Ellis, H. 1987. *The Criminal*. New York: Charles Scribner.

Ellis, L. 1982. "Genetics and criminal behavior." *Criminology*, 20: 43–66.

Ellsberg, Daniel. 1988. Remarks presented at the session, "The Growth of the National Security State," at the conference on Anti-Communism and the U.S.: History and Consequences, sponsored by the Institute for Media Analysis, Inc., Harvard University, November 11–13.

Ermann, David and Richard Lundman. 1982. *Corporate and Governmental Deviance: Problems of Organizational Behavior in Contemporary Society*. New York: Oxford University Press.

Ewen, S. 1988. *All Consuming Images: The Politics of Style in Contemporary Culture*. New York: Basic Books.

Falk, Richard. 1988a. *Revolutionaries and Functionaries: The Dual Face of Terrorism*. New York: E. P. Dutton.

———. 1988b. Remarks presented at the session, "The Growth of the National Security State," at the conference on Anti-Communism and the U.S.: History and Consequences, sponsored by the Institute for Media Analysis, Inc., Harvard University, November 11–13.

———. 1989. "United States foreign policy as an obstacle to the rights of people." *Social Justice*, 16, 1: 57–70.

Faris, R. E. 1967. *Chicago Sociology, 1920–1932*. San Francisco: Chandler.

Farnworth, M. and M. J. Lieber. 1989. "Strain theory revisited: economic goals, educational means, and delinquency." *American Sociological Review*, 54: 259–279.

Fayetteville Observer-Times. 1991a. "Mutilator seemed so normal." July 28, p. 7A.

———. 1991b. "Ultimate stage mom faces trial." August 25, p. 6A.

Ferrell, Jeff. 1990. "Bombers' confidential: Interview with Eye Six and Rasta 68." (Part Two) *Clot*, 1: 10–11.

———. 1991. "The Brotherhood of Timber Workers and the culture of conflict." *Journal of Folklore Research*, 28: 163–177.

———. 1993. *Crimes of Style: Urban Graffiti and the Politics of Criminality*. New York: Garland.

Ferrell, Jeff and Kevin Ryan. 1985. "The Brotherhood of Timber Workers and the southern trust: Legal repression and worker response." *Radical America*, 19: 54–74.

Feyerabend, Paul. 1975. *Against Method*. London: Verso.

Field, Hubert. 1978. "Attitudes toward rape: A comparative analysis of police, rapists, crisis counselors, and citizens." *Journal of Personality and Social Psychology*, 36: 156–179.

Fishbein, D. H. 1990. "Biological Perspectives in Criminology." *Criminology*, 28: 27–72.

———. 1992. "The psychobiology of female aggression." *Criminal Justice and Behavior*, 19: 99–126.

Fiske, John. 1991. "An interview with John Fiske." *Border/Lines*, 20/21: 4–7.

Flax, Jane. 1990. "Postmodernism and gender relations in feminist theory." In Linda J. Nicholson (Ed.), *Feminism/Postmodernism*. New York: Routledge, Chapman and Hall.

Flowers, Ronald Barri. 1988. *Minorities and Criminality*. New York: Praeger.

Flynn, Kevin. 1990. "Plan aims to quiet booming car stereos." *Rocky Mountain News*, October 11, 6.

Foley, E. and D. Warren. 1985. *Dropout Prevention: A First Step: The Story of New York City's Implementation of Education Law 3602 (D) Relating to Attendance Improvement and Dropout Prevention*. New York: The Public Education Association.

Fonow, Mary Margaret and Judith A. Cook. 1991. *Beyond Methodology: Feminist Scholarship as Lived Research*. Bloomington: Indiana University Press.

Foster, Hal. 1985. *Postmodern Culture*. London: Pluto Press.

Foucault, M. 1977. *Discipline and Punish*. New York: Pantheon.

———. 1980. *Power/Knowledge: Selected Interviews and Other Writings, 1972– 1977*. New York: Pantheon Books.

Fraser, Nancy and Linda J. Nicholson. 1990. "Social criticism without philosophy: An encounter between feminism and postmodernism." In Linda J. Nicholson (Ed.), *Feminism/Postmodernism*. New York: Routledge, Chapman and Hall.

Friedrichs, D. 1980. "The legitimacy crises in the United States: A conceptual analysis." *Social Problems*, 27: 540–554.

Furstenberg, Frank, James Peterson, Christine Winquist Nord, and Nicholas Zill. 1983. "The life course of children of divorce: Marital disruption and parental contact." *American Sociological Review*, 48 (October): 656–668.

Gadwa, K. and S. A. Griggs. 1985. "The school dropout: Implications for counsellors." *The School Counsellor*, 33, 1: 9–17.

Gagnier, Regena. 1990. "Feminist post-modernism: The end of feminism or the ends of theory." In Deborah L. Rhode (Ed.), *Theoretical Perspectives on Sexual Difference*. New Haven, CT: Yale University Press.

Garfinkel, Harold. 1956. "Conditions of successful degradation ceremonies." *American Journal of Sociology*, 61: 420–424.

Garnaas, Steve. 1988. "Sprocket spikes go on graffiti alert." *Denver Post*, August 11, 1, 20.

Garofalo, J. and J. Laub. 1978. "The fear of crime: Broadening our perspective." *Victimology*, 3, 3/4: 242–253.

Gelsthorpe, Loraine and Allison Morris. 1988. "Feminism and criminology in Britain." *British Journal of Criminology*, 28, 2: 93–110.

———. (Eds.). 1990. *Feminist Perspectives in Criminology*. Milton Keynes: Open University Press.

Gibbons, D. 1972. "Observations on the study of crime causation." *American Journal of Sociology*, 17: 262–279.

———. 1989. *Criminal Justice: Annual Additions 89/90*. Guilford, CT: Dushkin.

Gibbs, J. 1987. "The state of criminological theory." *Criminology*, 25: 821–840.

———. 1989. "Conceptualizations of terrorism." *American Sociological Review*, 54: 329–340.

Giddens, A. 1968. "Power in the recent writings of Talcott Parsons." *Sociology*, 2: 257–272.

———. 1981. *A Contemporary Critique of Historical Materialism*. Cambridge: Polity Press.

Gilsinan, James. 1989. "They is clowning tough: 911 and the social construction of reality." *Criminology*, 27, 2: 329–344.

Ginsburg, R. and H. Greenly. 1978. "Competing theories of marijuana use: A longitudinal study." *Journal of Health and Social Behavior*, 19: 22–34.

Glasser, W. 1969. *Schools Without Failure*. New York: Harper and Row.

Glick, Brian. 1989. *War at Home: Covert Action Against U.S. Activists and What We Can Do About It*. Boston: South End Press.

Goffman, E. 1967. *Interaction Ritual*. New York: Anchor Books.

Goode, E. 1990. "Review of seductions of crime: Moral and sensual attractions of doing evil." *Contemporary Sociology*, 15: 5–12.

Goodrich, P. 1984. "Law and language: An historical and critical introduction." *Journal of Law and Society*, 11: 173–206.

Goodrich, P. 1990. *Languages of Law: From Logics of Memory to Nomadic Masks*. London: Weidenfeld and Nicolson.

Gordon, Margaret T. and Stephanie Riger. 1991. *The Female Fear: The Social Cost of Rape*. Urbana: University of Illinois Press.

Gottfredson, Michael and Travis Hirschi. 1987. "The methodological adequacy of longitudinal research on crime." *Criminology*, 25 (August): 581–614.

Gottlieb, Alan. 1990. "City leaders vow to persevere in battle against graffiti." *Denver Post*, May 12, 6B.

Gottschalk, L. A. et al. 1991. "Abnormalities in hair trace elements as indicators of aberrant behavior." *Comprehensive Psychiatry*, 32: 229–237.

Gouldner, A. 1970. *The Coming Crisis of Western Sociology*. New York: Basic Books.

Gove, Walter and Robert Crutchfield. 1982. "The family and juvenile delinquency." *Sociological Quarterly*, 23 (Summer): 301–319.

Graham, R. B. 1990. *Physiological Psychology*. Belmont, CA: Wadsworth.

Granfield, R. and T. Koenig. 1990. "From activism to pro bono: The redirection of working class altruism at Harvard Law School." *Critical Sociology* 17: 57–80.

Greenberg, David F. 1977. "Delinquency and the age structure of society." *Contemporary Crises*, 1: 189–223.

Greenblatt, 1982. "Filthy rites." *Daedalus*, 3: 1–16.

Greendlinger, V. and D. Byrne. 1987. "Coercive sexual fantasies of college men as predictors of self-reported likelihood to rape and overt sexual aggression." *The Journal of Sex Research*, 23: 1–11.

Griffin, Susan. 1971. "Rape: The all-American crime." *Ramparts*, June, 26–35.

Groves, W. and M. Lynch. 1990. "Reconciling structural and subjective approaches to the study of crime." *Journal of Research in Crime and Delinquency*, 27, 4: 348–375.

Groves, W. B. and R. J. Sampson. 1987. "Traditional contributions to radical criminology." *Journal of Research on Crime and Delinquency*, 24, 3 (August): 181–214.

Guerin, Daniel. 1970. *Anarchism*. New York: Monthly Review Press.

Gusfield, J. R. 1987. "Passage to play: rituals of drink in American society." In Mary Douglas (Ed.), *Constructive Drinking: Perspectives on Drinking from Anthropology*. Cambridge: Cambridge University Press.

Habermas, J. 1975. *Legitimation Crises*. Boston: Beacon Press.

———. 1984. *The Theory of Communicative Action*. Vol. One: *Reason and the Rationalization of Society*. trans. T. McCarthy. Boston: Beacon Press.

Hagan, J., A. R. Gillis, and J. Simpson. 1985. "The class structure of gender and delinquency: Toward a power control theory of gender and delinquency." *American Journal of Sociology*, 90: 1151–1178.

———. 1987. "Class in the household: A power control theory of gender and delinquency." *American Journal of Sociology*, 92: 788–816.

Hager, Steven. 1984. *Hip Hop: The Illustrated History of Break Dancing, Rap Music, and Graffiti*. New York: St. Martin's Press.

Hall, Stuart and Tony Jefferson (Eds.). 1976. *Resistance through Rituals*. London: Hutchinson.

Hamilton, P. 1983. *Talcott Parsons: Key Sociologist*. London: Tavistock.

Hanson, C., S. Henggeler, W. Haefele, and J. D. Rodick. 1984. "Demographic, individual, and familial relationship correlates of serious and repeated crime among adolescents and their siblings. *Journal of Consulting and Clinical Psychology*, 51: 528–538.

Harding, Sandra. 1986. *The Science Question in Feminism*. Milton Keynes: Open University Press.

———. 1987. *Feminism and methodology*. Bloomington: Indiana University Press.

Hariton, Barbara. 1973. "The sexual fantasies of women." *Psychology Today*, 6, 10: 39–44.

Harris, M. Kay. 1987. "Moving into the new millennium: Toward a feminist vision of justice." *The Prison Journal*, 67, 2: 27–38.

Harter, S. 1988. "The construction and conservation of the self: James and Cooley revisited." In D. K. Lapsley and F. C. Power (Eds.), *Self, Ego, and Identity: Integrative Approaches*. New York: Springer-Verlag, 43–70.

———. 1990. "Developmental differences in the nature of self-representations: Implications for the understanding, assessment, and treatment of maladaptive behavior." *Cognitive Therapy and Research*. Special issue on representations of the self in emotional disorders: A cognitive behavioral perspective.

Haug, W. F. 1986. *Critique of Commodity Aesthetics: Appearance, Sexuality and Advertising in Capitalist Society*. Cambridge: Polity Press.

Haugeland, J. (Ed.). 1985. *Mind Design*. Cambridge, MA: The MIT Press.

Hawkes, R. 1975. "Norms, deviance and social control: A mathematical elaboration of concepts." *American Journal of Sociology*, 80: 886–908.

Heath, S. 1981. *Questions of Cinema*. Bloomington: Indiana University Press.

Hebdige, Dick. 1979. *Subculture: The Meaning of Style*. London: Methuen.

Heidensohn, Frances. 1986. "Models of justice: Portia or Persephone? Some thoughts on equality, fairness and gender in the field of criminal justice." *International Journal of the Sociology of Law*, 14: 287–298.

———. 1987. "Women and crime: Questions for criminology." In Pat Carlen and Anne Worrall (Eds.), *Gender, Crime and Justice*. Philadelphia: Open University Press.

Helliwell, Christine. 1990. Unpublished anthropological lectures on her field work in Borneo.

Henig, J. R. 1980. "Gentrification and displacement within cities: A comparative analysis." *Social Science Quarterly*, 61: 638–652.

Henry, S. and D. Milovanovic. 1991. "Constitutive criminology." *Criminology*, 29: 293–315.

Herman, Edward. 1982. *The Real Terror Network: Terrorism in Fact and Propaganda*. Boston: South End Press.

Hershorn, M. and A. Rosenbaum. 1985. "Children of marital violence: A closer look at the unintended victims." *American Journal of Orthopsychiatry*, 55: 260–266.

Herzog, Elizabeth and Cecelia Sudia. 1973. "Children in fatherless families." In B. Caldwell and H. Ricciuti (Eds.), *Review of Child Development Research*, Vol. I. Chicago: University of Chicago Press, 141–232.

Hess, Robert and Kathleen Camara. 1979. "Post-divorce family relationships as mediating factors in the consequences of divorce for children." *Journal of Social Issues*, 35, 4: 79–96.

Hilgard, E. R. 1987. *Psychology in America*. New York: Harcourt Brace Jovanovitch.

Hindelang, M. J. 1973. "Causes of delinquency: A partial replication and extension." *Social Problems*, 20: 471–487.

Hindelang, M. J., T. Hirschi, and J. G. Weis. 1979. "Correlates of delinquency: The illusion of discrepancy between self-report and official measures." *American Sociological Review*, 44: 995–1014.

————. 1981. *Measuring Delinquency*. Beverly Hills, CA: Sage Publications.

Hirschi, T. 1969. *Causes of delinquency*. Berkeley: University of California Press.

Hochschild, A. R. 1983. *The Managed Heart: Commercialization of Human Feeling*. Berkeley: University of California Press.

hooks, bell [Gloria Watkins]. 1990. *Yearning: Race, Gender and Cultural Politics*. Boston, MA: South End Press.

Humphries, Drew and Susan Caringella-MacDonald. 1990. "Murdered mothers, missing wives: Reconsidering female victimization." *Social Justice*, 17, 2: 71–89.

Howell, F. M. and W. Frege. 1982. "Early transition into adult roles: Some antecedents and outcomes." *American Research Journal*, 19: 51–73.

Husserl, Edmund. 1975. *Ideas*. Trans. W. R. Boyce Gibson. New York: Collier Books.

Hyde, Janet Shibley. 1982. *Understanding Human Sexuality*, 2nd ed. New York: McGraw-Hill.

Iran-Nejad, A. 1990. Active and dynamic self-regulation of learning processes. *Review of Educational Research*, 60, 4: 573–602.

Jackson, B. 1991. *Law, Fact and Narrative Coherence*. Mersyside, England: Deborah Charles Publications.

Jackson, P. I. 1991. "Crime, youth gangs, and urban transition: The social dislocations of postindustrial economic development." *Justice Quarterly*, 8, 3: 379–397.

Jacobs, D. 1981. "Inequality and economic crime." *Sociology and Social Research*, 66: 12–28.

Jacobson, R. 1971. "Two aspects of language and two types of aphasic disorders." In R. Jacobson and M. Halle (Eds.), *Fundamentals of Language*. Paris: Mouton.

Jameson, F. 1984. "Post modernism, or the cultural logic of late capitalism." *NLR* July/August, No. 146.

———. 1985. "Postmodernism and consumer society." In Hal Foster (Ed.), *Postmodern Culture*. London: Pluto Press, 111–125.

Janowitz, M. 1978. *The Last Half-Century: Societal Change and Politics of America*. Chicago: University of Chicago Press.

Jeffery, C. R. 1990. *Criminology*. Englewood Cliffs, NJ: Prentice-Hall.

Jemail, Jay Ann and James Geer. 1977. "Sexual scripts." In R. Gemme and C. C. Wheeler (Eds.), *Progress in Sexology*. New York: Plenum.

Jencks, Charles. 1977. *The Language of Post-Modern Architecture*. New York: Rizzoli.

Jenkins, Philip. 1988. "Whose terrorists? Libya and state criminality." *Contemporary Crises*, 12, 2: 1–11.

Jensen, G. F. and M. L. Erickson. 1977. "Peer commitment and delinquency: New tests of old hypothesis." Unpublished Manuscript.

Jessor, R., J. A. Chase, and J. E. Donovan. 1980. "Psychosocial correlates of marijuana use and problem drinking in a national sample of adolescents." *American Journal of Public Health*, 70: 604–613.

Jessor, R. and S. L. Jessor. 1977. *Problem and Psychological Development: A Longitudinal Study of Youth*. New York: Academic Press.

Johnson, James and Lee Jackson. 1988. "Assessing the effects of factors that might underlie the differential perception of acquaintance and stranger rape." *Sex Roles*, 19, 1/2: 37–45.

Johnson, R. E. 1979. *Juvenile Delinquency and Its Origins: An Integrated Approach*. Cambridge: Cambridge University Press.

Johnson, Richard. 1986. "Family structure and delinquency: General patterns and gender differences." *Criminology*, 24, 1: 65–84.

Jurik, Nancy C. 1985. "An officer and a lady: Organizational barriers to women working as correctional officers in men's prisons." *Social Problems*, 32, 4: 375–388.

Kalat, J. W. 1992. *Biological Psychology*, 4th ed. Belmont, CA: Wadsworth.

Kandel, D. B. (Ed.). 1978. *Longitudinal Research on Drug Use*. New York: Wiley.

Kandel, Elizabeth and Mednick Sarnoff. 1991. "Perinatal complications predict violent offending." *Criminology*, 29, 3: 519–529.

Kaplan, H. I. and B. J. Sadock. 1991. *Synopsis of Psychiatry*. Baltimore: Williams and Wilkins.

Kapsis, R. E. 1978. "Residential succession and delinquency." *Criminology*, 15, 4: 459–486.

Kasarda, J. D. and M. Janowitz. 1974. "Community attachment in mass society." *American Sociological Review*, 39: 328–339.

Katz, Jack. 1988. *Seductions of Crime: Moral and Sensual Attractions in Doing Evil*. New York: Basic Books.

Kelley, Earl. 1962. *In Defense of Youth*. Englewood Cliffs, NJ: Prentice-Hall.

Kelley, T. M. 1990. "A neo-cognitive model of crime." *Journal of Offender Rehabilitation*, 16(1/2): 1–26.

Kellner, D. 1990. *Jean Baudrillard: From Marxism to Postmodernism and Beyond*. Stanford, CA: Stanford University Press.

Kennedy, D. 1982. "Legal education as training for hierarchy." In D. Kairys (Ed.), *The Politics of Law*. New York: Pantheon Books, 40–61.

Kennedy, Leslie and David R. Forde. 1990. "Routine activities and crime: An analysis of victimization in Canada." *Criminology*, 28, 1: 137–152.

Kethinini, S. R. 1990. "Adolescent drug use in India." Unpublished Dissertation, Rutgers University.

Kirkpatrick, J. T. and J. A. Humphrey. 1991. "Theoretical formulations of the stress criminal violence relationship." Paper presented at the 1991 American Society of Criminology annual meetings, San Francisco.

Klahr, D. 1982. "Nonmonotone assessment of monotone development: An information processing analysis." In S. Strauss (Ed.), *U-shaped Behavioral Growth*. New York: Academic Press.

Klein, H. A. 1977. "Towards more effective behavioral programs for juvenile offenders." *Federal Probation*, 31: 45–50.

Klemmark, S. H. and D. L. Klemmark. 1976. "The social definition of rape." In M. J. Walker and S. C. Brodsky (Eds.), *Sexual Assault*. Lexington, MA: D. C. Heath.

Knudten, R. 1970. *Crime in a Complex Society*. Homewood, IL: The Dorsey Press.

Kohfeld, Carl and John Sprague. 1990. "Demography, police behavior, and deterrence." *Criminology*, 28, 1: 111–136.

Kojeve, A. 1980. *Introduction to the Reading of Hegel*. Ithaca, NY: Cornell University Press.

Kornhauser, R. R. 1978. *Social Sources of Delinquency: An Appraisal of Analytic Models*. Chicago: University of Chicago Press.

Koss, M. P., C. A. Gidycz, and N. Wisniewski. 1987. "The scope of rape: Incidence and prevalence of sexual aggression and victimization in a national sample of higher education students." *Journal of Consulting and Clinical Psychology*, 55: 162–170.

Koss, M. and C. Oros. 1980. "Hidden rape: A survey of the incidence of sexual aggression and victimization on a university campus." Paper presented at the Annual Meetings of the Midwestern Psychological Association, St. Louis.

Kropotkin, Peter. 1975. *The Essential Kropotkin*, Emile Capouya and Keitha Tompkins (Eds.). New York: Liveright.

Krot, S. 1983. "The adolescent in the transitional family: How the schools can help." *Educational Horizons*, 61: 205–208.

Kruttschnitt, Candace. 1984. "Respectable women and the law." *Sociological Quarterly*, 23: 221–234.

Kruttschnitt, Candace and Donald E. Green. 1984. "The sex-sanctioning issue: Is it history?" *American Sociological Review*, 49: 541–551.

Kuhn, T. S. 1962. *The Structure of Scientific Revolutions*. Chicago: University of Chicago Press.

Lacan, J. 1977. *Ecrits: A Selection*, trans. A. Sheridan. New York: Norton.

———. 1981. *The Four Fundamental Concepts of Psycho-Analysis*. New York: W. W. Norton.

Lachmann, Richard. 1988. "Graffiti as career and ideology." *American Journal of Sociology*, 94: 229–250.

Laclau, M. and E. Mouffe. 1985. *Hegemony and Socialist Strategy*. New York: Verso.

Ladd, G. T. 1887. *Elements of Physiological Psychology*. New York: Scribners.

LaFree, Gary. 1989. *Rape and Criminal Justice: The Social Construction of Sexual Assault*. Belmont, CA: Wadsworth.

LaFree, Gary and Christopher Birkbeck. 1991. "The neglected situation: A cross-national study of the situational characteristics of crime." *Criminology*, 29, 1: 73–98.

LaGrange, Randy L. and Kenneth F. Ferraro. 1989. "Assessing age and gender differences in perceived risk and fear of crime." *Criminology*, 27, 4: 697–719.

Lander, B. 1954. *Towards an Understanding of Juvenile Delinquency*. New York: AMS Press.

Leavitt, G. 1990. "Relativism and cross-cultural criminology: A critical analysis." *Journal of Research in Crime and Delinquency*, 27, 1: 5–29.

Lecercle, J. 1990. *The Violence of Language*. New York: Routledge.

Lee, J. 1990. *Jacques Lacan*. Amherst: University of Massachusetts Press.

Lefebvre, H. 1971. *Everyday Life in the Modern World*. New York: Harper Torchbooks.

Lemaire, A. 1977. *Jacques Lacan*, trans. D. Macey. New York: Routledge and Kegan Paul.

Leonard, Eileen B. 1982. *Women, Crime and Society: A Critique of Criminological Theory*. New York: Longman.

LeVine, R. A. 1959. "Gusii sex offenses: A study in social control." *American Anthropologist*, 61: 965–990.

Lewis, D. O. 1986. "Psychiatric, neurological, and psychoeducational characteristics of 15 death row inmates in the United States." *American Journal of Psychiatry*, 143: 838–845.

Lewis, D. O. et al. 1988. "Neuropsychiatric, psychoeducational, and family characteristics of 14 juveniles condemned to death in the United States." *American Journal of Psychiatry*, 135: 584–589.

Light, I. 1977. "Numbers gambling among blacks: A financial institution." *American Sociological Review*, 42: 892–904.

Linden, E. and J. C. Hackler. 1973. "Affective ties and delinquency." *Pacific Sociological Review*, 16: 27–34.

Liska, A. 1987. "A critical examination of macro perspectives on crime control." *Annual Review of Sociology*, 13: 67–88.

Lochman, J. E., L. B. Lampron, P. R. Burch, and J. F. Curry. 1985. "Client characteristics associated with behavior change for treated and untreated aggressive boys." *Journal of Abnormal Child Psychology*, 13, 4: 527–538.

Loeber, R. and T. Dishion. 1984. "Boys who fight at home and school: Family conditions influencing cross-setting consistency." *Journal of Consulting and Clinical Psychology*, 52: 759–768.

Lugones, Maria C. and Elizabeth V. Spelman. 1983. "Have we got a theory for you! Feminist theory, cultural imperialism and the demand for 'the woman's voice.' " *Women's Studies International Forum*, 6, 6: 573–581.

Luyt, Clifford. 1989. "The killing fields: South Africa's human rights record in Southern Africa." *Social Justice*, 16, 2: 89–115.

Lyng, S. 1990. "Edgework: a social psychological analysis of voluntary risk taking." *American Journal of Sociology*, 95: 887–921.

———. 1991. "Edgework revisited: Reply to Miller." *American Journal of Sociology*, 96: 1534–1539.

MacCabe, C. 1985. *Tracking the Signifier*. Minneapolis: University of Minnesota Press.

MacDonald, A. 1893. *Criminology*. New York: Funk and Wagnalls.

Maher, Frances. 1984. "Appropriate teaching methods for integrating women." In Bonnie Spanier, Alexander Bloom, and Darlene Boroviak (Eds.), *Toward a Balanced Curriculum*. Cambridge, MA: Schenkman.

Malamuth, N. M. 1981. "Rape proclivity among males." *Journal of Social Issues*, 37: 138–157.

Manning, P. 1979. "Metaphors of the field: Varieties of organizational discourse." *Administrative Science Quarterly*, 24: 660–671.

Marcuse, Herbert. 1965. "Repressive tolerance." In R. Wolff, B. Moore and H. Marcuse, *A Critique of Pure Tolerance*. Boston: Beacon, 81–123.

Marques, J. K. and C. Nelson. 1989. "Elements of high-risk situations for sex offenders." In D. R. Laws (Ed.), *Relapse Prevention with Sex Offenders*. New York: Guilford.

Marsh, R. 1967. "Prospects for comparative sociology." In R. Merton (Ed.), *Comparative Sociology*. New York: Harcourt.

Martin, Del. 1976. *Battered Wives*. New York: Simon and Schuster.

Martin, Susan. 1980. *Breaking and Entering: Policewomen on Patrol*. Berkeley: University of California Press.

Maslow, A. H. 1970. *Motivation and Personality*. New York: Harper and Row.

Matsueda, Ross and Karen Heimer. 1987. "Race, family structure, and delinquency: A test of differential association and social control theories." *American Sociological Review*, 52 (December): 826–840.

Maume, D. J. 1989. "Inequality and metropolitan rape rates: A routine activity approach." *Justice Quarterly*, 513–527.

May, Todd. 1989. "Is post-structuralist political theory anarchist?" *Philosophy and Social Criticism*, 15: 167–182.

Mayhew, B. H. 1980. "Structuralism versus individualism: Part 1, shadowboxing in the dark." *Social Forces*, 58: 335–375.

Mayo, S. 1991. *Confessions*. London: Marshall Pickering.

McCaul, Devin, Lois Veltum, Vivian Boyechko, and Jacqueline Crawford. 1990. "Understanding attributions of victim blame for rape: Sex, violence, and foreseeability." *Journal of Applied Social Psychology*, 20: 1–26.

McCombs, B. L. 1991. "Metacognition and motivation for higher level thinking." Paper presented at the Annual Meeting of the American Educational Research Association, Chicago.

McCombs, B. L. and R. J. Marzano. 1990. "Putting the self in self-regulated learning: The self as agent in integrating will and skill." *Educational Psychologist*, 25, 1: 51–69.

McCord, Joan. 1991. "Family relationships, juvenile delinquency, and adult criminality." *Criminology*, 29, 3: 397–417.

McCord, W. and J. McCord. 1959. *Origins of a Crime: A New Evaluation of the Cambridge-Somerville Study*. New York: Columbia University Press.

McRobbie, Angela. 1980. "Settling accounts with subcultures: A feminist critique." *Screen Education*, 34: 37–49.

———. 1986. "Postmodernism and popular culture." In *ICA Documents 4: Postmodernism*. London: Institute of Contemporary Arts, 54–58.

———. (Ed.). 1989. *Zoot Suits and Second-Hand Dresses*. Houndmills, UK: Macmillan.

Meade, A. C. and M. E. Marsden. 1981. "An integration of classic theories of delinquency." In A. C. Meade (Ed.), *Youth and Society: Studies of Adolescent Deviance*. Chicago: Institute for Juvenile Research.

Mednick, S., T. Moffitt, and S. A. Stack (Eds.). 1987. *The Causes of Crime: New Biological Approaches*. Cambridge: Cambridge University Press.

Mednick, S. and J. Volovka. 1980. "Biology and crime." In N. Morris and M. Tonry (Eds.), *Crime and Justice*. Chicago: University of Chicago Press.

Medvedev, P. and M. Bakhtin. 1978. *The Formal Method in Literary Scholarship*. Baltimore: John Hopkins University Press.

Meichenbaum, D. H. 1977. *Cognitive-behavior modification: An integrative approach*. New York: Plenum Press.

Melbin, M. 1978. "Night as frontier." *American Sociological Review*, 43: 3–22.

———. 1987. *Night as Frontier*. New York: The Free Press.

Menkel-Meadow, Carrie and Shari Seidman Diamond. 1991. "The content, method and epistemology of gender in sociolegal studies." *Law and Society Review*, 25, 2: 221–238.

Mennell, S. 1985. *All Manner of Foods*. Oxford: Basil Blackwell.

Merton, R. K. 1938. "Social structure and anomie." *American Sociological Review*, 3: 672–82.

———. 1968a. "Continuities in the theory of social structure and anomie." In R. K. Merton, *Social Theory and Social Structure*, enlarged ed. New York: The Free Press.

———. 1968b. "Social structure and anomie." In R. K. Merton, *Social Theory and Social Structure*, enlarged ed. New York: The Free Press.

Merton, R. K. and A. S. Rossi. 1968. "Contributions to the theory of reference group behavior." In R. K. Merton, *Social Theory and Social Structure*, enlarged ed. New York: The Free Press.

Metro Wide Graffiti Summit. 1990. Author transcription, May 11. Denver.

Metz, C. 1982. *The Imaginary Signifier*. Bloomington: Indiana University Press.

Michalowski, Raymond. 1985. *Order, Law, and Crime: An Introduction to Criminology*. New York: Random House.

Mies, Maria. 1991. "Women's research or feminist research?: The debate surrounding feminist science and methodology." In Mary Margaret Fonow and Judith A. Cook (Eds.), *Beyond Methodology: Feminist Scholarship as Lived Research*. Bloomington: Indiana University Press.

Miller, Eleanor M. 1986. *Street Women*. Philadelphia: Temple University Press.

Miller, E. 1991. "Assessing the risk of inattention to class, race, ethnicity and gender: comment on Lyng." *American Journal of Sociology*, 96: 1530–1534.

Miller, G. A., E. Galanter, and K. H. Pribram. 1960. *Plans and the Structure of Behavior*. New York: Holt.

Mills, C. W. 1959. *The Sociological Imagination*. New York: Oxford University Press.

Mills, R. C. 1987. "Relationship between school motivational climate, teacher attitudes, student mental health, school failure and health damaging behavior."

Paper presented at the American Educational Research Association Annual Conference, Washington, D.C.

———. 1988. *Modello Early Intervention Project: Second Quarter, Quarterly Report*. Metro-Dade Department of Youth and Family Development. Miami: Bureau of Criminal Justice Assistance.

———. 1990. Substance abuse, dropout and delinquency prevention: The Modello-Homestead Gardens public housing early intervention project. Paper presented at the 9th Annual Conference on the Psychology Of Mind, St. Petersburg, FL.

Mills, R. C., R. G. Dunham, and G. P. Alpert. 1988. "Working with high-risk youth in prevention and early intervention programs: Toward a comprehensive wellness model." *Adolescence*, 23, 91: 643–660.

Milovanovic, D. 1986. "Juridico-linguistic communicative markets: Towards a semiotic analysis." *Contemporary Crises*, 10: 281–304.

———. 1987. "The political economy of 'liberty' and 'property' interests." *Legal Studies Forum*, 11: 267–293.

———. 1988. "Jailhouse lawyers and jailhouse lawyering." *International Journal of the Sociology of Law*, 16: 455–475.

———. 1989. *Weberian and Marxian Analysis of Law: Structure and Function of Law in a Capitalist Mode of Production*. Aldershot, England: Gower Publishers.

———. 1991. "Images of unity and disunity in the juridic subject." In R. Quinney and H. Peipinsky (Eds.), *Criminology as Peacemaking*. Bloomington: Indiana University Press, 209–227.

———. 1992. *Postmodern Law and Disorder: Pyschoanalytic Semiotics, Chaos and Juridic Exegeses*. Merseyside, England: Deborah Charles Publications.

Milovanovic, D. and Jim Thomas. 1989. "Overcoming the absurd: Legal struggle as primitive rebellion." *Social Problems*, 36(1): 48–60.

Minow, Martha, 1990. *Making All the Difference: Inclusion, Exclusion and American Law*. Ithaca, NY: Cornell University Press.

Mintz, S. W. 1985. *Sweetness and Power: The Place of Sugar in Modern History*. New York: Viking.

Mizrahi, Marilyn. 1981. "Up from the subway." *In These Times*, October 21–27: 19–20.

Moore, Kristin, James Peterson, and Frank Furstenberg. 1986. "Parental attitudes and the occurrence of early sexual activity." *Journal of Marriage and the Family*, 48 (November): 777–782.

Morash, M. and M. Chesney-Lind. 1991. "A reformulation and partial test of the power-control theory of delinquency." *Justice Quarterly*, 8: 347–377.

Morgan, G. 1980. "Paradigms, metaphors, and puzzle solving in organizational settings." *Administrative Science Quarterly*, 25: 605–622.

———. 1983. "More on metaphor: Why we cannot control tropes in administrative science." *Administrative Science Quarterly*, 28: 601–607.

Morris, Allison and Loraine Gelsthorpe. 1991. "Feminist perspectives in criminology: Transforming and transgressing." *Women & Criminal Justice*, 2, 2: 3–26.

Morris, D. 1967. *The Naked Ape*. New York: Dell Publishing.

Muehlenhard, Charlene, Debra Friedman, and Celeste Thomas. 1985. "Is date rape justifiable? The effects of dating activity, who initiated, who paid, and men's attitudes toward women." *Psychology of Women Quarterly*, 9, 3: 297–310.

Mugford, S. K. and P. O. O'Malley. 1991. "Heroin policy and the limits of Left Realism." *Crime, Law and Social Change: An International Journal*, 15: 19–36.

Munch, R. 1987. *Theory of Action: Towards a New Synthesis Going Beyond Parsons*. London: Routledge.

———. 1988. "Parsonian theory today: In search of a new synthesis." In A. Giddens and J. Turner (Eds.), *Social Theory Today*. Stanford, CA: Stanford University Press, 115–155.

Myers, Martha A. and Susette M. Talarico. 1987. *The Social Contexts of Criminal Sentencing*. New York: Springer-Verlag.

Mynatt, C. and E. Allgeir. 1985. "Attribution of responsibility by victims of sexual coercion." Paper presented at annual meeting of the Scientific Study of Sex, New York City.

Naffin, N. 1985. "The masculinity-femininity hypothesis." *British Journal of Criminology*, 25, 4: 365–381.

Naroll, R. 1983. *The Moral Order*. Beverly Hills, CA: Sage Publications.

Nelson-Pallmeyer, Jack. 1989. *War Against the Poor: Low-Intensity Conflict and Christian Faith*. Maryknoll, NY: Orbis Books.

Newman, G. 1976. *Comparative Deviance*. New York: Elsevier.

———. 1990. "Review of seductions of crime: Moral and sensual attractions of doing evil." *Contemporary Crises*, 14: 179–184.

Nye, F. Ivan. 1958. *Family Relationships and Delinquent Behavior*. New York: Wiley.

O'Conner, O. 1985. "Dropout prevention programs that work." *Oregon School Study Council Bulletin*, 29, 4: 7–13.

Palen, J. J. 1981. *The Urban World*. New York: McGraw-Hill.

Park, R. E. and E. W. Burgess. 1969. *Introduction to the Science of Sociology*. Chicago: University of Chicago Press.

Parker, R. and C. Loftin. 1983. "Poverty, inequality, and type of homicide: A reconsideration of unexpected results." Paper presented at the 1983 American Society of Criminology annual meeting, Denver.

Parks, Ron. 1990. "Busking." *Border/Lines*, 19: 7–8.

Parsons, P. A. 1909. *Responsibility for Crime*. New York: AMS Press.

Parsons, T. 1942. "Age and sex in the social structure of the U.S." *American Sociological Review*, 7: 604–616.

———. 1947. "Certain primary sources and patterns of aggression in the social structure of the western world." *Psychiatry*, 10: 167–181.

———. 1951. *The Social System*. New York: The Free Press.

———. 1960. "Pattern variables revisited: A response to Robert Dubin." *American Sociological Review*, 25: 466–484.

———. 1966. *Societies: Evolutionary and Comparative Perspectives*. New York: The Free Press.

———. 1971. *The System of Modern Societies*. Englewood Cliffs, NJ: Prentice-Hall.

———. 1978. *Action Theory and the Human Condition*. New York: The Free Press.

Parsons, T., R. Bales, and E. Shils. 1953. *Working Papers in the Theory of Action*. New York: The Free Press.

Parsons, T. and G. Platt. 1973. *The American University*. Cambridge, MA: Harvard University Press.

Parsons, T. and D. Gerstein. 1977. "Two cases of social deviance: Addiction to heroin, addiction to power." In E. Sagarin (Ed.), *Deviance and Social Change*. Beverly Hills, CA: Sage Publications, 19–57.

Parsons, T. and E. Shils. 1951. *Toward a General Theory of Action*. Cambridge, MA: Harvard University Press.

Passas, N. 1987. "Anomie and relative deprivation." Paper presented at the 1987 Eastern Sociological Society annual meetings.

Patterson, G. R. 1982. *Coercive Family Process*. Eugene, OR: Castalia Publishing Co.

Patton, P. forthcoming. *Post-Modern Subjectivity: The Problem of the Actor*.

Pearlin, L. I., E. G. Menaghan, M. A. Lieberman, and J. T. Mullan. 1981. "The stress process." *Journal of Health and Social Behavior*, 22: 337–356.

Pearson, F. and N. A. Weiner. 1985. "Toward an integration of criminological theories." *Journal of Criminal Law and Criminology*, 76 (Spring): 116–150.

Pecheux, M. 1982. *Language, Semantics and Ideology*. New York: St. Martin's Press.

Peck, N., A. Law, and R. C. Mills. 1987. *Dropout Prevention: What We Have Learned*. Coral Gables, FL: University of Miami, Center for Dropout Prevention.

Penfield, W. 1975. *The Mystery of the Mind*. Princeton, NJ: Princeton University Press.

Pepinsky, Harold E. 1978. "Communist anarchism as an alternative to the rule of criminal law." *Contemporary Crises*, 2: 315–327.

———. 1989. "The contribution of feminist justice to criminology." *Feminist Teacher*, 4, 1: 18–23.

———. 1991. *The Geometry of Violence and Democracy*. Bloomington: Indiana University Press.

Pepinsky, Harold E. and Paul Jesilow. 1984. *Myths That Cause Crime*. Cabin John, MD: Seven Locks Press.

Pepinsky, Harold E. and Richard Quinney (Eds.). 1991. *Criminology as Peacemaking*. Bloomington: Indiana University Press.

Peterson, James L. and Nicholas Zill. 1986. "Marital disruption, parent-child relationships, and behavior problems in children." *Journal of Marriage and the Family*, 48, 2: 295–307.

Peterson, Richard A. (Ed.). 1990. "Symposium: The many facets of culture." *Contemporary Sociology*, 19: 498–523.

Phelps, J. L. 1987. "Understanding wisdom and creativity: A psychology of mind perspective." Paper presented at the American Psychological Association Annual Meeting, New York.

Phillips, E. L. 1968. "Achievement place: Token reinforcement procedures in a homestyle rehabilitation setting for predelinquent boys." *Journal of Applied Behavior Analysis*, 1: 213.

Platt, Tony. 1974. "Prospects for a radical criminology in the United States." *Crime and Social Justice*, Spring–Summer: 2–10.

Polk, K., and S. Kobrin. 1972. *Delinquency Prevention Through Youth Development*. Washington, DC: U.S. Department of Health, Education and Welfare.

Polk, K. and W. E. Schafer (Eds.). 1972. *Schools of Delinquency*. Englewood Cliffs, NJ: Prentice-Hall.

Polsky, Ned. 1969. *Hustlers, Beats and Others*. Garden City, NY: Doubleday.

Pransky, G. S. 1990. *Divorce Is Not the Answer*. Blue Ridge Summit, PA: TAB Books.

Presdee, M. 1985. "Agony or ecstasy." University of South Australia occasional papers I.

———. 1992. "The Muck of Ages." Unpublished paper.

Provonost, G. 1986. "Introduction: Time in historical perspective." *International Social Science Journal*, 107: 5–18.

Purser, Valerie. 1990. Author interview with Valerie Purser, Executive Director, Keep Denver Beautiful, December 17. Denver.

Radzinowicz, L. 1966. *Ideology and Crime*. New York: Columbia University Press.

Ragland-Sullivan, E. 1986. *Jacques Lacan and the Philosophy of Psychoanalysis*. Chicago: University of Illinois Press.

Rankin, Joseph. 1983. "The family context of delinquency." *Social Problems*, 30, 4: 466–479.

Rankin, Joseph and L. Edward Wells. 1987. "The preventive effects of the family on delinquency." In Elmer H. Johnson (Ed.), *Handbook on Crime and Delinquency Prevention*. Westport, CT: Greenwood Press, 257–277.

Raskin-White, H., E. Labouvie, and M. Bates. 1985. "The relationship between sensation seeking and delinquency." *Journal of Research in Crime and Delinquency*, 22: 197–211.

Raskin-White, H., R. Pandina, and R. LaGrange. 1987. "Longitudinal predictors of serious substance use and delinquency." *Criminology*, 25: 715–740.

Reckless, W. 1967. *The Crime Problem*. New York: Appleton-Century-Crofts.

Reeves, Richard. 1990. "S&L disaster rips off taxpayers." *The Montgomery Advertiser*, April 23 (*Washington Post* reporter).

Rennie, Y. 1978. *The Search for Criminal Man*. Lexington, MA: D. C. Heath.

Richards, P. 1981. "Quantitative and qualitative sex differences in middle-class delinquency." *Criminology*, 18: 453–470.

Richardson, D. C. and J. Campbell. 1982. "Alcohol and rape: The effect of alcohol on attribution of blame for rape." *Personality and Social Psychology Bulletin*, 8: 468–476.

Robinson, D. N. (Ed.). 1977. *Significant Contributions to the History of Psychology*. Vol IV: *H. Maudsley*. Washington, DC: University Publications of America.

Robinson, P. 1978. "Parents of beyond control adolescents." *Adolescence*, 13: 116–119.

Rocky Mountain News. 1991. "Crackdown on cruising nets 18 arrests." May 29, 16.

Rosen, Lawrence and Kathleen Neilson. 1982. "Broken homes." In Leonard Savitz and Norman Johnson (Eds.), *Contemporary Criminology*. New York: Wiley, 126–135.

Rosenblum, Nina (Producer). 1990. *Through the Wire* (Film). Public Broadcasting Service.

Russell, Diane E. H. 1982. *Rape in Marriage*. New York: Macmillan.

Rutherford, R. B. 1975. "Establishing behavioral contracts with delinquent adolescents." *Federal Probation*, 39: 29.

Ryan, Kevin and Jeff Ferrell. 1986. "Knowledge, power and the process of justice." *Crime and Social Justice*, 25: 178–195.

Sagarin, Edward. 1973. "The research setting and the right not to be researched." *Social Problems*, 21: 52–64.

Samenow, S. 1984. *Inside the Criminal Mind*. New York: Times Books.

Sampson, R. 1985. "Structural sources of variation in race-age-specific rates of offending across major U.S. cities." *Criminology*, 23: 647–673.

Sanday, Peggy. 1981. "The socio-cultural context of rape: A cross-cultural study." *Journal of Social Issues*, 37, 1: 5–27.

Sargent, Alice G. 1984. *Beyond Sex Roles*. New York: West Publishing.

Saussure, F. de. 1966. *Course in General Linguistics (Course de linguistique generale)*. New York: McGraw-Hill.

Schaefer, E. S. 1959. "A circumplex model for maternal behavior." *Journal of Social Psychology*, 59: 226–235.

Schatzberg, A. F. and J. O. Cole. 1991. *Manual of Clinical Psychopharmacology*. Washington, DC: American Psychiatric Press.

Schiller, Herbert. 1989. *Culture, Inc.: The Corporate Takeover of Public Expression*. New York: Oxford.

Schniedewind, Nancy. 1983. "Feminist values: Guidelines for teaching methodology in women's studies." In Charlotte Bunch and Sandra Pollack (Eds.), *Learning Our Way: Essays in Feminist Education*. Trumansburg, NY: Crossing Press.

Schwendinger, Herman and Julia Schwendinger. 1970. "Defenders of order or guardians of human rights?" *Issues in Criminology*, 5, 2 (Summer): 123–157.

———. 1985. *Adolescent Subcultures and Delinquency*. New York: Praeger.

Sciulli, D. and D. Gerstein. 1985. "Social theory and Talcott Parsons in the 1980s." *Annual Review of Sociology*, 11: 369–387.

Scott, Peter. 1989. "Northwards without North: Bush, counterterrorism, and the continuation of secret power." *Social Justice*, 16, 2: 1–30.

Scott, James C. 1990. *Domination and the Arts of Resistance: Hidden Transcripts*. New Haven: Yale University Press.

Seabrook, J. 1988. *The Leisure Society*. Oxford: Basil Blackwell.

Second January Group, The. 1986. *After Truth: A Post-Modern Manifesto*. London: Inventions Press.

Seligman, C., J. Brickman, and D. Koulack. 1977. "Rape and physical attractiveness: Assigning responsibility to victims." *Journal of Personality*, 45: 555–563.

Selman, R. L. 1976. "Toward a structural analysis of developing interpersonal relations concepts: Research with normal and disturbed pre-adolescent boys." In A. Pick (Ed.), *Minnesota Symposium on Child Psychology*, Vol. 10. Minneapolis: University of Minnesota Press.

Seltzer, J. A. and D. Kalmuss. 1988. "Socialization and stress explanations for spouse abuse." *Social Forces*, 67: 473–491.

Session Laws of Colorado. 1989. Chapter 153: "An act concerning the war on gangs and gang-related crime." Denver: Bradford, 872–878.

Shaw, C. R. and H. D. McKay. 1942. *Juvenile Delinquency and Urban Areas*. Chicago: University of Chicago Press.

Shelley, L. 1981. *Crime and Modernization*. Carbondale, IL: Southern Illinois University Press.

Sherman, L. W. 1987. "Repeat calls to police in Minneapolis." *Crime Control Reports*. Washington, DC: Crime Control Institute.

Sholle, David. 1990. "Resistance: Pinning down a wandering concept in cultural studies discourse." *Journal of Urban and Cultural Studies*, 1: 87–105.

Short, J. 1985. "The level of explanation problem in criminology." In R. Meier (Ed.), *Theoretical Methods in Criminology*. Beverly Hills, CA: Sage Publications.

Shrout, P. E., B. G. Link, B. P. Dohrenwend, A. E. Skodal, A. Stueve, and J. Mirotznik. 1989. "Characterizing life events as risk factors for depression: The role of fateful life events." *Journal of Abnormal Psychology*, 98: 460–467.

Shuford, R. 1986. "An exploratory study to determine the effectiveness of a neo-cognitive treatment approach when utilized in a clinical setting." Unpublished doctoral dissertation, University of Oregon.

Shuford, R. and A. Crystal. 1988. "The efficacy of a neocognitive approach to positive psychological change: A preliminary study in an outpatient setting." Paper presented at the Seventh Annual Conference on the Psychology of Mind, Coral Gables, FL.

Shure, M. B. and G. Spivack. 1982. "Interpersonal problem solving in young children: Cognitive approach to prevention." *American Journal of Community Psychology*, 10, 3: 42–59.

Sigler, R. 1987. "Social disorganization on Bimini: Impact of the drug trade." *International Journal of Comparative and Applied Criminal Justice*, 2, 1: 133–142.

Silverman, I. and S. Dinitz. 1974. "Compulsive masculinity and delinquency: An empirical investigation." *Criminology*, 11, 4: 498–515.

Silverman, K. 1983. *The Subject of Semiotics*. New York: Oxford University Press.

Simmel, G. 1950. *The Sociology of Georg Simmel*. Glencoe, IL: The Free Press.

Simon, John K. 1991. "Michel Foucault on Attica: An interview." *Social Justice*, 18 (Fall): 26–34.

Simpson, Sally S. 1989. "Feminist theory, crime, and justice." *Criminology*, 27, 4: 605–631.

Sjoberg, Gideon and Paula J. Miller. 1973. "Social research on bureaucracy: Limitations and opportunities." *Social Problems*, 21: 129–143.

Skinner, B. F. 1971. *Beyond Freedom and Dignity*. New York: Knopf.

Smart, Carol. 1989. *Feminism and the Power of Law*. New York: Routledge.

Smelser, N. and R. Warner. 1976. "Talcott Parsons' theory of deviance and social control." In N. Smelser and R. Warner (Eds.), *Sociological Theory: Historical and Formal*. Morristown, NJ: Silver Burdett, 179–204.

Smith, P. 1988. *Discerning the Subject*. Minneapolis: University of Minnesota Press.

Smith, R. and J. Walters. 1978. "Delinquent and non-delinquent males' perceptions of their fathers." *Adolescence*, 13: 21–28.

Soto, Natalie. 1991. "Gang policy at Elitch's questioned by parents." *Rocky Mountain News*, June 16, 6.

Spelman, Elizabeth V. 1988. *Inessential Woman: Problems of Exclusion in Feminist Thought*. Boston: Beacon Press.

Sroufe, L. A. 1979. "The coherence of individual development: Early care, attachment, and subsequent development issues." *American Psychologist*, 34: 834–841.

Sroufe, A., B. Egeland, and M. Erickson. 1983. "The development consequence of different patterns of maltreatment." *International Journal of Child Abuse and Neglect*, 1, 4: 459–469.

Stacey, Judith and Barrie Thorne. 1985. "The missing feminist revolution in sociology." *Social Problems*, 32, 4: 301–316.

Stack, S. 1984. "Income inequality and property crime: A cross-national analysis of relative deprivation theory." *Criminology*, 22: 229–257.

Stallybrass, P. and A. White. 1986. *The Politics and Poetry of Transgression*. Methuen: London.

Stanley, Liz and Sue Wise. 1983. *Breaking Out: Feminist Consciousness and Feminist Research*. London: Routledge and Kegan Paul.

Stark, R. 1986. *Crime and Deviance in North America: Show Case*. Seattle: Cognitive Development.

———. 1987. "Deviant places: A theory of the ecology of crime." *Criminology*, 25, 4: 893–909.

Stern, D., J. Catterall, D. Alhadeff, and M. Ash (Eds.). 1985. *Report to the California Policy Seminar on Reducing the Dropout Rate in California*. Berkeley: University of California, School of Education.

Stewart, D. 1985. "Affective states as the key variable in determining student mastery of basic reading skills." Paper presented at the Fourth Annual Conference on the Psychology of Mind, Kahuku, HI.

Stitt, B. G. and D. J. Giacopassi. 1992. "Trends in the connectivity of theory and research in *Criminology*." *The Criminologist*, 17, 4 (July–August): 1, 2–6.

Stouffer, S. 1962. *Social Research to Test Ideas*. New York: The Free Press.

Straus, Murray A., Richard J. Gelles, and Susan K. Steinmetz. 1980. *Behind Closed Doors: Violence in the American Family*. Garden City, NY: Anchor/Doubleday.

Suarez, E. M. 1985b. "Neo-cognitive Psychotherapy." Book manuscript in preparation.

———. 1985a. "The efficacy of a neo-cognitive approach to psychotherapy." Paper presented at the Hawaii Psychological Association Annual convention, Honolulu.

Suarez, E. M. and R. C. Mills. 1982. *Sanity, Insanity, and Common Sense: The Missing Link in Understanding Mental Health*. West Allis, WI: Med-Psych Publications.

———. 1987. *Sanity, insanity, and common sense*. New York: Ballantine Books.

Suarez, E. M., J. L. Phelps, and J. K. Blevens. 1987. "Thought as agency: A neo-cognitive view of an unrecognized dimension." Paper presented at the American Psychological Association annual meeting, New York.

Sutherland, E. 1939. *Principles of Criminology*. Philadelphia: J. B. Lippincott.

Sutherland, Edwin. 1949. *White Collar Crime*. New York: Holt, Rinehart and Winston.

Sykes, G. and D. Matza. 1957. "Techniques of neutralization: A theory of delinquency." *American Sociological Review*, 22: 664–670.

Taylor, I. 1990. *The Social Effects of Free Market Politics*. London: Harvester.

Taylor, L. 1984. *Born to Crime*. Westport, CT: Greenwood Press.

Taylor, Robert B. 1973. *Cultural Anthropology*. Boston: Allyn and Bacon.

Thio, A. 1975. "A critical look at Merton's anomie theory." *Pacific Sociological Review*, 18: 139–158.

Thompson, Hunter S. 1966. *Hell's Angels: A Strange and Terrible Saga*. New York: Ballantine.

Tifft, Larry. 1979. "The coming redefinition of crime: An anarchist perspective." *Social Problems*, 26: 392–402.

Tifft, Larry and Lyn Markham. 1991. "Battering women and battering Central Americans: A peacemaking synthesis." In Harold E. Pepinsky and Richard Quinney (Eds.), *Criminology as Peacemaking*. Bloomington: Indiana University Press, 114–153.

Tifft, Larry and Dennis Sullivan. 1980. *The Struggle to be Human: Crime, Criminology and Anarchism*. Orkney, England: Cienfuegos Press.

Timm, J. and D. Stewart. 1990. *The Thinking Teacher's Guide to Self-Esteem*. Tampa: Advanced Human Studies Institute.

Tittle, C. 1980. *Sanctions and Social Deviance*. New York: Praeger.

Todorov, T. 1984. *Mikhail Bakhtin: The Dialogical Principle*. Minneapolis: University of Minnesota Press.

Toulmin, S. 1990. *Cosmopolis: The Hidden Agenda of Modernity*. New York: The Free Press.

Tumin, M. 1965. "The functionalist approach to social problems." *Social Problems*, 12, 4: 379–388.

USA Today. 1991a. "Nationline: Book thief." August 1, p. 3A.

USA Today. 1991b. "BCCI: Story of intrigue worthy of a novel." August 15, p. 8B.

USA Today. 1991c. "Police fear killings span 10 years." July 26.

USA Today. 1991d. "Drifter: I killed 60 people." August 15, p. 1A.

U.S. Congress, Senate Select Committee to Study Governmental Operations with Respect to Intelligence Activities. 1976. *Intelligence Activities: Senate Resolution 21*, Vol. 6. Washington, DC: U.S. Government Printing Office.

Van Voorhis, Patricia, Francis Cullen, Richard Mathers, and Connie Chenoweth Garner. 1988. "The impact of family structure and quality on delinquency: A comparative assessment of structural and functional factors." *Criminology*, 26 (May): 235–260.

Vaux, A. and M. Ruggiero. 1983. "Stressful life change and delinquent behavior." *American Journal of Community Psychology*, 11: 169–183.

Vaz, E. (Ed.). 1967. *Middle-Class Juvenile Delinquency*. New York: Harper and Row.

Veblen, T. 1953. *The Theory of the Leisure Class*. New York: Mentor Books.

Vold, George B. and Thomas J. Bernard. 1986. *Theoretical Criminology*, 3rd ed. New York: Oxford Press.

Volosinov, V. 1986. *Marxism and the Philosophy of Language*. Cambridge, MA: Harvard University Press.

Vygotsky, Lev. 1962. *Thought and Language*. Cambridge, MA: MIT Press.

Walters, G. D. 1990. "Heredity, crime, and the killing-the-bearer-of-bad-news syndrome: A reply to Brennan and Mednick." *Criminology*, 28, 4: 657–662.

Walters, G. D. and T. W. White. 1989a. "Heredity and crime: Bad genes or bad research?" *Criminology*, 27: 455–486.

———. 1989b. "The thinking criminal: A cognitive model of lifestyle criminality." *Criminal Justice Research Bulletin*, 4, 4: 1–9.

Warming, E. 1909. *Oecology of Plants: An Introduction to the Study of Plant Communities*. Oxford: Oxford University Press.

Warr, Mark and Mark Stafford. 1991. "The influence of delinquent peers: What they think or what they do?" *Criminology*, 29 (November): 851–865.

Waugh, N. C. and D. A. Norman. 1965. "Primary memory." *Psychological Review*, 72: 89–104.

Wehlage, G. G. and R. A. Rutter. 1986. "Dropping out: How much do schools contribute to the problem?" *Teachers College Record*, 87, 3: 374–392.

Weiler, Kathleen. 1988. *Women Teaching for Change: Gender, Class and Power*. South Hadley, MA: Bergin and Garvey Publishers.

Weiner, B. 1990. "History of motivational research in education." *Journal of Educational Psychology*, 82, 4: 616–622.

Weinstein, James. 1989. "Now that it's out in the open, the underlying principles should be debated." *In These Times*, October 11–17.

Wells, L. Edward and Joseph Rankin. 1985. "Broken homes and juvenile delinquency: An empirical review." *Criminal Justice Abstracts*. 17, 2: 249–272.

———. 1986. "The broken homes model of delinquency: Analytic issues." *Journal of Research in Crime and Delinquency*, 23, 1: 68–93.

———. 1988. "Direct parental controls and delinquency." *Criminology*, 26, 2: 263–285.

———. 1991. "Families and delinquency: A meta-analysis of the impact of broken homes." *Social Problems*, 38 (February): 71–93.

West, D. J. and D. P. Farrington. 1973. *Who Becomes Delinquent?* London: Heinemann Educational Books.

———. 1977. *The Delinquent Way of Life*. London: Heinemann Educational Books.

Westkott, Marcia. 1979. "Feminist criticism of the social sciences." *Harvard Educational Review*, 149, 4: 422–430.

Wheeler, Stanton, Kenneth Mann, and Austin Sarat. 1988. *Sitting in Judgment: The Sentencing of White-Collar Criminals*. New Haven, CT: Yale University Press.

White, R. 1990. *No Space of Their Own*. Cambridge: Cambridge University Press.

Wilkins, L. 1965. *Social Deviance*. London: Tavistock.

Willis, P. 1990. *Common Culture*. Milton Keynes: Open University Press.

Williams, F. 1984. "The demise of criminological imagination: A critique of recent criminology." *Justice Quarterly*, 1: 91–106.

Wilson, J. Q. and R. Herrnstein. 1985. *Crime and Human Nature*. New York: Simon and Schuster.

Wilson, Nanci K. 1991a. "Feminist pedagogy in criminology." *Journal of Criminal Justice Education*, 2, 1: 81–93.

———. 1991b. "Recycling offenses, the routine ground of everyday activities, and Durkheimian functionality in crime." Paper presented at the annual meeting of the Academy of Criminal Justice Sciences, Nashville.

Winfree, L. T., H. E. Theis, and C. T. Griffiths. 1981. "Drug use in rural America: A cross cultural examination of complementary social deviance theories." *Youth and Society*, 12, 4: 465–489.

Wolf, J. (Ed.). 1981. *Fear of Fear: A Survey of Terrorist Operations and Control in Open Societies*. New York: Plenum.

Wolfe, Alan. 1973. *Repression: The Seamy Side of Democracy*. New York: McKay and Company.

Wolfgang, M. E. 1972. "Cesare Lombroso." In H. Mannheim (Ed.), *Pioneers in Criminology*. Montclair, NJ: Patterson-Smith.

Wonders, Nancy A. 1990. "A sociological approach to sentencing disparity." Unpublished doctoral dissertation. Rutgers University.

Wonders, Nancy A. and Susan L. Caulfield. 1993. "Women's work?: Reflections on the 'Women and the Criminal Justice System' course." *Journal of Criminal Justice Education*, 4, 1: 79–100.

Wood, A. 1961. "A socio-structural analysis of murder, suicide and economic crime in Ceylon." *American Sociological Review*, 26: 744–753.

Wright, Robin. 1989. "U.S. redefining ban on assassinations." *The Montgomery Advertiser and Alabama Review Journal*, October 15.

Wundt, W. 1873. *Principles of Physiological Psychology*. New York: Macmillan.

Yllo, Kersti. 1988. "Political and methodological debates in wife abuse research." In Kersti Yllo and Michele Bograd (Eds.), *Feminist Perspectives on Wife Abuse*. Beverly Hills, CA: Sage Publications, 28–50.

York, Peter. 1980. *Style Wars*. London: Sidgwick and Jackson.

Yudofsky, S. C. and R. E. Hales. 1992. *Textbook of Neuropsychiatry*. Washington, DC: American Psychiatric Press.

Zwerman, Gilda. 1989. "Domestic counterterrorism: U.S. government response to political violence on the left in the Reagan era." *Social Justice*, 16, 2: 31–63.

Index

About the Contributors

TED ALLEMAN currently holds a joint appointment with the Departments of Sociology and Administration of Justice at Pennsylvania State University. He has worked in maximum security prisons as a college instructor, developed one of the first computerized prison management systems emphasizing prisoner rehabilitative treatment, and established a press specializing in the writings of prisoners.

GREGG BARAK is the department head of Sociology, Anthropology, and Criminology at Eastern Michigan University. He has been involved in local and national efforts to resist homelessness. His most recent books include *Crimes by the Capitalist State: An Introduction to State Criminality* (1991), and *Gimme Shelter: A Social History of Homelessness in Contemporary America, Choice* Outstanding Academic Book, 1991.

VELMER S. BURTON, JR. is an Assistant Professor of Criminal Justice at Sam Houston State University. He has published in the areas of corrections, mental health, criminological theory, and is coauthor of the forthcoming book *Contemporary Criminological Theory*.

SUSAN CAULFIELD is an Assistant Professor of Sociology at Western Michigan University. Her articles on the role of the state in the perpetuation of violence and the role of the "women and crime" courses in criminal justice education have appeared in *The Journal of Prisoners on Prison* and the *Journal of Criminal Justice Education*, respectively.

R. GREGORY DUNAWAY is an Assistant Professor in the department of Sociology, Anthropology, and Social Work at Mississippi State University.

He has published in the areas of corrections and socialization and is currently conducting research on social class and adult criminality.

JEFF FERRELL is Associate Professor of Sociology at Regis University, Denver. He has published a variety of studies exploring topics such as secondhand popular culture, social and labor history, workers' culture, popular music videos, and the social dynamics of the criminal justice system. He is the author of *Crimes of Style: Urban Graffiti and the Politics of Criminality* (1993), from which his chapter in this volume is derived.

C. RAY JEFFERY is a Professor of Criminology and Criminal Justice at Florida State University. He is the past president of the American Society of Criminology, the founding editor of *Criminology*, a Fulbright-Hays Research Fellow to the Netherlands, and a George J. Beto Professor of Criminal Justice at Sam Houston State University. His books and other publications have included work in the areas of crime prevention and environmental design as well as on biology and crime.

THOMAS M. KELLEY is an Assistant Professor in the department of Sociology and Criminal Justice at Wayne State University. He is also a licensed clinical psychologist and certified social worker in the State of Michigan. His major research interest is the application of the Neo-Cognitive learning perspective to the understanding and prevention of crime and delinquency.

DRAGAN MILOVANOVIC teaches in the Department of Criminal Justice and coordinates the Honors Program at Northeastern Illinois University. He has co-edited *The Critical Criminologist* and is the editor of the journal *Humanity and Society*. He has authored *Sociology of Law, Weberian and Marxian Analysis of Law*, and *Postmodern Law and Disorder: Psychoanalytic Semiotics, Chaos and Juridic Exegeses*.

STEPHEN MUGFORD is Senior Lecturer in Sociology at the Australian National University, Canberra. Much of his work and publications have been concerned with the development of progressive policies for dealing with illicit drug use, with research into patterns and cultures of use among leisure consumers of psychotropic drugs, and investigating the place of violence in sport with special focus on the accounts of men and women players in comparative activities.

THOMAS O'CONNOR is Assistant Professor of Criminal Justice at Mercyhurst College, Pennsylvania. His interests are theory development, comparative deviance, justice systems and ethics.

PAT O'MALLEY is Professor of Legal Studies at Latrobe University, Melbourne. His research work and publications include the development of models of crime prevention that reflect critical criminological concerns, fieldwork into cross-cultural crime prevention among Aborginal people in remote regions of the Great Sandy Desert, and analysis of the place of excitement in modern culture.

MIKE PRESDEE is currently a Senior Lecturer in the School of Social and International Studies at the University of Sunderland, in England. He has written several important ethnographic and analytical studies of youth, poverty, and crime, including chapters in Ian Taylor's *The Social Effects of Free Market Policies* and in *The Sociology of Youth and Youth Policy*, edited by Claire Wallace and Malcolm Cross.

JOSEPH H. RANKIN is Professor of Sociology at Eastern Michigan University. His major research interest includes the etiology of juvenile delinquency, especially those causal factors involving the family. Recently published articles on this subject have appeared in *Social Problems*, the *Journal of Research in Crime and Delinquency*, and *Criminology*.

FRANK SCHMALLEGER is Chair of the Department of Sociology, Social Work and Criminal Justice at Pembroke State University in North Carolina. He is the author of many articles and books, including *Criminal Justice Today* (1993) and *Computers in Criminal Justice* (1990). As editor of *Criminal Justice Ethics* (1991), *Ethics in Criminal Justice* (1990), and *The Social Basis of Criminal Justice* (1981), he has worked to focus attention within the justice field on ethical concerns. He was the founding editor of the journal, *The Justice Professional*.

JEFFERY T. WALKER is an Assistant Professor of Criminal Justice at the University of Arkansas at Little Rock. In addition to his work in criminology, he has researched and written in the area of computers in criminal justice and police work. His previous publications include the book, *Briefs of Leading Cases in Law Enforcement*, and he is the editor of *ACJS Today* (the Academy of Criminal Justice Sciences).

L. EDWARD WELLS is Associate Professor of Criminal Science at Illinois State University. His research focuses on theoretical models of juvenile delinquency and victimization, as well as decision-making in criminal justice organizations. Recent publications have focused on the effects of family structure and family relations on juvenile delinquency.

NANCY WONDERS is an Assistant Professor of Criminal Justice at Northern Arizona University. Her scholarship explores the link between criminology and political sociology, with special emphasis on the relationship between social inequality, law, and justice. She has coauthored chapters in *Political Crime in Contemporary America* and *Law and Structural Contradictions*.